Power and Persuasion

Power and Persuasion
Ideology and Rhetoric in Communist Yugoslavia 1944–1953

Carol S. Lilly

NEW YORK AND LONDON

First published 2001 by Westview Press

Published 2018 by Routledge
605 Third Avenue, New York, NY 10017
4 Park Square, Milton Park, Abingdon, Oxon OX14 4RN

Routledge is an imprint of the Taylor & Francis Group, an informa business

Copyright © 2001 Taylor & Francis

All rights reserved. No part of this book may be reprinted or reproduced or utilised in any form or by any electronic, mechanical, or other means, now known or hereafter invented, including photocopying and recording, or in any information storage or retrieval system, without permission in writing from the publishers.

Notice:
Product or corporate names may be trademarks or registered trademarks, and are used only for identification and explanation without intent to infringe.

Library of Congress Cataloging-in-Publication Data
Lilly, Carol S., 1959–
  Power and persuasion : ideology and rhetoric in communist Yugoslavia, 1944–1953 / by Carol S. Lilly.
    p. cm.
  Includes bibliographical references and index.
  ISBN 0-8133-3825-5
  1. Yugoslavia—Politics and government—1945–1980. 2. Yugoslavia—Cultural policy. 3. Rhetoric—Political aspects—Yugoslavia. 4. Comminication—Political aspects—Yugoslavia. I. Title

DR1302.L55 2000
949.702—dc21   00-048470
                                                                        CIP

ISBN 13: 978-0-8133-3825-5 (pbk)

Contents

Acronyms vii
Acknowledgements xi

Introduction 1

Note About Sources, 9
Notes, 11

Part One

1 Setting the Stage 17

   Historical Review, 17
   External and Internal Constraints, 25
   Notes, 31

2 Tools of the Trade: The Apparatus for Cultural Change 35

   The Communist Party, 35
   The State, 42
   Mass Organizations, 48
   Notes, 54

3 Problems of Persuasion 61

   Internal Disunity, 61
   "Kadrovi Rešavaju Sve"—Cadres Determine Everything, 66
   Notes, 71

Part Two

4 Taking Power: Cultural Manipulation and
   Revolutionary Change 77

   Compromise and Moderation, 77
   Partisanstvo in Postwar Rhetoric, 86
   Pragmatism and Partisanstvo, 92
   Conclusion, 105

Notes, 107

5   Constructing the Framework: Mobilization and Control   115

    Shockwork and Competition, 118
    Youth Volunteer Labor Brigades, 120
    Economic Tasks and Education, 124
    Culture and the Media, 128
    Notes, 132

6   The Cultural Transformation Begins   137

    New Goals and New Expectations, 138
    Culture and Ideology, 140
    Educating the Educators, 148
    Conclusion, 153
    Notes, 154

7   The Cultural Transformation Delayed   161

    The Soviet-Yugoslav Split, 162
    Two Steps Backward, 165
    Three Steps Forward, 175
    Conclusion, 189
    Notes, 191

8   The Cultural Transformation Transformed   198

    1950: A Turning Point, 198
    Further Reforms, 208
    The Sixth Party Congress and the Fourth
       Congress of the People's Front, 210
    Playing by New Rules, 214
    Notes, 222

9   The Cultural Transformation Abandoned   229

    Youth and Culture After the Soviet-Yugoslav Split, 229
    Conclusion, 240
    Notes, 242

    Conclusion   245

Bibliography   253
Index   00

Acronyms

The following abbreviations for archives, archival funds, individual works, organizations, and institutions have been employed in the text and in footnotes.

ACKSKJ	Arhiv Centralnog komiteta Saveza komunista Jugoslavije (Archives of the Central Committee of the League of Communists of Yugoslavia)
AFW/AFŽ	Anti-fascist Front of Women/Anti-fašistički front žena
AJ	Arhiv Jugoslavije (Archives of Yugoslavia)
AVNOJ	Anti-fašističko vijeće narodnog oslobodjenja Jugoslavije (Anti-fascist Council of the People's Liberation of Yugoslavia)
CC/CK	Central Committee/Centralni komitet
CKKPH	Centralni komitet Komunističke partije Hrvatske (Central Committee of the Communist Party of Croatia)
CKKPHAP	Centralni komitet Komunističke partije Hrvatske, Agitprop (Central Committee of the Communist Party of Croatia, Department of Agitation and Propaganda)
CKKPJ	Centralni komitet Komunističke partije Jugoslavije (Central Committee of the Communist Party of Yugoslavia)
CKSKOJ	Centralni komitet Savez komunističke omladine Jugoslavije (Central Committee of the League of Communist Youth of Yugoslavia)
CO	Centralni odbor (Central Council)
CPSU	Communist Party of the Soviet Union
CPY	Communist Party of Yugoslavia
CRPP	Croat Republican Peasant Party
CV	Centralno vijeće/veće (Central Council)
DFJ	Demokratska federativna Jugoslavije
FNRJ	Federativna Narodna Republika Jugoslavija (Federal People's Republic of Yugoslavia)
GK	Gradski komitet (City Committee)

HDA	Hrvatski Državni Arhiv (Croatian State Archives, previously Archives of the Insitute for the History of the Workers' Movement of Croatia)
JSRNJ	Jedinstveni Sindikat Radnog Naroda Jugoslavije (United Trade Union of the Working People of Yugoslavia)
KDAŽH	Komitet za društvenu aktivnost žena Hrvatske (Committee for the Social Activity of Women of Croatia)
KK	Kotarski komitet (Regional Committee)
KKU	Komitet za kulturu i umetnost (Committee for Culture and Art)
KPH	Komunistička partija Hrvatske (Communist Party of Croatia)
KPJ	Komunistička partija Jugoslavije (Communist Party of Yugoslavia)
KPO	Kulturno-prosvetno odeljenje (Cultural-Educational Department)
KPS	Komunistička partija Srbije (Communist Party of Serbia)
KŠN	Komitet za škole i nauku (Committee for Schools and Science)
KUD	Kulturno-umetničko društvo (Cultural-Artistic Society)
LCY	League of Communists of Yugoslavia
LFVV	Lični fond Veljka Vlahovića (Personal fund of Veljko Vlahović)
LTU	League of Trade Unions
MK	Mesni komitet (Local Committee)
MNK	Ministarstvo za nauku i kulturu
MP	Ministarstvo prosvete (Ministry of Education)
NFH	Narodni front Hrvatske (People's Front of Croatia)
NFJ	Narodni front Jugoslavije (People's Front of Yugoslavia)
NOJ	Narodna omladina Jugoslavije (People's Youth of Yugoslavia)
NOB	Narodnooslobodilačka borba (People's Liberation Struggle)
NOH	Narodna omladina Hrvatske (People's Youth of Croatia)
NSO	Narodna studentska omladina (People's Student Youth)
OK	Okružni/Oblasni komitet (District/Regional Committee)
OO	Okružni/Oblasni odbor (District/Regional Council)
PB	Politburo
PC	People's Council
PFY	People's Front of Yugoslavia
PK	Pokrajinski komitet (Regional Committee)
PKSKOJ-H	Pokrajinski komitet Savez komunističke omladine Jugoslavije za Hrvatsku (Regional Committee of the League of Communist Youth of Yugoslavia for Croatia)

PWC	Peasant Working Cooperative
PYY	People's Youth of Yugoslavia
RKSSRNH	Raionski komitet Socijalističkog saveza radnog naroda Hrvatske (Regional Committee of the Socialist League of the Working People of Croatia)
SAWPY	Socialist Alliance of the Working People of Yugoslavia
SKJ	Savez komunista Jugoslavije (League of Communists of Yugoslavia)
SKOJ	Savez komunističke omladine Jugoslavije (League of Communist Youth of Yugoslavia)
SRZ	Seljačka radna zadruga (Peasant Working Cooperative)
SSJ	Savez sindikata Jugoslavije (League of Trade Unions of Yugoslavia)
SSOJ	Socijalistički savez omladine Jugoslavije (Socialist League of Youth of Yugoslavia)
SSRNJ	Socijalistički savez radnog naroda Jugoslavije (Socialist League of the Working People of Yugoslavia)
UK	Univerzitetski komitet (University Committee)
UNRRA	United Nations Relief and Rehabilitation Administration
UPA	Uprava za propagandu i agitaciju (Administration for Propaganda and Agitation)
USAOH	Ujedinjeni savez anti-fašističke omladine Hrvatske (United League of Anti-Fascist Youth of Croatia)
USAOJ	Ujedinjeni savez anti-fašističke omladine Jugoslavije (United League of Anti-Fascist Youth of Yugoslavia)
VSSH	Vijeće Savez sindikata Hrvatske (Council of the League of Trade Unions of Croatia)
YPA	Yugoslav People's Army
ZV	Zemalsjko vijeće (Land Council)

Acknowledgements

As I sat down to write these acknowledgements, I found myself overwhelmed by the magnitude of the task. That enormity stems in part from the many years that this work has been in progress; I chose the topic for my dissertation thesis in 1985. In the subsequent fifteen years, a great many people, as well as many academic and funding institutions, facilitated the research and writing of this study. I am grateful to all of them and fear that I may forget some. Should I do so, I apologize for it now.

To begin with I must thank the library, staff, and, of course, faculty of Yale University where this project began. In particular, my thanks go to Professor Ivo Banac, my thesis advisor, who taught me more than I can say and without whose exacting guidance this work, however flawed now, would undoubtedly include many more errors. Thanks also to my unofficial advisors at Yale, Paul Bushkovitch and Susan Woodward, who offered considerable additional advice and criticism, as well as moral support. Dr. Woodward, in particular, provided invaluable assistance thanks to her incredible breadth of knowledge and remarkable listening and teaching skills.

Research for this monograph then continued at numerous libraries and archives in the United States and the former Yugoslavia. The librarians at the library and archives of the Hoover Institution in Stanford were especially gracious and helpful. I thank them all, but especially Linda Wheeler. In the former Yugoslavia, my work was greatly facilitated by the professional and friendly staff at the University Library and the Institute for the Contemporary History of Croatia in Zagreb, and in Belgrade at the Institute for Contemporary History, the Archives of the Central Committee of the League of Communists of Yugoslavia, the Archives of Yugoslavia, and the National Library of Serbia. As important as their help, of course, was the funding which made that research possible. Over the last 15 years, I have been fortunate to receive generous grants from the International Research and Exchanges Board, The American Council of Learned Societies, and the University of Nebraska at Kearney's Research Services Council. I am extremely grateful to all of them!

On a more personal note, I would like also to thank all those in the former Yugoslavia who made my research trips there not just productive but absolutely fun! Two families in particular have given more to me than I can ever repay and, perhaps most important, formed within me a reserve of faith in and love for the people of that region strong enough to survive the miseries and tragedies of the last decade. My deepest thanks then go to Lela Baća and her family in Zaprešić, Croatia, and Momčilo Pavlović and his family in Sremčica and Lebane of the Federal Republic of Yugoslavia.

A second reason for the size of my debt of gratitude is my firm belief in the values (at least for me) of collaboration. What that means in practice is that over the past years I have begged, bribed, or bullied numerous friends and colleagues into reading and critiquing my work. At the top of my list of regular readers are, of course, Melissa Bokovoy and Jill Irvine, my two closest colleagues in the field as well as two of my best friends. Close behind them are Nick Miller and Tom Clark, followed by James German, Charles Hanson, and back in the earliest stages of my research, John Buchanan and Carla Schmidt. Others who provided extremely valuable critiques were Gary Cohen, Martin Johnson, Dennison Rusinow, and the anonymous reviewers at Westview Press. Their comments have been enormously helpful and have clearly contributed a great deal to whatever virtues this book may possess. Its flaws and errors, of course, remain my own. In addition, of course, I thank Rob Williams, Carol Jones, Michelle Trader, and the rest of the professional staff at Westview Press for their work in bringing my manuscript to print.

Finally, I thank all those whose daily friendship, support, and love helped me maintain a sense of perspective and carry out my work with commitment and even, on occasion, intensity but not obsession. They facilitated and encouraged my research and writing but also refused to let me neglect those other aspects of life that bring joy and satisfaction. For these gifts, I am especially grateful to my parents, Douglas and Judith Lilly, and to my husband and children, Rick, Daniela, and Max Garvue.

Introduction

When the Communist Party of Yugoslavia (CPY) took power after the Second World War, it had a vision for a new and better society—a society in which all humans would live together in peace and prosperity and in which their mutual exploitation would be eliminated. Based on the ideology of Karl Marx and Friedrich Engels (as amended by Vladimir Lenin), that vision was the party's ultimate goal and main source of legitimacy. Consequently, many party policies sought to achieve the social and cultural transformation inherent in that vision. Yet party leaders also faced innumerable practical and political problems associated first with maintaining power and rebuilding the Yugoslav economy, and later with retaining independence and economic viability in the face of Soviet and Eastern European hostility. Moreover, party leaders in Yugoslavia were not acting in a vacuum but had to take into account the preexisting societies and cultures.[1] Indeed, Yugoslav Communists faced a particularly complex task as they confronted not one but a whole series of preexisting cultures based around the country's numerous constituent nations and national minorities. Hence, every attempt at change faced an array of deeply entrenched structures, institutions, values, and behavioral habits. In each case, Yugoslavia's Communists had to decide whether and how to undermine the extant cultures or to adopt and manipulate them for their own purposes. Postwar CPY policies thus reflect the party's struggle to find and hold a balance between its long-term goal of transforming society and culture[2] and its immediate political and economic needs, between its revolutionary desire for change and its pragmatic need for security and stability.

In its efforts to attain both political security and social change, the CPY employed a number of tools, including economic incentives, force, and persuasion. While party leaders often counted on the first two to realize political goals, they also saw persuasion as crucial for securing public acceptance of and participation in their political agenda. Persuasion was even more important to the social and cultural transformation required by the party's long-term vision for the future. After all, the party's ultimate goal required changes not only in the country's political and economic structure, but in its citizens—in their values, morals, goals, aesthetics, and social behavior.³ These new citizens would be strong, courageous, and hardworking, but also intelligent, educated, and highly cultured. Most of all, they would be people who recognized that the needs of society as a whole were more important than the needs of any one individual and who were prepared to give their all for that greater good, understanding that in so doing they would also be serving their own best interests. While party leaders did not hesitate to use force to achieve their ends, they believed that the final goal of communism could only be built with the voluntary cooperation and participation of the vast majority of the population. Consequently, persuasion was a vital component of the party's activities and party leaders desperately wanted it to succeed.

This monograph documents the CPY's use of persuasive rhetoric by oral, written, and visual means for both its long-term transformative and short-term political goals in the years between the establishment of Communist power in Yugoslavia with the liberation of Belgrade in October 1944 and the end of the party's first reform era at the June 1953 Second Plenum of the Central Committee of the League of Communists of Yugoslavia (LCY, formerly the CPY). It considers both the intentions and accomplishments of the party's persuasive strategies and shows the evolution of their content and form during the first nine years of Communist rule.

In the process, it modifies existing historiography on early postwar Yugoslavia in several ways. Most historians of Yugoslavia designate the period from 1944 to 1949 as the "Stalinist" era, during which time the Yugoslav Communists were rigid and dogmatic ideologues who unreservedly drew nearly all their policies and institutions directly from Soviet models and imposed them on a helpless and passive population. The June 1948 split between Tito and Stalin, they then explain, brought about the next "reformist" era of Yugoslav history, from late 1949 to the Sixth Party Congress of November 1952. According to traditional views, the split caused a political and economic crisis that forced CPY leaders to renounce their Soviet-based policies and initiate a series of innovative political, social, and economic reforms. These reforms were designed to justify the continued tenure of CPY leaders in power despite Soviet hostility, secure Western economic aid, and pacify an increasingly dissatisfied population.⁴ These scholars clearly delineated the main events and issues relating to the Soviet-Yugoslav split and have offered many valuable insights into the development of communism in Yugoslavia. Their research established a solid foundation of knowledge on which all future studies of the topic must rely. For a variety of reasons, however (some clearly relating to the availability of sources), nearly all of these earlier scholars concentrated on the Soviet-Yugoslav split and its accompanying political and ideological changes, neglecting in the process the years between 1944 and 1948.[5]

My research into the 1944–1948 era led me to question many of the assumptions about the so-called Stalinist period. First of all, my study of rhetoric showed that while party leaders unquestionably drew on the Soviet experience, they were fully conscious well before 1948 that not all features of the Soviet example were worthy of emulation or suited to Yugoslavia's needs and conditions. Moreover, the evolving form and content of CPY rhetoric revealed party leaders who, even before the split, were not just ideologues committed to a Marxist-Leninist vision of the future but also very practical power politicians, willing and able to modify their policies in response to unexpected events and reactions from below. Likewise, the populace was more influential and effective than previously assumed. Albeit on an unequal basis and within certain boundaries, ordinary people engaged in a process of negotiation with party leaders, resulting in clearly visible consequences for both the party's rhetoric and its more general policies.

The traditional periodization and depiction of postwar Yugoslav history thus raises a number of questions. After all, if CPY leaders had been blindly dogmatic ideologues, more Stalinist than Stalin himself, up until 1948, their metamorphosis into flexible and innovative reformers by 1950 would seem improbable. The transformation of the passive and impotent populace of the 1940s into dangerous masses that party leaders tried to pacify is equally baffling. It is my contention that while the split was a defining moment in postwar Yugoslav history, its significance and the content of subsequent reforms can be properly understood only in the context of those years preceding the split. Only by combining evidence from the two eras can we devise a portrait of the CPY and Yugoslav society that resolves these dilemmas.

By placing equal emphasis on the years before and after the split, this monograph reveals the line of continuity that joined them and that makes the post-1948 reforms intelligible. In the process, it modifies the significance of 1948, which then ceases to represent a kind of "iron curtain" separating two apparently unconnected regimes. For while many of the changes that took place in CPY policies after 1948 were stimulated by external events, the direction and form that those changes took flowed from the party's previous experiences and internal development. The split created both a crisis and an opportunity that allowed and even required policy changes; yet the nature of those changes was rooted in the party's previous successes and failures. Without denying the significance of the Soviet-Yugoslav split, my study allows us to see another criterion of equal importance for the evolution of the Yugoslav Communist regime—the tension between the party's desire for revolutionary social and cultural change and its concurrent need for political security and stability.

Just as important, my study revises our understanding of the complex and evolving dynamic between the party-state and Yugoslav society in the postwar era. Cold war–era historiography of Communist regimes has tended to perceive them as monolithic behemoths that persistently imposed their policies on helpless and passive subjects. More recent studies, especially those based on newly available archival sources, have begun to modify that perspective, revealing the kinds of pressure from below that various social forces have been able to assert even in clearly dictatorial regimes. My study belongs in that latter category, as it will describe the ways in which the party-state and Yugoslavia's inhabitants responded to and influenced one another. While I do not pretend that the relationship was an equal one, neither was it entirely one-sided. After all, precisely because CPY leaders were committed to their vision for the future, they wished to engage Yugoslavia's citizens in its construction. Yet seeking to ensure their own political security, party leaders also insisted on a degree of social control that served to stifle popular initiative and activism. These simultaneous and contradictory goals competed in party rhetoric and directly influenced the nature of state-society relations.

The party's long-term vision for the future, which involved the transformation of society and culture, required that all Yugoslav citizens learn and adopt Marxist-Leninist ideology as a way of understanding the world, a vision for the future, and a program of action. It also required that they become active participants in the construction of socialism. Rhetorical strategies designed to attain that goal were both motivational and pedagogical. They sought to inspire the populace with the party's vision for the future, but also provide them with the knowledge and skills necessary to achieve that vision. The party's concurrent need for stability required quite a different kind of rhetoric—one that stressed absolute adherence to the program established from above and indeed an absence of alternatives to that program. It offered both positive and negative directions, informing the public not only what it must do but what it must not. It was, most often, supported by the open threat of coercion.

The tension between the opposing goals in CPY rhetoric reflected the party's graduated strategy for the construction of socialism in Yugoslavia. According to that strategy, party leaders focused first on securing political power, second on achieving economic stability, and only third on transforming society and culture in accordance with Communist values. Although this phased program of action was referred to only rarely in print (and then only after 1948), it clearly dictated what party leaders understood to be their immediate and long-term goals. By referring to that strategy, then, we may better understand why certain policies were implemented, continued, modified, or abolished at particular times.

Reference to that strategy also helps explain changes in the party's persuasive activities. In the first two phases, as party leaders sought to consolidate power and reconstruct the economy on a socialist basis, the glorious future and the importance of Marxist-Leninist ideology remained secondary to the demands of daily politics in party rhetoric. Even then, party leaders could not afford completely to neglect their long-term vision for the future. After all, it represented their main source of legitimacy. Nonetheless, it was only when the party embarked on the third phase of transforming society and culture that Marxist-Leninist ideology began to play a stronger and more public role in CPY rhetoric. Here again, however, party leaders, while giving more emphasis to their long-term goals, could not afford to risk their immediate position in power. And so the balancing act continued.

Yet even while adhering to their strategy, CPY policies and rhetoric were necessarily limited by existing conditions, institutions, and social relations in postwar Yugoslavia as well as by the international constellation of power. Such "internal and external constraints," to use Stephen Lukes's terminology, often forced party leaders to modify their approach and adopt policies contrary to their guiding ideology.[6] The most important external force, the Soviet-Yugoslav split, interrupted and delayed the planned transformation of society and culture, while it simultaneously allowed CPY leaders to expand their notions about how to achieve that transformation. Nonetheless, it did not change the basic strategy. Moreover, the direction taken by many reforms in the 1950s was clearly determined by the party's domestic experiences—in particular, its past successes and failures in the field of persuasion.

Public response to party rhetoric also influenced its form and content. When urged to take up the party's vision and help make it happen, some Yugoslav citizens were inspired and acted with enthusiasm and vigor. Yet they did not always do so in an orderly or acceptable manner. Very often, when such citizens heeded the call to "show greater initiative," they made "mistakes." Moreover, the party's calls for engagement sometimes resulted in disagreements over strategy and goals or even open dissent. This kind of activism clearly countered the party's need for political security and stability. Yet when party rhetoric sought to resolve these problems by offering increasingly specific and restrictive instructions about how to participate, it only dampened public interest and enthusiasm; discussion ceased and Yugoslav citizens adopted a strategy of public accommodation and private resistance. That is, they would do precisely as much as they had to and refrain from forbidden activities, but also withdraw from activism into the private sphere and avoid contact with the party-state as much as possible. Obviously, these responses to CPY rhetoric, even while offering greater political stability, sabotaged the party's plans for social and cultural change.

The party's need to maintain power and its desire to inspire public enthusiasm for communism thus meant that party leaders often had to adjust both their policies and their rhetoric in response to such feedback from below. These modifications, as well as numerous internal reports, offer clues about popular opinion and reveal the existence of active or passive resistance. When a particular approach or policy worked well, party leaders talked about and encouraged further use of it. When, on the contrary, it met with popular resistance, they talked about that too and sometimes either modified or discontinued it. In either case, we learn much about the party, the populace, and the complex relationship between state and society. We can gauge the sensitivity of CPY leaders toward public opinion and clarify the limits of their flexibility, while simultaneously discerning the level of public support or tolerance for party policies, the methods by which people expressed their opinions, and the degree to which they were able to influence party policy.

This analysis relies upon a modified view of state-society relations in Communist, fascist, and other dictatorial revolutionary regimes. For if even within the heavily restrictive cultural and ideological milieu of early postwar Yugoslavia, the population was neither passive nor impotent but able to express its views and influence the party's long- and short-term plans, it seems likely that a similar process of negotiation (however unequal) may also have developed in other systems typically termed "totalitarian." In this sense, my research contributes to the civil society literature on Eastern Europe that recognizes apolitical means of social pressure.[7] It differs, however, in that those authors tend to focus on the activities of organized interest groups of the 1970s–1980s, while Yugoslav citizens of the 1940s–1950s expressed their views in ways that were less coherent and deliberate. It comes closer to supporting James Scott's conclusion that subordinate classes resist the dominant culture in small ways, "in ridicule, in truculence, in irony, in petty acts of noncompliance, in foot dragging, in dissimulation, in resistant mutuality, in the disbelief in elite homilies, in the steady, grinding efforts to hold one's own against overwhelming odds," except that he, like those theorists who describe culture as an ideological battleground, assumes a class basis to these acts of resistance.[8] In Yugoslavia, by contrast, those resisting the party's ideological and cultural agenda were not always its "class enemies" but were often among those most favored and coddled by the CPY, including workers, intellectuals, and youth. The material thus describes state-society relations as a complex and often unpredictable dynamic between ruling elites and their constituents.

While this study focuses on persuasion, its role within the party's program for change should not be overstated. Coercion was also crucial and it, too, reflected the party's graduated strategy for the construction of socialism. Party leaders expected to use coercion especially during the first and second phases of their program in order to secure power and restructure the economy according to socialist principles. During those periods in particular, party leaders relied heavily on their monopoly over the state's organs of force. They arrested, imprisoned, or shot open, active, or potentially dangerous opponents of the regime, sometimes in horrifyingly large numbers. Meanwhile, they severely restricted the civil liberties of the rest of the population. Whatever the claims of some CPY rhetoric, there was no real freedom of assembly, speech, or press.

The party's use of coercion clearly affected the nature and impact of its persuasive policies as well as the character of state-society relations. Party rhetoric obviously backed up by the threat of force had very different consequences than that which was purely persuasive. The coercive element of the party's program for change thus reminds us of the limits to popular resistance in dictatorial regimes. Yet, the party's changing emphasis on coercion also points to its boundaries. For while party leaders relied on force during the first two phases of their program, they expected to reduce its usage over time. Coercion, they believed, could help realize the party's political and economic policies but it could not effect the long-term cultural transformation of society.

In fact, however, it appeared that neither could persuasion. By tracing the evolution of party rhetoric, this book presents also a case study in the goals and achievements of Communist party persuasion and informs us about its value as a means of bringing about change. It offers a particularly enlightening case, moreover, since persuasive methods in Yugoslavia changed so radically and so quickly but with so little apparent success. Further, the question of persuasion's utility is particularly intriguing now that we have witnessed the demise (or transmogrification) of most Communist parties but see also some evidence of their lingering popularity. Finally, an evaluation of propaganda's persuasive effect is clearly germane given its recent and flagrant application by several new nationalist regimes in Yugoslavia's successor states.

Among the persuasive means employed by party leaders in the 1940s–1950s were newspaper and journal articles; public speeches; educational curricula and course content; posters; insignia; group activities like parades, workplace competitions, and volunteer labor brigades; and the works, monuments, and production of both high and popular culture. While the importance of the public media and education as methods of indoctrination is well known, the persuasive value of cultural monuments and rituals has stimulated much debate among both those who would use it and those who study it. A belief in culture's educational and persuasive potential has been adopted by a wide variety of religious, political, and commercial organizations since the beginning of time. The Catholic Church sought to maintain its monopoly on most culture in order to direct people's attention toward God; Jacobin idealists strove to alter French citizens' fundamental values and associations by creating a new revolutionary calendar; and American advertisers have used the power of popular music to promote their products. Yet the effect of such efforts remains uncertain. Can cultural manipulation change people's minds? And if so, how and to what extent? Most recently, this question has been addressed in the form of an ongoing debate among 20th-century U.S. historians about the nature of the relationship between the producers and consumers of mass or popular culture. Is the Hollywood entertainment industry imposing its own warped values and cheap aesthetic tastes on the public, or is it only responding to preexisting popular tastes and demands? Further, to what extent are the consumers of culture able to make it their own, adapting it to their interests and imbuing it with their values, regardless of its producer's original intent?[9]

The debate is clearly relevant to a discussion of state-society relations in Yugoslavia, where, as in all Communist-dominated countries, the state held a monopoly over the production and distribution of culture and manipulated it with the clear intent of directing and changing the values and aesthetic tastes of its citizenry. My investigation into the successes and (more often) failures of the party's manipulation of culture and other more direct persuasive methods supports the hypothesis of several previous scholars that such suasive efforts are effective only or mainly when they seek to build upon already existing values and beliefs and are much less so when they try to change people's values or create new ones for them.[10] In other words, party rhetoric could confirm and sometimes manipulate the existing culture, but was generally unable to transform it.[11]

For example, Yugoslavia's citizens proved remarkably adept at finding ways of appearing to comply with the demands of the party while simultaneously satisfying their own personal needs and interests. Yugoslavia's youth might indeed join volunteer labor brigades in the desired numbers but did not always use that opportunity so much for their moral and ideological development as for avoiding parental discipline. Similarly, musicians might conform to the party's insistence that they compose songs about the heroic wartime efforts of the Partisans or the contributions of workers to the construction of socialism, but would then set the politically correct lyrics to "decadent" jazz music. In other words, even as the Communist rulers of Yugoslavia sought to manipulate the extant culture, Yugoslavia's citizens manipulated with equal or greater success that culture imposed upon them from above.

Ultimately, the party's apparent inability to transform society and culture altered not only the form and content of its persuasive rhetoric, but eventually its entire approach to the construction of socialism. Thus, the party's relaxation of cultural controls beginning in 1950 was motivated not so much by the consequences of the Soviet-Yugoslav split as by negative responses to its previous policies and the rhetorical strategies designed to justify them. The reforms of the early 1950s were intended to reactivate Yugoslavia's citizens and engage them in the cultural transformation. Again, however, the party's response to feedback from below could go either way. While such feedback inspired certain reforms, it ended others. By mid-1953, top CPY leaders began to back away from many recently adopted political reforms, not so much due to external events like the death of Stalin but because domestic reactions to the new persuasive approach had convinced them that those reforms could endanger the party's hold on power. Those reactions also gradually convinced party leaders that they would never effect the transformation of society by means of persuasion. As a result, the party's political security came to acquire a position of absolute priority, while its long-term vision was consigned to an increasingly distant future.

Note About Sources

The activities and strategies described in this monograph were called by the Communists *agitation* and *propaganda* or *agitprop*.[12] These terms did not carry the pejorative connotation among Communists that they do among Western observers but were seen to be a legitimate and natural part of politics. Indeed, persuasion and rhetoric are inherent in political activity. When applied by Communist regimes, however, the activity takes on a more suspicious nature and is often considered to be simply lying or a means of distracting public attention from despotic government. Certainly, rhetoric can be and often is used for such purposes (both by Communist and non-Communist parties). Nonetheless, my comparison of official published rhetoric with internal party documents and meetings revealed that in most cases CPY propaganda accurately reflected the party's short-term and/or long-term goals and intentions. Although party rhetoric did offer some outright lies, they tended to fall into certain categories (statistics on production or broad generalizations about popular support for the party or its policies) and were easily recognized. Otherwise, because it represented the party's most direct means of communicating with not only the broader public but also its own membership, CPY rhetoric had to and did describe party goals with reasonable accuracy.

Indeed, through such rhetoric one may clearly discern the party's entire political, economic, and cultural program. Its changing form and content mirrored changes in CPY goals and priorities. Moreover, my research shows that the party's persuasive policies not only accurately reflected its goals, but in some cases even determined them. That is, public response to some rhetorical strategies convinced CPY leaders to make fundamental changes in their overall approach and general policies. In such cases, rhetoric did not just mirror or justify party policies, but actually inspired and influenced them. An examination of such rhetoric thus clearly contributes to a fuller and more sophisticated understanding of the regime.

Information for this study was drawn largely from the archival funds in Belgrade and Zagreb of various party, state, and mass organizations as well as from numerous public forms of persuasion, such as periodical and nonperiodical publications, film, radio, speeches, educational programs and curricula, official celebrations, and high and popular culture—including literature, art, sculpture, music, theater, and dance. I also made use of a growing supply of memoir literature and I conducted interviews with a select number of participants in the party's persuasive activities. In terms of secondary sources, I relied not only on other historians, but also on experts in the fields of political science, anthropology, literature, the arts, and education.

At archives in Zagreb and Belgrade, the more important funds were those of the politburo and the departments of agitation and propaganda from the central committees of the CPY and Communist Party of Croatia; archives of the People's Front and of women's, youth, and trade union organizations; and archives of the ministry of education and Committee for Schools and Science. Access to these archives was available in Yugoslavia already by the late 1980s.

Among the more important newspapers consulted were *Borba* (the official organ of the CPY), *Politika* (an ostensibly independent but clearly Communist-dominated newspaper), *20. oktobar* (the organ of the People's Front of Belgrade), *Rad* (the organ of the united trade unions' organization), and *Republika* (the organ of the non-Communist but cooperative Republican party). Particularly relevant journals included *Komunist* (the party's theoretical journal), *Naša književnost*, *NIN*, and *Republika* (Serb- and Croat-based literary journals), *Mladost* (a youth literary journal), and *Savremena škola* (journal of the Union of Educational Workers).

Most of the internal documents and many of the public ones examined were of an all-Yugoslav nature and presented the conclusions of central organs, usually based on numerous reports received from throughout the country. Except as otherwise stated, these conclusions and the policies based on them were meant to be applied in the same way in all regions of the country. This does not mean, of course, that all policies *were* applied uniformly throughout the country. On the contrary, it is one of the basic conclusions of this work that policy implementation varied widely de-

Introduction

pending on a number of factors, including the age, educational level, class, gender, religious background, and national identity of those involved. Any attempt to provide a comprehensive social history of the era would have to address these differences in a systematic manner.

Notes

1. *Culture* in this work refers both to works and monuments of artistic creation and to what Geertz calls "mass culture," defined as "the half-formed, taken-for-granted, indifferently systematized notions that guide the activities of normal men in everyday life." Clifford Geertz, *The Interpretation of Cultures* (New York: Basic Books Inc., 1973), 14, 362.

2. Given Yugoslavia's complex national makeup, it would undoubtedly be more accurate to speak of efforts to realize the transformation of cultures, not culture. The Communists, however, made no such distinction and for the sake of simplicity, unless the distinction is absolutely necessary, neither will I.

3. For this paper, I use the term *citizens* to mean only "members of a state." While some may reasonably dispute its implication of sovereignty, it is, even so, a less problematic term than the most obvious alternative, *Yugoslavs*.

4. Phyllis Auty, *Yugoslavia* (New York: Walker and Company, 1965); George W. Hoffman and Fred Warner Neal, *Yugoslavia and the New Communism* (New York: Twentieth Century Fund, 1962); Dennison Rusinow, *The Yugoslav Experiment, 1948–1974* (Berkeley, CA: University of California Press, 1977). Yugoslav historians have generally followed a similar approach. While less critical of CPY leaders before the split, they nonetheless blame all flaws in the early years of party rule on its adherence to the Soviet model. Vladimir Dedijer, *Tito* (New York: Simon and Schuster, 1953); Milovan Djilas, *Conversations with Stalin* (New York: Harcourt Brace Jovanovich, 1962); Pero Morača and Stanislav Stojanović, eds., *Povijest Saveza komunista Jugoslavije* (Belgrade: Izdavački centar Komunist, 1985).

5. Certain aspects of the period have been addressed in larger histories, memoirs, and isolated monographs, but most often only in a brief and clearly introductory manner. See Dušan Bilandžić, *Historija Socijalističke Federativne Republike Jugoslavije: Glavni procesi, 1918–1985* (Zagreb: Školska knjiga, 1985); Branko Petranović, *Političke i pravne prilike za vreme privremene vlade DFJ* (Belgrade: 1964); Branko Petranović, *Istorija Jugoslavije 1918–1978* (Belgrade: 1980); Morača and Stojanović; Vladimir Dedijer, *Novi prilozi za biografiju Josipa Broza Tita*, Vol. 3 (Belgrade: Rad, 1984); Djilas, *Conversations with Stalin*; Milovan Djilas, *Rise and Fall* (New York: Harcourt Brace Jovanovich, 1983); Vladimir Dedijer, *The Battle Stalin Lost, Memoirs of Yugoslavia, 1948–1953* (New York: Viking Press, 1970); A. Ross Johnson, *The Transformation of Communist Ideology, The Yugoslav Case, 1945–1953* (Cambridge, MA: The MIT Press, 1972); Ivo Banac, *With Stalin Against Tito, Cominformist Splits in Yugoslav Communism* (Ithaca, NY: Cornell University Press, 1988); Adam B. Ulam, *Titoism and the Cominform* (Cambridge, MA: Harvard University Press, 1952). Only recently, stimulated by a new availability of archival materials, has more detailed study of the 1944–1948 period been initiated by a number of young Yugoslav scholars as well as by a few Americans. See Melissa

Bokovoy, *Peasants and Communists: Politics and Ideology in the Yugoslav Countryside, 1941–1953* (Pittsburgh: University of Pittsburgh Press, 1998); Katherine M. McCarthy, "Peasant Revolutionaries and Partisan Power: Rural Resistance to Communist Agrarian Policies in Croatia, 1941–1953," Ph.D. Dissertation, University of Pittsburgh, 1995; Vojislav Koštunica and Kosta Čavoški, *Party Pluralism or Monism, Social Movements and the Political System in Yugoslavia, 1944–1949* (Boulder, CO: Westview Press, 1985); Ljubodrag Dimić, *Agitprop kultura, Agitpropovska faza kulturne politike u Srbiji, 1945–1952* (Belgrade: Rad, 1988); Rajko Danilović, *Upotreba neprijatelja: Politička sudjenja 1945–1991 u Jugoslaviji* (Valjevo: Valjevac, 1993); Sonja Bokun-Djinić, *Na sudilištu agitpropa: Etatizam i književno nasledje, 1944–1952* (Belgrade: Filip Višnjić, 1997); Radmila Radić, *Verom protiv vere: Država i verske zajednice u Srbiji, 1945–1953* (Belgrade: INIS, 1995); Marko Lopušina, *Crna knjiga: Cenzura u Jugoslaviji, 1945–91* (Belgrade: Fokus, 1991); Momčilo Pavlović, *Srpsko selo 1945–1952: Otkup* (Belgrade: Institut za savremenu istoriju, 1997).

6. Stephen Lukes, *Essays in Social Theory* (London: MacMillan Inc., 1977), 3–13.

7. See, for example, Vaclav Havel et al., *The Power of the Powerless* (Boston, MA: Faber and Faber, 1987) and Vladimir Tismaneanu, *Reinventing Politics: Eastern Europe from Stalin to Havel* (New York: Free Press, 1992).

8. James C. Scott, *Weapons of the Weak: Everyday Forms of Peasant Resistance* (New Haven, CT: Yale University Press, 1985), 350. See also Antonio Gramsci, *The Modern Prince and Other Writings* (New York: International Publishers, 1957); Stuart Hall, "Notes on Deconstructing 'The Popular'," in *People's History and Socialist Theory,* ed. Raphael Samuel (London: Routledge and Kegan Paul, 1981), 227–240.

9. For a clear and unapologetic expression of both views see the introductory chapters by Bernard Rosenberg and David Manning White in their edited volume, *Mass Culture Revisited* (New York: Van Nostrand Reinhold Co., 1971), 3–21. For a more recent discussion of the issue, see the articles by Lawrence W. Levine, Robin D.G. Kelley, Natalie Zemon Davis, and T. J. Jackson Lears in *American Historical Review,* 97 (December 1992): 1369–1430.

10. See, for example, Jacques Ellul, *Propaganda, the Formation of Men's Attitudes* (New York: Alfred A. Knopf, 1965), 295; Oliver Thomson, *Mass Persuasion in History, An Historical Analysis of the Development of Propaganda Techniques* (Edinburgh: Paul Harris Publishing, 1977); Ian Kershaw, "How Effective Was Nazi Propaganda?" in *Nazi Propaganda, the Power and the Limitations,* ed. David Welch (UK: Croom Helm Ltd., 1983), 180–205.

11. This conclusion may be seen as either encouraging or discouraging in the current post-Communist context. An optimist might conclude that the obviously absurd rhetorical claims recently set forth by various nationalist groups in Yugoslavia's successor states are clearly doomed to failure. A pessimist, on the other hand, might worry more about what the apparent successes of such nationalist propaganda seem to suggest about the preexisting values and beliefs of the local population.

12. The separate functions of *agitation* and *propaganda* as terms relating to methods of Communist indoctrination were first elaborated by G. V. Plekhanov, who stated that "the propagandist presents many ideas to one individual, or to several individuals. The agitator presents one idea only, or a few ideas, but he presents them to a whole mass of persons." Lenin later explained that propa-

ganda was primarily ideological—explaining the bases of class society and the inevitability of class struggle—while agitation was to be both economic and political. But if Plekhanov and Lenin differentiated between the two techniques, CPY leaders (at least up until 1950) did not and generally referred to their persuasive activities using the lump term *agitprop*. G. V. Plekhanov cited in Leonard Schapiro, *The Communist Party of the Soviet Union*, 2d ed. (New York: Random House, 1971), 23; V. I. Lenin, "Zadachi russkikh sotsial-demokratov," in *Polnoe sobranie sochinenii* 2: 6–7 (Moscow: 1958–1965).

Part One

While this monograph offers a primarily chronological argument, it does not provide a full account of all events and policies in the years between 1944 and 1953. Therefore and in order to help readers place the changing themes and forms of party persuasive policies in context, Chapter 1 provides a brief summary of events leading up to the establishment of Communist rule and sketches the main political and economic developments in Yugoslavia from 1944 to 1954. Some of these later developments will be described in considerably more detail in subsequent chapters. This chapter also describes the domestic and international context within which the CPY's efforts to remake society took place.

Chapter 2 specifies the individuals, institutions, and organizations involved in party persuasive activities—including the Communist party, the state, and the mass organizations—and describes the methods by which they sought to realize the party's short-term and long-term agenda. Essentially, then, this chapter displays the nuts and bolts of party persuasion, explaining who carried it out and by what means.

Finally, Chapter 3 describes several common problems that CPY leaders faced in their efforts to transform society and culture by persuasive means, including an occasional lack of unity in decision making at the top and a far more pervasive lack of consistency in policy application below.

1

Setting the Stage

Historical Review

The liberation of Belgrade from German occupation by the combined efforts of Tito's Partisans and the Soviet Red Army on October 20, 1944, represented the symbolic beginning of Communist rule over the second "new" Yugoslavia. Although there had been and would be dates of more legal importance, control over the country's political center not only suggested the solidity of the Communist organization, but provided it with the secure basis and administrative apparatus necessary for governance.[1]

The first "old" Yugoslavia, which had perished in the Second World War, had been formed on December 1, 1918, as an alliance of several South Slavic and other nations. Originally entitled "The Kingdom of Serbs, Croats, and Slovenes," the new state really combined members of over a dozen ethnic groups, each with its own culture, history, and in some cases, language and religion. While the unification of these groups made a certain amount of sense given the geographic, demographic, and political makeup of the region, it was nonetheless at odds with the exclusivist atmosphere typical of many 19th-century nationalist ideologies. Moreover, the newly formed entity rested on shaky foundations since each of the predominant member nations joining it held different concepts of state organization. While the Croats hoped the Yugoslav state would be a loose federation of equal and autonomous nations, the Serbs envisioned and successfully established it as a highly centralized, unitaristic entity dominated by Serbian governing institutions. As a result, many citizens of the new state never accepted its legitimacy and even fewer came to see themselves as members of a new "Yugoslav" nation. The resultant clashes between these conflicting notions of the new state, combined with the concurrent growth of national intolerance and the monarchical government's increasingly oppressive and autocratic style, made for a turbulent interwar experience.[2] Eventually, faced by the growing threat from Nazi Germany in the late 1930s, the prewar government recognized the dangers of its internal dissension and made some concessions aimed at reconciliation and unification. But these measures were both too little and too late and with the onset of the Second World War the festering national tensions exploded into violence.

The Communist Party of Yugoslavia, first formed in 1919, had remained, throughout the history of interwar Yugoslavia, a relatively small and inconsequential force. Outlawed by the government after 1921 and torn by internal dissension (mostly over the national question), the party came close to being dissolved by the Soviet-dominated Communist International, or Comintern, in 1937. CPY fortunes began to improve only in the next few years thanks both to its adoption of the Comintern's new "popular front" line, which helped end the party's previous self-imposed isolation, and to the naming of Josip Broz Tito as general secretary of the party. Tito's purges and "bolshevization" of the party made it a firmer, more disciplined, and more monolithic body than ever before, yet the CPY remained relatively small and weak, counting on the eve of the Second World War only 12,000 members.[3]

In the course of the war, however, the balance of forces in Yugoslavia altered radically and the CPY found itself in an advantaged position to lead a Partisan movement for liberation from foreign occupiers. The party's vast interwar experience in illegal activity, together with its consolidation and bolshevization under Tito, made the CPY uniquely well suited to develop an underground opposition to the foreign occupiers. Even more important, the CPY was the only prewar party in Yugoslavia not associated with any one national group. In the bloody fratricidal conflict that developed concurrently with foreign occupation, the CPY's apparent ability to stand above nationalism and call for the "brotherhood and unity" of all Yugoslav nations and nationalities was enormously effective.

Moreover, during the war, the party's popular front policy finally began to bear fruit. Although CPY efforts to cooperate with other opposition parties in prewar Yugoslavia had met with little success, under conditions of foreign occupation and civil war, the party's call for unity in the struggle against fascism regardless of political, national, or religious affiliation gained new impetus. Consequently, and particularly as the party's military successes grew, increasing numbers of ordinary citizens, including many with no ties to or interest in communism, joined the Partisan forces. This union of peasants, workers, and others—led by the CPY, but fighting for the common goals of liberation from foreign occupation, national equality, and a better future—formed the basis of the United People's Liberation Front, later renamed the People's Front of Yugoslavia (PFY). By 1947, the PFY had grown into a mass organization of 7 million members and was the CPY's strongest pillar of support.

As the war progressed, the Communist party gradually but insistently created and affirmed its own governing organizations at all levels of society. At the lowest level, the CPY first established local governing bodies, known as People's Councils (PCs), in all liberated regions to stimulate and coordinate the gathering of supplies for the Partisan army. Originally considered temporary, in September 1942 the Central Committee of the CPY declared the PCs permanent and "the germ from which the future government will develop."[4] By the end of the war, an entire system of PCs, beginning at the bottom with local or village councils and progressing upward through townships, cities, districts, and regions, not only secured supplies for the army, but also acted as fully functioning organs of government.

CPY construction of its higher organs of power began on November 26–27, 1942, with the first meeting of the Anti-fascist People's Liberation Council of Yugoslavia (AVNOJ—Anti-fašističko vijeće narodnog oslobodjenja Jugoslavije). Acting on Soviet advice, AVNOJ did not immediately establish itself as an organ of power in opposition to the prewar Yugoslav government, now in exile in London, but only as a general political, national, and anti-fascist body. One year later, however, at its second meeting on November 29–30, 1943, and in defiance of Soviet instructions, AVNOJ officially declared itself the highest legislative, executive, and judicial organ of power in Yugoslavia.

The party's next goal was to obtain international recognition of its new government. In the early part of the war, the Western allies had offered their support exclusively to the royalist Yugoslav government-in-exile and to the Četniks, a Serbian organization loyal to King Petar and led by Colonel Draža Mihailović. Although originally a resistance movement, Mihailović's Četniks ended by collaborating with the Germans, and in 1943 the British transferred their support to the Partisans as it had become clear that they were more effective at fighting Germans. The CPY and the British government held prolonged negotiations throughout 1944, eventually agreeing to a compromise government based on AVNOJ, but including also representatives from the government-in-exile and the prewar Yugoslav Parliament. The June 1944 "Tito-Šubašić Agreement" also obliged the CPY to permit free activity of other political parties and to hold free elections for a constitutional assembly.

The Red Army's approach through Romania in the fall of 1944 offered the CPY an opportunity to enlist Soviet aid for the liberation of Belgrade. In late September, Tito secretly flew to Moscow to negotiate the joint action and one month later a combined force of Soviet and Partisan soldiers drove the Germans from Belgrade. On October 20, 1944, Tito's Supreme Staff took control over Yugoslavia's capital city. Although the war in Yugoslavia continued to rage for almost seven more months until the final expulsion of German troops from Croatia and Slovenia in May 1945, the liberation of Belgrade greatly enhanced the CPY's position as the leading force in Yugoslavia. The party, nonetheless, restated its commitment to the compromise reached with Britain, and the new government of "Democratic Federated Yugoslavia," created March 7, 1945, included three members of the Yugoslav government-in-exile. Likewise, AVNOJ—now designated the new government's provisional assembly—accepted into its ranks 118 "non-compromised" prewar politicians and people's deputies.

Officially, the new government's main function was to maintain order while presiding over the promised free elections to a constitutional assembly. Held on November 11, 1945, the elections themselves were, according to most observers, relatively free and clean. The preelection campaign, however, certainly was not. The CPY had designed the electoral law to benefit its own candidates, exerted tight control over the media, carried out systematic terror against opposition elements, and issued barely veiled threats against any "neutral" or "apolitical" citizens. Under these conditions, the opposition chose to boycott the elections, turning them into a one-horse race. Yet despite the farcical nature of the election, the party's intense political activity paid off when the elections achieved both high voter turnout and a 90 percent victory for the Communist-backed candidates.[5]

On November 29, 1945—on the second anniversary of the Second Meeting of AVNOJ—the newly elected Constitutional Assembly declared King Petar formally deposed and Yugoslavia a "Federal People's Republic." Two months later, on January 31, 1946, it formally adopted a new constitution, modeled on that of the Soviet Union. The Constitutional Assembly then refashioned itself as new Yugoslavia's first parliament.

Once it had secured victory through elections, the new regime relaxed its concern for the Western allies' democratic sensitivities and became far less restrained in its treatment of opposition elements. By the spring of 1946, Četnik leader Draža Mihailović, had been captured, tried, and executed, and in the fall of that year the party also arrested and imprisoned the Croatian Catholic archbishop of Zagreb, Alojzije Stepinac, ostensibly for collaborating with the Croat fascist organization known as the Ustaša. The following summer saw the arrest, trial, and imprisonment of prewar Serb politician Dragoljub Jovanović, who, although a member of the People's Front, had proved to be unacceptably stubborn in his refusal to accept all party policies without question.

In the meantime, the party had launched a series of legislative and economic policies designed to bring about the socialist transformation of society. Already in August 1945, the Provisional Assembly had passed a law on agrarian reform and colonization that ultimately resulted in the redistribution of some 800,000 hectares of land among 316,000 peasant families.[6] In December 1946, Parliament passed its first law on nationalization, covering such enterprises of "national importance" as banking, transportation, and wholesale commerce, although, in fact, 80 percent of Yugoslav industry had already been confiscated either directly from wartime occupiers or from their Yugoslav owners on often dubious grounds of collaboration. A second nationalization law passed in April 1948 finally completed the process, realizing state control over even minute enterprises. Meanwhile, in April 1947, the government had unveiled its first Five Year Plan for economic development, which, again following the Soviet example, called for extremely high levels of investment, especially in the infrastructure and in heavy industry.

In the spring and summer of 1948, CPY progress toward socialist development was suddenly interrupted by its developing conflict with the Soviet Union and "People's Democracies" of Eastern Europe. After a tense meeting between top CPY leaders and Stalin in February 1948, Tito's pictures were suddenly removed from all public places in Romania. Then on March 18, the Soviet Union abruptly recalled its high level military and diplomatic personnel from Yugoslavia, claiming that they were "surrounded by an absence of comradeship."[7] In the weeks and months that followed, Soviet leaders carried on a heated correspondence with the Central Committee of the CPY. In their letters, Stalin and Molotov accused Yugoslav leaders of a variety of sins, from anti-Soviet attitudes to coddling the peasantry. Some of the accusations were clearly ludicrous while others bore more relationship to reality. Top CPY leaders, however, correctly surmised that the conflict had nothing to do with these specific accusations but was intended to destroy the independence of the party, making it into a more obedient and predictable satellite.

In their responses, therefore, CPY leaders refused to admit error, while nonetheless insisting on their loyalty to the Soviet Union and the cause of socialism. They declined, moreover, to discuss their case at a special meeting of the Communist Information Bureau or Cominform (an organization in which Yugoslavia's Communists had previously held a position of leadership) convened in Bucharest, Romania, on June 28, 1948. The resolution passed at that meeting restated the Soviet accusations and called on "healthy elements" in the party to remove their leaders and return Yugoslavia to the socialist fold. In response, CPY leaders first published the resolution and their entire correspondence with Soviet leaders and then instituted a campaign to root out Cominform supporters, while at the same time still declaring loyalty to the Soviet Union and socialist bloc.

The split, formalized by the Cominform resolution of June 28, 1948, thus did not end Yugoslavia's efforts at socialization. It did, however, change them, though not all at once and not always in the expected manner. The immediate impact of the split was a tightening up of party controls on Yugoslav society, seen most clearly in the arrest and imprisonment of some 14,000 Communists as Cominformist agents. In addition, the considerable economic hardships imposed by the Cominform blockade of Yugoslavia, together with the country's heightened defense needs, led the party to accelerate its plan for socialization of the countryside through the often forcible creation of Peasant Working Cooperatives. Yet, it was also during this period that party leaders began to express increasingly sharp criticisms of the Soviet Union and its party leadership. Beginning in the spring of 1949, that leadership was consistently described as imperialistic, chauvinistic, and bureaucratic, while its policies were now said to deviate substantially from the theories of Marx, Engels, and Lenin.

It was also in mid-1949 that party leaders began rereading the classics of Marx and Engels in order to provide ideological justification for their acts of independence. As they did so, they developed a new approach to the political and economic construction of socialism, as well as a more sophisticated and thoughtful understanding of social and cultural change. Consequently, while the immediate post-split era did show increased levels of repression and higher demands for the mobilization of labor, it also served as an incubator for new ideas about how to achieve the transformation of society.

One of the embryos nurtured in that incubator would emerge by June 1950 as the Law on Worker's Self-Management or, according to its official title, "The Basic Law on the Management of State Economic Enterprises and Higher Economic Associations by the Work Collectives." Introduced and defended by Tito and passed by the National Assembly on June 27, 1950, the new law was intended to begin the process of the "withering away of the state" and bring Yugoslav socialism closer to the model envisioned by Marx and Engels. The law officially ended state ownership of the means of production, turning it over to "society" in the care of elected workers' councils and management boards. In practice, however, the enterprise director, though officially a nonvoting member of the management board, maintained considerable authority. Most important, as an agent of the state, he was responsible for ensuring the enterprise's compliance with central economic planning.

Yet even if the Law on Self-Management did not lead to true workers' management of the economy, it provided the ideological basis for more influential changes in the structure and modus operandi of party organizations—especially at the district and local levels. Accordingly, the reform of party organizations passed on June 20, 1950, sought to establish a clearer boundary between party and state apparati. In the past, it explained, district party and government positions had been almost inseparable and the party had exercised its leading role in society through direct control over the most important branches of the state. While claiming that this approach had been both necessary and correct in the first years of socialist construction, the Central Committee admitted that it had now become a barrier to socialist democracy as it had prevented the development of independence by government organizations and stifled the initiative of the masses.[8] The reform also reduced the size of the administrative apparati in all party organizations, hoping to minimize bureaucratization. As a result, whereas in 1950 there had been 11,930 professional party functionaries, by November 1952 that number had been reduced to 4,599.[9]

Meanwhile, party leaders strengthened efforts to stimulate ideological debate at the Fourth Plenum of the Central Committee of the CPY held in June 1951. The plenum's "Resolution on theoretical work in the CPY" now stated that the opinions of top party leaders need not be obligatorily studied or adopted by lower party forums unless so ordered by a Politburo directive. The Fourth Plenum also urged substantial progress in the development of a more independent and professional legal system after a stunning report by Aleksandar Ranković admitted to numerous violations of legality in the previous years by the party, the courts, and especially the secret police, otherwise known as UDBa.[10] Various speeches by top party leaders in the early 1950s also now referred to the future "withering away" of both the state and the party. All agreed that such an occurrence would not mean their elimination but only a withering away of their functions. Nonetheless, the very existence of such discussions reflected a revised interpretation of the party's guiding ideology.

The high point of the party's reform policies came at the Sixth Party Congress held November 2–7, 1952, and at the Fourth Congress of the People's Front in late February 1953. The Sixth Party Congress represented a culmination and official endorsement of the trends and reforms carried out in the previous two years. First, it offered a severe criticism of the Stalinist system, unequivocally describing it as an aggressive imperialist force, state-capitalist, and bureaucratic. More importantly, however, party leaders now moved beyond criticizing Stalinist revisionism to articulate openly and officially their own interpretation of Marxist theory for the Yugoslav case based on workers' self-management, the separation of party and state, and the guiding (but not ruling) role of the Communist party. To make tangible this new approach, the Central Committee changed the party's name from the Communist Party of Yugoslavia to the League of Communists of Yugoslavia (LCY). The party, its leaders now declared, would unquestionably maintain its leading role in society, but would realize it by different, less Stalinist, means.[11]

The Fourth Congress of the People's Front (now renamed the Socialist Alliance of the Working People of Yugoslavia—SAWPY) held in February 1953 marked a further step forward in expanding the party's view of its role. All agreed that SAWPY now represented the main political organization in the country. The LCY, meanwhile, would represent only its "most ideologically consistent section" and would seek to realize its goals through that organization.

The congress also prepared the ground for the official abandonment of the collective farms, describing Stalin's collectivization drive as the "cruel exploitation of the masses" and the "barbaric theft of the peasantry." According to the "Decree on Property Relations and Reorganization of Peasant Working Cooperatives," on March 30, 1953, peasants could choose freely to leave the cooperative, taking with them whatever equipment and land they had brought into it. Predictably, most did. In some areas, two-thirds of the peasants in Peasant Working Cooperatives left them within the first nine months. By 1957, the amount of arable land in the socialist sector had declined from 25 percent in 1952 to only 9 percent.[12]

Although collective farms were never reestablished in Yugoslavia, the party almost immediately thereafter embarked on an era of retrenchment toward tighter party control. The crucial turning point away from reform came at the Second Plenum of the Central Committee held on Tito's island retreat of Brioni in June 1953. The plenum's purpose was to evaluate and reinterpret the conclusions of the Sixth Party Congress. In marked contrast to plenums and congresses earlier in the 1950s, which worried about excessive bureaucratization, the use of administrative methods, and the danger of developing state capitalism, the directive letter that followed the Brioni Plenum expressed concern over the growing and dangerous influence of the bourgeois West. The Brioni Plenum of 1953 thus marked the end of the reform period of the 1950s. Indeed, less than a year later at another Brioni Plenum in January 1954, Milovan Djilas, the foremost proponent of the reforms, would be first expelled from the party and later arrested. The party, it was now made clear, would not "wither away," nor would it turn over its leading role in the country to any other organization.

Nonetheless, throughout the following decades, Yugoslavia would become known for the greater degree of freedom and economic prosperity it offered. In stark contrast to those in the Soviet Union and its Eastern European allies, Yugoslavia's citizens enjoyed the right to travel abroad and had considerable access to Western material and cultural imports. Thanks to Western loans, Yugoslav citizens also enjoyed a much higher standard of living than did their counterparts in the Warsaw Pact. Yet, the country also retained its socialist system and while other periods of reform came and went, none was as innovative or idealistic as that of the early 1950s, and none ever caused any further wavering in the party's determination to maintain its monopoly on power.

External and Internal Constraints

The events outlined above developed as the result of a complex mixture of forces, including ideology, international events, and Yugoslavia's domestic circumstances. This monograph focuses mainly on the ideological element, that is, on CPY efforts to realize its vision for the future. Those efforts, however, were necessarily conditioned by the party's position within the matrix of domestic and international power relations, as well as by Yugoslavia's postwar economic and social circumstances. While not the sole determinants of CPY policy, these relations and circumstances defined the boundaries within which the party sought to realize its ideological agenda. Party policies could not help but be affected by the emerging cold war atmosphere, the Soviet-Yugoslav split, Yugoslavia's changing but nearly always desperate economic situation, the high level of national tension in the country, and a generally unstable political and social environment.

Within the emerging postwar division of power between the Soviet Union and the West, and despite a wartime agreement between Stalin and Churchill evenly splitting future political influence in Yugoslavia, the CPY's rise to power firmly affixed Yugoslavia to the Soviet camp. New Yugoslavia's loyalty to the Soviet Union derived mainly from the CPY's Communist ideology and its adherence to the general line of the Communist movement. Up until the end of the Second World War, the Soviet Union had been the only major country in the world ruled by Communists, providing it an essentially unchallenged position of authority among other aspiring Communist parties. Soviet predominance in the Comintern, first formalized at its Second Congress by the mandatory adoption of Lenin's "21 Conditions," grew even further under Stalin, when defense of the Soviet Union became the first duty and requirement of all Comintern members.

The CPY had joined the Comintern already in 1919 and its adherence to the Comintern line was never seriously questioned. Indeed, Soviet leaders commonly and directly interfered in the CPY's internal organization and policy determination throughout the interwar period. Even during the war, after Soviet leaders had dissolved the Comintern, they continued to send regular advice and directives to the CPY through communiqués, couriers, and radio transmissions. After the war ended, the CPY remained closely attuned to the Soviet Union in the determination and execution of its domestic and foreign policies.

It is also true, however, that almost from the very outset of the war, the CPY showed considerably more independence in its relations with the Soviet Union than did any of the other Communist parties in Eastern Europe. Even in the early stages of the war, CPY leaders took a number of decisions separate from or in opposition to the Soviet line, and as the party's position of authority in Yugoslavia increased, so too did its independence. The CPY certainly did not consciously set itself up in opposition to the Soviet Union. On the contrary, Yugoslav party leaders clearly considered themselves to be Stalin's most loyal and devoted disciples. Up until the Soviet-Yugoslav split and even for six months after it, CPY leaders regularly hailed the Soviet Union as the first country of socialism and publicly recognized its position of authority. Treatment of the Soviet Union by the Yugoslav media was voluminous and unfailingly complimentary, glorifying it as the most just, democratic, freedom-loving, and progressive nation in the world. Nonetheless, in the years from 1944 to 1948, several disputes arose between the two governments concerning their mutual economic relations, the behavior of Soviet military personnel in Yugoslavia, and especially the CPY's radical foreign policies. Although CPY loyalty to the Soviet Union remained unshaken until after the 1948 split, its earlier adherence to the Soviet line could be considered neither unquestioning nor unconditional.[13]

Meanwhile, CPY relations with the West grew increasingly tense after the end of the war. In part, Yugoslavia's relations with the West reflected only the changing international scene in which the United States and the Soviet Union, with their vastly differing political ideologies, emerged as the predominant world powers. Already by late 1944 and early 1945, the entire wartime alliance system was disintegrating in disputes over the construction of peace and the postwar organization of Europe. Despite what is now seen as Stalin's relatively conservative foreign policy, the Western allies' fear of proliferating Communist-dominated governments resulted by early 1946 in Churchill's declaration of a "crusade against communism" and by 1947 in Truman's promise to help Greece and Turkey ward off the Communist threat.

The CPY, in particular, regularly provoked Western hostility through its radical domestic polices, its intransigent stance with regard to Trieste, and its continued aid to Communist insurgents in Greece. Although Stalin often opposed these CPY policies, Western allies clearly believed they had originated in Moscow. Thus the Western allies tended to treat Yugoslavia as a fully obedient satellite of the Soviet Union and a testing ground in the battle between Soviet and Western ideologies.

As a result of both the CPY's inflexible policies and Western misconceptions about their significance, ill feelings between Yugoslavia's Communist regime and the West began to surface already in 1943 and increased steadily in the years following the war. Consequently, Yugoslavia's postwar relations with the West were characterized by an extreme degree of uncertainty, and Yugoslav leaders apparently considered a new war possible in the near future. In a Politburo meeting in December 1945, for example, Tito warned that given the extremely tense situation in Trieste, the party must be militarily prepared for anything, and internal reports throughout the early postwar era worried that the press too often published material that might be useful to an unnamed enemy in case of war.[14]

Even so, it would be inaccurate to suggest that the West had no influence on CPY policies before 1948. For even if party leaders steadfastly rejected Western political, economic, and cultural models, the same could not be said of Yugoslavia's citizens. While CPY opponents who promoted Western political and economic solutions might be dealt with relatively easily, party leaders had a much harder time countering the influence of Western high and popular culture on Yugoslavia's intellectuals and ordinary citizens.[15]

In the years following the Soviet-Yugoslav split, Yugoslavia's position in this international dichotomy necessarily changed. Expelled from the Soviet bloc and the target of an almost complete economic blockade by the Soviet Union and Eastern European countries, Yugoslavia's leaders were forced to reorient their foreign policies toward the West. While retaining a socialist system and claiming continued loyalty to the socialist cause, party leaders nonetheless reduced the level of their anti-Western rhetoric and ended their support of Greek insurgents. Simultaneously, they began cautious conversations with Western diplomats in search of economic aid. By September 1949, they had secured their first U.S. loan of $20 million. In the following years, party leaders would accept large amounts of additional Western economic and even military aid. While always claiming that this aid came "with no strings attached," the increased contact with the West unquestionably influenced the political and cultural realm, while the loans themselves offered new opportunities in the economic sphere.[16]

While clearly conditioned by the conflict between East and West in the international sphere, CPY policies were more directly affected by Yugoslavia's domestic needs and circumstances. Yugoslavia's impoverished economic status, in particular, placed almost overwhelming demands on the new regime in the years immediately following the war. Largely agrarian and seriously underdeveloped, Yugoslavia's prewar per capita income had been only between 60 and 70 U.S. dollars, compared with $521 in the United States and $236 in France.[17] This state of poverty was further exacerbated by the war, in which a total of 1.7 million people died and another 3.5 million were left homeless. The country's infrastructure suffered enormous devastation as over 50 percent of rail lines were destroyed, along with 35 percent of prewar industry, 50–70 percent of prewar livestock, and 80 percent of ploughs and harvesting equipment. Many villages had been entirely destroyed and difficult living conditions prevailed even in the major cities. Worse yet, two years of drought immediately following the war and another in 1950 raised the threat of mass starvation.[18]

The new government's first and most pressing responsibility, then, was to prevent a famine and begin rebuilding the country by reestablishing lines of communication and distribution, as well as agricultural and industrial production. In these early efforts, despite significant and crucial aid from UNRRA, the new government stood almost entirely alone. For although CPY leaders had originally hoped for massive Soviet aid, they soon had to accept that the Soviet Union itself had been badly damaged by the war and was unable (or unwilling) to raise Yugoslavia out of its poverty.

Consequently, economic tasks occupied a major proportion of the new government's energy, and party leaders regularly warned that failure in the economic sphere could threaten to overturn all their wartime moral and political victories. Immediately following the liberation of Belgrade, various party documents had begun to stress the overwhelming importance of economic activities. Youth leader Milijan Neorečić, for example, stated,

> Today a good member of the party and SKOJ [the Communist youth organization] is one who is a good merchant. A good member of the party is one who knows to bring food products to Belgrade and to sell them at regulated prices. Today we must be good grocers, good engineers, and good merchants. The survival of the broad popular masses depends upon it.[19]

By late 1947, the country's economic status, while far from prosperous, seemed at least relatively stable. Following the Soviet-Yugoslav split, however, economic issues were once again the subject of enormous concern. Now bordered by unfriendly nations on all sides, Yugoslavia faced greatly increased defense needs, while at the same time the Soviet and Eastern European economic blockade inhibited the party's ability to carry out its economic agenda as specified by the Five Year Plan. These considerations altered CPY policies in a number of areas. For example, according to Susan Woodward, economic requirements (though caused by a change in the country's international status) were primary in both the party's disastrous decision to accelerate its campaign for the socialization of the countryside in 1949 and its later introduction of workers' self-management.[20]

A second circumstance that inevitably shaped the form and content of CPY domestic policies was the national question. From the moment of its formal inception in December 1918, Yugoslavia's fate was inextricably connected with the relations between its constituent nations and nationalities. Despite claims to the contrary, Yugoslavia's recent conflicts have not resulted from "ancient ethnic hatreds." It is true that a degree of tension has long existed between many of the peoples of Yugoslavia; yet that tension has only periodically produced violence. During much of their long history, Yugoslavia's ethnic groups have managed to coexist on the Balkan peninsula reasonably peacefully, if not harmoniously. Indeed, during the 19th and 20th centuries the growth of Serb, Croat, Slovene, and other national ideologies was accompanied by the development of "Yugoslavism" as a kind of South Slavic national identity. The precise content of the Yugoslav national idea varied considerably over time and among different national groups; nonetheless, its popularity among many in the region should not be dismissed.

Unfortunately, much of that appeal was squandered during the interwar period by the Serbian-dominated government's insensitive and bullying approach to the country's other constituent peoples. Even so, the strongest expression of hostility among Yugoslavia's nations came only during the Second World War with the genocidal policies of the Croatian fascist Ustaša and the subsequent massacres of Croats and Muslims by Serbian Četnik organizations. The legacy of hatred caused by those events was perhaps the greatest challenge that Yugoslavia's postwar Communist party would face. Indeed the Communist regime deserves some credit for tempering those hostilities and maintaining peace among the Yugoslav nations for nearly 50 years. Yet, as is now clear, the Communists may also be blamed for failing ultimately to face the national problem head on and find a lasting solution.

The position of the CPY concerning the national question had varied during the interwar period from complete indifference and unitarism to advocating the mandatory dissolution of Yugoslavia as an artificial creation of Versailles. By the beginning of the war, however, the party had finally settled on a federal solution to the problem within a united Yugoslavia. From the very beginning of Yugoslavia's occupation, the party spoke out for national self-determination and the equality, brotherhood, and unity of all Yugoslav nations within a federal structure that ultimately included the six sovereign republics of Serbia, Croatia, Slovenia, Bosnia-Hercegovina, Macedonia, and Montenegro, the autonomous province of Vojvodina, and the autonomous region of Kosovo-Metohia.

The federal structure of new Yugoslavia did not provide the individual republics with any real independence since decision making within the party and state remained highly centralized. Yet even if largely a formality, the party's federal solution did show that it valued each constituent nation, and CPY adherence to it was a key source of its postwar legitimacy.

Yet CPY policies concerning the national question were often inconsistent as the party sought a balance between its more popular support for decentralized federalism and its ideologically based centralism. On the one hand, party leaders consistently stressed the equality of all nations in new Yugoslavia, insisting that all Serbs, Croats, and so on were both citizens of a common homeland and free within their federal units. They also sought to pacify national hostilities and fears by stressing the importance of national tolerance and, especially, the "brotherhood and unity" of Yugoslavia's nations and nationalities.[21] Yet, in seeking to paper over Yugoslavia's national question, the Communist regime refused fully to confront the atrocities committed during the war, treating them only as additional signs of the prewar bourgeois government's moral and political bankruptcy.[22]

Moreover, for all their talk of national self-determination, party leaders were not about to permit the dissolution of Yugoslavia. After all, without a united Yugoslavia, there was no role for a ruling Communist party of Yugoslavia. Nor, in these early years at least, would party leaders allow any such decentralization or "local particularism" as might hinder their ability to control and direct the country. As Tito explained in several speeches during the spring of 1945, federalism did not imply any form of separatism or particularism and no federal unit should become strong at the expense of the others. Rather, he said, the point was to create out of them all one powerful Yugoslav national state.[23] In practice, of course, the party's attempts to balance national equality and Yugoslav unity met with mixed success at best.

A final characteristic of the domestic scene confronting CPY leaders as they took power was the generally chaotic social and moral atmosphere caused by four years of foreign occupation and civil war. Despite CPY attempts to forge unity, a variety of national, religious, political, and social factors deeply divided the Yugoslav population. The massacres committed by various factions could not be forgotten overnight, nor could members of such wartime political enemies as the Partisans, Četniks, Ustaše, Ljotićists, and Slovene or Croat Home Guards be easily reconciled. In addition, individuals who had taken active part in the struggle or had seen their villages burned and loved ones murdered often had little but contempt for those who had waited out the war in comfort either abroad or in the major occupied cities. It is no surprise, therefore, that high levels of emotional intensity and irrational outbursts of anger characterized postwar Yugoslav society.

Even discounting the elements of fratricide and revolution, the very atmosphere of war—where fear and death were daily occurrences, and lies and deception could represent supreme virtues—was enough to cause serious social dislocation and massive uncertainty and trepidation. One contemporary of the time has suggested that even the enormous enthusiasm characteristic of the postwar period was the result of collective psychosis. The fear and trauma were so great, he argues, that they required some outlet and the only safe and possible one was positive.[24]

The fear and uncertainty that saturated Yugoslav society may be most clearly perceived in the myriad rumors that spread through the country after the war. Most of these rumors concerned the likelihood of a new war. Many, for example, anticipated some sort of alliance between local allies or enemies (Četniks, Ustaše, etc.) and the Western powers, leading to a change in government and massive reprisals against all who had cooperated with the Communist regime. Fear of bombing attacks remained so strong that long after the war had ended some people still ran for cover when Yugoslav planes passed overhead. Others, meanwhile, whispered that America had invented a gas that would put the entire population of the country asleep for 24 hours.[25]

Other prevalent rumors found their source in domestic political events or in folk or religious superstitions. Some people feared the immediate communization of all property and families, or even that their children would be rounded up and sent to Russia. Several rumors implied the existence of national conflicts between top CPY leaders, while others referred to assassination attempts on Tito. Finally, many peasants in several parts of the country believed that a meteorite would soon fall from the sky, wiping out the entire Yugoslav population.[26]

It was in this war-torn and impoverished land, caught between East and West, with a society rent by national, religious, political, and social tensions and a population in fear of imminent war or falling meteorites, that the CPY dreamed of creating its Communist utopia. The precise outlines and dimensions of the party's policies of persuasion depended, however, not only on the circumstances within which it operated, but also on the media and agents entrusted to implement those policies.

Notes

1. It may be argued with some justification that CPY efforts to remake society in Yugoslavia actually began either in November 1943 with the second meeting of

AVNOJ or with the final liberation of Yugoslavia in April 1945. I have chosen the median date based on the liberation of Belgrade not only for its symbolic importance, but also because in the former period so much of the party's attention focused on efforts to liberate the country, while to begin the examination only in April 1945 would exclude from consideration the extremely vigorous persuasive campaigns that developed in the winter of 1944–1945.

2. Among the more important English-language sources for the interwar period in Yugoslavia are Ivo Banac, *The National Question in Yugoslavia: Origins, History, Politics* (Ithaca, NY: Cornell University Press, 1984); Aleksa Djilas, *The Contested Country: Yugoslav Unity and Communist Revolution* (Cambridge, MA: Harvard University Press, 1991); J. B. Hoptner, *Yugoslavia in Crisis, 1934–1941* (New York: Columbia University Press, 1962); Andrew Wachtel, *Making a Nation, Breaking a Nation: Literature and Cultural Politics in Yugoslavia* (Stanford, CA: Stanford University Press, 1998).

3. On the Communist Party of Yugoslavia in the interwar era see Ivan Avakumović, *The History of the Communist Party of Yugoslavia*, Vol. 1 (Aberdeen: Aberdeen University Press, 1964); Banac, *The National Question*; Djilas, *The Contested Country*; Jill Irvine, *The Croat Question: Partisan Politics in the Formation of the Yugoslav Socialist State* (Boulder, CO: Westview Press, 1993).

4. Josip Broz Tito, cited in Pero Morača and Stanislav Stojanović, eds., *Povijest Saveza komunista Jugoslavije* (Belgrade: Izdavački centar Komunist, 1985), 233.

5. For information on and analyses of the elections see Branko Petranović, *Političke i pravne prilike za vreme privremene vlade DFJ* (Belgrade: 1964), 186–205; *Informativni priručnik o Jugoslaviji, Opšti podaci o političkom, privrednom, socijalnom, kulturnom i prosvetnom životu u Federativnoj narodnoj republici Jugoslaviji*, November-December 1948 (Belgrade: 1948–1951), 61–64; Rajko Kuzmanović, *Privremena narodna skupština DFJ* (Belgrade: 1981), 76–87, 143–149; Stojan T. Tomić, "Izbori u vrijeme revolucionarnog etatizma 1945–1953," in *Skupštinski izbori u Jugoslaviji, 1942–1982* (Belgrade: 1983), 75–101; Vojislav Koštunica and Kosta Čavoški, *Party Pluralism or Monism, Social Movements and the Political System in Yugoslavia, 1944–1949* (Boulder, CO: Westview Press, 1985), 125–126.

6. Dužan Bilandžić, *Historija Socijalističke Federativne Republike Jugoslavije: Glavni procesi, 1918–1985* (Zagreb: Školska knjiga, 1985), 115.

7. Cited in Robert Barry Farrell, *Yugoslavia and the Soviet Union 1948–56* (Hamden, CT: Shoestring Press, 1956), 69.

8. "Odluke i direktive CK KP, Svim Centralnim komitetima KP Republika," 22 June 1950, *Partijska izgradnja*, 6 (1950): 55–60.

9. Morača and Stojanović, 376.

10. "Rezolucija Četvrtog plenuma CKKPJ o teorijskom radu u KPJ," and Milovan Djilas, "O teorijskom radu naše partije," 3–4 June 1951, in Branko Petranović, Ranko Končar and Radovan Radonjić, eds., *Sednice Centralnog komiteta KPJ (1948–1952)* (Belgrade: Izdavački centar Komunist, 1985), 639, 589–597; Predrag J. Marković, *Beograd izmedju istoka i zapada, 1948–1965* (Belgrade: 1996), 173–174.

11. "Značaj Šestog Kongresa Saveza Komunista Jugoslavije," *Komunist*, 5, no. 1 (1953): 5–8.

12. Dennison Rusinow, *The Yugoslav Experiment, 1948–1974* (Berkeley, CA: University of California Press, 1977), 78.

13. For more information on these conflicts see Vladimir Dedijer, *The Battle Stalin Lost, Memoirs of Yugoslavia, 1948–1953* (New York: Viking Press, 1970), 31–35, 48–54, 73–96; Milovan Djilas, *Conversations with Stalin* (New York: Harcourt Brace Jovanovich, 1962), 8–11, 87–124, 133–142, 173–184; Milovan Djilas, *Rise and Fall* (New York: Harcourt Brace Jovanovich, 1983), 77–98, 145–153, 163–172; Ivo Banac, *With Stalin Against Tito, Cominformist Splits in Yugoslav Communism* (Ithaca, NY: Cornell University Press, 1988), 4–44.

14. "Sednica CK KPJ sa Birom CK KP Slovenije," 4 Dec. 1945, ACKSKJ, III/9; Letter to editorial boards from Ivan Šibl, December 1946, HDA, CKKPHAP; "Dnevne direktive i zadaci u agitaciji i štampi 1948," 1948, ACKSKJ, VIII II/1-a-14; "Instrukcija CK KPJ o čuvanju državnih tajna u štampi, filmu i na radiju," 1948, ACKSKJ, VIII I/1-a-9.

15. For an excellent analysis of the impact of Western and Soviet ideologies on the population of Belgrade between 1948 and 1965 see Marković.

16. For a thorough description of precisely how the CPY adjusted its economic policies in response to international events see Susan Woodward, *Socialist Unemployment: The Political Economy of Yugoslavia 1945–1990* (Princeton: Princeton University Press, 1995).

17. An estimated 75 percent of the population made its living from agriculture while manufacturing accounted for only 26.8 percent of the GNP. Rusinow, xviii.

18. Rusinow, 19.

19. Milijan Neorečić, "Savetovanje PK SKOJ za Srbiju," Spring 1945, ACKSKJ, CKSKOJ IIa–2/1.

20. Woodward, 98–163.

21. "Drug Tito govorio u Celju i Osijeku," *Rad,* 9 June 1945; "Ekspoze pretsednika Ministarskog saveta Maršala Tita," *Selo,* 6 Aug. 1945; Milovan Djilas, Speech at the Second Plenum of the USAOJ, 5–8 Sept. 1945, AJ, SSOJ-27; "Govor Maršala Tita u Čajetini," *Politika,* 9 July 1946.

22. For a description of how the party avoided these issues in its educational curriculum see Wolfgang Höpken, "History Education and Yugoslav (Dis-)Integration," in Melissa Bokovoy, Jill Irvine, and Carol Lilly, eds., *State-Society Relations in Yugoslavia: 1945–1991* (New York and London: St. Martin's Press, 1997), 79–104.

23. "Iz govora generalnog sekretara KPJ Josipa Broza Tita na osnivačkom kongresu KP Srbije," 8–12 May 1945, in Branko Petranović and Momčilo Zečević, *Jugoslovenski federalizam: Ideje i stvarnosti,* Vol. 2 (Belgrade: 1987), 158–159; "Prvi govor Maršala Tita u oslobodjenom Zagrebu," *Politika,* 23 May 1945; "Govor Maršala Tita u Ljubljanu," *Slobodna Vojvodina,* 28 May 1945.

24. Milo Gligorijević, *Odgovor Mica Popović* (Belgrade: 1984), 35. See also "Information about Human Rehabilitation of Children and Young People," March 1945, AJ, MP-3; Dušan Baranin, "Psihoza straha," *Selo,* 15 April 1945.

25. "Izvještaj OK SKOJ za Gorski kotar," 4 July 1945, HDA, PKSKOJ-H; "Neprijateljske parole od marta 1946 g. do aprila 1947 g. na teritoriju FNRJ," 14 April 1947, ACKSKJ, VIII VI/2-h-2.

26. See "Izveštaj OK KPH Gorski kotar," 9 June 1945, HDA, CKKPH; "Izvještaj političke situacije" from OO Bjelovar, 4 July 1945, HDA, RKSSRNH-1; "Izvještaj OK SKOJ Varaždin," 4 Aug. 1945, HDA, PKSKOJ-H-1; "Mesečni izveštaj OK SKOJ Požarevac," 13 April 1946, ACKSKJ, CKSKOJ III b-1/6; "Neprijateljske parole."

2

Tools of the Trade: The Apparatus for Cultural Change

CPY efforts at social and cultural change in Yugoslavia unfolded within a complex, multilayered, and interconnected apparatus headed by three institutional entities: the party, the state, and the mass organizations. These entities, while institutionally distinct, were joined by the overriding power and influence of Communist party members in each. Indeed, the CPY carefully secured its leadership in all institutions with a persuasive agenda by placing party members in the leading positions of nearly all public and state forums, including the army, the media, mass organizations, film production companies, state publishing agencies, and the ministry of education.[1] Persuasive policies thus originated at the top levels of the party. They were implemented, however, by a wide variety of committees and councils within not only the party, but also the state and various mass organizations.

The Communist Party

The Communist Party of Yugoslavia was unquestionably the primary source of cultural and persuasive policies in the new state. In accordance with the new federal structure of postwar Yugoslavia, the CPY was organized on both a federal and a hierarchical basis. Slovenia and Croatia had formed their own individual Communist parties already in 1937, while the remainder of Yugoslavia's new federal units formed separate parties during and just after the war. The existence of separate parties did not, however, imply their independence, since the principle of democratic centralism obligated all lower bodies to carry out decisions adopted by central organs. Thus, directives and instructions traveled downward through the party hierarchy, from the Politburo and Central Committee of the CPY, to the central committees of the federal units, and then through regional, district, township, city, and local party committees.

The main decision-making body of the postwar CPY was an ad hoc, informally selected Politburo whose actual membership was unclear even to the top leaders. (Evidently some leaders were not sure whether they had attended its meetings as regular members or as occasional guests.)[2] The top four leaders of the Politburo, however, and those with ultimate power and responsibility were Josip Broz Tito, Edvard Kardelj, Aleksandar Ranković, and Milovan Djilas.

Josip Broz Tito clearly stood out as top man in the party whose authority and position of respect were absolutely unquestioned.[3] Tito's authority derived from a broad combination of factors, including his social origin (as one of the few top CPY leaders who had actually been a worker), his considerable experiences in the Soviet Union, his success in unifying and bolshevizing the CPY, his demonstrated abilities as a politician and to a lesser extent as a military leader, and last, but not least, his own personal charisma. Tito attracted the loyalty of other CPY leaders and ordinary Yugoslav citizens alike apparently as much by his personal qualities as by his leadership skills. It is typical, for example, that one of the most popular wartime songs about Tito referred to him not as a powerful military figure or an impressive politician but as a "little white violet."[4] Every official policy required Tito's approval and in cases of uncertainty or internal disagreement, Tito represented the ultimate arbiter. Yet, Tito was not himself a theoretician and was not always deeply involved even in policy formation, much less implementation. Thus, although Tito's aura hangs over all CPY activities, his name arises only sporadically throughout this work.

The names of Edvard Kardelj and Aleksandar Ranković also appear only occasionally in this work, although both men were crucial to the development of postwar Yugoslav policies. As a well-educated intellectual and seasoned Communist, Kardelj was the primary theoretician and ideologist of the CPY. But Kardelj tended to concentrate on large-scale political and economic activities and was often only peripherally involved in the more detailed and culturally oriented policies covered by this work. Ranković, meanwhile, as head of the Yugoslav secret police, supervised the enforcement of many policies addressed in this study. But while it is worth remembering that Ranković and the secret police stood behind each policy, the focus of this work lies on the persuasive rather than the coercive element of CPY activity.

The CPY leader who directed the party's persuasive and cultural policies was Milovan Djilas. The character and personality of this enigmatic Montenegrin, who went from being a top leader in the Yugoslav Communist movement to its most celebrated and outspoken dissident, have been the source of considerable interest and speculation. Was he a true idealist who suddenly realized that the party had somehow gone astray, a born fanatic genetically inclined toward rebellion, or a political opportunist interested only in remaining in the limelight?[5] Certainly up until the split with the Soviet Union, Djilas appeared to be one of the most severe and dogmatic leaders of the CPY, utterly devoted to Stalin, the Soviet Union, and the ultimate cause of communism. What then could explain his remarkable transformation into an avid proponent of democratization? My own sense is that Djilas was ruled by his belief in the value of consistency with one's principles, over and above issues of either humanity or practicality. Thus, when he accepted the principles associated with Stalinism (especially the notion that the ends justify the means), he was ruthless in their application. Later, however, when he adopted the principles of democratization, he sought to apply them with equal vigor and consistency, regardless of the consequences for his party or himself. In any case, it is also true that even when spouting the Stalinist party line in the mid-1940s, Djilas's essays displayed a level of sophistication not found in the writings of many of his colleagues. Certainly Djilas was no elevated Marxist theoretician, but he was able to perceive or construct certain nuances within the party line and to express them through manipulation of the written word.[6]

Besides Djilas, a broad variety of other leading Communists and intellectuals like Radovan Zogović, Vladimir Dedijer, Rodoljub Čolaković, Veljko Vlahović, Mitra Mitrović, Milijan Neorečić, and Bora Drenovac directly influenced the party's persuasive and cultural policies. The decision-making process at these top levels took place in an extremely informal manner, often through personal conversations, the conclusions of which were only subsequently (if ever) formalized in written documents. Entitled "reports" or "circular letters," these documents often lacked any claim of authorship. In many cases, the individual author was indeed irrelevant, as the document simply repeated the party line in the official Communist terminology.

After all, top leaders generally agreed about the ultimate goals of the party, its correct political and ideological line, and—with some important exceptions—even the essential program required to attain those goals.[7] At lower levels, too, party leaders in many regions worked together very closely. The intimacy among CPY leaders resulted in part from their common wartime experiences; it continued after the war both out of necessity and due to a sort of siege mentality among party members. For while Communists bore responsibility for all political, economic, social, and cultural activity in a region, they often made up only a tiny minority of the local population. Consequently, each available activist held multiple positions and they all worked closely together to both maintain their grasp on power and fulfill the ever-increasing tasks assigned from above.

The Departments of Agitation and Propaganda

The main organs for cultural change within the Communist party were the departments of agitation and propaganda, or agitprop. As Djilas explained in September 1945, the goal of the agitprop apparatus was "to concentrate, directly or indirectly, all political, cultural, educational, and scientific life in the hands of the party"; to channel correctly the aspirations of the populace for culture; and to prevent all efforts by enemy elements to direct cultural life toward their interests.[8]

While no unified or fully organized agitprop department had existed in the prewar CPY, already from the early stages of the war, an agitprop department attached to the Supreme Staff consciously managed cultural and educational life in both Partisan units and liberated territory.[9] The postwar organization of agitprop departments properly commenced in June 1945 with the division of the party's Central Committee into 12 departments and commissions, including a department of agitation and propaganda headed by Milovan Djilas.[10] Agitprop departments, commissions, or sections were also to be formed at all levels of the party hierarchy. The organizational development of agitprop bodies proceeded at different speeds and with varying degrees of success in different parts of the country, but within a relatively short period most party organizations had created some internal body to help realize party tasks by cultural and educational means.

The internal structure of agitprop departments went through several preliminary stages, but most often included four main sectors, each with several subdepartments. According to the system established in the spring of 1946, the departments consisted of a sector for agitation and the press to transmit and interpret party decisions and the party line through the press and by other oral and visual means; a theoretical sector to verify the ideological purity expressed in party rhetoric, to guard against deviations from orthodox Marxism-Leninism, and to ensure the correct Marxist-Leninist education of both the masses and party cadres; a cultural sector that was responsible for the organization and development of all cultural life including the theater, film, music, art, various exhibits, and literary presentations and publications; and an organizational sector that handled the material and financial aspects of the department, as well as organizing its statistics and bookkeeping.[11] The number of professional party functionaries required to staff agitprop departments varied over time and place, but generally increased in the period from 1945 to 1950.

The primary tasks of agitprop departments were determined in Belgrade most often through informal agreements among top CPY leaders. These duties were then elaborated in the central department of agitprop and passed downward to regional and local agitprop bodies by a variety of methods. The central agitprop department sent regular memos to regional party, state, and mass organizations providing them with material, information, and recommendations. Or, if the matter was urgent, one of the leaders of the central agitprop department, such as Djilas, Radovan Zogović, or Stefan Mitrović, would simply telephone a corresponding leader in the regional or local agitprop department and transmit the necessary instructions.

Since, in theory, agitprop commissions of higher and lower bodies were not directly connected to each other, memos of the central agitprop department were generally issued by the Central Committee, endowing them with a distinctly obligatory tone. Essentially, then, these memos were directives that articulated the party line on all manner of issues and events. An agitprop memo might explain the party's views on some recent domestic or foreign political event, establish the correct policy for theatrical or radio repertoires, provide the curricula and reading lists for party or professional courses, make recommendations for publishing houses, or provide "theses for the press" and exemplary slogans for upcoming celebrations. The degree of specificity in the directives varied considerably. In theory, the central agitprop department was to provide only the basic line and content, leaving each local body sufficient leeway to develop its own initiative and tailor each topic to the concrete conditions of its region. In some cases, however, the instructions were extremely detailed.

One directive from Djilas to the department of agitation and propaganda of the Central Committee of the Communist Party of Croatia, for example, instructed that no publications begun by the Ustaše were to continue no matter what, that as many realist writers as possible should be published as cheaply as possible, and that the publication of "decadent," "semi-pornographic," and "pessimistic" literature must be avoided at all costs. In another, Djilas deleted specific works from Croatia's publishing plan for 1947 as insufficiently important, politically unreliable, or—often—without any explanation whatsoever. That such interference was not always restricted to obviously political materials may be seen by the Croatian agitprop department's request to central agitprop for a decision on whether or not to publish Ivan Supek's *A History of Physics from Oldest Times to Atomic Energy*.[12]

Another centrally produced document, entitled "Directive Letter from the Central Committee of the CPY to all Central Committees and Regional Committees in Connection with the Celebration of the Tenth Anniversary of the Death of the Writer Maxim Gorky," provided detailed instructions for celebrating the June 18 event. According to this directive, all agitprop departments were to supervise the following preparations to publicize the life of this Russian author whose works were considered models of the new socialist literature. All theaters were to prepare something by Gorky and before the performance give a short lecture about him; all schools were to hold special assemblies with lectures on Gorky and readings from his works; all villages were to hold public assemblies or lectures involving the best known educational workers of that area; all factories and workshops were to hold short assemblies; and all institutions of higher learning were to hold assemblies involving specialists in Gorky's work. The June or July issue of every literary journal was to be devoted entirely to Maxim Gorky and should include two or three essays on his literary activity, several excerpts from his writings, some memoir or personal essay about him, original literature contributed in Gorky's honor, a bibliography of his works in the Yugoslav languages, information about the censorship of Gorky in prewar Yugoslavia, and information about his publications in the Soviet Union. All other journals were also to include at least one article commemorating Gorky, and the daily papers were to dedicate a large section of their June 18 issue to him. The writers' unions were also to hold meetings, lectures, and readings in celebration of the author; cinemas were to show a Soviet movie, preferably one based on one of Gorky's works; and, finally, the press was to follow and record all of the cultural presentations and manifestations held for this event.[13]

Agitprop leaders also transmitted party policy by publishing articles in various newspapers and journals. Articles appearing in the party's main directive organ, *Borba*—especially those by top leaders of the Central Committee—represented the official party line. According to Djilas, each agitprop department was to carefully study and rework such articles, making them accessible to the masses. Meanwhile, the leader of each agitprop department's section for the press monitored the content of both the local and central press to ensure that "the local press correctly applies and interprets the directives of the central press. . . . He takes into account which people should join the editorial boards of party and other newspapers and journals, and if necessary, himself joins certain important editorial boards."[14]

Ultimately, party forums and individual members were expected to take any and all measures necessary to realize the decisions expressed in the press.[15] An example of how this might work is provided by Marko

Lopušina in his book on censorship in Yugoslavia. According to Lopušina, Djilas effectively killed the drama *Knez od Zete* by publishing an anonymous critique of it in *Borba*. Even though the article was unsigned, the Zagreb theater's directors knew that anyone writing in *Borba* had to be powerful and so they withdrew the play from their repertoire. Lopušina also claims that the play's director, Oskar Danon, received a party punishment, while its composer, Jovan Konjović, gave up the theater for a safer occupation tending a fruit orchard.[16] Incidentally, a later critique of the play by Natko Devčić (a non-Communist but cooperative composer and professor of the Musical Academy in Zagreb) explained that the Zagreb masses had been so disgusted by the play that *they* closed it down, thus proving that the Yugoslav public had high standards and would not tolerate bad art.[17]

A third way that agitprop departments conducted policy was in direct meetings with the leaders of relevant institutions. Agitprop departments maintained constant contact with the heads of all important bodies and held irregular meetings as needed with various cultural bodies, including the cultural sectors of youth, women's, or trade union organizations; music schools; or the Radio Committee. The central agitprop department also held regular meetings with the editorial boards of all major newspapers and journals (paying particular attention to *Borba*) in order to discuss current events, their correct political interpretation, and any problematic matters.

Finally, agitprop departments transmitted information and policy by sending their own members out into the field in order to provide "more direct supervision and aid."[18] The departments might send out individual members or, on occasion, they would create *actives* for this purpose. These bodies of especially qualified party members temporarily convened to fulfill a particular persuasive task could be used strictly for internal party purposes, as for giving lectures to various party organizations, or for giving lectures and promoting the party line among the wider public.

Although the departments of agitation and propaganda were by far the most important source of persuasive and cultural policies within the CPY, certain other party commissions—including the women's commission and the commission for schools—also provided forums for the elaboration and transmission of party rhetoric. Within such bodies, Communists with a particular interest in women's issues or education could work out the details of party policy in those areas, hold meetings with the relevant state or mass organizations, and prepare articles and directives for publication or transmission to lower bodies. One final source of persuasive activity closely connected to the CPY was its Communist youth organization, SKOJ (Savez komunističke omladine Jugoslavije).

SKOJ

Yugoslav Communists considered youth and children to be especially important for both the immediate success of their policies and the eventual achievement of communism. In the short run, the party valued youth as a reserve of enthusiastic, energetic, and highly impressionable actors on whom it could call to fulfill various concrete tasks. In the long run, however, youth and children were even more important as those who would eventually realize the goals and dreams of the party. If, as the Communists believed, the attitudes and values necessary to make communism possible would develop only under conditions of socialism, children raised in a socialist system would be the first to possess those new values and would ensure the future of the country and of social progress worldwide. Youth and children would ultimately create the Communist society, while those raised under capitalism could only prepare the ground for them.

Attention to the role of youth in the Yugoslav Communist party led to the formation of the League of Communist Youth of Yugoslavia, SKOJ, in October 1919. The party's popular front line in the late 1930s, along with the growing threat from fascism, facilitated SKOJ's development and by the end of 1940 it claimed a membership of close to 30,000—more than twice the number enrolled in the CPY.[19] Thanks to the extremely widespread participation of youth in the wartime Partisan movement, SKOJ's membership further grew to 150,000 by the end of the war and over 330,000 by mid-1948.[20]

Theoretically, SKOJ operated under the direct supervision of party leaders who provided it with concrete tasks and instructions for work. SKOJ's goals were to help realize party policies among youth, to provide a reservoir of future party cadres through theoretical and ideological education of its members, and to provide leadership for non-Communist youths in schools and in the broader youth organization, the People's Youth of Yugoslavia (PYY).

Indeed, SKOJ members were extremely active in promoting party policy, especially with regard to the struggle against religion and bourgeois concepts in culture. In addition, SKOJ members actively campaigned for party-approved candidates in federal, republic, and local elections; helped mobilize youth for volunteer labor actions; and assisted the government in carrying out various economic and agricultural policies, including the organization of factory competitions and grain requisitioning.

The State

Although most persuasive activities in new Yugoslavia originated within the party, the CPY also used the enormous resources provided by its control over the state to realize its program for social change. After all, according to one internal report, the first question of revolution—that is, of the transition from one stage of social development to another—was power. Only party control over the legislative, judicial, and executive functions of government could ensure real social and economic progress. "Without a good state apparatus which will stubbornly work for the mobilization of the masses," Djilas explained, "we would not be able to realize the tasks which stand before us."[21]

State power provided the party with both the opportunity to create new laws and the ability to enforce those laws. While many of the regime's new laws were concerned with strictly political or economic issues, others were designed to bring about changes in the existing social and cultural order. Control over the state also, of course, gave the CPY the monopoly over the organs of justice and force necessary to eliminate all opposition to its regime. Party members were placed in the leading positions of the army, police, secret police, and judicial system in order to ensure their compliance with party dictates.[22] Finally, state control offered party leaders the chance to establish a broad moral, social, and cultural agenda for the Yugoslav population and to promote that agenda through publishing and the press, the educational system, and official policies toward religion and the family.

Publishing and the Press

The new state was especially concerned to establish its control over the mass media and all publications. Yugoslav officials regularly insisted in public that the press and all other publications were legally free in postwar Yugoslavia and that "there are no organs of state administration which could direct the press or exercise control by means of censorship or in any other way."[23] In fact, however, the party and the state clearly regulated the media and publishing through a complex network of direct and indirect means.[24]

First of all, although the Communist regime did not immediately nationalize printing presses, publishing agencies, or movie theaters, it did manage to confiscate most of them on usually shaky grounds that their owners had collaborated with the occupiers during the war. Moreover, while Article 1 of the "Law on the Press," passed in August 1945, stated that "no one can be prevented from the free expression of his/her opinion by means of the press," it also added, "except in those cases provided for by this law." Then, in an unapologetic attempt to make possible a purge of journalists and to forbid publication activity to those who "used the press for immoral and filthy purposes," the law required prospective publishers of newspapers and periodicals to apply for permission to the public prosecutor 14 days in advance. Articles 6 and 11 of the law supplied the long list of conditions under which an editor could be denied the right to publish or a publication could be denied distribution. Many of these conditions were so vaguely stated that, as Djilas pointed out, "there was nothing that could not be prohibited."[25] For example, in March 1946 three British newspapers or journals were specifically denied entry and distribution in Yugoslavia because they were said to be full of insults and slanders and "systematically spread false and alarming news, which is in conflict with Article 11 of the Law on the Press."[26]

The state evidently considered books somewhat less influential than the periodical press, as their publication or distribution required no prior application or approval. Yet books, too, could be withdrawn from distribution under the provisions of the Law on the Press, and the party soon devised new methods of sabotaging private publishers and booksellers. Already in February 1945, a group of Belgrade booksellers complained that, while they welcomed the founding of new "people's" publishing companies and were looking forward to selling the new books, they hadn't been able to get hold of any because the publishing companies were opening their own stores and selling the new books only through them. Somewhat later the editors of the independent newspaper of the Republican party, *Republika*, reported that many newspaper distributors not only were not selling their newspaper but were harassing and intimidating any prospective customers.[27]

Foreign periodicals published in the Yugoslav languages or directed at the Yugoslav people had to obtain prior governmental approval, while most other foreign newspapers and periodicals were permitted free entrance into the state, but could be distributed only by government-authorized personnel.[28] By late 1946, all foreign publications passed through the state publishing agency Jugoslovenska knjiga, which, according to one document from the central agitprop department, distributed only a few of them in major cities. Up to September 1946, it declared, only 25,000 copies of the British press had entered the country, and only 50 percent of them had been sold while the rest would be returned to their publishers.[29] The CPY also exploited the government's exclusive right to designate those who would sell foreign publications, as evidenced by the following "strictly confidential" memo from the agitprop department of the Communist Party of Croatia to the District Party Committee of Karlovac:

> Find in the city of Karlovac one comrade, a member of the Communist party, who directs or owns a bookstore or tobacco shop, one that is not the property of the People's Front but is private. Entrust that comrade with the sale of Anglo-American newspapers and journals. He should not sell great quantities of the received newspapers but only a small number, while the

majority should be sent back with a notation that the people do not buy those newspapers because of their reactionary writings, and with a request that in the future as few of them as possible be sent to him.[30]

Finally, although most individual newspapers, journals, and publishing firms theoretically fell under the control of various mass and political organizations, such as the People's Front, the People's Youth, or even the Croat Republican Peasant Party, the Communist-dominated government provided financial support and publishing supplies. Therefore, it could and did prevent the publication of many "undesirable" items through denial of paper or a printing press, or by various bureaucratic and delaying actions. Zogović, for example, specifically recommended the use of such techniques in order to prevent the publication of religious literature directed at youth. Djilas has also recalled an encounter with the editor of the non-Communist newspaper *Republika*. "[The editor] came to me and said, 'Hey, don't sabotage us by not giving us paper,' and I said, 'No, really, there isn't any paper, its going badly!' But the truth was that we were giving the paper first of all to our own press."[31]

Education and Culture

The CPY exercised its control over education and cultural and artistic activities through local governmental bodies known as the People's Councils and through the federal and republic ministries of education. Even during the war, while the main purpose of People's Councils had been to secure supplies for the Partisans, direct economic life, and carry out communal and social services, they had also organized the cultural and educational life of their region. This aspect of state activity continued beyond the war and local organs of government took on such cultural tasks as opening and supplying schools, creating adult literacy courses, organizing cultural centers, and forming amateur cultural groups.

At the federal and republic levels, the ministries of education took on full responsibility for financing, opening, and supplying the new state schools. Although the Communists permitted the continued existence of a few religious schools (mainly at the university level), they abolished most with the argument that it was necessary to unify and democratize education, eliminating the existence of separate and clearly unequal schools for the rich and poor.[32] In fact, of course, the act was intended mainly to ensure party control over the form and content of all education. In addition, a directive from the central ministry of education in February 1945 stated that religious studies classes must no longer be considered an obligatory part of the school curriculum.[33] Student participation in the optional religious studies courses varied over time and place, but gradually regime resistance to them increased until they were abolished in 1952.³⁴

Meanwhile, the Communist-dominated state determined the class curricula and course content for state schools. All textbooks, for example, had to be approved by the republic ministries of education, which forbade the use of many, requiring their replacement by more ideologically correct texts often translated from Russian. In addition, since the ministries of education also controlled employment policy, they could ensure that those teachers who opposed the new regime would lose their positions, allowing others who were more loyal (even if less qualified) to replace them. The party also paid considerable attention to the teachers' schools, greatly increasing their numbers and shortening their duration of training in an effort to increase the pool of educational cadres as quickly as possible.

The party used similar methods to exercise direct and indirect supervision over cultural-artistic personnel and their productions or performances. Immediately after the war, the new government took possession of drama theaters, opera houses, and concert halls and closely supervised the future management of these institutions. In addition, the state offered financial support to officially approved artistic organizations, sponsored various cultural performances and artistic exhibitions, and held artistic competitions in the fields of literature, drama, the fine arts, film, and music. The obvious stick that accompanied the carrot was, at best, loss or denial of the official financial and moral support and, at worst, the threat of imprisonment or execution. Uncooperative artists could be denied admission to official trade unions and while not forbidden to create, they then lost out on its material benefits. Those who needed further persuasion had only to recall that a number of artists accused of collaborating with the occupier had been fired, imprisoned, or even shot by the new regime.

Religion and the Family

Finally, the party used its control over the state in an effort to penetrate even the private lives of Yugoslavia's citizens. In particular, the Communist-dominated state used legislative means against the party's main ideological and cultural rival—religion. Officially, the new Yugoslav Constitution of 1946 guaranteed full freedom of conscience and religious belief, established full equality of all citizens regardless of religion, and permitted the performance of religious rites and the training of religious personnel. At the same time, however, and ostensibly in response to the allegedly divisive role religion had played in the region throughout history, the constitution banned churches from the field of politics, stating that "it is forbidden to misuse the church and religion for political ends, or to establish political organizations on a basis of religion."[35]

The state's main blows against the church, however, landed in the fields of education and economics. We have already seen how the state established its control over education. In economic terms, the land reform law of August 1945 legalized the confiscation of 85 percent of all church holdings without compensation, while the December 1946 "Law on the Nationalization of Private Economic Enterprises" deprived churches not only of the charitable foundations from which they had drawn considerable income but also of their printing presses, making them dependent on the government-owned publishers and printers.[36]

The degree of legal coercion applied against the churches varied considerably. Certainly, many priests were arrested and imprisoned, usually on dubious charges that they had collaborated with the Nazis or their domestic quislings. According to statistics provided by Serb historian Rada Radić, from the end of the war to April 1953, 1,403 religious leaders from all of Yugoslavia's religious communities were convicted of serious political crimes. Among the Orthodox priests, 38 percent were convicted for collaborating with the occupier or domestic quislings, 22 percent for conspiring with traitors, 32 percent for spreading enemy propaganda, 1 percent for espionage, and 7 percent as Cominform bureau agents or for other unspecified reasons.[37] The most famous case concerns the archbishop of Zagreb, Alojzije Stepinac, who was sentenced to 16 years in prison for his purported collusion with the Ustaša. Leaving aside the still debatable truth of that accusation, there can be no doubt that Stepinac's real crime was his refusal to cooperate with and indeed his open criticism of the Communist regime.[38]

Finally, the state also employed legislative measures in its efforts to erode the bases of Yugoslavia's traditional patriarchal culture. Marxist-Leninist ideology includes among its principles the full legal, economic, and social equality of women. Accordingly, the new Yugoslav Constitution stipulated that "all citizens, regardless of sex ... who are over eighteen years of age have the right to elect and be elected to all organs of state authority." Moreover, Article 24 was entirely devoted to the legal status of women, specifying their full equality with men in all fields, and providing working mothers with special economic protection, including the right to equal pay for equal work and three months' paid maternity leave. The "Law on Marriages" further stipulated full equality of both partners in all spheres, while the "Law on the Rights and Duties of Parents" declared them to be the same for both the mother and the father regardless of whether or not they were married. The new state also passed laws allowing for more accessible divorce and providing full legal equality for legitimate and illegitimate children, even though similar laws had been rescinded or limited in the Soviet Union some 10 years previously.[39] Finally, the state vowed to take responsibility for establishing day care centers and cafeterias to ease the double burden suffered by working women.[40]

Mass Organizations

Beyond relying on party and state institutions, party leaders implemented their persuasive and cultural policies through the mass organizations of the People's Front of Yugoslavia (PFY), the League of Trade Unions (LTU), the People's Youth of Yugoslavia (PYY) and the Anti-fascist Front of Women (AFW). Unlike the CPY, which, despite enormous increases in membership, remained a party of cadres comprising less than 2 percent of registered voters, the PFY, LTU, PYY, and AFW were truly mass organizations that could count as members sometimes up to 80 percent of their constituent populations.[41]

These mass organizations propagated the party line in a broad variety of media, public educational programs, and cultural activities directed either at the broad public or particular segments of it. Each published newspapers, journals, and brochures; held public lectures, mass meetings, literacy and other courses, reading groups, study circles, and debate clubs; and organized cultural-educational and cultural-artistic societies, gymnastics and sports organizations, reading rooms, libraries, and "houses of culture" for their members.

The importance of mass organizations as a medium for CPY persuasive policies was best described in an unsigned party document from 1947. The document began by stressing the persuasive character of CPY work among the masses and raised the question of how, specifically, the party could carry out its policies among them. In response, it traced the history of the People's Front from 1935 onward, asking, "Why did the Party want to create these organizations? So that it could feel the pulse of the masses and revolutionize them through party members located in these organizations, and so that, acting within the midst of these organizations, it could transmit its political concepts into life." If the party fulfilled its tasks only through its own members, the document continued, the road to victory would be long. By serving as examples among the masses and especially among youth, however, party members could accomplish much. After all, the document continued, "socialism is not built by a few individuals but by millions. . . . that means that it is necessary to transform millions of people, the masses, into active builders of the new society."[42]

Since the party intended mass organizations, and especially the People's Front, to provide the political pillar of the new government, it put considerable effort into securing broad public participation in and support for them. Consequently, the CPY often set its revolutionary plans and ideas on the back burner when dealing with these organizations. Their programs did not call for class struggle or socialist construction but focused on such generally accepted domestic and foreign policies as preserving the independence and unity of Yugoslavia; deepening the "brotherhood and unity" of the nations of Yugoslavia while guarding their complete equality; establishing brotherhood and cooperation with the Slavs and all "progressive" peoples (particularly the USSR); defending peace in the world; struggling against fascism and reaction and for increased democracy; providing general, political, and economic education for the masses; guaranteeing the equality of women; securing rights and opportunity for youth; establishing close ties between intellectual and physical workers; and helping the government with social problems. The program also, however, included several policies that were more clearly intended to serve the specific needs and interests of the Communist-dominated government. The Front was asked, for example, to help secure the position of the new government, to supervise governmental work, to explain official policies to the masses, to mobilize them for the fulfillment of those tasks, and to help develop the consciousness and initiative of the people through persuasive means.[43]

The People's Front of Yugoslavia

The flagship of the party's mass organizations was the People's Front of Yugoslavia. Membership in the PFY, which had reached 7 million by mid-1947, was not predicated on one's political affiliation, religious beliefs, or worldview, and the Front included not only individual members but also other political parties and mass organizations. It accepted into its ranks, for example, a number of prewar political parties, including the Agrarian Party, the People's Peasant Party, the Social-Democratic Party, the Yugoslav Republican Party, the Independent Democratic Party, the Socialist Party, and the Croat Republican Peasant Party. The Front accepted these parties both in order to prevent them from uniting in opposition to it and to ease Western concerns about the spread of communism.[44] The CPY, on the other hand, although clearly the leading force in the PFY, did not formally belong to it, apparently out of leftover conspiratorial habits. When asked point-blank by an American journalist why the CPY was not registered in the PFY, Tito responded only that that was a formal issue and the PFY was not a formal coalition but was created from below and led by the CPY throughout the war.[45]

In fact, the nature of the PFY and the role of political parties within it were a matter of some controversy between non-Communist leaders and the CPY. The leaders of non-Communist parties tended to describe the

PFY as a coalition within which all parties would have equal rights.⁴⁶ The CPY, on the other hand, always insisted that the PFY—despite its broad character and multiparty composition—was not a coalition. Rather, it claimed, the PFY was a unified political organization, created from below during the war, to which political leaders and parties other than the CPY had only subsequently attached themselves.⁴⁷ The CPY thus demanded that each member-party or -group cooperate with others in common efforts and put aside its own narrow class or party interests, working only for the joint program of the Front.

But while party leaders insisted that the CPY *also* had no narrow party interests and no program other than that of the PFY, in fact the reverse was true.⁴⁸ For if the PFY was not a composite body or a power-sharing coalition, neither was it a "common people's political organization" as the CPY claimed. The CPY had accepted other parties into the Front primarily to neutralize their opposition and dilute their individuality, and was not about to share its leading role with them. As Djilas explained to a small group of intellectuals who had complained of their unequal status in the Front: "You're not equal and you can't be! Behind us Communists stand fifty divisions and a terrible war. You're only one little group. You have the wrong idea of equality. What's needed here isn't equality but understanding!"⁴⁹ Finally, at the Fifth Party Congress in 1948, in response to Cominform accusations that the CPY had dissolved into the PFY, Moša Pijade publicly explained that "the words of Comrade Tito that the Party has no other program outside of the program of the People's Front mean just the opposite, that the program of our Party is also the program of the People's Front."⁵⁰

Here was clearly a case where party leaders sought to manipulate preexisting institutions for their own purposes. They especially valued peasant parties like the Agrarian Party, the People's Peasant Party, and the Croat Republican Peasant Party as "transmission belts between the avant garde of democracy [i.e., the Communist party] and the peasant masses."⁵¹ Agitprop leaders in Croatia, for example, urged local activists to support the cultural organization of the Croat Republican Peasant Party as "one of the most suitable forms for gathering the village into the great work of our Republic."⁵² Indeed, although after the first year of Communist rule no one harbored any further illusions about CPY leadership of the PFY, it did draw many Yugoslav citizens into educational and cultural activities, particularly if they were not too heavily political or ideological.

The League of Trade Unions

As a member of the PFY, the League of Trade Unions took on responsibility for spreading the party's message among all workers and employees in the new state. While during the interwar period, the various trade union organizations had been disunited and subject to not only Communist but also Social Democratic and non-Marxist influences, already by January 1945 they had been fully united under the leadership of the CPY within the United League of Workers and Employees of Yugoslavia, later renamed the League of Trade Unions of Yugoslavia.[53] The CPY clearly expected its influence among the working class and in the trade unions to be decisive and exclusive; the League of Trade Unions was to serve as a helping agent or transmission belt in the party's activity with the working class and must under no circumstances put itself above the party. As one party document put it, "the working class has many detachments—trade unions, cultural societies, etc.—but the only leading unit is the party. It is the conscious Marxist unit. Only it can determine the direction of class struggle."[54]

Unable to offer workers immediate improvements in their living and working conditions, party leaders theoretically understood that they must consciously encourage and nurture worker enthusiasm for the construction of a new and more just socialist society.[55] In practice, however, CPY leaders often seemed to neglect persuasive activities among workers, apparently taking their support for granted. The party did, however, develop relatively vigorous cultural-educational policies toward the working class, hoping to raise their general, cultural, and ideological level and prepare them for their eventual leading role in society. By providing workers with the correct view of work and the world, CPY rhetoric sought to make them more efficient, as well as more conscious, creative, and willing to work for society. Trade union organizations thus offered workers a variety of educational opportunities, including lectures, reading groups, and Marxist-Leninist study circles. They even created a certain number of schools specifically for workers to educate them about the natural sciences, math, hygiene, Russian language, history, the new constitution, and so on.

The unions also endeavored to raise the workers' cultural level by negotiating reduced prices on books and cultural events so that workers could afford them and by arranging collective, and sometimes free, visits to the theater, cinema, exhibits, museums, and concerts. In one case, students from the Musical Academy in Belgrade presented a program of pieces that were popular and "close to the workers," and then asked the workers to let them know what they liked and what they did not. The event was considered a great success since the workers were given the opportunity to enjoy musical art after a hard day's work, and the artists were able to get closer to the people they served.[56]

Trade unions provided workers with additional access to cultural materials in the workers' clubs and "red corners" of each enterprise. Although the financial resources available to trade union cultural-educational departments were quite small, many were at least able to provide a few copies of Soviet socialist realist literature (most commonly, Ostrovskii's *How Steel Was Tempered*), a radio for listening to musical and literary programs, and an occasional movie. Finally, the unions tried to involve workers in the creation of high culture within cultural-artistic societies so as to enable them to use the country's scientific and cultural means and heritage, and thus make high culture really and truly "the property of the masses."[57]

The People's Youth of Yugoslavia

Given CPY recognition of the importance of youth, the predominant role played by the mass organization of youth is unsurprising. During the Second World War and in accordance with the party's general anti-fascist line, the Communist youth organization had begun to create broader, mass-based *actives* and councils, and in December 1942 it organized the founding congress of the United League of Anti-Fascist Youth of Yugoslavia (USAOJ), later renamed the People's Youth of Yugoslavia. Indeed, youth played a particularly important role during the Second World War and in the CPY's rise to power. They were among the first to join the Partisans and constituted 75 percent of its members. Over half of the leading cadres in the war were under the age of 26 and 90 percent of the martyred People's Heroes declared up to 1951 were under 23.[58]

While clearly organized and directed by Communist youth, the PYY was a much broader organization than SKOJ, counting by September 1948 1,415,763 members, or approximately 80 percent of youth in the country.[59] Understanding that its goals could not be realized just through the efforts of Communists, the party ordered that almost all political, educational, and cultural work among youth be carried out within the youth organization. PYY organizations clearly were important agents for the party's program of social and cultural change, especially in rural areas where they not only participated in but often even directed village political, educational, and cultural life. PYY bodies in the villages cooperated with and aided the government in carrying out grain requisitions, mobilized youth to participate in volunteer labor brigades, played a significant role in the struggle to eradicate illiteracy, and often initiated the formation of various amateur cultural and sports societies. In urban areas, too, the PYY was particularly active in the creation and management of various cultural-educational, cultural-artistic, and gymnastic and sports organizations. It was, moreover, an ever-present promoter of party policies in the schools, where it created special suborganizations for work among secondary school youth and university student youth. A special subsidiary of the PYY, the Pioneer Organization, acted as the party's agent among children under 15, protecting them from "alien and harmful influences" and securing their education in the values and tasks established by the new regime.

The Anti-fascist Front of Women

Finally, party policies penetrated the consciousness of over half of Yugoslavia's postwar population through the Anti-fascist Front of Women. Founded in 1942 as a means of including women in the Communist-led struggle against national and social oppression, the AFW was never intended to represent women's interests or to fight for their rights.[60] Rather, as Djilas explained, the question of women's equality was to be approached in such a way that it would "activate women to participate in the general people's public life and in the government, *not as representatives of women but as the best children of the people.*"[61]

After the war, although considering that the state had solved the women's question by providing them with legal equality, the party insisted on the continuing need for special work among women. The AFW was still important, according to one unsigned document, not as some separate "women's" organization struggling for their equality, but as an organization through which the party could approach the masses of women made backward by class society.[62] In other words, the party considered the AFW just another mass organization that drew its tasks directly from the PFY and the party. Indeed, although the AFW had drawn fire during the war for separating itself from the broader tasks of the PFY, by the end of the war any feminist and separatist tendencies within the movement had been crushed.

Among the main tasks of the postwar AFW was to raise the general educational and cultural level of women, providing numerous courses, lectures, and brochures on everything from better housekeeping to the construction of the new state. Certain AFW leaders, particularly Vida Tomšić, Cana Babović, and Mitra Mitrović, also consistently propagated not only social work and the maternal activities of women, but also their full and equal inclusion in the economic and political life of the country. Official CPY and state support for women's inclusion in the economy was much less consistent and increased only after the adoption of a Five Year Plan that specified a greatly increased need for labor.[63] That need for female labor eventually also brought party and AFW leaders to a different understanding of the association of women with motherhood, impelling them to focus on the need for adequate and affordable day care.

These, then, were the myriad party, state, and mass organizations on which CPY leaders relied to help realize the cultural transformation of

Yugoslav society. In many ways, all of these organizations, including the state, represented only "transmission belts" for the party leadership. Yet, lest one be inclined to dismiss them on that account, it should be remembered that each, too, had its own membership, established goals, and vested interests. As we have seen, they were often targeted at certain segments of the population. Indeed, CPY official rhetoric most often categorized Yugoslavia's citizens as belonging to one of the following five groups: workers, peasants, people's intelligentsia, women, and youth.[64] Internal party documents also differentiated between those who belonged to the Communist party or Communist youth organization and those who did not. Some degree of overlap was occasionally acknowledged, resulting in articles or speeches directed, for example, at young female workers. More often, however, party rhetoric and persuasive personnel adhered to these formal categories rather narrowly. Hence, each organization approached its assigned tasks in particular ways and presented CPY leaders with unique challenges.

Notes

1. "O agitaciono-propagandnom radu KPJ," late 1945, early 1946, ACKSKJ, VIII I/2-a-35.

2. Dennison Rusinow, *The Yugoslav Experiment, 1948–1974* (Berkeley, CA: University of California Press, 1977), 22, n. 38.

3. For more information on Tito see Stevan K. Pavlowitch, *Tito–Yugoslavia's Great Dictator* (Columbus, OH: Ohio State University Press, 1992); Vladimir Dedijer, *Tito* (New York: Simon and Schuster, 1953); Vladimir Dedijer, *Novi prilozi za biografiju Josipa Broza Tita*, Vol. 3 (Belgrade: Rad, 1984); Milovan Djilas, *Tito, The Story from Inside* (New York: Harcourt Brace Jovanovich, 1980); Phyllis Auty, *Tito: A Biography* (New York: McGraw Hill, 1970).

4. "*Druže Tito, ljubičice bjela*," folk melody arranged by J. Š. Slavenski, score and lyrics published in *Rad*, 8 Sept. 1945, p. 3.

5. For more information on Djilas see Jevrem Brković, *Anatomija morala jednog Staljiniste* (Zagreb: 1988); Stephen Clissold, *Djilas, The Progress of a Revolutionary* (UK: Maurice Temple Smith, 1983); Vladimir Dedijer, *Veliki buntovnik, Milovan Djilas, Prilozi za biografiju* (Belgrade: 1991); Momčilo Djorgović, *Djilas, Vernik i Jeretik* (Belgrade: Akvarijus, 1989); Vasilije Kalezić, *Djilas, kontroverze pisca i ideologa* (Belgrade: 1986); Dennis Reinhartz, *Milovan Djilas: A Revolutionary as Writer* (New York: East European Monographs, distributed by Columbia University Press, 1981).

6. Djilas's persuasive writing skills may be seen also in his memoirs, making their interpretation a rather tricky matter. Yet even while many of his later writings are obviously self-serving and occasionally offer outright falsifications, they often confirm information and evaluations offered elsewhere and provide numerous useful insights concerning the basic ideas and motivations behind CPY policies. Djilas's memoirs include *Land without Justice* (New York: Harcourt Brace

Jovanovich, 1958); *Memoirs of a Revolutionary* (New York: Harcourt Brace Jovanovich, 1973); *Wartime* (New York: Harcourt Brace Jovanovich, 1977); *Conversations with Stalin* (New York: Harcourt Brace Jovanovich, 1962); *Tito, Story from the Inside* (New York: Harcourt Brace Jovanovich, 1980); *Rise and Fall* (New York: Harcourt Brace Jovanovich, 1985). The latter has been especially useful for this study.

7. Woodward argues for more serious differences between party leaders over the party's political-economic strategy. Susan Woodward, *Socialist Unemployment: The Political Economy of Yugoslavia 1945–1990* (Princeton: Princeton University Press, 1995). On differences within the CPY over the socialization of agriculture see Melissa Bokovoy, *Peasants and Communists: Politics and Ideology in the Yugoslav Countryside, 1941–1953* (Pittsburgh: University of Pittsburgh Press, 1998), and A. Ross Johnson, *The Transformation of Communist Ideology, The Yugoslav Case, 1945–1953* (Cambridge, MA: The MIT Press, 1972). For a discussion of disagreements with Croat Communist leader Andrija Hebrang, see Jill Irvine, *The Croat Question: Partisan Politics in the Formation of the Yugoslav Socialist State* (Boulder, CO: Westview Press, 1993).

8. Milovan Djilas, "Svim CK-ima i PK-ima o reorganizaciji agitacije i propagande," 6 Sept. 1945, HDA, CKKPH.

9. See, for example, Zlata Knežević, *Kulturno stvaralaštvo u revoluciji* (Zagreb: 1981).

10. The 12 departments and commissions formed within the Central Committee of the CPY were:
   I) Organizational and Instructor's Department
   II) Cadres Department
   III) Department of Agitation and Propaganda
   IV) Trade Union Commission
   V) Military Commission
   VI) Women's Commission
   VII) Foreign Policy Commission
   VIII) Commission for Economic Policy
   IX) Commission for Schools
   X) Commission for the Construction of People's Power
   XI) Commission for Social Policy
   XII) Control Commission.

The central committees of the federal units were similarly organized but lacked the Foreign Policy Commission and the Control Commission. "Sednica CK KPJ," 30 June 1945, ACKSKJ, III/4.

11. 1: Sector for Agitation and the Press
   a) dept. for information (Radio, TANJUG)
   b) dept. for the press (to control, criticize, and help the daily press)
   c) dept. for agitation (to prepare conferences, meetings, and oral agitation, and to fight enemy propaganda originating in Yugoslavia)
   d) dept. for the struggle against foreign enemy propaganda
2: Theoretical Sector
   a) dept. for party schools and courses
   b) dept. for Marxist-Leninist education in mass organizations
   c) dept. for theoretical lectures (to collect materials, help lecturers)

3: Cultural Sector
   a) dept. for film, theater, and music
   b) dept. for literature
   c) dept. for art
   d) dept. for cultural work in mass organizations
4: Organizational Sector (to deal with cadres, technical issues, and publishing)
Djilas, "Svim CK-ima i PK-ima o reorganizaciji"; "O agitaciono-propagandim radu KPJ." In 1946, a radio committee was also formed under supervision of the central agitprop department to run Radio-Belgrade and to determine the line for radio stations in other republics. "Imenovanje članova Radio komiteta," *Politika*, 5 July 1946; "Osnovni nedostaci, greške, i propusti u programu naših radio-stanica," 14 Nov. 1946, ACKSKJ, VIII II/5-c-74.

12. "Primjedbe uz nacrt plana," December 1945, HDA, CKKPHAP; Letter from Milovan Djilas to Agitprop CK KPH, 17 Jan. 1947, HDA, CKKPHAP; Letter to Agitprop CK KPJ in Belgrade, 21 Jan. 1946, HDA, CKKPHAP.

13. "Direktivno pismo CK KPJ upućeno svim CK-ima i PK-ima u vezi obeležavanja 10-godišnjice smrti književnika Maksima Gorkog," 16 May 1946, ACKSKJ, CKKPJAP VIII I/1-a-4.

14. Ibid.

15. Djilas, "Svim CK-ima i PK-ima o reorganizaciji."

16. Marko Lopušina, *Crna knjiga: Cenzura u Jugoslaviji, 1945–91* (Belgrade: Fokus, 1991), 224.

17. Natko Devčić, "Gotovčev *Kamenik* u Zagrebačkoj operi," *Borba*, 5 Feb. 1947.

18. "O agitaciono-propagandnim radu KPJ."

19. On the development of SKOJ in the interwar period see Pero Morača and Stanislav Stojanović, eds., *Povijest Saveza komunista Jugoslavije* (Belgrade: Izdavački centar Komunist, 1985), 65–168 passim; Ivan Avakumović, *The History of the Communist Party of Yugoslavia*, Vol. 1 (Aberdeen: Aberdeen University Press, 1964), 159–184; Slavoljub Cvetković, *SKOJ, 1919–1929* (Belgrade: 1979); Miroljub Vasić, *SKOJ 1929–1941* (Belgrade: 1979); *Revolucionarni omladinski pokret Jugoslavije, 1919–1979* (Zagreb: 1979); Miroljub Vasić, ed., *Kongresi, konferencije i sednice Centralnih organa SKOJ-a 1919–1924*, and *1925–1941* (Belgrade: Izdavački centar Komunist, 1984); Miroljub Vasić, ed., *Četvrti kongres SKOJ-a i Zajednički kongres SKOJ-a i NOJ, 1948* (Belgrade: Izdavački centar Komunist, 1985).

20. Morača and Stojanović, 308.

21. "Partija i Narodni odbori," 1945, ACKSKJ, X2-IV/2; Milovan Djilas, "Izopačivanje karaktera narodne vlasti," *Komunist*, October 1946, in Milovan Djilas, *Članci, 1941–1946* (Belgrade: 1947), 295.

22. For more information on CPY manipulation of the judicial system, see Rajko Danilović, *Upotreba neprijatelja: Politička sudjenja 1945–1991 u Jugoslaviji* (Valjevo: Valjevac, 1993).

23. Vladislav Ribnikar, "Medjunarodna konferencija za slobodu štampe i informacije u Ženevi," *Borba*, 27 March 1948. While formal censorship generally did not exist, there were two exceptions to that rule. First of all, in its desire to provide children with literature "which develops healthy fantasies, a correct understanding of nature and society, and which raises people who are conscious of their power and who do not fear any kind of difficulties," the government passed a law permitting official censorship over children's literature in the spring of

1947. In addition, the government exercised formal control over the film industry, where a censorship commission (including representatives from the ministry of defense, the ministry of information, and the ministry of education) previewed and approved or denied production and distribution of all domestic and foreign films. See Luka Soldić, "Povodom donošenje zakona o izdavanju i rasturanju omladinske i dečje književnosti i štampe," *Mladost*, 3, no. 5 (May 1947); "Zakon o izdavanju i rasturanju omladinske i dečje književnosti i štampe," No. 216, *Službeni list*, 3, no. 29 (8 April 1947): 328; "Uredba o osnivanju filmskog preduzeća DFJ," No. 411, *Službeni list*, 46 (3 July 1945). See also "Predlog za privatna dječja izdanja koja bi trebalo zabraniti," 1947, ACKSKJ, VIII VI/2-g-8; Čedo Vuković, "Privatna izdanja dečje literature," *Mladost*, 3, no. 1–2 (Jan.-Feb. 1947); Milovan Djilas, "Obrazloženje predloga Zakona o izdavanju i rasturanju omladinske književnosti i štampe," *Borba*, 22 March 1947.

24. For more information on censorship of press, publications, films, and music in postwar Yugoslavia see Lopušina who delineates four forms of censorship that operated between 1945 and 1991: legal (carried out through the judicial system); self-managed (carried out in the name of the working class); political (carried out in forums of party or front organizations); and police (mainly works published abroad carried out with the help of customs agents at the country's borders). According to Lopušina's statistics, during the period encompassed by this study, police censorship was the most common with 84 cases, then political with 67, followed at a great distance by judicial censorship with 4 cases and self-managed with 1. Such numbers must not be taken too seriously, for as Lopušina admits, even his detailed listing cannot be considered complete. Indeed, I ran across several additional cases of what he would likely term "political censorship" in my research.

25. "Zakon o štampi," No. 611, *Službeni list*, 65 (31 Aug. 1945): 633–635; "Jedanaesta sednica," 23 Aug. 1945, in Slobodan Nešović, ed., *Rad zakonodavnih odbora Pretsedništva AVNOJ i Privremene narodne skupštine DFJ (3. aprila–25. oktobra 1945)* (Belgrade: 1952); Djilas, *Rise and Fall*, 30.

26. "Rešenje o zabrani ulaska i rasturanja pojedinih stranih listova i časopisa," No. 164, *Službeni list*, 2, no. 26 (29 March 1946): 303.

27. "Rezolucija knjižara doneta na konferenciji Beogradskih knjižara," 28 Feb. 1945, AJ, MP-4; Stasa Milijanović, "Godinu dana *Republike* u republici," *Republika*, 5 Nov. 1946.

28. "Zakon o štampi," *Borba*, 25 Aug. 1945; "Zakon o potvrdi i izmjenama zakona o štampi," No. 381, *Službeni list*, 2, no. 56 (12 July 1946): 641–643.

29. "Informacija o inostranoj propagandnoj delatnosti u našoj zemlji," 30 Oct. 1946, ACKSKJ, VIII VI/2-h-1.

30. Memo from the agitprop department of the CK KPH to OK Karlovac, 7 Feb. 1946, HDA, CKKPHAP.

31. Radovan Zogović, "O problemu crkvene i privatne izdavačke djelatnosti," 15 Dec. 1948, ACKSKJ, VIII II/5-c-76; Milovan Djilas, Interview with the author, Belgrade, 17 Nov. 1988. See also "Zapisnik sa sastanka Agitpropa," 12 Dec. 1947, ACKSKJ, VIII II/2-b-4. In a more direct approach just after the war, the Yugoslav secret police evicted the editors of a cultural newspaper for the Hungarian minority in Croatia from their building on grounds that they were not using it in the agreed-upon fashion. Zdenko Štambuk, "Izvještaj o listu *Magjarujšag*, o knjizi Mladena Ivekovića, i o knjizi *Nova biologija*," 10 Dec. 1945, HDA, CKKPHAP.

32. According to the 1946 Constitution all schools were state schools, but private schools could be formed with special legal permission. Radmila Radić, *Verom protiv vere: Država i verske zajednice u Srbiji, 1945–1953* (Belgrade: INIS, 1995) 162.

33. "Verska štampa o ukidanju verske nastave u našim školama," 21 Sept. 1945, AJ, MP-1.

34. After that, religious studies courses could be held only on church property and never during school hours. Radić, 160, 315.

35. "Zakon o zabrani izazivanja nacionalne, rasne i vjerske mržnje i razdora," No. 322, *Službeni list*, 36 (29 May 1945). The new state also created a special agency, the Commission for Religious Affairs, presumably to direct and restrict the activities of Yugoslavia's religious communities. Unfortunately, that archive was inexplicably unavailable for examination on both of my research trips to Yugoslavia.

36. Stella Alexander, *Church and State in Yugoslavia Since 1945* (Cambridge: Cambridge University Press, 1979), 156–159, 213 n. 9; Djoko Slijepčević, *Istorija srpske pravoslavne crkve*, Vol. 3 (Cologne: 1986), 319–331.

37. Radić, 306.

38. Radić, 229; Djilas, *Rise and Fall*, 39. See also O. Aleksa Benigar, *Alojzije Stepinac: Hrvatski kardinal* (Rome: Ziral, 1974), and Richard Pattee, *The Case of Cardinal Aloysius Stepinac* (Milwaukee, WI: The Bruce Publishing Co., 1953).

39. Articles 23 and 24, *Constitution of the Federal People's Republic of Yugoslavia*, 1946, Hoover Institution Library; Jelena Janković, "Žena i majka danas," *20. oktobar*, 4 Jan. 1946; Blaženka Mimica, "Brak i porodica," 1946, HDA, AFŽ, 5/641. Concerning the development of official attitudes toward these issues in the Soviet Union see Wendy Goldman, *Women, the State, and Revolution: Soviet Family Policy and Social Life, 1917–1937* (New York: Cambridge University Press, 1993).

40. *Constitution*; "Referat Vide Tomšić," at the Second Plenum of the AFW, 19–20 Sept. 1948, AJ, AFŽ 141-6-14.

41. At the time of the November 1945 elections the number of registered voters was 8,383,455. *Jugoslavija 1945–1964, Statistički pregled* (Belgrade: 1965), 25.

42. "Narodna fronta kao platform partiskog masovnog rada," 1947, HDA, RKSSRNH-1.

43. Dragoljub Jovanović, "Koji su danas zadaci NOF," *Politika*, 25 July 1945; "Referat Edvarda Kardelja," *Politika*, 6 Aug. 1945; "Program NFJ," *Borba*, 8 Aug. 1945; "Front će potpomoći narodnu vlast," *20. oktobar*, 7 Sept. 1945; Sreten Žujović, "Izveštaj o radu NFJ od I. Kongresa do danas," 27 Sept. 1947, AJ, SSRNJ F2/J4-6; "Narodna fronta kao platform."

44. It has even been said that Tito was willing to accept the quasi-fascist prewar Yugoslav National Party of Milan Stojadinović into the PF until outrage from some of the other non-Communists in the Front dissuaded him. Dragoljub Jovanović, "Ka saradnju u Narodnom frontu i narodnoj vlasti," in book 7 of *Političke uspomene–memoari*, AJ, Lični fond Dragoljuba Jovanovića, 255.

45. "Odgovori maršala Tita na pitanja američkih novinara," *Politika*, 17 Oct. 1946.

46. "Izjava Miloša Carevića o Frontu kao političkoj organizaciji," *Politika*, 5 Aug. 1945; Jovanović, "Ka saradnju," 209, 212; "Pretsednik Zemljoradničke stranke, Kosan Pavlović-Brdjanski, o kongresu JNOF," *Selo*, 29 July 1945. For

more information on the role of non-Communist political parties in the PFY see Vojislav Koštunica and Kosta Čavoški, *Party Pluralism or Monism, Social Movements and the Political System in Yugoslavia, 1944–1949* (Boulder, CO: Westview Press, 1985).

47. Edvard Kardelj, "Kongres Osvobodilne fronte Slovenije," *Politika*, 18 July 1945; "Referat Edvarda Kardelja."

48. "Odgovori Maršala Tita na pitanja američkih novinara"; Milovan Djilas, "U ime Komunističke partije," 1945, HDA, RKSSRNH-1.

49. Djilas, "U ime Komunističke partije"; Djilas, *Rise and Fall*, 7.

50. Moša Pijade, "O projektu programa Komunističke partije Jugoslavije," in *Peti kongres Komunističke partije Jugoslavije, Izvještaji i referati* (Belgrade: Izdavački centar Komunist, 1948), 546. Even so, the CPY did not officially join the PFY until 1953, by which time both organizations had been renamed and the relationship between them reconsidered.

51. "Referat Edvarda Kardelja."

52. "Organizacija, dosadašnji rad, i zadaci kulturno-prosvjetnog rada na selu," 1947, HDA, CKKPHAP.

53. On the history of the trade union movement in interwar Yugoslavia see Avakumović, passim; E. Hasanagić, *Nezavisni Sindikati* (Belgrade: 1951); Josip Cazi, *Komunistička partija Jugoslavije i sindikati* (Belgrade: 1959); Josip Cazi, *Nezavisni sindikati, 1921–1929*, 2 vols. (Zagreb: 1962–1964); Nadežda Jovanović, *Sindikalni pokret u Srbiji, 1935–1941* (Belgrade: 1984). Membership in the League of Trade Unions grew quickly from 225,000 at the beginning of 1945 to 1,015,000 by the end of 1947. "Statistics on trade unions," 1948, AJ, CVSSJ-F1/J1–3.

54. "Šta je i kakva treba da bude naša komunistička partija," 15 Aug. 1945—but clearly written much earlier, between June 1941 and May 1943, HDA, CKKPH." See also "Izvještaj OK KPH Bjelovar," 5 Oct. 1945, HDA, CKKPH; "Izvještaj u vezi priprema za Kongres," report from the district committee of the KPH for Dalmatia, 25 Feb. 1946, HDA, CKKPH; Milovan Djilas, "O daljem radu na ideološkom i političkom podizanju komunista i ideološkom i političkom podizanju radnih masa," 21 Sept. 1946, ACKSKJ, VIII I/1-a-6; Mišo Pavičević, "Značaj šestog plenuma za dalji razvoj Jedinstvenih sindikata," *Rad*, 8 April 1948.

55. Djuro Špoljarić, "Šta treba da znaju naši funkcioneri," *Rad*, 28 Nov. 1945; Marjan Krleža, "Kulturno-prosvjetni zadaci i problemi," 1946, HDA, VSSH-1-KPO; "Sprovedimo odlučniju borbu za ideološko jačanje naših sindikata," *Rad*, 28 Sept. 1946.

56. "Naši umetnici medju radnicima," *Politika*, 18 April 1946. See also "Pitanja i problemi kulturnog prosvetnog rada," 17 Sept. 1946, AJ, CV SSJ F1/J3 KPO; "Organizacione primjedbe na našu agitaciju i propagandu," 1947, HDA, ZV NOH-29.

57. Mišo Pavičević, "Zadaci kulturno-prosvetnih aktivista sindikata u borbi za ostvarenje Petogodišnjeg plana," *Rad*, 27 May 1947, p. 6.

58. Dušan Bilandžić, *Historija Socijalističke Federativne Republike Jugoslavije: Glavni procesi, 1918–1985* (Zagreb: Školska knjiga, 1985) 88; Morača and Stojanović, 198, 236.

59. Morača and Stojanović, 308, 325, 328.

60. For information on the Yugoslav women's movement during and after the war from an anthropological and feminist perspective see Lydia Sklevicky, "Eman-

cipated Integration or Integrated Emancipation: The Case of Post-Revolutionary Yugoslavia," unpublished manuscript; "Kulturnom mijenom do žene 'novog tipa' Antifašistička fronta žena," *Gordogan*, 6, no. 15–16 (January-April 1984); "Organizirana djelatnost žena Hrvatske za vrijeme narodnooslobodilačke borbe 1941–1945," *Povijesni prilozi*, 3, no. 1 (1984).

61. Milovan Djilas, "Izgledi na razvoj AFŽ," from *Žena u borbi*, No. 3–4, no date, HDA, AFŽ-7. Italics in the original.

62. "Informacija o položaju žena radnica i nameštenica u FNRJ," June 1948, AJ, AFŽ 141-11-57. See also Aleksandar Ranković, "Pismo CK KPJ, " 23 Oct. 1945, AIHRPH, CKKPH.

63. Mara Naceva, "Ulaženje u industriju i stručno uzdizanje žena," *Žena danas*, 51 (November-December 1947); "Izglasanje rezolucija i izbor Centralnog i Izvršnog odbora AFŽ-a," *Politika*, 28 Jan. 1948; Report of the AFW on its activities, June 1948, HDA, KDAŽH-18.

64. Significantly, while class, occupation, age, and gender were all considered legitimate forms of identity, nation and ethnicity were not.

3

Problems of Persuasion

The party, state, and mass organizations described in the previous chapter provided both the institutions and the personnel through which the CPY carried out its rhetorical strategies. Working together they elaborated and presented to the public the party's short- and longer-term goals. Given the pervasive nature of these institutions and their seemingly broad opportunities to influence the population, one might have expected the party's persuasive efforts to achieve stunning results. In fact, however, party leaders were often frustrated in their efforts to bring about social and cultural change. Indeed, despite their position in power, party leaders often found that they could not always even realize their short-term political agenda, to say nothing of their long-term transformative one. While one might argue that their ambitions were inherently unrealistic and unrealizable, there were also several tangible problems that inhibited the party's ability to carry out its program for change.

Internal Disunity

The first element that hindered party success in achieving its goals by means of persuasion concerned occasional cases of disunity and ambivalence about the party's persuasive strategy at the very top levels of the CPY. As noted above, party leaders generally agreed about their ultimate goals and overall strategy for the construction of socialism. Differences between leaders did sometimes emerge, however, concerning their choice of methods and priorities. In some cases these differences derived only from individual personalities, while in others they related to a given leader's national affiliation or functional position within the party.[1]

One such dispute developed in the field of education almost immediately following the war. While party leaders generally agreed on the kinds of subjects that should be offered in the new state schools as well as on their correct ideological content, they often disagreed over the appropriate degree of centralization in educational policy. Up until the November 1945 elections, the central government provided for a federal ministry of education to construct the general line and principles of educational policy for the entire country. Each republic, however, also had its own ministry of education, which held full responsibility for and independence in applying the overall policy.[2] Already in mid-1945 a debate developed over the relative rights and responsibilities of the federal and republic ministries of education.

At an August 1945 meeting of the educational council of the ministry of education, the opening speaker, Martin Mencej, who favored centralized and unified preparation and publication of textbooks, met considerable resistance from Slovenian, Croatian, and some Serbian delegates. These delegates argued that as each republic had its own history and literature and was operating under unique educational conditions, each unit should individually prepare and publish its own texts. Delegates from Montenegro, Macedonia, and Bosnia-Hercegovina, on the other hand, stressed the need for uniform education, pointing out that they, at least, could not possibly prepare or publish their own texts in the near future. Ultimately Mencej decided the issue, insisting that if the Soviet Union with its many regional differences could have unified texts, so too could Yugoslavia. And while recognizing that some individuals clearly feared centralization, he insisted that unified texts represented "centralization in the interests of youth, schools, and our people. We cannot be afraid of such centralization."[3]

Later documents, however, suggest that in deference to national sensitivities, a compromise solution permitted federal units to prepare their own texts in the field of language arts and in history.[4] Then, in January 1946, the party moved further in the direction of decentralization, forming a new government that included no federal ministry of education. As the federal ministry was replaced only by the weaker Committee for Schools and Science, many educational responsibilities, including, apparently, preparation and production of textbooks, now devolved onto the individual republic ministries.[5] The resulting discrepancies in the educational program have been documented by Andrew Wachtel in his recent monograph on cultural politics in Yugoslavia. According to Wachtel, history teachers in Croatia received detailed instructions about how to handle the question of interwar Yugoslavia, while those in Bosnia-Hercegovina were advised to accord it rather less attention, and Serbia's teachers were given full latitude on the matter.[6]

By the fall of 1947, such discrepancies had become sufficiently worrisome that party leaders initiated a new shift in the party's policy toward education. An article in *Borba* by Kosta Grubačić now noted problems in the educational policies of certain republics, which, he said, not only engaged in insufficient communication and exchange of information but refused to contribute to the educational development of poorer republics by sharing teaching cadres.[7] More to the point, participants in a discussion of the new class program the following spring noted that over time each republic had made significant changes in the local curricula so that they were now far from uniform. And according to a "strictly confidential" report of a meeting between the central agitprop department and the Committee for Schools and Science, many republic courses on history and literature had even become openly nationalistic. "Our youth," it insisted, "must be educated in a common Yugoslav [opštejugoslovenski] spirit." The report, therefore, recommended the formation of a federal body to supervise the work of republic textbook commissions and to work out a unified plan for national and Yugoslav histories. In addition, the Committee for Schools and Science now created a unified class program for elementary and secondary schools for the 1948/49 academic year in order to eliminate many of the "previous errors."[8] In December 1948, the government replaced the Committee for Schools and Science with a federal Ministry of Science and Culture in order to compensate for the lack of unified leadership and coordination in work. This organizational form, however, also proved to be short-lived and was replaced in 1950 by the Council for Science and Culture. By that time, as we shall see, the party's entire approach to education had significantly changed.[9]

These debates and the constantly shifting policies clearly reflected the party's uncertainty about how best to negotiate the national question within the field of education. Party leaders quite reasonably aspired to create some sense of common historical identity through their educational curriculum; but they also sought to avoid any hint of the unitarism that had been so unpopular in the interwar period.[10] In a sense, then, these debates foreshadowed the Yugoslav Communist party's long postwar history of vacillation between centralization and decentralization. Meanwhile, the constantly changing educational policies offered teachers ample opportunities to deviate from the party line on the relative cultural and political roles played by various nations and nationalities historically, particularly during the interwar period and Second World War.

Another point of conflict in the determination and realization of CPY policy derived from individual leaders' functional positions in the party or in society. As we have seen, party leaders after the war were assigned to a variety of party, state, and mass organizations that dealt with specific aspects of party policy, such as trade unions, education, youth, women's issues, and so on. Not surprisingly, these leaders soon began to establish priorities in terms of their offices instead of for the party. Functional differences operated at all levels—not only among departments, but even among individual sectors of those departments.

One conflict apparently developed within the youth movement over the role and importance of the volunteer labor brigades. Volunteer labor brigades, first formed during the war, continued after its end to help with street and park reconstruction, collection actions, social work, building renovation, road building, woodcutting, spring sowing, fall harvest, and so on. Although originally valued for their contribution to the renovation and reconstruction of the country, party leaders increasingly stressed their role in the political, ideological, professional, and cultural education of youth. The frequent use of forced recruitment techniques, however, soon undermined the moral influence of the brigades. In late 1946, this question of forced recruitment became the subject of a disagreement between two prominent leaders of the youth movement. At a September meeting, Mihailo Švabić, who was formally in charge of youth brigades, remarked that, since there had been too few volunteers for the last shift of the Brčko-Banovići Brigade, "we held people over from the first shift, and even some who came just to tour the brigades, we arrested them as it were!" In response, Rato Dugonjić, his superior who was in charge of the entire youth movement, had retorted, "You're still bragging about that!" and criticized Švabić for excessive confidence and a lack of self-criticism.[11] The following spring, Dugonjić spoke out even more openly against Švabić's methods and insisted that the use of force and pressure in recruitment for youth brigades must cease. More significantly, he told local youth organizations that they should not be afraid of failing to fill brigade quotas established by local party organizations because to do so by means of forced mobilization would destroy the entire meaning of volunteer labor. Similarly, in a later meeting, despite complaints by some that many brigade quotas had not been filled, Dugonjić again argued that it was better to send fewer brigades than to use forced mobilization.[12]

The differences between Švabić and Dugonjić in this case most likely stemmed from their differing functions in the youth movement. Švabić was specifically responsible for youth brigades and was therefore naturally more inclined to concentrate on ensuring their success, at least in terms of membership and accomplishments. Dugonjić, on the other hand, headed the entire youth movement and was more likely to recognize the harmful effects of forced mobilization techniques on the party's policies and reputation within the movement as a whole. Their disagreement was only one of several cases in which position in the party apparently affected a person's understanding of CPY policies and the appropriate rhetorical strategies to achieve them.[13] Such disagreements, while not necessarily fatal, could not help but obscure the party's message and likely confused both activists and ordinary citizens alike.

Finally, divergences in the attitudes and policies of certain party leaders seem to have reflected an inherent ambivalence within the party over its most immediate goals. For while some Communists apparently had adopted the party's early "Popular Front" line with ease, others were clearly frustrated by the need to dilute revolutionary radicalism in the interests of social unity and power politics. Such may have been the case, for example, with Radovan Zogović—leader of the Serbian agitprop department until mid-1948—who quickly showed himself to be one of the harshest and most ideologically dogmatic members of the CPY.[14]

Zogović's invariably acrid and uncompromising statements were clearly at odds with the more moderate cultural line of the party as a whole, and were surrounded by the calmer, less antagonistic remarks of other agitprop leaders. Yet no party leader ever denied the validity of Zogović's comments or rebuked him for them. On the contrary, Zogović's authority in cultural matters was recognized both in and outside the CPY, often creating the impression that *his* methods and style best represented the party line. To some extent, other party leaders may have tolerated Zogović's harsh line out of respect for his strict personal asceticism and ideological purity. It is also likely, however, that by acceding to the Zogović line, some leaders were simply responding to that current within the CPY that favored a less gradual and more vigorous approach to socialism.

A similar case concerned the party's relationship with its Communist youth organization, SKOJ, whose members were extraordinarily active in promoting the party line. But while SKOJ proved itself a valuable instrument in the revolutionary struggle, as the party's sword it turned out to be equally sharp on both sides. Postwar party documents referring to SKOJ were peppered with criticisms and complaints about the organization as extremist, sectarian, radical, and unreliable. Indeed, the vigorous and often violent methods employed by SKOJ members caused the new regime considerable embarrassment and frustration as they belied its claim to represent the interests of the whole people. Moreover, SKOJ members failed in their roles as both students of Communist theory and teachers of non-Communist youth. Raised and stimulated by the heroism of the Second World War, the young activists apparently found theoretical work uninspiring and were soon renowned for their indifference to self-improvement. As the political secretary of Belgrade University's party committee put it, "SKOJ members love to work, but they do not love to study."[15] Other reports were even less complimentary and mentioned increasing problems with discipline among SKOJ members, many of whom were accused of irresponsibility, frequent drunkenness, and tardiness for work, school, and meetings.[16]

Further, SKOJ members, who were supposed to exercise influence over non-Communist youth mainly through their exemplary behavior, were often accused of stifling youth initiative and adopting a commandeering style. The party instructed SKOJ members to adopt the popular front line and not to harass or frighten non-Communist and "passive" youth, but to court them and draw them into greater activity. Now was not the time for civil war, one document insisted, but for flexibility and maneuvering. Yet, complaints about SKOJ members' condescending attitudes and dictatorial behavior persisted even beyond the organization's final merger with the People's Youth in December 1948.[17]

While many of SKOJ's problems could be blamed on the intemperance of youth, CPY leaders must also bear some responsibility. For even though party leaders urged SKOJ to adopt a more moderate popular front line, they also valued SKOJ's revolutionary enthusiasm and were initially reluctant to stifle its initiative through excessive restrictions. Moreover, the radicalism shown by SKOJ members was mirrored by many within the party who also resented the compromises that had been made in the name of unity.

Although these conflicts often surfaced over issues of style and tactics rather than content and strategy, they undoubtedly did affect the implementation and reception of party rhetoric. Zogović's unyielding and aggressive posture in the field of culture, however unrepresentative, received considerable (and largely negative) public attention. More than anyone else, Zogović is responsible for the popular perception of CPY cultural policies in the 1940s as dogmatic and Stalinist. Moreover, his rhetorical strategies encouraged other impatient activists to apply similar methods, frightening many non-Communist cultural figures into silence and passivity.

Likewise, while party leaders may have hoped to pacify those frustrated by the need to conform to political realities by tolerating SKOJ extremism, in so doing they sabotaged many of their own persuasive policies. The constant threat or use of force that accompanied SKOJ rhetoric may have attracted some youths, but it frightened and repelled many others, leading them to retreat from the public sphere and contributing to the party's reputation as dogmatic and despotic.

"Kadrovi Rešavaju Sve"—Cadres Determine Everything

While disagreements over policy making at the top undoubtedly inhibited the realization of party goals, a far greater impediment to effective persuasion lay in the gap between policies as dictated at the center and as applied in the field. Contacts between higher and lower party organizations in Yugoslavia's poor and war-torn infrastructure were often minimal. Many local committees received the party line in only its most basic outlines since they lacked regular access to detailed instructions or even to the party's central organ, *Borba*. Moreover, even when Djilas's finely tuned directives made it to the local level, his careful nuances were often completely lost on the rank novices assigned to implement them.

Such deficits arose primarily out of the character and composition of the postwar CPY—especially its middle and lower cadres. As the party evolved from an illegal sectarian group of minor importance to the leader of a popular mass movement, it found that it needed more cadres in more places. Several party reports during the war called for greater party membership through reduced entrance requirements and the elimination of "sectarian attitudes." Indeed, although 9,000 of the original 12,000 prewar Communists perished in the war, CPY membership increased twelve-fold, reaching 141,066 by the war's end and 468,175 by mid-1948.[18]

The enormous and rapid increase in CPY membership meant that the great majority of party members after the war were completely new to the game and lacked a solid backing in Communist ideology. As one internal circular dedicated to constructing a solid party apparatus admitted, many members had "entered while the battle was in full bloom and do not know what is accurate. They don't know what the party is or how it should be."[19] Moreover, since the vast majority of new recruits came from the village, they were not only usually unfamiliar with Marxism-Leninism but often only poorly educated, or even illiterate. Finally, as youth had made up some 75 percent of all Partisan units, the new members were also generally very young. Even within the leadership, over half the cadres were under 26.[20] Consequently, both party leaders and ordinary members were often excessively optimistic about the possibilities for rapid social change, while their methods tended to be unsophisticated and immoderate.

The youth, low educational level, and relative inexperience of most CPY members were especially evident within the party's agitprop departments. Admittedly, the very top leaders of the central and republic agitprop departments often were not only leading members of the CPY but also such highly educated and gifted intellectuals as Djilas, Zogović, and Dedijer. At the lower levels, however, the situation was less promising, and although party leaders sought for their agitprop departments "people who know how to write well, to speak well, who are ready-made Marxists and agitators," in fact, they had to admit, "there are no such people, or only a very few."[21]

Faced with such a dilemma, some party organizations simply failed to form agitprop departments, while others formed them out of cadres who, as one party leader from Dalmatia put it, were ready to die for socialism but didn't know what to do. Another report from Dalmatia also noted that out of 180 agitprop leaders, only 20 had passed through even lower- and middle-level party courses.[22] Leaders of agitprop departments regularly complained that they were assigned either the least desirable personnel available—who were unsuited for any other work—or persons already overburdened with other tasks. Agitprop personnel were also regularly assigned and then reassigned to other fields, causing extreme organizational instability.[23] The sum total of well-educated, seasoned Communists being rather small, the few reliable and competent cadres available, especially at lower levels, simply were assigned to more pressing tasks.[24]

Similar cadre problems also existed within trade unions and the fields of mass communications and education. Although the Communist party theoretically represented working-class interests, its ideological influence among workers was far from complete. Party activists working with the League of Trade Unions frequently referred to "left-over," "incorrect," and "anarcho-syndicalist" views among trade-union functionaries as well as ordinary workers.[25] A 1946 report from the Central Committee of the Communist Party of Croatia to the Central Committee of the CPY openly admitted that due to a lack of experienced cadres who understood the new attitude of trade unions toward production, administration, and the state, the trade union organizations in Croatia were "not firmly in the hands of the Party."[26]

Similarly, despite the state's unquestioned ability to exert its control over the press, postwar Yugoslavia's newspapers and journals did not always accurately reflect CPY interests and beliefs. Once again the problem lay in the lack of educated and experienced cadres, which forced the party to rely on many non-Communists for its persuasive work in the press. Even if the editors of postwar newspapers were reliable Communists, the journalists often were not. One report from the agitprop department of Rijeka described the editor of that city's newspaper as politically loyal, but young, inexperienced, and under the influence of older prewar journalists, who did not always accept instructions and sometimes did the opposite of what they were told. Likewise, the Communist in charge of the central agitprop department's sector for agitation and the press, Zdenka Šegvić, noted that in the Yugoslav news agency Tanjug, although the managing director was both loyal and experienced, "politically unqualified" individuals much lower down in the organization made many important choices concerning news selection.[27]

The situation in education was even more serious. Through its enormous attention to education, the government had created a vast new reserve of students before it had the educational cadres to handle them. For example, while the number of elementary school students in Bosnia-

Hercegovina increased from 1939/40 to 1949 by 76.2 percent, the number of teachers decreased by 29.6 percent due to both wartime deaths and party purges of the school system. Likewise, while the number of students at Belgrade University increased from 9,972 before the war to 24,364 in June 1948, the number of professors and instructors fell from 577 before the war to only 374 by the end of 1947.[28]

Not only were teachers in short supply, but they were unevenly distributed. Few educators, it turned out, were willing to work in the countryside, where they were most needed, but where remote villages were often unconnected by roads, railways, or telephones and lacked the most elementary public utilities, such as electricity, plumbing, health care facilities, and stores. Even those who had originally come from a village saw higher education as a means of escape from it and preferred to seek employment—of whatever kind—in the cities. According to one article in the Belgrade city newspaper, over 1,000 elementary and secondary school teachers resided in Belgrade after the war although the city needed only 500.[29]

As state employees, teachers theoretically had to work wherever the state sent them. In practice, however, most did everything in their power to avoid relocation. Some found powerful friends, others secured false health documents certifying them as unfit for harsh country life, and yet others left the teaching profession altogether.[30] The CPY relied almost entirely on moral persuasion to induce teachers to accept rural employment. Countless articles appealed to the civic and professional duty of teachers, stressing the dire need for their services in the provinces and imploring them to accept personal sacrifices for the good of the community. Others, meanwhile, reviled those teachers who avoided relocation, calling them selfish, irresponsible, and even reactionary. Nonetheless, the "Law on State Employees," which made avoidance of relocation a criminal offense, was not strictly enforced. Nor did the new government institute civil mobilization of teachers, as it had with doctors and veterinarians.[31] Here was a case where the party's persuasive rhetoric, unsupported by any convincing threat of force, proved remarkably ineffective.

But if the government seemed unwilling to use the stick on recalcitrant teachers, it was even less forthcoming with the carrot. Admittedly, the state could not radically improve conditions in the village overnight, but it could have offered greater material incentives to village teachers. Instead, many teachers were so badly paid that they had to take on second jobs for strictly financial reasons, while the state piled ever more obligations on their shoulders. Although teachers in provincial regions often had over 200 students, they were expected to augment their work in the classroom with public service in literacy courses and people's universities, and they were frequently instructed to perform such extraneous tasks for state and mass organizations as passing out ration cards and helping collect agricultural surplus.[32]

Moreover, the government's treatment of existing teachers often sabotaged its efforts to increase future educational cadres. Already by mid-1945, some teachers had begun advising students to stay away from the profession as it would condemn them to life in the village forever; and in 1947, only 856 students out of a planned 2,050 enrolled in higher pedagogical schools. Reports throughout 1948 also complained that many of those enrolled in teachers' schools had no real love for the profession and were there only because they had been unable to gain entrance elsewhere.[33]

The consequences of these personnel problems were extremely serious. Within agitprop departments, the paucity of well-educated cadres ensured that the political and ideological level of their rhetoric would remain low. At best, inexperienced agitprop cadres, who did not themselves really understand the issues, were likely to concentrate more on the fulfillment of concrete tasks than on the promotion of new ideas. At worst, it meant, as one report from the ministry of education put it, that often "things are decided in a bureaucratic manner."[34] This rather mild statement takes on a more ominous tone when it is remembered that "in a bureaucratic manner" was a euphemism for "by force." Indeed, there can be no doubt that when agitprop leaders failed to achieve a desired goal by means of persuasion, many were inclined to adopt more reliable, coercive methods. This kind of substitution was undoubtedly facilitated by the often incestuous nature of party activists in many regions. The leader of an agitprop department, for example, was likely to be on close personal terms with the leader of the secret police, if indeed both jobs were not held by the same person.

The lack of reliable cadres in mass communications was less likely to result in coercion, but it certainly hindered the party's ability successfully to promote even its short-term, to say nothing of its long-term, agenda. If the journalists were Communists, they were often lacking in professional journalistic skills and produced crude and often nearly unreadable articles. If non-Communists, they were more sophisticated and eloquent, but less likely to promote the proper Communist values. In precisely the same way, the shortage of educational personnel meant that most teachers were lacking the professional and/or ideological qualifications necessary to fulfill their persuasive mission.

Indeed, many acting educators in the first postwar years were only minimally educated themselves. Often teachers had received only one year's training from a normal four-year pedagogical school, and in some places the need for teachers was so acute that any literate person was likely to be drafted into service. In Montenegro, for example, 353 of the more literate peasants were used as teachers, and in Kosovo, literacy courses were taught by schoolchildren who had only recently become literate themselves.[35] Even among the better educated teachers, very few were Communists, and they were generally young, inexperienced, and lacking in authority. Many had been rather hastily accepted into the party and lacked a solid understanding of or loyalty to its principles. According to the president of the Belgrade University party committee, for example, the professors' party cells didn't seem like Communist organizations at all, since the members addressed one another by their official titles.[36]

Finally, even had CPY persuasive policies been determined above and implemented below with absolute consistency, it seems unlikely that they would have successfully achieved the desired transformation of society and culture. As the remainder of this study will show, Yugoslavia's citizens proved remarkably resistant to party attempts to mold their attitudes and values. In some cases, they simply refused to read, hear, view, or accept the party's instructions for or models of correct socialist thinking. In others, they successfully manipulated the party's persuasive agenda for their own purposes. While it is as difficult to prove the utter failure of the party's persuasive agenda as it would be to prove its success, the evidence suggests that CPY rhetoric succeed only in convincing people of those ideas in which they already believed.

Notes

1. For further examples of such differences see Carol Lilly, "Problems of Persuasion: Communist Agitation and Propaganda in Yugoslavia, 1944–1948," *Slavic Review*, 53, no. 2 (Summer 1994): 395–413.
2. "O agitaciono-propagandnim radu KPJ," 1945, ACKSKJ, VIII I/2-a-35.
3. "Prilozi prvom zapisniku Prosvetnog saveta pri MP savezne vlade," 6–16 Aug. 1945, AJ, MP-9; "Na zasedanju Prosvetnog saveza Jugoslavije zaključeno je da se pitanje udžbenika najhitnije reši," *Borba*, 19 Aug. 1945.
4. Report of the ministry of education, 1945, ACKSKJ, X2-II/4.
5. N. N., "Zadaci Komiteta za škole i nauku," *Savremena škola*, 1, no. 1 (July 1946); "Reč Borisa Ziherla," at the First Congress of the Union of Educational Workers, 14 July 1946, AJ, KŠN-17.
6. Andrew Wachtel, *Making a Nation, Breaking a Nation: Literature and Cultural Politics in Yugoslavia* (Stanford, CA: Stanford University Press, 1998), 136–137.
7. Kosta Grubačić, "O nekim nedostacima rada na polju narodne prosvjete," *Borba*, 4 Oct. 1947.
8. Franc Ostanek, "Nastavni planovi i programe za osnovne škole," *Savremena škola*, 3, no. 2–3 (1948): 22–37; "Zapisnik sa savjetovanja sa drugovima iz KŠN," Strictly Confidential, 2 March 1948, ACKSKJ, VIII II/4-d-10; "Savezna konferencija o pitanjima opšteobrazovanih srednjih škola znači krupan doprinos u

razvoju našeg novog školstva," *Prosvetni radnik*, 1 June 1948; "Obrazovanje našeg čoveka," 1949, ACKSKJ, VIII II/8-d-35.

9. "Deveta sednica Prezidijuma Narodne skupštine FNRJ," 11 Dec. 1948, in Slobodan Nešović, ed., *Sednice Prezidijuma Narodne skupštine FNRJ (prvog i drugog saziva, 4. februar 1946–9. januar 1953)* (Belgrade: 1956).

10. For further information on the relationship between education and the national question in Yugoslavia see Charles Jelavich, *South Slav Nationalisms: Textbooks and Yugoslav Union before 1914* (Columbus, OH: Ohio State University Press, 1990); Wolfgang Höpken, "History Education and Yugoslav (Dis)-Integration," in Melissa Bokovoy, Jill Irvine, and Carol Lilly, eds., *State-Society Relations in Yugoslavia, 1945–1992* (New York and London: St. Martin's Press, 1997); Leopoldina Plut-Preglj, Aleš Gabrić and Božo Repe, "The Repluralization of Slovenia in the 1980's: New Revelations from Archival Records," The Donald Treadgold Papers, no. 24 (Seattle: University of Washington, 2000).

11. "Zapisnik o idejno političkom radu na Omladinskoj pruzi," 12–13 Sept. 1946, AJ, SSOJ F37.

12. Rato Dugonjić, "Diskusija o referatu Švabića," 15–16 April 1947, AJ, SSOJ-37; "Zapisnik sa pretsednicima glavnih odbora," 24 June 1947, AJ, SSOJ F57.

13. The women's and youth organizations were also accused at various points of subordinating the larger interests of the party to those of their own particular organizations. One internal report complained that even the department of agitation and propaganda worked "according to 'its own agitprop line,' approaching party problems in a one-sided manner." "Direktivno pismo Uprave za agitaciju i propagandu," 1948, ACKSKJ, VIII II/1-a-13.

14. Radovan Zogović is undoubtedly one of the more intriguing characters in the cast of CPY cultural policies. A poet of unquestioned talent (Krleža called him "brilliant"), the Montenegrin Communist was also notorious as Yugoslavia's prime defender of socialist realism and the theories of Todor Pavlov and Andrei Zhdanov. Although Zogović's contemporaries invariably noted his acidic and unyielding temperament in their descriptions, they also usually expressed admiration for his absolute dedication to the cause of communism and for his incorruptible nature. But although top CPY leaders were reputedly "fond" of Zogović and willing to forgive him much, eventually his refusal to bend brought him down. Having received already a "serious reprimand" during the Second World War for "leftist errors," Zogović was expelled from the CPY in late 1948 as a Cominformist supporter. See Milomir Marić, "Prkosne strofe Radovana Zogovića," 3 parts, *Duga*, nos. 311–313, 25 Jan.–22 Feb. 1986; Josip Pavičić, "Uz smrt Radovana Zogovića: Trajno ime poezije," *Vjesnik*, 7 January 1986, p. 11; Milovan Djilas, *Wartime* (New York: Harcourt Brace Jovanovich, 1977), 163–164; Milovan Djilas, *Rise and Fall* (New York: Harcourt Brace Jovanovich, 1983) 223.

15. V[j]era [Kovačević], "Zapisnik sa sastanka UK," 21 June 1946, in Momčilo Mitrović and Djordje Stanković, eds., *Zapisnici i izveštaji univerzitetskog komiteta Komunističke partije Srbije, 1945–1948* (hereafter ZIUKKPS) (Belgrade: 1985), 77–79. See also "Političko-organizacijoni izvještaj OK SKOJ Biokovo-Neretva," 26 May 1945, HDA, PKSKOJ-H; "O vaspitnom radu SKOJ-a," 20 Dec. 1945, ACKSKJ, CKSKOJ VI-1/3; "Zapisnik sa sastanka UK," 13 Feb. 1947, *ZIUKKPS*, 163.

16. "Stenografske beleške sa Savetovanja CK SKOJ," 28 Sept. 1946, ACKSKJ, CKSKOJ IIa-1/1; "Četvrti sastanak Pretsedništva CV NOJ," 15–17 Sept. 1947, AJ,

SSOJ-37; "Zapisnik sa sastanka UK," 18 Sept. 1947, *ZIUKKPS*, 258; "Izveštaj o radu PK SKOJ za Srbiju u toku 1947 g.," 21 Jan. 1948, ACKSKJ, CSKOJ III b-1/10.

17. "Zapisnik sa sastanka PK SKOJ," 21 July 1945, HDA, PSKOJ-H-1; Rato Dugonjić, "Rezime po pitanju odbora USAOJ-a," March 1945, ACKSKJ, CKSKOJ IIa-1/2;"Izvještaj OK SKOJ Srednje Dalmacije," 29 May 1945, HDA, PKSKOJ-H; "Izvještaj OK KPH Bjelovar," 5 Oct. 1945, HDA, CKKPH; Rato Dugonjić, Discussion at the Third Plenum of the USAOJ, 11 Jan. 1946, AJ, SSOJ-27; "O Savezu komunističke omladine Jugoslavije," 1947, ACKSKJ, CKSKOJ IIc-1/42.

18. Josip Broz Tito, "Narodno-oslobodilačka borba i organizaciono pitanje naše partije," *Proleter*, 14–15 (April 1942): 53–62; Dušan Bilandžić, *Historija Socijalističke Federativne Republike Jugoslavije: Glavni procesi, 1918–1985* (Zagreb: Školska knjiga, 1985), 101; Pero Morača and Stanislav Stojanović, eds., *Povijest Saveza komunista Jugoslavije* (Belgrade: Izdavački centar Komunist, 1985), 322.

19. "Šta je i kakva treba da bude naša komunistička partija," 15 Aug. 1945— but clearly written much earlier, between June 1941 and May 1943, HDA, CKKPH.

20. Bilandžić, *Glavni procesi*, 88.

21. "Referat o ideološkom odgoju komunista," 8 Dec. 1946, HDA, CKKPH.

22. "Zapisnik sa sastanka Agitpropa PK KPH za Dalmaciju," 7 June 1947, HDA, CKKPHAP; "Opći pregled rada agitpropa OK KPH-a za Dalmaciju," 2 Nov. 1946, HDA, CKKPHAP.

23. See "Izvještaj OO USAOH za Dalmaciju," 30 Aug. 1945, HDA, USAOH-17; "Opći pregled rada agitpropa OK KPH-a za Dalmaciju"; "Organizacione primjedbe na našu agitaciju i propagandu," 1947, HDA, ZV NOH-29; "Zapisnik sa savjetovanja po pitanju teoretskog rada," 22 Nov. 1947, ACKSKJ, VIII II/4-d-a; Veljko Zeković, "Marksističko-lenjinističko vaspitanje kadrova," *Borba*, 8 July 1948.

24. Milovan Djilas, Interview with the author, Belgrade, 17 Nov. 1988. A recent article on agitprop work on the Soviet home front during the Second World War argues that there, too, agitprop work was considered "inferior work, the province of those who had failed at other activities." Richard J. Brody, "Ideology and Political Mobilization: The Soviet Home Front during World War II," Carl Beck Papers in Russian and East European Studies, No. 1104 (Pittsburgh, PA: 1994).

25. "Izveštaj o kulturno-prosvetnim radu JSRNJ," 3 Dec. 1945, AJ, CVSSJ F1/J3 KPO; "Izvještaj u vezi priprema za Kongres" from the OK KPH za Dalmaciju, 25 Feb. 1946, HDA, CKKPH; "Teze za referate na Sindikalnim konferencijama povodom I. Kongresa," 1948, AJ, CVSSJ F1/J1-3 Konferencija; Ivan Božičević, "Uloga i zadaci JSRNJ," at I. Kongres, 24–29 Oct. 1948, AJ, CVSSJ F3.

26. "Izvještaj o radu CK KPH," 17 March 1946, HDA, CKKPH. See also "O kulturno-ideološkom radu u sindikatima," no date, HDA, CKKPHAP.

27. "Izvještaj agitpropa MK KPH Rijeka," 19 Sept. 1947, HDA, CKKPHAP; Zdenka Šegvić, "Referat o radu *TANJUGa*," 15 Sept. 1945, ACKSKJ, VIII II/5-d-85.

28. "Stanje nastavnog kadra u školama," 1949, ACKSKJ, VIII II/8-d-36; "Iz godišnjeg izveštaja CK KPS za 1947 godinu," December 1947, *ZIUKKPS*, 311–314. See also "Maršal Tito predao Beogradskom univerzitetu darove praškog i bratislavskog univerziteta," *Borba*, 30 March 1946; Ljubodrag Dimić, *Agitprop kul-*

tura, Agitpropovska faza kulturne politike u Srbiji, 1945–1952 (Belgrade: Rad, 1988), 113–114.

29. "Raspored stručnjaka treba pravilno izvršiti," *20. oktobar,* 20 April 1945; Jelena Popović, "Prosveta nije privilegija povlašćenih," *20. oktobar,* 5 Oct. 1945.

30. "Raspored stručnjaka." See also "Izveštaj o stanju srednjih i osnovnih škola NR Crne Gore," May 1946, AJ, KŠN-77; Pavle Radoman, "Prosvetno-politički zadaci Saveza," 15 July 1946, AJ, KŠN-17; "Osnovne smjerice naše prosvjetne političke," 1947, HDA, CKKPHAP; "Izveštaj sa obilaska srednjih i sredno-stručnih škola, February 1948, AJ, SSOJ-98.

31. Memo from the Secretariat of the Government of the FNRJ for Personnel, 10 March 1948, AJ, KŠN-45. On the other hand, relocation to the hinterland was occasionally used by the government as a form of punishment or for political reasons. "Izveštaj o stanju učiteljskog kadra," no date, AJ, SSOJ-102.

32. "Izveštaj o stanju srednjih i osnovnih škola NR Crne Gore"; Radoman, "Prosvetno-politički zadaci Saveza"; Martin Mencej, "U novu školsku godinu," *Prosvetni radnik,* 15 Sept. 1947; Puniša Perović, Concluding speech at the federal conference of the KŠN on the question of teachers' schools, 14–15 Oct. 1948, AJ, SSOJ-98; "Izveštaj o stanju nastavnog kadra u gimnazijama," no date, AJ, SSOJ-102; "Društveni položaj učitelja i profesora," no date, AJ, SSOJ-102.

33. Trifun V. Trivunac, "Omladino, više ljubavi za učiteljski poziv, inteligencijo, više razumevanje za selo," *Selo,* 23 Sept. 1945; "Izveštaj sa obilaska srednjih i sredno-stručnih škola"; "O nekim problemima učiteljskih škola," *Prosvetni radnik,* 1 April 1948; Milislav Mijušković, "Srednjoškolska omladina pred izborom poziva," *Prosvetni radnik,* 15 June 1948.

34. "Izveštaj o radu Ministarstva prosvjete," Oct.-Nov. 1945, ACKSKJ, X2-II/4.

35. "Otpočeo je rad Prosvetnog saveta Jugoslavije," *Borba,* 8 Aug. 1945; "Agitaciono-politički rad," report from Kosovo-Metohia, 26 Oct. 1948, ACKSKJ, VIII II/2-c-67; "Survey of the Conditions under Which Educational Work Has to Be Organized in Yugoslavia Today," 16 April 1945, AJ, MP-3.

36. Dragiša M. Ivanović, "Zapisnik sa pretkongresne konferencije partijske ćelije nastavnika i administratora Beogradskog univerziteta," 19 June 1948, ZIUKKPS, 386; "Mesnom komitetu KPS," 5 Nov. 1946, ZIUKKPS, 118–120; "Zapisnik sa sastanka UK KPS, 3 April 1947, ZIUKKPS, 178; "Zagrebačko sveučilište," Dinko Tomašić Collection, Hoover Institution.

Part Two

Having described the historical context and institutional structure that delineated the party's postwar persuasive enterprise, we may now turn our attention to a chronological description of its specific content and activities. The succeeding chapters thus follow the evolution of party persuasion from the liberation of Belgrade in October 1944 through the Soviet-Yugoslav split in June 1948 to the end of the party's subsequent reform era in June 1953. In the process, they describe changes in CPY persuasive policies and rhetoric in response not only to the evolving domestic and international context, but also to the party's graduated strategy for the construction of socialism and feedback from below. These changes inevitably influenced the nature of state-society relations in postwar Yugoslavia.

CPY rule over Yugoslavia commenced from liberated Belgrade in an atmosphere characterized by social tension and violence but also by enormous enthusiasm, energy, and hope for the future. By late 1947, that atmosphere had been replaced by one of repression, order, and increasing monotony. In the party's struggle to balance revolutionary idealism with its desire for social stability, the latter seemed to have won out. Beginning in late 1947, however, persuasive activists began to shift their emphases from the party's short-term political goals to its long-term transformative agenda. CPY persuasive policies during the first three years after the war document the progress of that transition. In the first year, from the fall of 1944 through the fall of 1945, party rhetoric blended elements of revolutionary radicalism with a broad, relatively tolerant approach to social change. In the following two years, the party worked to channel postwar enthusiasm into socially useful activity, while simultaneously reducing the extent of political and cultural pluralism. In other words, although party leaders willingly exploited the unsettled conditions of the first postwar years, they also worked to increase regime control and prevent any unexpected developments. In the final stage, party leaders sought to increase the role of Communist ideology in Yugoslavia, hoping thereby to initiate the planned transformation of society. They wished to do so, however, by strictly pedagogical means, without losing any of the control and stability already acquired. Thus, in the period from late 1947 to mid-1948, party leaders sought a new balance that would give more weight to long-term goals and reinspire Yugoslavia's population with their vision for the future. Despite evident uncertainty about exactly how to realize the cultural transformation, CPY persuasive policies reflected the changing emphasis and by early 1948 had begun to pay more attention to issues of ideology.

4

Taking Power: Cultural Manipulation and Revolutionary Change

In the first years of CPY rule, beginning even before the war had ended, party leaders and members both reflected the prevailing social tensions and simultaneously strove to control or direct them. On the one hand, the party's fledgling government had a direct interest in creating and maintaining a sense of order and stability, while building popular support for its program of change. At the same time, however, party members were still very much engaged in the revolutionary struggle and the effort to remake society from top to bottom. CPY rhetoric from the liberation of Belgrade up through the November 1945 elections reflected this complex dynamic. Accordingly, in some areas, CPY persuasive policies were clearly moderate and compromising; in others, they were radical and extremist; and in others yet the two approaches coexisted and contradicted one another. Thus, while some persuasive activities and rhetoric sought only to manipulate the existing values and culture for party purposes, others revealed the party's much more ambitious goal of revolutionary social and cultural change.

Compromise and Moderation

The primary goal of the CPY in the months following the October 1944 liberation of Belgrade was to maintain and secure its position in power. To do so, the party needed at least the passive compliance, if not the active cooperation and participation, of a large segment of the population. Therefore, the party could not afford to frighten its citizens (or provoke the Western allies) with too much talk of communism, and it tended to concentrate instead on those aspects of its program that were already popular. Party leaders in this early period never admitted their socialist intentions and when pressed, Tito flatly denied the Communist character of the government.[1] Inasmuch as socialist values and goals appeared in the party's public program, they were couched in a "popular front"–style vocabulary. The new order, party rhetoric claimed, was building a people's democracy (not socialism), based on the unity of the Yugoslav population (not class conflict), in opposition to fascist occupiers and fascist or pro-fascist domestic quislings (not the class enemy).

Seeking a degree of social stability, party leaders also strove in this period to defuse the explosive wartime atmosphere and to reconcile certain opposing elements of the population. Among the first laws passed was one that forbade the incitement of racial, national, or religious hatred; and early amnesty acts for Četniks and Croat and Slovene Home Guards were intended to show that there would be no further mass acts of vengeance by the new government.[2] Meanwhile, newspaper articles and speeches promised that conditions in the country would gradually improve and that no one would be allowed to starve. One article from January 1946, for example, reassured the population that according to precise scientific analyses, the upcoming winter would be unusually mild, with lowest temperatures reaching only –16 degrees Celsius (3 degrees Fahrenheit) and with averages between –5 and +5 degrees Celsius (23–41 degrees Fahrenheit).[3]

Most of all, however, the party worked to further broaden its basis of support and ensure the victory of PFY candidates in the November 1945 elections. Rhetorical strategies in this period reflected that goal and were primarily designed to nurture mass enthusiasm for a new and better Yugoslavia. In many ways, CPY persuasive policies in this early period surpassed any that would follow; their educational component was high and they presented the party's vision for a new society in the broadest possible format.[4] Accordingly, the ideas presented by CPY rhetoric in this period were not based strictly on Communist ideology and did not touch on all aspects of the party's program. Rather, they reflected most often those goals and values for which the party had already gained strong support. Such rhetoric was not so much trying to change Yugoslavia's culture as to build upon and manipulate those aspects of the existing culture that roughly coincided with the party's own program for change. Moreover, the ideas expressed in that rhetoric wisely focused attention not on the immediate future, which was sure to be difficult and full of hardship, but more on the distant goal of a free, prosperous, and just Yugoslavia.

The most important of the new values conveyed by early CPY rhetoric was that the good of the whole is greater and more important than the good of the one; the rights of the group are of greater worth and significance than the rights of the individual; and community service is humanity's most noble function. This one broad value or principle provided the core for an entire system of related values and principles. A new appreciation for community service, for example, implied also a new attitude toward labor, which would no longer be seen as a daily grind necessary for the maintenance of life, but a force for the enrichment of the community and the means by which people fulfill their most noble function. The related cult of labor portrayed work not only as humanity's most honorable and natural function but also as the essential measure of its worth. The "people" of Yugoslavia were the *working* people, and those who did not work (and thus did not contribute to the new state and society) were not the "people" but their enemy. Mass participation in government and society also made up an integral part of this value system; for if all citizens practiced the ideal of self-sacrifice and community service, they would all become actively involved in the organization and functioning of community life, that is, in government and society. Further, art could no longer be seen as something personal, belonging to the artist and only coincidentally of value to others, because art and artists also had to serve the community, responding to its needs and wishes. Acceptance of this system did not imply complete neglect of the self since it was an individual's solemn duty to develop his/her physical and mental capabilities to their fullest and to exhibit enormous self-initiative. One should do so, however, not for reasons of personal satisfaction or enrichment, but only in order better to serve the community.

Political rhetoric, meanwhile, described the principles that would lead to the new and improved society as the "Heritage of the People's Liberation Struggle" (the new regime's official designation for the Partisan uprising during the Second World War). The first item in the heritage was the full sovereignty and independence of Yugoslavia in its international relations, including the clear assertion that Yugoslavia would never again serve as a plaything to the Great Powers, but also accepting reliance in foreign relations on the Soviet Union. The second principle was "People's Power," which was not only the official name of the new government but claimed to signify full sovereignty of the people. It included abolition of the prewar monarchy, full enfranchisement of all persons over 18 years of age, regular elections with the right to recall all government officials, and democracy—not such "formal" democracy as existed in the West, it was stressed, but a new, deeper, and more substantial democracy based on mass participation in government. The third important principle included in the heritage was the "brotherhood and unity" of the nations of Yugoslavia based on their voluntary and equal participation in a federation that admitted the right to national self-development but excluded any form of national chauvinism or separatism. All citizens of the new state were to develop a sense of "true" Yugoslav patriotism, as opposed to "chauvinistic nationalism." Finally, party rhetoric explained that in order for Yugoslavia to attain the goals of that heritage, it would have to be industrialized and made more technologically advanced, while the population would have to attain a higher level of education and culture. In short, the party's early persuasive policies were designed to appeal to the broadest segments of the population. Party rhetoric in this first year was unquestionably idealistic; it was not, however, especially ideological. Rather than seeking to change Yugoslav culture, it sought to increase popular support for the CPY on the basis of certain preexisting values and principles. Indeed, in many specific areas CPY rhetoric diverged substantially from the party's Marxist-Leninist ideology. Three such cases concerned the party's rhetoric toward class struggle, the All-Slavic Movement, and women's rights.

Class Struggle

One area where the party's rhetoric most obviously contradicted its ideological program was in its apparent denial of class conflict in new Yugoslavia. While stressing the "bourgeois" nature of prewar Yugoslav society, the party rarely admitted in public the class basis of its own state. Party leaders were fully aware, after all, that in a predominantly agrarian country such as Yugoslavia, Communists could not gain and maintain power by relying solely on the working class. Therefore, and in harmony with the popular front line, which sought to unite all progressive forces regardless of social background, CPY rhetoric generally emphasized the need for class cooperation rather than conflict. Party leaders especially encouraged cooperation between the working class and the peasantry, but also included the "progressive" or "people's" intelligentsia within the alliance. Although party leaders were generally less sanguine about the possibilities of cooperation with the members of the "bourgeoisie"—insisting that they had collaborated en masse with the fascist occupiers and their quislings—one Communist trade union official referred to an alliance that included not only the workers, peasants, and people's intelligentsia, but also "one part of the patriotic bourgeoisie."[5] Tito himself expressed this unitarist line most clearly in a June 1945 speech that declared that peasants, workers, and the people's intelligentsia were the three most important factors in the country. "Not one of those three factors can be favored, not one can be higher than another, but all are equal."[6]

The net effect of such tactical associations was to minimize the leading role and revolutionary aims of the working class in CPY rhetoric. Even internal party documents, while insisting that the CPY was a workers' party, urged a policy of class cooperation over conflict and emphasized the need to achieve some degree of consensus within Yugoslav society. Djilas, for example, specifically advised party members not to provoke artificial differentiation among the masses, "because differentiation can separate one part of the masses and cause confusion among us ourselves."[7]

CPY public statements were even more cautious; several authors insisted that the working class was not acting on the basis of its own selfish class interests but saw its interests in those of the entire people. An article in the central trade union newspaper *Rad*, for example, insisted that as a member of the Front, the League of Trade Unions did not approach the upcoming elections for the Constituent Assembly with its own special program. "The elaboration of a particular program of the working class would play into the hands of those who want to break up the People's Front."[8]

Moreover, party leaders never referred to the working class in isolation but only in conjunction with the other social groups. In fact, they most often replaced the phrase *working class* with *working masses* or *working people*, and described "people's power" not as a dictatorship of the proletariat but as the government of the working people or, at most, the working class and the working people. Party rhetoric in 1945 even hailed the traditional worker's holiday May 1 as an "All-People's Celebration."[9]

While de-emphasizing the leading role of the working class, party rhetoric simultaneously accentuated peasant participation in the struggle against fascism and in the construction of a new state. Although the union of workers and peasants is an article of faith in orthodox Marxism-Leninism, it found especially broad application in Yugoslavia. Moša Pijade, for example, once insisted that there was no contradiction of interests between workers and peasants. Likewise, Djilas argued that as a result of the war, the peasants of Yugoslavia could not be compared with those of any other country. "The experience of this war tells us that enormous progressive revolutionary forces are hidden within the peasantry."[10] Djilas later recalled that in describing the course of the uprising in Yugoslavia to members of the Soviet agitprop department, he "practically reduced the uprising in Yugoslavia to a tie between a peasant rebellion and the Communist avant-garde."[11]

Recognizing that peasants would not respond positively to Marxist-Leninist ideology, the party adopted a "soft-sell" approach in rhetoric directed at them and carefully avoided any narrow Communist terminology. The party was also quite cautious in its treatment of several prewar peasant parties, and especially the Croat Republican Peasant Party (CRPP). For while the masses in interwar Serbia had been divided among several different parties, the CRPP had been Croatia's only significant prewar political party and thus encompassed not only the vast majority of Croatia's peasants, but also most of its intelligentsia and middle classes. It was also politically very sensitive since its most recent leader, Vladko Maček, had refused all cooperation with the CPY and was one of its most dangerous rivals. In the course of the war, however, the CPY had successfully split the CRPP and cooperated with one branch while seeking to isolate those still loyal to Maček.[12]

Djilas later concluded that the CPY overestimated the postwar strength of the CRPP; at the time, however, party leaders clearly felt they had to work with the peasant party, although keeping it within certain boundaries. Thus, they not only allowed the CRPP formally to reestablish itself as a party but included several CRPP members in federal, Croatian republic, and local organs of government. Further, they authorized and funded publication of its newspaper, *Slobodni dom* (*Free Home*), and the activities of its cultural organization, Seljačka sloga (Peasant Harmony).[13] Tito established both the limits and the purpose of such concessions at a Central Committee meeting in late 1945. "We *must not* have in Croatia a peasant movement, which is now at the boiling point. It is not necessary to be sectarian in relation to certain personalities from the CRPP. . . . We must win over the peasant masses in Croatia and Serbia, then no one can do anything to us."[14]

Consequently, party rhetoric was careful in this early stage to emphasize aspects of its political program that roughly coincided with those of the CRPP—including, in particular, land reform, the cooperative movement, anti-clericalism, and Slavism. Party leaders treated the deceased founders of the CRPP, Ante and Stjepan Radić, with great respect, almost as honorary Communists. One internal document from the Croatian agitprop department contained a list of approved quotes from the Radić brothers to be used in party rhetoric; and Djilas advised youth activists to exploit the essentially "progressive and revolutionary" Radićist traditions among the Croat peasantry. At the first postwar conference of the CRPP one Communist sympathizer, Vladimir Nazor, even interrupted shouts of "Long Live Tito" to say,

> There is one other name which now hovers above us all. . . . Also hovering on our lips is the name of the leader of you all, the one who gathered you here. That is the name of Stjepan Radić. (Shouts of: Glory to Stjepan Radić!)
>
> *Stjepan Radić is celebrating a day of victory today such as he never experienced while he was alive.* He is celebrating today his greatest victory. He is celebrating because he sees that that for which he gave the greatest sacrifice and that all that is good, everything he ever wanted for the Croat peasant, and everything for which he struggled has come true today.[15]

The CPY tried to appropriate for itself the mystique and popularity not only of Stjepan Radić but also of Matija Gubec, the martyred leader of a 16th-century peasant uprising in Croatian and Slovenian lands. Tito's name, for example, was regularly attached to those of Gubec and Radić, and at official gatherings in Croatia his picture often hung between theirs to form a trinity of the "Best Sons of the Croat People." Party rhetoric relating to these class issues shows a keen appreciation for the country's social structure and dominant values. It reveals also the pragmatism of party leaders, who were prepared to minimize certain aspects of their program in hopes of winning broad popular support.

The All-Slavic Movement

Another area where the CPY showed an appreciation for the power of existing culture, whatever its discordance with Communist ideology, concerned the postwar Slavic movement. Created by the Soviet Union in 1941 to unify all Slavs in opposition to the German threat, the "All-Slavic Movement" (*Sveslavenski pokret*) also found enormous application in Yugoslavia's postwar politics. Indeed, while all of the Slavic "People's Democracies" obediently adopted Slavism, Yugoslav Communists were especially prominent in the movement from the moment of its inception up to the Soviet-Yugoslav split. One of the CPY's leading representatives in Moscow, Veljko Vlahović, had prepared the program of the first All-Slavic meeting held in 1941, and after the war, Belgrade became the movement's official headquarters. Abundant articles in the Yugoslav press loudly heralded Slavic solidarity, often replacing the title of the "Soviet Union" with "Russia," "Great Slavic Russia," or "Mother Russia." Even the First of May—traditionally a class-based workers' holiday—was described in *Borba* in 1945 as "a celebration of united Slavdom."[16]

Beyond showing loyalty to the Soviet line, CPY leaders supported the Slavic movement in order to facilitate public acceptance of Yugoslavia's new alliance system. Thus, although Yugoslavia's relations with the Soviet Union and newly emerging Communist-dominated states of Eastern Europe clearly derived from their common ideological foundations, party rhetoric often described them in terms of their common Slavic heritage. After all, Communist ideology remained alien to the peasant masses of Yugoslavia, while Slavic sentiment—expressed especially in friendship with and reliance on Russia—had numerous and deep roots in the country.[17] Finally, while no documents directly support this conjecture, it seems plausible that the party leaders also hoped a sense of Slavism would further cement the unity of those Slavic nations within Yugoslavia.

The party's effort to generate cooperation based on Slavism appeared, for example, in Tito's May 1945 speech about church-state relations in new Yugoslavia. In it, he explained, "We want to create a great community of South Slavs. In this community there will be both Orthodox and Catholic, who must be closely linked with all the other Slavs."[18] Indeed the party's Slavic/Russian card proved remarkably effective. Even more important than the attention Slavism received at the hands of Communists was that which it was granted by various non-Communist supporters of the new government. Prominent intellectuals, leading representatives of several non-Communist parties, and members of the Orthodox and Catholic clergy all packed their speeches and articles with references to Slavism.

The Orthodox clergy were especially pro-Russian and pro-Slavic. Patriarch Gavrilo of the Serbian Orthodox Church, though no stooge of the Communist party, warmly greeted the first Congress of the All-Slavic Movement held in Belgrade in December 1946 with the following words:

> Slavic solidarity which is, happily, so divinely manifested, today more than ever, in all Slavic countries, led by our century-long defender and patron Mother Russia (applause) and under the brilliant leadership of the great and powerful Russian people, headed by the great Stalin (All rise and wildly and lengthily applaud) . . . that Slavic solidarity is the strongest guarantee for the future development and majesty of all Slavic peoples. (Applause). . . The Serbian Orthodox Church sends warm prayers, that the Blessed Almighty follow the work of the Slavic Congress so that its noble efforts may be crowned with full success for the good of all Slavic peoples and for the good of all humanity. (Lengthy applause)[19]

In addition, Monsignor Svetozar Rittig, the most important Catholic to cooperate with the Communists, apparently did so largely on the basis of their common faith in Slavism and Yugoslavism. A former secretary of Bishop Strossmayer, Rittig was a true believer in South Slavic unity and Slavic solidarity; he valued the People's Front mainly because it had rescued the South Slavic peoples from internal dissension.[20] An article he wrote in the spring of 1944 noted that while Cyril and Methodius had been the first to see the importance of the Slavs for the development of mankind, no Slavic king had moved the South Slavic tribes along the path taken by the English, Germans, and French to become the leading people of the world. The People's Liberation Struggle, he then explained, would realize that wasted medieval opportunity to create a new educational and political power out of the mosaic of Slavic tribes in the Balkans.[21]

Women and the Family

A final area where party rhetoric conformed to existing values, rather than seeking to change them, concerned the role of women. Although CPY leaders declared the full legal equality of men and women, they clearly adopted and promoted certain culturally accepted views about women. CPY leaders, male and female, generally believed that differences between the sexes were biologically preordained rather than socially constructed, and should be accepted and encouraged, not repressed. Thus, nearly every article and official statement regarding women throughout this period referred to them first as mothers, then as sisters and wives. Only rarely were they accorded an identity separate from and outside of the family.

Peasant mothers were particularly revered in party rhetoric. The ideal AFW activist and loyal female citizen was a peasant Partisan woman often barely literate, dressed in simple garb, and with rough hands. A prime example was Kata Pejnović, a peasant woman from the Lika region of Croatia who had only minimal education but who had joined the Communist party already in 1938. At the outset of the Second World War she lost her husband and three sons to Ustaša terror and joined the Partisan movement. She became a leading figure in the Croatian People's Front during and after the war and was a perfect symbol of the Partisan woman as bereaved mother, hardworking peasant, and loyal Communist, appearing at all official functions in her traditional black peasant's scarf.[22]

Certainly, the party and AFW made no attempt to eliminate the division between "men's" and "women's" work, and if anything, confirmed those divisions. As elaborated by Tito at the First Congress of the AFW in June 1945, the primary tasks of women included not only such standard PFY fare as providing support for and supervising the work of the state, affirming the "brotherhood and unity" of the nations of Yugoslavia, and aiding in rebuilding the country, but also and especially educating children and youth in a spirit of love for the homeland, the heritage of the People's Liberation Struggle and the government, and caring for orphans, refugees, invalids, and the ill and wounded.[23]

Meanwhile, the party made little attempt substantially to raise women's ideological and political consciousness, considering them unprepared for such activity and fearing to provoke their more useful and powerful menfolk. As a result, in these first years after the war, women remained woefully underrepresented in all state and party organizations, especially at the higher levels.[24] Nor did the party and AFW make any serious effort to reeducate men. Not a single article or speech ever suggested that perhaps men should take up some of the burden of housework. On the contrary, in one case, the women's press in Croatia was criticized for suggesting that men "should seek less comfort, that [women] shouldn't clean their shoes, bring them coffee in bed, and so on."[25] Clearly, whatever the party's ideological claim to realize the equality of women, it was unprepared or unwilling to risk alienating half (the powerful half!) of the population and stimulating unwanted social conflict. In this case, the party's need for social stability overruled its desire for social transformation.

Partisanstvo in Postwar Rhetoric

While CPY rhetoric often worked to stabilize postwar Yugoslav society and projected an atmosphere of tolerance and conciliation, it also reflected the prevailing unsettled and revolutionary atmosphere. Accordingly, CPY persuasive policies that emphasized lines of concord between the existing culture and party values coexisted with rhetoric condemning the old culture and its values as "bourgeois," "decadent," and antithetical to the new regime. Similarly, the moderation and tolerance typical of many early postwar policies were often overshadowed by the extremist and often violent behavior of many party activists. Without doubt, a strong current of revolutionary radicalism, voluntarism, and "partisanstvo"—a kind of spontaneous, on-the-spot activism associated with the Partisan struggle—ran through much of the party's immediate postwar activity. After all, not only were most members and leaders of the new regime extremely young, but they had also just succeeded in defeating both foreign and domestic opponents largely by their own efforts. Numerous participants in the Partisan movement have described their feelings of optimism and self-confidence at the end of the war.[26]

Such feelings of optimism and an inclination toward radicalism inevitably colored CPY rhetoric, endowing it with a spirit of genuine enthusiasm and energy, but also a measure of primitivism and violence. Certainly, the events of the war and revolution stimulated in many a true sense of hope for the future and a readiness to sacrifice for its construction. In those early postwar years, the CPY could and did rely on the willingness of much of the population to engage in community service and provide voluntary labor to renovate and reconstruct the Yugoslav economy. Party leaders especially called on youth to participate in these volunteer labor brigades, hoping in that way to maintain and channel the enormous energies and enthusiasm they had displayed during the war. As youth leader Rato Dugonjić explained it, just as youth had been motivated during the war by the slogan of the struggle against fascism and for liberation, they were now to be stimulated by "the construction of the country, its defense, and the affirmation and broadening of the democratic heritage."[27]

Indeed, in direct contradiction to their program of stabilization and pacification, party leaders simultaneously sought to preserve the wartime sense of urgency in order to justify their demands for continued self-sacrifice. Party leaders regularly complained about enemy slogans that said that since the war was over, there was no longer any need to work so hard.[28] Thus, far from putting the war behind them, CPY leaders kept it constantly in the foreground as a source of great inspiration, and they frequently couched peacetime tasks in military terminology. The battle, Dugonjić argued, had simply been transferred from the military to the political, economic, and ideological fields and youth must continue to work in a spirit of persistence, initiative, courage, decisiveness, endurance, ingenuity, collective work, and organization. One female participant in a major youth action even remarked in her diary that work there reminded her fondly of the best days among the Partisans. "Here it is really just like in battle. The explosions, the shrieking, the screaming remind one of battle and the fighting assault."[29]

Although CPY revolutionary rhetoric could be considered constructive in some such cases, it also served further to aggravate the already anarchic and potentially violent social tensions within the country. The main opposition newspaper, *Demokratija*, frequently complained that the party's heavy-handed political campaigns only exacerbated social conflict. Likewise, the non-Communist but pro-PFY *Republika* worried about the excessive use of unreliable and vengeful informers in political trials.[30] Clearly, not all enemies would be forgiven and coercion played a significant role in postwar party policies. CPY rhetoric thus mercilessly attacked all those who opposed its program as "fascists," "collaborators," and other "anti-people types." Articles in *Borba* regularly reported the arrest, conviction, and condemnation of various political and economic "criminals." The new regime called on its supporters to help root out such "enemies of the people," with one prominent leader, Sreten Žujović, even encouraging people to take matters into their own hands. "Do not wait for any kind of decision or law, but grasp the speculator by the throat and throw him in prison."[31]

In this immediate postwar period, then, the party did not hide the coercive element of its program, but displayed it proudly as a necessary component of the social transformation. Nonetheless, the Communist regime was certainly responsible for a great many more arrests and executions than it admitted to in *Borba*. Particularly as the war was ending, Partisan units simply shot without delay the members of many opposition groups, including some who clearly had collaborated with the fascist occupiers, but also many whose wartime activities were less clear but who represented an organized and often armed alternative to the Communists. The most famous such case concerns the Partisan murder of several thousand members of the Croat Home Guard in the Austrian town of Bleiburg just before the end of the war in the spring of 1945.[32]

Moreover, while some party rhetoric established connections between the existing culture and the party, it more often dichotomized nearly all people, institutions, and values in the country into "new" and "old," often reducing them to "good" and "bad." In public speeches and articles, party leaders proudly displayed everything good in the country as proof of the rightness of the new program, while they condemned everything bad as a remnant of the old order. Stressing that there could be no return to the old, journalists and speakers consistently devoted much attention to "unmasking" the evils of prewar Yugoslavia, which they described as economically, socially, and nationally oppressive; corrupt; incompetent; and pusillanimous in its international relations. This aggressive style of persuasion (if it can be called that) was perhaps most visible among the activities of youth, particularly in the schools.

In their struggle to create a new society and especially new and more socialist people, CPY leaders relied heavily on youth.[33] As noted previously, party leaders valued young people in the short run for their natural rebelliousness and high level of energy and in the long run as those who would ultimately create the Communist society envisioned and described by Marx. Moreover, the CPY was fully aware and extremely appreciative of youth's contribution to its victory, and the new government quickly enacted legislation designed to benefit them, including stricter labor laws and universal suffrage for all citizens 18 and over. Even children under 18 were permitted to vote if they had participated in the Partisan struggle. The new regime also declared its determination to defend and help realize all rights won by youth during the war and to secure full possibilities for their educational and spiritual development. The interests of young people were further addressed through youth-oriented newspapers and journals and in various cultural, educational, sports, and leisure-time associations.[34] Indeed, an examination of party activity and rhetoric in the first years after the war might lead one to believe that youth, and not the working class, was the favored social group of the CPY.[35]

In return for these favors, CPY leaders clearly expected youth to remain the party's most ardent supporters and contribute to the fulfillment of its program. Indeed, young people were extremely active in promoting party policies. SKOJ members, in particular, were nearly always the first to "unmask" the "counterrevolutionary" and "collaborationist" activities of clergy members, small-business owners, schoolteachers, and other potential "enemies of the people." In addition, SKOJ members actively campaigned for party-approved candidates in federal, republic, and local elections, often going door to door to "convince" all "patriotic citizens" to vote for the "right" candidates. SKOJ members were also prominently involved in furthering the government's economic policies: they helped mobilize youth for volunteer labor actions (by force if necessary) and assisted in carrying out the grain requisitioning program and in organizing factory competitions and shockwork. PYY members likewise participated in renovation and reconstruction of the country; played a significant role in the struggle to eradicate illiteracy; created and managed various educational, artistic, and gymnastic and sports organizations; and tirelessly promoted party policies in the schools, covering their walls with banners and slogans and holding countless meetings, often during school hours.

Education in new Yugoslavia was, in fact, heavily politicized at all levels. The material used in many literacy courses consisted primarily of political slogans or stories and poems from the war, while public lectures in people's universities, houses of culture, and cooperative centers addressed such current political topics as the new law on agrarian reform, some youth leader's recent visit to the Soviet Union, or the Slavic heritage of the disputed region of Istria. Political activity also permeated the school system. The party rapidly injected its political message into the class curriculum, often replacing old texts with Soviet translations and adding a new course on the history of the People's Liberation Struggle so that children would learn of the crimes committed by "enemies of the people" and of the courage and self-sacrificing efforts of the Partisans to secure freedom for the people.[36]

Beyond such positive measures, CPY leaders also relied heavily on more negative and coercive means of shaping the new educational system. One of the first tasks established by the party in the immediate postwar period was to purge from public life all those who could be accused of collaborating with the occupier or holding fascist or pro-fascist sentiments. Party leaders considered this cleansing mission especially important in schools, since they were expected to imbue students with new socialist values. Therefore, all teachers had to pledge loyalty to the heritage of the People's Liberation Struggle and the new government, and the party ruthlessly purged any suspect or hostile teachers and students.

The youth organizations, SKOJ and PYY, played a predominant role in these purges, encouraging students of all ages to take the initiative in "unmasking and eliminating the enemies within." Leaders of the SKOJ organization in Croatia instructed their members to "carry to its end the democratization of the schools and throw out of school those professors who want to provoke us." And an early article proudly reported the expulsion from a school in Tuzla of nine students accused by their colleagues of belonging to Ustaša and Četnik societies.[37] Within the universities, the student youth organization formed a special commission to gather information and facilitate the purges. As a result of its work, in the 1945/46 academic year, 36 teachers at Belgrade University were dismissed, and the former rector was sentenced to six years' imprisonment and forced labor. Department conferences in early 1946 recommended that 119 students be expelled from the university.[38]

A number of articles on education in this period also urged that the educational system be transformed by creating a new relationship between students and teachers based on mutual respect, cooperation, comradeliness, and conscious discipline imposed by the students themselves and not by teachers or administrators using threats or physical punishment. Rules and regulations, while necessary, were now to be phrased in new ways so as to emphasize the students' own responsibility. Rather than stating that such-and-such is "forbidden" or that the student "must not" do something, rules were to advise that "the student is obliged," or "has a responsibility," to behave in a certain way. According to one article about developments in a provincial Croatian high school, teachers were no longer being seen as sheriffs and judges but as older, more experienced, and educated helpers who respected each student's individuality.[39]

In practice, however, the behavior of many youth activists failed to reflect the anticipated "conscious discipline" and was characterized instead by insubordination, arrogance, and even physical violence. Hence, the party's relations with youth, despite its great hopes, were often turbulent. Countless articles criticized the generally anarchic atmosphere in which students came to class late, left early, and held meetings during school hours. As a SKOJ report from the Croatian town of Varaždin admitted, the relationship between teachers and students had indeed changed in the sense that "individual students understood that they were now something higher."[40]

Those youths who had fought in the war were particularly difficult to control, especially since they often insisted on wearing their pistols to school. Empowered by participation in the Partisan struggle, they clearly reveled in their new superior status and saw no need for moderation or discretion in their treatment of old enemies or rivals. Taking matters into their own hands, such youth activists not only threatened but physically attacked other youths and professors. In one case, a professor was beaten for giving out bad grades, and at a student assembly, youth activists not only condemned some fellow students, "but they beat them and busted some heads."[41]

The CPY leadership soon came to oppose youth, and especially SKOJ's, radicalism in the schools as anarchic and counterproductive. After all, the party's initial priority was to win broad popular support. Open enemies of the regime were not to be tolerated but, as one Croatian SKOJ leader put it, "cadres must know how to maneuver. The basic slogan with which we shall act and through which we will look at every provocation is *separation* or *unification* of youth forces." As youth leader Stana Tomašević explained at the First Congress of the PYY in March 1945, young activists must prevent "the enemy" from creating two fronts and destroying the unity of young people, and hence should "lead the sharpest struggle against every attempt to introduce politicization and political struggles into the schools, against national chauvinism in the schools, and against struggles which would be established on religious or any other bases."[42]

Yet this was one directive that many other youth leaders preferred to ignore. Not only did SKOJ activists clearly encourage students to root out political enemies, some appeared openly resistant to official policy. In two separate documents from late 1945, SKOJ leaders criticized the organization of high school youth as insufficiently sharp in its relations with the enemy, because its leadership was opportunistically "following a 'tactical' line toward them in 'the interests of preserving unity'." Serbian Minister of Education Mitra Mitrović also later admitted to some disagreement over this issue between the outside (party and state) leadership and the Belgrade University Party Committee, which was dominated by SKOJ members.[43]

Nor was education the only arena of conflict between SKOJ and the party. Party leaders expected SKOJ members to be the most enthusiastic participants on youth brigades; yet such was not always the case. One local report said that of some 22,000 SKOJ members in the region, only 850 had applied for admission to the brigades; another complained that when reluctant party and SKOJ members had been assigned to the brigades, some had even refused; and a third reported that youth on the railway sang:

> USAOJci prugu izgradjuju
> a SKOJevci prugom se vozaju[44]
> *USAOJ [former title of the PYY] members build the railroad*
> *But SKOJ members ride on it*

Conflicts like these made plain the dangers inherent in youth activism. Hence, CPY leaders, while continuing to demand youth's participation in the transformation of society, also increasingly sought to limit and control it.

One should note that the often inappropriate behavior exhibited by Yugoslav youth was not unique for this period. A conference of the allied ministers of education held before the end of the war established a Commission for the Human Rehabilitation of Children and Young People in order to address the psychological damage to youth caused by the war. Among the issues it mentioned was the problem of children and youth "for whom normal values and codes have been reversed, for whom lying, deceit, stealing, destruction, spying and informing, and even killing have become the highest virtues," and who "have become addicts to the excitement and fascination of lawlessness."[45] Nonetheless, CPY rhetoric that emphasized revolutionary change and condemned traditional values as anachronistic and perhaps even traitorous only encouraged such behavior. It is unsurprising, then, that while CPY leaders condemned youth extremism as counterproductive to party goals, disorder and violence were common in many schools until at least mid-1946.

Pragmatism and Partisanstvo

While in some cases, party rhetoric clearly represented either the need to increase stability through compromises and moderation or a revolutionary desire to change society overnight, just as often it did both simultaneously. Thus, for example, in the fields of culture and religion, we find conciliatory and persuasive rhetoric competing with voices that were predominantly radical and coercive in tone. As such cases are difficult to evaluate from a historical perspective, how much more baffling and disturbing must they have been to those living at the time. It is no wonder that state-society relations in this period were so unpredictable and uneasy.

Culture

CPY leaders placed enormous emphasis on the role of both high and popular culture in the transition to socialism. Perhaps for that very reason, its policies and rhetoric toward culture and cultural personnel were simultaneously exacting and conciliatory. Communists in Yugoslavia, as elsewhere, had a utilitarian rather than an aesthetic view of culture. From the perspective of the Communist party, culture's primary function lay in its political-educational potential and not in its value as an expression of beauty or a source of entertainment.[46] All forms of culture—including literature, film, theater, painting, sculpture, music, and dance—represented tools by which the party would realize its political, social, and cultural agenda. Not only could these tools assist in the completion of concrete political and practical tasks, they would work to effect lasting changes in the values, attitudes, aesthetic tastes, moral principles, and behavioral norms of the Yugoslav population. Thus CPY leaders expected writers, artists, and musicians to instill new and "correct" values in people and to develop their social consciousness, becoming, in Stalin's words, "engineers of the human soul."

Partly leaders expected cultural personnel to fulfill this improbable mission by adhering to the theories of the Bulgarian ideologist Todor Pavlov (who had defined culture as the "subjective reflection of objective reality") and the Soviet cultural tsar, Andrei Zhdanov (the founder of "socialist realism"). Without showing every element of reality in photographic detail, socialist realist culture was meant to extract, synthesize, and express from a particular point of view all that was *typical* of that reality. Modernist artistic trends like impressionism, futurism, and cubism, since they presented deliberate deformations of objective reality, and abstract art, since it reflected *no* objective reality, were automatically excluded from the Communist definition of culture.

In order to fit the Communist definition of "realism," culture also had to provide the correct ideological bias; that is, it was not to portray reality with false "objectivity" but only in a Marxist historical and ideological framework. After all, as the Communists had always maintained, culture was a weapon either of progress or of reaction; it affected people either positively or negatively and had to be evaluated accordingly. In internal reports and public articles, party activists described art's magical yet potentially dangerous influence and revealed with horror the harmful effects of ostensibly apolitical art. Western popular music, they said, would divert people from the political and ideological struggle. Based on imitations of primitive music, "it lulls one's conscience to sleep, inflaming wild instincts by means of such 'modern' dances as the 'sphinx,' 'boogie-woogie,' 'rumba,' and so on." Likewise, pure entertainment films were said to serve foreign propaganda by "awakening an interest in superficial pleasures, drawing out lower instincts, and popularizing the kind of 'art' that is harbored in nighttime bars to distract the thoughts of millions of film viewers from reality, from the present, from serious problems, from the fate of the country and the people."[47]

The party, therefore, had to ensure that culture used its influence in a strictly positive manner and served party ends by spreading socialist values and perspectives among the masses. It should not only reflect the new reality but help create it by providing models of socialist heroism, inspiring the masses to acts of self-sacrifice, encouraging the development of community values, and arousing a sense of hope and optimism for the glorious socialist future to come.

But since, according to Communist ideology, the interests of the party and the people were identical, party propagandists confidently declared that the main function of culture was to serve the people. Party leaders had no tolerance for the theory of "art for art's sake," nor would they allow an artist to create merely for his or her own enjoyment. Rather, they demanded that cultural personnel speak in a language accessible to the people, formulate problems close to them, and reflect their aspirations. For if the official culture did not reach the masses, it could not possibly transform them.

This insistence that all culture be made accessible and appealing to the broad public represented an effort to abolish the distinction between popular and high culture.[48] The elite in most societies presume that high culture need not necessarily appeal to the broader population, many of whom lack the education, training, or sophistication to appreciate its finer points. In such societies, high culture may openly claim to represent mainly, if not exclusively, the interests, needs, and tastes of the individual artist, writer, or musician. In Communist societies, such an approach was considered both elitist and reactionary. Art that did not serve the people and was not loved by them, the party insisted, was not art at all.

In theory, at least, CPY leaders did not wish to achieve this identity between high and mass culture by lowering high culture's aesthetic quality. Rather, they hoped eventually to raise popular tastes to the level of high culture. Consequently, a further task of cultural personnel (and especially of literary, art, and film critics) was to develop high aesthetic tastes among the people.[49] Simultaneously, however, party leaders regularly and explicitly demanded that high culture—while retaining its artistic quality—be made accessible to the masses at their current level of education. In essence then, the CPY made three concurrent demands of culture—that it be ideologically correct, of high aesthetic quality, and popular.

The party sought to achieve these ends and exercise its control over the production and distribution of culture through its network of party and state organizations. Intellectuals were unquestionably among those from whom party leaders most desired and expected support in this endeavor. Not only had intellectuals played a considerable role in the war (of the 212 martyred People's Heroes proclaimed up to 1951, 109 were from the ranks of the intelligentsia), but party leaders understood that they would be indispensable in both immediate and long-term efforts to transform society and humanity.[50] Therefore, most leading party figures (who were, after all, usually intellectuals themselves) welcomed the cooperation of intellectuals and actively sought their support.

This tactical approach was particularly evident in CPY relations with the cultural intelligentsia. During the war, the party had welcomed into its movement artists from all backgrounds, regardless of political or aesthetic orientation, as long as they were willing to fight the occupying forces and their domestic quislings. Indeed a great many artists joined the Partisan struggle, placing their skills at its disposal. The modernist painter Vojo Dimitrijević for example, joined the Partisans and was put to work creating sketches and posters. Likewise in 1942, six members of the State Theater in Zagreb fled to the Partisans where they formed the Theater of People's Liberation and performed skits, excerpts, and one-act plays for the soldiers.[51] One of the most publicized artists to join the Partisans was the 70-year-old Croat poet Vladimir Nazor, who had to flee Zagreb in the dead of night in order to do so.[52] Overall, the party was extremely proud of its wartime cultural activities and often claimed that among the Partisans, the old adage "When the guns roar, the muses are silent" did not apply.

The party's early postwar expectations for artistic creation continued these efforts to appear moderate and willing to compromise. For example, although party cultural personnel clearly adopted the main principles of Soviet socialist realism, they once again rephrased them in less ideologically aggressive terms. Party rhetoric called art's appropriate form "new realism" (not "socialist realism"), suggesting that it be combined with elements of "fighting" (not "revolutionary") romanticism. It asked that new art in Yugoslavia serve "the people" (not "the party" or "the working class"), "democracy" (not "socialism"), and "progress" (which was rather vaguely defined). And while insisting that art was inevitably tendentious, party leaders most often singled out the Germans as the enemy and not the bourgeoisie. Finally, in one 1944 speech, Croat Communist author Marijan Stilinović reworked the Soviet maxim that art should be "national in form and socialist in content" to read "national in form and generally humanist [općečovječanska] and democratic in content."[53]

CPY rhetoric also tried to emphasize a line of continuity between pre- and postwar Yugoslav culture, as long as that prewar culture could be considered relatively progressive and as long as its creator was not among the party's political opponents. Thus, in that same 1944 speech, Stilinović explained that the new culture would build not only on the experiences of the People's Liberation Struggle, but also on the cultural foundations of Croatia's history from its Glagolitic period, through the Dalmatian renaissance, to the Radić brothers, and Vladimir Nazor.[54] And while "new realism" was expected to show a particular ideological bias, the content of that bias in the early years was often rather vague. A call for an early competition among screenplays, for example, said only that the entrants should reflect the "spiritual renaissance" of the people and satirically show the mistakes and machinations of the enemy. Even Zogović, in an article from December 1944, stated only that artists must love their homeland, be conscious of the meaning of freedom, serve the truth, listen to their hearts, and be fighters for democracy and progress.[55] Who could argue with that?

Other signs of pluralism in the field of culture may be found in the non-Communist press of the early postwar era. The Republican party's newspaper, for example, offered a rather different approach to art than did the Communist press, arguing that art fulfilled a universal need for beauty and referring to its source as an "internal urge." Likewise, cultural performances sponsored by the Croat Republican Peasant Party were often far from Communist and concentrated mainly on village life, love, and even religion.[56] In the field of the fine arts, several differing trends briefly coexisted, and a great proportion of the films shown in 1945 and even 1946 were Western and American, including such classics as *Of Mice and Men, The Three Musketeers,* and *The Hunchback of Notre Dame,* but also many of more dubious quality like *Andy Hardy, The Cisco Kid, Tarzan, That Girl from Paris, In the Wild West,* and *Hawaii Calls*.[57] While comprising only a minute percentage of all cultural presentations, the existence of such non-Communist perspectives did indicate a degree of cultural tolerance at least in the first year after the war.

Meanwhile, CPY leaders actively sought the voluntary cooperation of many cultural figures. To do so, the government provided artists with considerable financial incentives. It sponsored cultural-artistic unions throughout the country and offered approved union artists high-level ration cards, apartments, health care, vacations, studios, and artistic supplies. Not all these benefits were available immediately, but considering the extremely difficult material conditions of the time, writers, artists, musicians, and other cultural-artistic personnel were treated with great care and many were probably better off after the war than they had been before it. As one speaker at the Congress of the Writers' Association of Croatia stated, "Today the writer has the right, and what is just as important, the conditions to devote his life to literature."[58]

In addition, the state and party offered cultural-artistic personnel a great deal of moral support. Far from anti-intellectual, most members of the top leadership had great respect for culture and valued its role in their program for change. Consequently, cultural figures, especially artists and writers, netted considerable attention in the daily press, which printed theoretical and critical articles, reported all manner of cultural events, and even published original works of art. The May 1 issue of *Borba* in 1945, for example, included poems by Vladimir Mayakovsky, Dušan Kostić, Radovan Zogović, Marko Ristić, and Eli Finci, a short piece by Branko Ćopić, an excerpt from a book by Ivo Andrić, a number of sketches by various artists, and a photograph of a sculpture by Antun Augustinčić. The recognition granted to cultural figures as highly significant and influential members of society had to be gratifying and was a form of intellectual flattery that few are able to resist.

Party leaders particularly desired to win over certain prominent and highly influential cultural figures who might be willing to cooperate with the new regime, regardless of past differences. For example, the famous Croat Communist writer, Miroslav Krleža, had feared party leaders might settle accounts with him after the war by means of a shotgun due to his prewar disagreements with Djilas and Zogović. In fact, however, they were eager for his support and invited him to Belgrade immediately after the war to meet with Tito.[59] Likewise the party welcomed the support of author Ivo Andrić despite his official presence at the signing of the Tripartite Pact with Germany. Indeed, according to Djilas, at Andrić's own request, party leaders removed the photograph revealing his presence at the signing of the pact from a postwar exhibit.[60]

Moreover, Andrić was given full opportunity to create without government or party interference, as long as he did not challenge CPY authority, and Krleža was even invited to edit the Croat literary journal, *Republika*. In fact, Krleža's opening article in *Republika*, while consistent with party policy in many ways, certainly did not provide a typical rendition of the postwar tasks of literature. The entire essay was imbued with an oppressive sense of gloom, and his description of how most men reacted to the repression of interwar and wartime Yugoslavia stood in sharp contrast to the more typical eulogies about the heroism of the masses. He spoke of the people as "dark and cold empty wells" and "warped unfortunates" who had been crippled, degraded, and poisoned by social relations based on private ownership of the means of production. Literature, he said, would "know how to paint this enormous composition of general moral-political poverty, when our average citizen lost himself completely in passive lethargy and in a depressed inability to cope in space and time." While understandably less than enthusiastic about this article, the party leadership let it pass both because Krleža—who had been instructed to prepare something literary, not programmatic—had effectively presented them with a fait accompli, and because the Croatian agitprop department felt that Krleža had "the conditions to master our line."[61] The flexibility that party leaders demonstrated in their relations with Krleža was not an anomaly. Recognizing that they were not yet in a position to transform culture, party leaders sought to incorporate and claim as their own any aspects of the existing culture that they considered compatible with their future goals and capable of increasing their basis of support.

Yet despite such policies and rhetoric designed to elicit cooperation from Yugoslavia's cultural figures, the field of culture also represented something of a battleground in the first year after the war. Early postwar culture in Yugoslavia reflected mainly the values, interests, and experiences of the regime's new recruits and displayed their obsession with wartime themes. Already in December 1944 the new government had published a collection of 67 songs and poems from the war with chapters on Tito, the Partisans, the CPY, mothers, youth, Stalin, and the Soviet Union. Most early artistic sketches, paintings, and sculptures depicted wartime events, while musicians composed and orchestrated Partisan songs and marches. Meanwhile, the poetic efforts of many new recruits were packed with terms like "bomb," "Partisan," "freedom," and "hateful occupier."[62]

Partisanstvo in art meant placing greater emphasis on correct political-ideological content and mass participation than on aesthetic form or artistic skill. After all, one of the party's main goals was to make culture really and truly the property of the people. CPY rhetoric, therefore, worked ceaselessly to involve the entire Yugoslav citizenry in the work of artistic creation. Already during the war, Partisan units had formed their own artistic clubs. Now, after the war, villages, neighborhoods, factories, and mass organizations all formed amateur cultural-artistic societies, including choirs, theatrical groups, literary and film clubs, and so on. While the necessarily simple, spontaneous, and highly improvisational cultural works and presentations of the wartime and postwar amateur groups inevitably lacked technical sophistication, they nonetheless drew much official praise for their honesty and sincerity. Zogović, for example, once claimed that the performances of Partisan theater, though badly deficient in technical skill and quality, had often been better than those of postwar professional troupes. Partisan actors, he explained, had a more natural style and were better able to discern the essential from the nonessential in theatrical texts.[63]

A corollary to such praise of amateur artists was the often harsh criticism directed at many professional cultural personnel. Unsurprisingly, those cultural figures with clearly opposing political views drew the hottest fire. For example, immediately after the liberation of Belgrade, Nikola Popović, an actor and prewar theater director, was given a mandate to form a Commission for the Renovation of the Theater and investigate the wartime behavior of theatrical personnel. As a result, three actors were shot. A colleague of one of the executed men admitted that his coworker had indeed collaborated with the fascist regime but only out of cowardice and a love for gambling, not ideological affinity.[64] The new regime, however, was not interested in such nuances of guilt. Even a gifted Communist painter suffered a brief spell in prison after his letter expressing dissatisfaction with growing inequalities in the country was intercepted by a security officer.[65]

The party also drew a clear connection between an artist's political affiliation and aesthetic taste. While certain non-Communist cultural figures were allowed considerable leeway in their artistic creation, those artists, writers, and musicians (dead or alive) considered to be unalterable opponents of the new regime due to either their political convictions or aesthetic preferences were treated as absolute pariahs and "enemies of the people." One such pariah was Croat modernist poet Augustin Tin Ujević, who was viciously attacked by Zogović and others for both aesthetic and political crimes. Outraged to find Ujević's poetry included in a postwar literature textbook for high school students, Zogović sneered at his "strange mixture of jesuit serenity and decorative anarchism, verbalistic pathos and mystical resignation, Catholic mysticism and mysticized eroticism, virtuosity and tense, feeble verses." More damning yet was Ujević's service during the Second World War as the editor of a newspaper for Croat workers employed in Nazi Germany. With such behavior, Zogović continued, Ujević had shamed the literary profession and had properly been denied membership in the Union of Writers of Yugoslavia. He certainly must not be presented as a role model for either aspiring poets or Yugoslavia's youth. Indeed, a writer's aesthetic and political habits were generally seen as inextricably connected. Croat Communist writer Marin Franičević thus explained that Ujević's "explicitly reactionary approach to life and society, together with his ideological and practical . . . formalism led [him] naturally toward the Ustaša 'cultural' facade." Ultimately, Ujević was sentenced to five years in prison and in 1949 his complete works were banned from public use in schools and libraries.[66]

Finally, in some cases even merely apolitical professionals could be condemned for their lack of revolutionary idealism. As late as October 1946, Zogović attacked members of the Belgrade Ballet Troupe for their "empty, non-ideological, senseless, and purposeless dancing," which, he said, represented "classical formalism, the continuation of petty bourgeois performances." "Our ballet," he continued, "must, with new rhythms and new enthusiasm, speak, persevere, and develop in a noble struggle for man, for a new life and a new culture."[67]

Zogović's criticism of professional culture derived in part from a general Communist distrust of intellectuals that long persisted despite the party's official conciliatory approach toward them. That distrust had been especially prominent during the war when one party handbook plainly warned against the introduction into the party of "petty-bourgeois and bourgeois concepts" by intellectual members. Intellectuals, it conceded, could join the party, but must first prove that they had completely broken with the bourgeoisie and were willing to struggle for the proletarian cause. In any case, it concluded, the party must remain primarily a workers' organization and workers must master Marxism-Leninism in order better to supervise the unreliable intellectuals.[68]

Orthodox Communist suspicion of intellectuals was further enhanced by the social and cultural background of most new party members. Although admittedly, many high-level and prewar Communists were themselves intellectuals, those who had joined the party only during the war were not. One novelist has described the arrival in the major cities of these masses of poorly educated, peasant recruits to the party and new state as an invasion of barbaric "Huns and Visigoths" who had little appreciation for works of culture and science, and none at all for those who had created them.[69] Certainly the new Communists often believed that urban intellectuals suffered from hopeless passivism and corruption, while "the people" instinctively knew right from wrong and good from bad, and could thus take direct action against the enemy. Will and energy, they insisted, would more than compensate for any lack of educational or technical qualifications.[70] Even top party and government officials retained much of the populist anti-urban and anti-intellectual stance, in spite of the fact that or perhaps because they themselves were often urban intellectuals. Thus, they vigorously denied that state administration, politics, and economics needed to be carried out by "dignified" elegant people wearing gloves and top hats. Indeed, most Partisans, including those in the top leadership, continued to wear military uniforms and boots long after their active participation in the war had ended.[71]

Religion

A second area where the party's postwar policies and rhetoric included both elements of gradualism and radicalism concerned religion. The party's wartime popular front policy had already facilitated cooperation with Yugoslav religious communities, and individual members of many had joined the Partisans. After the war as well, *official* party policy discouraged frontal attacks on either religion or the clergy. Rather, while working to undermine the power and influence of the church through legal and economic measures and secular educational policies, party leaders generally tried to avoid open confrontation with the churches. Countless internal documents (from SKOJ organizations in particular) denounced the use of flagrantly anti-religious actions, saying that it was like "sticking our fingers in our own eyes" and would only provide priests with ammunition for their claim that they were a "dictatorship." Such measures, they insisted, would neither liberate youths from their religious ideas nor incline them toward Communist ones.[72] While the frequency of such declarations suggests that youth attacks on religious figures were widespread, it also confirms that party leaders discouraged such behavior in private as well as in public.

Moreover, party leaders also made conscious efforts to win the support of many religious figures. We have already seen that the postwar All-Slavic Movement contributed to that goal. The CPY also offered religious personnel certain financial incentives as well as the opportunity to continue their work as long as they cooperated fully with the new regime. Despite formal separation of church and state, the constitution also established that "the state may, at its discretion, give material assistance to religious communities." In practice, the state provided very little such financial support. Yet it could and did offer some material incentives to cooperative segments of the clergy.[73] One member of the extremely cooperative Association for Orthodox Priests, for example, seemed to call for a kind of quid pro quo relationship with the state: "Our government and leadership, for social motives and reasons, cares for all professions. . . . so it is necessary that our societies unite their forces in work for the general good, as do the other professions."[74]

The party's early attempts at conciliation with Yugoslavia's churches may also be seen in its attitude toward religious observances and festivities. During the war, the party had often deliberately paraded its religious tolerance by sanctioning official Partisan participation in holidays and celebrations. One Communist source described Partisan soldiers carrying yule logs for Christmas, while another recalled that as a Partisan he had once set an armed guard to stand watch before "Jesus' tomb" on Good Friday.[75]

Even after the war, while religious holidays like Christmas and Easter were not officially sanctioned, they often continued to receive notice in the press.[76] And in some cases, the party still sponsored the celebration of religious rituals and holidays, especially if they concerned rites for fallen soldiers, or when the celebration could be easily reconciled with the values of the party and the People's Front. The party approved, for example, the celebration in Serbian schools of St. Sava Day in 1945, citing the progressive role of the saint, who "is glorified as the defender of schools and the first fighter for cultural improvements," and "is for the Serbian people a symbol of education, knowledge, and freedom." Likewise, the Serbian ministry of education decreed that Cyril and Methodius Day be celebrated in schools on 24 May 1945, arguing that acceptance of Christianity had meant progress in relation to the previous paganism and had influenced not only the Serbs but also the Macedonians, Bulgarians, and Russians. "Thus the new belief connected the fraternal Slavic peoples on an ideological and cultural field."[77]

Perhaps the most extreme example of Communist participation in religious rituals occurred during a requiem liturgy held by the Serbian Orthodox Church in November 1944 for all Russian and domestic heroes who had fallen in the liberation of Belgrade. Among those representatives of the government listed by the Orthodox Synod's paper, *Glasnik,* as having taken part in the liturgy were longtime Communists Moša Pijade, Arso Jovanović, Peko Dapčević, and Ljubodrag N. Djurić. "At the end of the liturgy," *Glasnik* reported, "the president of AVNOJ [Ivan Ribar] approached the High Reverend, kissed the cross, and accepted the wafer, *and then the other representatives of government also kissed the cross and accepted wafers.*"[78]

Finally, party rhetoric often tried to exploit the powerful symbols attached to religious holidays for its own purposes. For Orthodox Christmas in 1945, *Politika* carried on its front page a drawing of the people of Yugoslavia following the victorious red star to a better future; the following year *20. oktobar* carried a drawing of six "wise men" in the national costumes of the six republics following a five-pointed star, with the caption, "We are six, but one star guides us all"; and for Easter 1946, *Politika* published a cartoon that showed a variety of Ustaše, Četniks, bandits, and priests looking into an empty grave over a caption that read, "Fascists over an empty grave from which freedom was recently resurrected vainly hatch new plots to bury it again."[79] Here again, party leaders clearly proved themselves willing and able to use existing cultural values for their own purposes.

At the same time, however, early party rhetoric toward religion also displayed a strong strain of revolutionary radicalism and partisanstvo. Officially, as noted above, the party opposed aggressive actions against religion, preferring that it die a natural death within the new socialist order. Nonetheless, the party worked tirelessly to discredit religious teachings and discourage people from attending religious ceremonies. While ordinary citizens were generally not punished for attending religious ceremonies, the new educational curriculum openly dismissed religious beliefs as the result of ignorance and superstition, promoting instead various atheistic and scientific theories. Moreover, party leaders passed by no opportunity to show the hypocrisy and villainy of those priests who might possibly be suspected of having collaborated with the occupier. All organs of the media devoted considerable attention to "unmasking the reactionary clergy," and Molière's acerbic satire *Tartuffe,* which showed the hypocrisy of many so-called holy men, was a standard in theatrical repertoires. As late as 1948 an internal report of the AFW in Croatia cited for her exemplary agitprop work a teacher in a village near Valpovo who heard children preparing for Communion. Rather than lecture the children on the virtues of atheism, she showed them two pictures in the recently published book, *Crimes of One Part of the Clergy.* One picture showed a kindly priest telling stories to children, while the other, right next to it, portrayed the Ustaše slaughtering children. In this way, the report declared, the teacher had "proved" the reactionary activities of the

Christmas 1945: The peoples of Yugoslavia through suffering the blackest slavery and the desolation of a destroyed country, united in struggle, follow the victorious red star toward a better and more beautiful future. Politika, 6–8 January 1945.

Christmas 1946: We are six, but one star guides us all. . . . 20. Oktobar, 4 January 1946.

УСКРС 1946

Easter 1946: Fascist executioners, over the empty grave from which freedom has recently been resurrected, vainly hatch plots to bury it again. Politika, 20–23 April 1946.

clergy and dissuaded the children from participating in Communion. Another example of "correct agitation" took place in the Croatian district of Sinj. A priest who had ridden his bike into town to propagate the faith was greeted by small boys who shouted "Pao Pop!"—"The Priest Fell!" The priest turned to look at them, slipped, fell in the mud, and left town in shame, never to return again.[80]

More importantly, especially in the first year after the war, religious figures often garnered much harsher physical abuse than the official line would suggest. Certainly party leaders did not hesitate to harass, arrest, imprison, and even execute those priests and religious officials who were unalterably opposed to the CPY, especially if any evidence of their misconduct during the war could be scraped up or manufactured.[81] Beyond such official actions, party leaders also tolerated a considerable degree of unofficial coercion against religious figures. Local party leaders frequently harassed, arrested, and executed even those religious figures who were aged, passive, or apolitical and who could not have represented any significant threat to the new government.[82] Moreover, in its concern to protect youth from religious influences, the party channeled much anti-religious propaganda through the overzealous SKOJ organizations. Many local SKOJ reports noted "unfortunate" occurrences of sectarianism and crude behavior, including throwing stones and breaking church glass.[83] Although CPY leaders opposed such actions, considering them self-defeating, they also considered much of this activity to be an integral part of its mopping-up operations, cleansing the country of "fascists," "collaborators," and other incorrigible opponents. Rhetorical strategies that treated the church and its officials as "enemies of the people" made such incidents likely, if not inevitable, and, in any case, party leaders often did very little to prevent them. As Rada Radić put it, "Any conduct that departed from legal regulations was interpreted as the result of inexperience, ineptitude, sectarianism and so on, but no representative of the local bureaucracy bore any responsibility for his conduct. The matter usually ended with a verbal reprimand."[84]

Conclusion

The CPY's combination of apparently conflicting rhetorical strategies, some of which worked for social unity through the use of existing cultural traditions, while others deliberately intensified social tensions in an effort to bring about revolutionary change, quickly entangles any neat characterization of the first year of Communist rule in Yugoslavia. For while the written record describes a policy of moderation, conciliation, and broadly targeted persuasion, contemporaries of the time best recall the intense atmosphere of hope and enthusiasm (if supporters of the new regime) or terror and coercion (if opponents). Ultimately, these contradictions only reflect the awkward transition of the Communist party from a revolutionary force in opposition into a ruling body in need of stability and broad popular acquiescence, if not active support.

State-society relations also reflect the ambiguity of this era. Without doubt, relations between the party-state and Yugoslavia's citizens were most dynamic in this first postwar year. On the one hand, that dynamism was characterized by the public's often enthusiastic participation in the party's agenda. Many citizens willingly joined volunteer labor brigades, participated in mass meetings about politics and culture, or joined violent mobs seeking revenge for past harm done.

On the other hand, however, the dynamism could be and often was expressed as opposition to party goals. Open and outspoken opponents of the regime did not last long before they were arrested or forced to flee the country, but they often made their opinions known at least locally first. The public statements of many Catholic church officials are particularly notable. For example, as the opening volley in his confrontation with the party-state, Archbishop Stepinac distributed in September 1945 a pastoral letter accompanied by a circular of similar content to be read by all priests before their congregations. It began by citing figures concerning the mistreatment of the clergy since the end of the war; continued with strongly worded objections to the laws on agrarian reform, nationalization, civil marriage, restrictions on religious education, the teaching of atheism, and the general moral atmosphere around youth; and concluded that lasting and peaceful cooperation could be realized only if the Catholic church were permitted full freedom for its religious schools, including obligatory religious studies courses in all grades, full respect for Christian marriages, and a return to the church of all factories and enterprises that had been confiscated.[85]

Similarly, Milan Grol, a prewar politician who was briefly included within the first postwar government, openly opposed many CPY policies. In his short-lived newspaper, *Demokratija* (which survived less than two months), Grol denounced the CPY's intolerance and totalitarian tendencies. Even the semi-official newspaper *Politika* published an article in which Grol criticized the proposed law about crimes against the state since it would only stir up people when the government ought to be pacifying them instead. During that fall, Grol became the target of increasingly vicious official and semi-official verbal abuse. Nonetheless, he continued his opposition activities until after the November 1945 elections.[86]

Moreover, in this brief period of pluralism before all means of expressing uncensored opinion had been eliminated, many citizens who had agreed to cooperate with the new regime but who nonetheless held rather differing values and goals for the future articulated their ideas and engaged in debates with CPY activists over party policies. Proof that such a dialogue, even if severely limited in scope, was still possible may be found among articles in those newspapers published by non-Communist political parties within the PFY. The organ of the Yugoslav Republican Democratic Party was especially outspoken. In it, one Republican leader, Vladimir Simić, criticized certain aspects of the proposed constitution, while another, Aleksandar Tomić, argued in favor of the continued existence of political parties, pointing out that "a party is only one part of a great whole . . . and never under any circumstances can it equate itself with the people and the state."[87]

As the party's grip on power tightened, however, its tolerance for such pluralism diminished. As a result, its rhetoric became increasingly directive and the Yugoslav population's willingness to participate in public life correspondingly declined. In the next phase of social transformation, from late 1945 to late 1947, CPY leaders ended all debate and focused their persuasive efforts directly on what they now saw as the most pressing tasks of economic renovation and construction.

Notes

1. Josip Broz Tito, "Razgovor s inostranim novinarima," *Borba*, 13 Aug. 1945, in Josip Broz Tito, *Govori i članci*, Vol. 2 (Zagreb: 1959), 21–24.
2. The Home Guards were the regular national armies of Croatia and Slovenia. While not specifically fascist organizations, they were subject to the command of the occupying armies during the war. In the spring of 1945 as the war drew to a close, many Croatian Home Guard units fled from the approaching Red Army and Partisan troops and crossed the Austrian border where they surrendered to British troops. In accordance with wartime agreements, however, the British turned these units over to the Partisans who massacred them by the tens of thousands in the subsequent weeks.
3. *Politika*, 2 Jan. 1946.
4. Indeed, in 1948 when Zdenka Šegvić prepared a retrospective report on the party press, she claimed that the best theoretical articles explaining the character of new Yugoslavia had come out in 1944 and 1945. Zdenka Ševgić, "Problemi naše štampe od oslobodjenja do danas i njezine slabosti," May 1948, ACKSKJ, VIII II/5-b-25.
5. Ibid.; Josip Cazi, "Učešće jedinstvenih sindikata u izbornoj borbi," *Rad*, 22 Sept. 1945.
6. "Reči Maršala druga Tita srpskom narodu Šumadije, " *Rad,* 23 June 1945.
7. "Šta je i kakva treba da bude naša komunistička partija," 15 Aug. 1945—but clearly written much earlier, between June 1941 and May 1943, HDA, CKKPH; "Partija i Narodni odbori," 1945, ACKSKJ, X2-IV/2. Milovan Djilas, "O medjunarodnoj i unutrašnjoj situaciji," 29 Sept. 1946, ACKSKJ, VIII IV-a-1.
8. "Govor druga Mihaila Švabića," 23–35 Jan. 1945, AJ, CV SSJ F1/J1-3; Cazi, "Učešće jedinstvenih sindikata"; J. L. "Rad u sindkatima ne sme da ide na štetu rada u Frontu," *20. oktobar*, 18 May 1945.
9. "Drugi Plenum," 12 April 1945, AJ CV SSJ F1-plenume; Milan Žugelj, "Prvi maj—općenarodni praznik borbe i rada," *Vjesnik*, 28 April 1945.
10. Milovan Djilas, Speech at the Second Plenum of the USAOJ, 5–8 Sept. 1945, AJ, SSOJ-27. See also Milijan Neorečić, "O radu USAOJ u selu," 5–8 Sept. 1945, AJ, SSOJ-27.
11. "Govor potpretsjednika Prezidijuma Narodne skupštine FNRJ Moše Pijade na mitingu birača prvog rajona Beograda," *Borba*, 25 Oct. 1947; Milovan Djilas, *Conversations with Stalin* (New York: Harcourt Brace Jovanovich, 1962), 30.
12. For a detailed description of this process see Jill Irvine, *The Croat Question: Partisan Politics in the Formation of the Yugoslav Socialist State* (Boulder, CO: Westview Press, 1993), and Zdenko Radelić, *Hrvatska seljačka stranka, 1941–1950* (Zagreb: 1996).
13. For a more detailed accounting of the CPY's use of *Seljačka sloga* see Katarina Spehnjak, "Hrvatsko seljačko prosvjetno društvo 'Seljačka sloga'," *Časopis za suvremenu povijest*, 29, no. 1 (1997): 129–146.
14. Milovan Djilas, Interview with the author, Belgrade, 17 Nov. 1988; J. B. Tito, "Sednica CK KPJ sa birom CK KPH," 5 Dec. 1945, ACKSKJ, PB III/10.
15. List of quotes from Stjepan and Ante Radić, 1945, HDA, CKKPHAP; Djilas, Speech at the Second Plenum of the USAOJ; "Govor Vladimira Nazora," *Slobodni dom*, 18 Sept. 1945 (italics in the original).

16. Veljko Vlahović, "August 1941," manuscript, no date, ACKSKJ, LFVV II/3-33; Veljko Vlahović, "Pripreme za Prvi Sveslovenski kongres," manuscript, no date, ACKSKJ, LFVV II/3-56; "Prvi maj," *Borba*, 1 May 1945.

17. Serbs and Montenegrins felt a special affinity with Russia due both to their common Orthodox religion and to Russia's moral and, in some cases, military support in earlier struggles for independence from the Ottoman Empire. A somewhat less Russocentric form of Slavism had strong roots in the 19th-century Illyrianist movement in Croatia. Moreover, Croatia's extremely popular prewar politician, Stjepan Radić, had shown strong Slavic sentiments and had visited the Soviet Union despite his ideological differences with the Communists. Finally, nearly all citizens of Yugoslavia felt a degree of unity with and gratitude toward Russia as a result of their most recent common battle against the Germans. While impossible to prove, it also seems clear that many CPY leaders supported the Slavic movement because it appealed to them as much as it did to the population as a whole. In an interview with the author, Djilas, while denying his interest in the Slavic movement, admitted to strong feelings of Slavic sentiment, insisting that similar feelings of solidarity must exist between, for example, all Anglo-Saxons. Conversations with other Yugoslav citizens also suggested that the concept of Slavic solidarity is so culturally pervasive among the South Slavs that most consider it absolutely natural and not in need of any particular defense or explanation. Obviously, however, such sentiments have not prevented Slavs from warring against one another.

18. Josip Broz Tito, "Crkva treba da bude nacionalna," *Borba*, 6 May 1945.

19. "Govor patrijarha Gavrila u ime Srpske pravoslavne crkve," *Politika*, 12 Dec. 1946. If one replaces the term "Slavic" in this excerpt with "Anglo-Saxon" the absurdity of Djilas's claim in note 17 becomes evident.

20. Radmila Radić, *Verom protiv vere* (Belgrade: INIS, 1995), 225.

21. Svetozar Rittig, "Maršal Tito na pozornici ratnih dogadjaja," *Naprijed*, 28 Aug. 1944; Svetozar Rittig, "Da se zadubimo u misli naše NOB-e," *Vjesnik*, 20 June 1944.

22. For biographical information see Marija Šoljan Bakarić, ed., *Kata Pejnović: monografija* (Zagreb: 1977); Milenko Predragović, *Kata Pejnović* (Kragujevac: 1978). In contrast, during the war, any "frivolity" in women had been openly condemned and some women were apparently expelled from the CPY simply for wearing lipstick. Lydia Sklevicky, "Emancipated Integration or Integrated Emancipation: The Case of Post-Revolutionary Yugoslavia," unpublished manuscript, 4.

23. Josip Broz Tito, "O novim zadacima žena," 16–19 June 1945, AJ, AFŽ 141-1-2. See also "Govor Maršala Tita na mitingu žena Srbije," *Borba*, 29 Jan. 1945. Indeed, AFW organizations were quite active in both social work and education, concentrating especially on the eradication of illiteracy not only among women but within the entire population.

24. According to statistics from 1948, for example, of all members of the Central Committees of Republican party organizations, less than 8 percent were women; only 3 out of 63 members of the Central Committee of the CPY elected at the Fifth Party Congress were women; and there were no women in the Polit-

buro. Likewise, fewer than 4 percent of all the members of the government were women, and none of them were among the federal ministers of the government. It is also evident from only a cursory glance at the names that a great many—although by no means all—of the most prominent women in the party and government were the wives or relatives of prominent male figures. Among the women activists who were the wives or other relatives of prominent male figures were Mitra Mitrović-Djilas, Vida Tomšić, Pepca Kardelj, Milica Dedijer, and Marija Šoljan Bakarić. It is not my intent to belittle their skills or leadership capabilities, but only to suggest something about the atmosphere of the times and the difficulties for unaffiliated women to rise through the ranks. *Informativni priručnik o Jugoslaviji, Opšti podaci o političkom, privrednom, socijalnom, kulturnom i prosvetnom životu u Federativnoj narodnoj republici Jugoslaviji,* September 1948 (Belgrade: 1948–1951), 16; Statistics on women in the party and government, 1948, AJ, AFŽ 141-13-71.

25. Braco Kosovac, "Izveštaj o pisanju ženskih listova," 1948, ACKSKJ, VIII II/5-b-26. Blaženka Mimica, "O našim ženskim listovima," *Žena danas,* 54 (May 1948).

26. Vladimir Dedijer, *Veliki buntovnik Milovan Djilas, Prilozi za biografiju* (Belgrade: 1991) 236; Milo Gligorijević, *Odgovor Mica Popović* (Belgrade: 1984), 49–53; Mitra Mitrović, Interview with the author, Belgrade, 13 April 1988.

27. Rato Dugonjić, "Zapisnik sa sastanka CK SKOJ-a," 9 Aug. 1945, in Petar Kačavenda, ed., *Kongresi, konferencije i sednice centralnih organa SKOJ-a* (hereafter *KKSKOJ, 1941–1948)* (Belgrade: Izdavački centar Komunist, 1984), 47.

28. See Milovan Djilas, "Povodom 27. godišnjice Oktobarske revolucije," November 1944, in Milovan Djilas, *Članci, 1941–1946* (Belgrade: 1947), 141–152; Političko-organizacioni izvještaj OK SKOJ Biokovo-Neretva," 26 May 1945, and "Izvještaj OK SKOJ Srednje Dalmacije," 29 May 1945, HDA, PKSKOJ-H; Report from Divisional Commander of KPH of 7th Shock Division of the JNA, 2 Aug. 1945, HDA, CKKPH; "Izvještaj OK KPH Banije," 9 April 1947, HDA, CKKPH.

29. Rato Dugonjić, "Omladina u novoj Jugoslaviji," 13 May 1946, AJ, SSOJ-2; Branko Bogunović, "Naša mladost na pruzi," *Žena danas,* 49 (July-August 1947).

30. "Završeno je treće zasedanje," *Politika,* 27 Aug. 1945; "Govor brojeva," *Demokratija,* 4 Oct. 1945; "Jedan jedini lik: sloboda," *Demokratija,* 1 Nov. 1945. See also numerous articles in *Republika,* especially in the summer of 1946.

31. "Govor Sretena Žujovića," *Politika,* 28 March 1945.

32. One of the first books to describe the massacre at Bleiburg was Borivoje Karapandžić's *Jugoslovensko krvavo proleće 1945: Titovi katini i gulazi* (Belgrade: 1990). Since the breakup of Yugoslavia numerous memoir accounts about Bleiburg have emerged, including Ante Beljo, *YU Genocide* (Toronto and Zagreb: 1995); Vinko Nikolić, *Tragedija se dogodila u Svibnju,* 2 vols (Zagreb: 1995); Mirko Valentić, ed., *Spomenica Bleiburg, 1945–1995* (Zagreb: 1995). As Danilović points out, however, the accuracy of such accounts is difficult to determine. Estimates of the numbers killed at Bleiburg vary from 60,000 to 250,000. Rajko Danilović, *Upotreba neprijatelja: Politička sudjenja 1945–1991 u Jugoslaviji* (Valjevo: Valjevac, 1993), 90–91.

33. The CPY's appreciation for the special qualities of youth was nothing new in the Communist or, for that matter, non-Communist world. On youth in the Soviet Union and other Communist countries see, among many others, V. I. Lenin, *On Youth* (Moscow: 1980); Jim Riordan, ed., *Soviet Youth Culture* (London: MacMillan Press, 1989); Isabel A. Tirado, *Young Guard! The Communist Youth League, Petrograd 1917–1920* (New York: Greenwood Press, 1988); Henry Gleitman, *Youth in Revolt: The Failure of Communist Indoctrination in Hungary* (New York: Free Europe Press, 1957); Paul Neuberg, *The Hero's Children: The Post-War Generation in Eastern Europe* (New York: William Morrow and Co. Inc., 1973).

34. "Osnovna programska načela NFJ," *Borba*, 8 Aug. 1945.

35. My use of the term *youth*, as a particular phase in the life cycle, resembles that of psychologists and sociologists, while historians have traditionally been interested in particular generations of youth united by common key experiences. My research does not trace the development of any one generation over time but examines the influence of persistent styles and attitudes among successive generations of youth. I have deliberately avoided using the term *youth culture* both because its existence is a matter of scholarly dispute and because the term encompasses a broader set of criteria than are relevant to my argument.

36. Memo from the ministry of education to all federal units, 14 March 1945, AJ, MP-2; "Godišnjica gimnazija u Glini," excerpt from *Naprijed*, 8 March 1945, HDA, AFŽ; "Nacrt jedinstvenog plana i programa za osnovnu školu," 26 July 1945, AJ, KŠN-77.

37. "Zapisnik sa sastanka PK SKOJ," 21 July 1945, HDA, PKSKOJ-H-1; "Školska omladina u Tuzli kažnjava sluge okupatora," *Politika*, 25 June 1945. See also Milutin Baltić, "O srednjim školama," 4 April 1945, AJ, SSOJ-55; "Nova škola mora da omogući zdravliji i bolji odnos nastavnika i djaka," *Glas*, 17 April 1945; "Zapisnike sastanka CK SKOJ-a," 24 April 1945, in *KKSKOJ, 1941–1948*, 7–9; "Izvještaj GK SKOJ Split," 1 June 1945, HDA, PKSKOJ-H-1; "Izvještaj o radu srednjoškolske omladine i pionira OK SKOJ Karlovac," 12 Aug. 1945, HDA, PKSKOJ-H-1.

38. "Izveštaj o radu Komisije za obnovu Univerziteta," 27 April 1945, in Momčilo Mitrović and Djordje Stanković, eds., *Zapisnici i izveštaji univerzitetskog komiteta Komunističke partije Srbije, 1945–1948* (hereafter *ZIUKKPS*) (Belgrade: 1985), 19–22; "Izvještaj odbora NSO Hrvatske," 31 July 1945, HDA, PKSKOJ-H-1; "Studenti Zagrebačkog univerziteta čiste svoje redove od ustaških i fašističkih elemenata," *Politika*, 26 Jan. 1946; "Oslobodjeni beogradski univerzitet uklanja sve tragove ropstva i fašizma," *Politika*, 23 May 1945; "Osudjen je dr. Nikola Popović bivši rektor Beogradskog univerziteta za vreme okupacije," *Politika*, 11 May 1946; "Mesnom komitetu KPS," 5 March 1946, *ZIUKKPS*, 37–39. See also "Zapisnik sa sastanka PK SKOJ, 21 July 1945, HDA, PKSKOJ-H-1; Report from the Council of the NSO of Croatia, 31 July 1945, HDA, PKSKOJ-H-1; "Izveštaj o prosvetnim problemima," 31 Oct. 1945, ACKSKJ, VIII VI/2-e-1.

39. "Nova škola mora da omogući"; "Godišnjica gimnazija u Glini." See also "Prilozi prvom zapisniku Prosvetnog saveta pri MP savezne vlade," 6–16 Aug. 1945, AJ, MP-9; "Rezolucija sa prve konferencije studenata Beogradskog univerziteta," 14 June 1945, *ZIUKKPS*, 23–24.

40. "Izvještaj OK SKOJ Varaždin," 4 Aug. 1945, HDA, PKSKOJ-H-1.

41. "Izvještaj GK SKOJ Split," 1 June 1945; "Zapisnik sa sastanka CK SKOJ-a," 22 April 1946, *KKSKOJ, 1941-1948,* 176-177, 182; "Referat Marice Kresojević na sastanku komisije na srednje škole," May 1946, AJ, SSOJ-2"; Danilo Purić, "Savetovanje OK SKOJ-a po pitanju rada srednjih škola," 1946, ACKSKJ, CKSKOJ II-a-2/3.

42. "Zapisnik sa sastanka PK SKOJ," 21 July 1945, HDA, PKSKOJ-H-1 (italics in the original); Stana Tomašević, "Zadaci rada sa školskim omladinom," March 1945, AJ, SSOJ-27.

43. Stevo Doronjski, "Zaključci prosvetnog saveta," 5–8 Sept. 1945, AJ, SSOJ-27; Brana Perović, "Zapisnik sa sastanka CK SKOJ-a," 20 Dec. 1945, *KKSKOJ, 1941-1948,* 92-98; Mitra Mitrović, interview with the author, Belgrade, 13 April 1988.

44. "Zapisnik sa sastanka organizacionih sekretara KK i GK SKOJ-a za Dalmaciju," 13 June 1946, HDA, PKSKOJ-H-2; "Izvještaj GK SKOJ Split," 1 June 1945; Četvrti sastanak Pretsedništva CV NOJ," 15–17 Sept. 1947, AJ, SSOJ-37.

45. "Human Rehabilitation of Children and Young People," 22 Feb. 1945, AJ, MP-3.

46. For information on Soviet cultural policies see Sheila Fitzpatrick, *The Commissariat of Enlightenment, Soviet Organization of Education and the Arts under Lunacharsky, October 1917-1921* (Cambridge: Cambridge University Press, 1970); Sheila Fitzpatrick, ed., *Cultural Revolution in Russia, 1928-1931* (Bloomington, IN: Indiana University Press, 1984); Peter Kenez, *The Birth of the Propaganda State* (Cambridge: Cambridge University Press, 1985); Richard Stites, *Revolutionary Dreams, Utopian Vision and Experimental Life in the Russian Revolution* (Oxford: Oxford University Press, 1989); and Denise J. Youngblood, *Movies for the Masses, Popular Cinema and Soviet Society in the 1920s* (Cambridge: Cambridge University Press, 1992). Youngblood's monograph includes a particularly interesting section on the "entertainment or enlightenment" debate of the 1920s.

47. Ivan Curl, "Muzika za ples," 16 Dec. 1946, HDA, CKKPH; Dušan Timotijević, "Naš budući domaći crtani film," *Film,* 2 (March 1947), 31–35. For more on the censorship of music see Marko Lopušina, *Crna knjiga: Cenzura u Jugoslaviji* (Belgrade: Fokus, 1991), 242–248.

48. See Lawrence Levine, *Highbrow/Lowbrow: The Emergence of Cultural Hierarchy in America* (Cambridge, MA: Harvard University Press, 1988).

49. Velibor Gligorić, "Zadaci književne kritike u 1948 godini," *Politika,* 1 Jan. 1948. In an interesting contrast, the chief architect of Nazi propaganda, Joseph Goebbels, banned art criticism in 1936, insisting that it be replaced by art reporting, which "should not be concerned with values, but should confine itself to description [which] should give the public the right to make up its own mind." Peter Adam, *Art in the Third Reich* (New York: Harry N. Abrams, Inc., 1992) 69.

50. Dušan Bilandžić, *Historija Socijalističke Federativne Jugoslavije: Glavni procesi, 1918-1985* (Zagreb: Školska knjiga, 1985), 88.

51. Vladimir Dedijer, *Novi prilozi za biografiju Josipa Broza Tita,* Vol. 3 (Belgrade: Rad, 1984), 218–219; "S glumcima kazališta narodnog oslobodjenja," *Slobodna Dalmacija,* 26 Aug. 1944.

52. For a discussion of Nazor's role in postwar efforts to create a "supranational Yugoslav culture" see Andrew Wachtel, *Making a Nation, Breaking a Nation:*

Literature and Cultural Politics in Yugoslavia (Stanford, CA: Stanford University Press, 1998), 149–151.

53. Marijan Stilinović, "U borbi za kulturni preporod," 25 June 1944, *Prvi kongres kulturnih radnika Hrvatske, Topusko, 25–27 juni 1944, Gradja* (Zagreb: 1976), 69–71.

54. Ibid.

55. "Konkurs sa filmski scenario," *Borba*, 24 Aug. 1945; Radovan Zogović, "Za mač i za pero!" *Borba*, 1 Dec. 1944, in Radovan Zogović, *Na poprištu* (Belgrade: 1947), 113.

56. Branislav Miljković, "Socijalistički realizam u književnosti," *Republika*, 27 Nov. 1945 and 4 Dec. 1945; Z. Cvetković, "Umetnost i društveni život," *Republika*, 29 Jan. 1946 and 5 Feb. 1946; Branislav Miljković, "Nekoliko reči o savremenom romanu," *Republika*, 26 Feb. 1946; Branislav Miljković, "Posle Kongresa književnika," *Republika*, 10 Dec. 1946; Tvrtko Čubelić, "Osvrt na glavnu smotru Seljačke sloge," reprint from *Vjesnik*, 28 Sept. 1946, in *Seljačka sloga* (October 1946).

57. "Obnovljeno udruženje likovnih umjetnika 'Zemlja'," *Naprijed*, 2 Jan. 1945; V. R. "Likovni život u oslobodjenoj Hrvatskoj," *Naprijed*, 25 April 1945.

58. By 1947 all members of the Writers' Union were supplied with R2 rationcards, the same as those given to skilled workers, while particularly influential writers got R1 cards, the highest available and the same as those given to workers employed in extremely important or dangerous industries. Zdenko Štambuk, "O našoj književnosti i književnim prilikama," *Republika*, 3, no. 3 (1947): 151; "Osnovan Savez likovnih umetnika Jugoslavije," *Borba*, 8 Dec. 1947. Even so, artists in new Yugoslavia were not always satisfied with what they got. The Zagreb film director Mirko Lukavac has recalled that he once complained about the lack of resources to Croatia's minister of finance, Anka Berus. She was friendly but told him, "Do you realize, my dear, how much we need for schools, hospitals, and highways, for the renovation of destroyed rail lines and factories, not to mention all the other things. You go on home nicely now and be happy with what you have received." Mirko Lukavac, "Prvi dani kinematografije u SR Hrvatskoj (1945–1946)," *Filmska kultura*, 100 (July 1975): 167.

59. "Miroslav Krleža o Milovanu Djilasu i Radovanu Zogoviću," in Enes Čengić, *S Krležom iz dana u dan* (Zagreb: 1985–1990), 197–211; Milovan Djilas, *Rise and Fall* (New York: Harcourt Brace Jovanovich, 1983), 48–49.

60. Djilas, *Rise and Fall*, 54–55. For more on the party's relations with Andrić and his role in the effort to create a Yugoslav culture see Wachtel, 156–172.

61. Miroslav Krleža, "Književnost danas," *Republika*, 1, no. 1–2 (1945): 159; "Izveštaj o listovima koji izlaze u Hrvatskoj," 1946, ACKSKJ, VIII VI/1-6-21.

62. "Zbirka narodnih pjesama," *Naprijed*, 19 Dec. 1944; Dušan Kostić, "O jednoj 'poeziji' koja nije poezija," *20. oktobar*, 17 Aug. 1945.

63. Radovan Zogović, "Poučna poredjenja," *Borba*, 1 March 1945, in Zogović, *Na poprištu*, 139.

64. Danilović, 93–94. See also "U Beogradu je osnovano novo gradsko pozorište," *Borba*, 3 Oct. 1945; "Jovan Popović koji je Beogradsko narodno pozorište stavio u službu okupatoru usudjen je na 4 godine prinudnog rada," *Politika*, 6 Sept. 1946; "Izvještaj o radu radio-direkcije za Hrvatsku," 9 June 1946, HDA,

CKKPHAP; Milomir Marić, "Prkosne strofe Radovana Zogovića," Part 2, *Duga*, no. 312 (February 1986): 62.

65. Gligorijević, 37–38.

66. Radovan Zogović, "Primjer kako ne treba praviti 'Primjere književnosti'," *Borba*, 8 May 1947 in Zogović, *Na poprištu*, 219–220; Marin Franičević, "O nekim negativnim pojavama u savremenoj poeziji," *Republika*, no. 7–8 (July-August 1947), in Marin Franičević, *Pisci i problemi* (Belgrade: 1948), 271; Lopušina, 28.

67. Radovan Zogović, "O kritici i o Beogradskom baletu," *Borba*, 16 October, 1946 in Zogović, *Na popristu*, 172.

68. "Šta je i kakva treba da bude."

69. Slobodan Selenić, *Očevi i oci* (Belgrade: 1988), 254.

70. See, for example, Speech of Professor Ivo Babić at the First Congress of the NF Hrvatska, 13 Oct. 1946, HDA, RKSSRNH-1; Marjan Krleža, "Kulturno-prosvjetni zadaci i problemi," 1946, HDA, VSSH-1-KPO.

71. Zogović was especially unforgiving and contemptuous of intellectuals, denouncing, in one article, "specialist fetishization," and insisting that "the people" knew perfectly well what was good and what was not in art. "O prosvetnim prilikama u FNRJ; Zogović, "O kritici i o Beogradskom baletu." See also Marić, "Prkosne strofe Radovana Zogovića," parts 1–3; Dedijer, *Novi prilozi*, Vol. 3, 129, 217–218; Stanko Lasić, *Sukob na književnoj ljevici* (Zagreb: 1970), 262–270; Gligorijević, 29–30. A similar disdain for civic and urban culture could be seen in party rhetoric which portrayed the prototypical female follower of the opposition as an attractive, well-dressed, well-groomed woman of obvious bourgeois background.

72. "Zapisnik sa sastanka PK SKOJ," 21 July 1945; "Zapisnik sa sastanka KK SKOJ Sinj," 8 April 1946, HDA, PSKSOJ-H-2; Pismo OK SKOJ-a za Dalmaciju," 18 Aug. 1948, ACKSKJ, CSKOJ II c-1/54.

73. "Article 25," *Constitution of the Federative People's Republic of Yugoslavia* (Belgrade: 1946).

74. Vitomir Vidaković, "Osnivačke skupštine pravoslavnog sveštenstva Jugoslavije," *Vesnik*, 1, no. 1 (March 1948). See also Milan D. Smiljanić, "Kojim putem?" *Vesnik*, 1, no. 1 (March 1948).

75. Gligorijević, 35–36; Ivan Šibl, *Sjećanja: Poslijeratni dnevnik*, Vol. 3 (Zagreb: 1986), 26–28. For other examples see Djoko Slijepčević, *Istorija srpske pravoslavne crkve*, Vol. 3 (Cologne: 1986), 176–181.

76. "Božić 1945," *Politika*, 6–8 Jan. 1945; "Sretan Uskrs!" *Vjesnik*, 31 March 1945; "Narodni običaji o Božiću," *20. oktobar*, 4 Jan. 1946; "Objašnjenje saopštenja o puštanju u slobodnu prodaju muških jaganjača o Uskrsu," *Politika*, 18 April 1946; "Povodom Božičnih praznika," *Politika*, 25 Dec. 1946. For a more detailed description of the celebrations of Christmas and New Year directly after the war see Lydia Sklevicky, "The 'New' New Year, or How a Tradition Was Tempered," *East European Politics and Societies*, 4, No. 1 (Winter 1990): 4–29.

77. "Svetosavske proslave u beogradskim osnovnim i srednjim školama," *Politika*, 28 Jan. 1946; "Odluke Ministarstva prosvete Srbije," 21 May 1945, AJ, MP-3.

78. "Parastos izginulim herojima za oslobodjena Beograda," *Glasnik*, 25, no. 10–12 (31 Dec. 1944) (emphasis added).

79. "Božić 1945"; "Božić 1946," *20. oktobar,* 4 Jan. 1946; "Uskrs 1946," *Politika,* 20–23 April 1946.

80. Godišnji izvještaj o radu Glavnog odbora i organizacije AFŽ-a u Hrvatskoj," 1948, AJ, AFŽ 141-13-67; "Zapisnik sa sastanka KK SKOJ Sinj," 8 April 1946.

81. Stella Alexander, *Church and State in Yugoslavia since 1945* (Cambridge: Cambridge University Press, 1979), 60–62, 131–136, 172–177; Slijepčević, *Istorija,* Vol. 3, 185–187; Pedro Ramet, "Catholicism and Politics in Socialist Yugoslavia," *Religion in Communist Lands,* 10, no. 3 (Winter 1982): 257.

82. Fr. Vladimir Rodzianko, "The Golgotha of the Orthodox Church in Yugoslavia, 1941–1951," *The Eastern Churches Quarterly,* 10, no. 2 (Summer 1953): 71–73.

83. Izvještaj OK SKOJ Varaždin," 4 Sept. 1945, HDA, PKSKOJ-H-1; "Izvještaj OK SKOJ Varaždin," 1 June 1945, HDA, PKSKOJ-H-1.

84. Radić, 322.

85. "Pastirsko pismo katoličkih biskupa Jugoslavije, izdan s općih Biskupskih konferencija u Zagrebu," in Branko Petranović and Momčilo Zečević, eds., *Jugoslovenski Federalizam: Ideje i stvarnosti,* Vol. 2 (Belgrade: 1987), 277–287.

86. Milan Grol, "Završeno je 3. zasedanje," *Politika,* 27 Aug. 1945. For more detail on Grol's treatment by the CPY see Vojislav Koštunica and Kosta Čavoški, *Party Pluralism or Monism: Social Movements and the Political System in Yugoslavia, 1944–1949* (Boulder, CO: Westview Press, 1985), 63–77.

87. Vladimir Simić, "Jugoslovenska republikanska demokratska stranka o nacrtu Ustava," speech at the 3rd meeting of the Constitutional Council of the Skupština held on 12 December 1945, *Republika,* 1 Jan. 1946; Aleksandar Tomić, "Političke partije i strančarstvo," *Republika,* 1 Jan. 1946.

5
Constructing the Framework: Mobilization and Control

The dynamism typical of state-society relations in the first year of Communist rule was both beneficial and harmful to the party's agenda. While party leaders clearly appreciated the enthusiasm displayed by much of the population, they also worried about its sometimes unpredictable and dangerous consequences. Once the November elections were behind them, party leaders moved more openly to remove any remaining rivals for power and eliminate that potential threat. Consequently, party rhetoric in the following two years from November 1945 to November 1947 became more injunctive and restrictive. Besides such modifications in tone, the content of party persuasive policies also now changed.

Persuasive policies in the first year of Communist rule had focused on aiding the party in its struggle for power and mainly, therefore, addressed political and vaguely ideological themes. Yet while rhetoric aimed at polarizing the political spectrum and popularizing the party's values and goals was crucial to the party's bid for power, it tended to neglect certain other important tasks. Already in early 1945, several internal reports on the party press complained that it was insufficiently connected to the economy and to concrete problems of renovation and construction, and tended to "get lost in ... some type of people's liberation phrase-mongering."[1] Likewise, an article in the Belgrade city paper complained that political meetings were too long and drawn out because participants very often began their speeches with lengthy introductions "about the evil acts of the occupier, about the struggle and suffering of our people and so on, only to conclude with the suggestion that it is necessary to replace the teachers in the daycare center or something like that."[2]

Indeed, since the solution of concrete economic problems was practically a matter of life and death, party rhetoric had targeted the achievement of numerous specific tasks from the very beginning. Reflecting the immediate need to feed the population, for example, a picture in one newspaper showed youths with their arms full of corn above the plea, "Youth! Don't let corn rot in Srem when hunger is reigning in other areas!"[3] In a speech from September 1945, Djilas stressed that problems in the economy "are today the *most important tasks,* to which are subordinated all other tasks," and he urged youth leaders to "mobilize youth for concrete questions, the question of good schools, the question of good work in factories, the question of coal production, the question of conscientious work on transport, the question of savings, the question of land cultivation."[4]

Emphasis on economic tasks greatly increased, however, once the CPY had secured its position in power through elections. Since the population had apparently accepted the story of Yugoslavia's wicked past and glorious future, party leaders saw no need to keep repeating it. Consequently, ever more articles and agitprop department reports accused the press of getting lost in abstractions and the general line, complained of its weaknesses in the areas of economics and mass mobilization, and urged it to publish more relevant, concrete, and interesting material from the field. In January 1946, Tito directly instructed youth leaders, for example, to include less politics in their press and more economics.[5]

As the leaders of agitprop departments responded to these complaints and refocused their attention on immediate tasks of economic survival and construction, grand ideas about the future of Yugoslavia retreated into the background. Not only did rhetoric now ignore the party's broader goals but until mid-1947, it still explicitly avoided any reference to Communist ideology. Even as late as December 1946 the central agitprop department criticized one newspaper for referring to "the struggle for the victory of socialism."[6] And an article in *Borba* on the spring sowing campaign of 1947 stated,

> Whoever looks at the problems of political work in the village and who also understands his tasks in connection with this year's spring sowing, will not speak abstractly and in vain about the problems of class struggle and differentiation in the village but will, himself, actively and successfully build our new state strong and free. He will simultaneously develop the new Yugoslav patriotism and build consciousness about each citizen's duty to fulfill wholeheartedly all tasks established by the Plan.[7]

Articles relating to the country's political situation certainly did not disappear but were now almost entirely pragmatic in their goals and orientation. Rather than elaborate on the political structure or ideological

Youth! Don't Let Corn Rot in Srem When Hunger is Reigning in other Areas. Glas, 6 March, 1945.

character of new Yugoslavia, they addressed specific themes such as Yugoslavia's territorial demands in the peace process (Istria, Trieste, and Carinthia) and the trials of prominent opposition figures (Draža Mihailović, Archbishop Alojzije Stepinac, and Dragoljub Jovanović). Djilas instructed even Communist party cells to focus their discussions not on theory but on "practical political and organizational work and the solution of those political and organizational tasks established by the party."[8]

In any case, the party's primary persuasive agenda throughout 1946 and 1947 appeared to be the mobilization of particular segments of the population to fulfill concrete tasks associated with economic renovation and construction—including especially factory shockwork and competitions, the activities of volunteer labor brigades, and preparations for and fulfillment of the Five Year Plan. In addition, party rhetoric now placed considerable emphasis on education, not so much because it would create people with new values, but because it would create people with new skills—the skills required by a modern industrialized state. As party persuasive personnel focused on these more pragmatic goals, their demands for absolute obedience to the party line in culture and the media also increased and their willingness to tolerate any signs of pluralism or independent thought declined.

Shockwork and Competition

The drive for increased production in the factories was unquestionably the most prominent theme in party rhetoric throughout 1946 and 1947. In this campaign, the working class took center stage as the main force that would rebuild the country's infrastructure and economy. Party rhetoric, therefore, strove to mobilize workers for the completion of economic tasks, explaining the new function of trade unions not as political organizations defending workers' rights (which, it said, were already guaranteed in new Yugoslavia), but as a force for economic renovation and construction.[9] As an administrative tool of the party for the mobilization of labor, trade unions relied especially on the techniques of shockwork and competition.

Based on the Russian Stakhanovite movement, shockwork—that is, the concentrated energy and overtime labor of an individual worker to overfulfill the expected production output by an enormous margin—achieved the same popularity in Yugoslavia after the war that it had in the Soviet Union in the 1930s.[10] In essence, party leaders hoped through the shockwork movement to foster continuation of such superhuman efforts as had occurred during the war. As SKOJ leader Milijan Neorečić put it, "During the war we had such heroes that the people were amazed. Now we need to have that in the factories." Likewise, trade union leader Djuro Spoljarić described Yugoslavia's shockworkers as "incredible heroes . . . who are able to work 20–30 hours under the most difficult circumstances, without a break, never asking is it cold or hot or do they have anything to eat." To be a shockworker, Tito explained, was to be a role model for the rest of society, "to have a high consciousness and to work for the community, for a better tomorrow, and for the entire people, it means giving all from oneself for the use of the entire people."[11] While shockworkers could be found among all types of enterprises, they were especially glorified in the fields of heavy industry, mining, and transportation. Shockworkers received enormous attention in the press and were rewarded for their efforts with bonuses, privileges, vacations, and enhanced opportunities for advancement.

A second extremely popular means of increasing worker enthusiasm and production was through competition. Organized competitions had developed during the war as a way of channeling and directing spontaneous working enthusiasm. These competitions, said to have nothing in common with capitalist competitions that only enslaved and destroyed the weak, were described as "comradely" events based on "the new attitude of workers toward each other and the technical intelligentsia, and the new content of the worker's attitude toward work in general."[12]

In the years after the war, competitions proliferated throughout Yugoslavia at all levels and in all spheres of activity, taking place in all imaginable enterprises not only between workers, factory brigades, and individual factories, but also between students, playwrights, cultural organizations, schools, and even governmental organizations. Again, the winners of such competitions gained public attention and praise, as well as some material rewards. In January 1946, for example, the barbers' and hairdressers' association of Belgrade competed to see who could work the fastest. The winner of the barbers' division completed a shave in 32 seconds to take home 40 percent of the entry fees, a small turkey, a liter of wine, and a diploma.[13]

While such lighthearted events suggest the popularity and universality of competitions in these first postwar years, the workers' response to party rhetoric was not always so positive. Certainly, workers knew that they were the favored social class of the CPY, at least in theory. And the new regime had provided workers with some immediate benefits, including legal limits on working hours, guaranteed vacations, paid maternity leave, legal protection for apprentices, and free education and health services. In addition, workers' representatives were included within the administrative bodies of all enterprises in order to guarantee their rights. In return, however, the party demanded from workers not only their political support but also, and especially, their raw hard labor. Moreover, in accordance with the overriding need for increased production, the new government had reintroduced many unpopular prewar policies like work norms, production quotas, and work books listing each employee's labor and production history. The party also insisted that workers and employees be compensated according to the quantity and quality of their work and its value to the community since even under socialism the maxim was not yet "each according to his needs," but only "each according to his work."

Although these policies did not necessarily represent new additions to Communist practice, they had not been publicized among workers in the interwar period when party rhetoric had emphasized instead the exploitative and unjust aspects of capitalism. Thus, although party leaders clearly imagined working-class support to be their due, the number and tone of articles explaining and justifying these policies suggests that many workers had expected something rather different from what was ostensibly *their* party. Evidence of worker resistance may also be found in articles that complained that despite laws intended to ensure proper remuneration of the technical intelligentsia and other qualified workers, salaries were too often determined *"according to the incorrect principle of equalization."*[14]

Clearly, shockwork and competitions also countered such egalitarian tendencies and may not have met with universal working-class support. While there is little evidence that workers openly opposed the techniques, party leaders did often complain that the workers' view of shockwork and competitions was too vague and needed to be concretized by the introduction of norms, contracts, and personal obligations. It was not sufficient merely to promise to produce "as much as possible," one must take on specific obligations and stick to them.[15] More often, however, party rhetoric attacked the trade unions' or workers' vision of competition as too narrow or harsh. For while the party leadership envisioned competition and shockwork as constant and regular methods of work, they were often treated as the subjects of campaigns. Workers outdid themselves (not always voluntarily) for two or three days, working up to 16 hours a day, and then collapsed from exhaustion. This approach, naturally, had an adverse effect on the workers' health, which, in turn, negatively influenced production. Moreover, it turned out that shockwork and competitions had sometimes reduced output by interfering with the organization of production.

The adoption of the Five Year Plan in April 1947, while further enhancing the emphasis in party rhetoric on increased productivity, did produce a somewhat more rational approach to the organization of shockwork and competitions. Trade union leaders were now instructed to prepare all competitions in cooperation with the administrators and engineers; in the event of any conflict, competitions were to be subordinated to the proper organization of production.[16] To put it another way, competitions thus far had relied on extensive means of increasing production—workers labored longer hours and used more material to produce more—when what party leaders really wanted was to increase the intensity of production. They wanted trade unions and workers to find faster, more efficient, less costly ways of producing more. Thus, they increasingly demanded that the unions not rely only on overtime work but encourage the development of innovators, inventors, and rationalizers.[17]

Youth Volunteer Labor Brigades

The second main focus of party rhetoric in 1946 and 1947 concerned youth participation in volunteer labor brigades. Indeed, the youth organization, PYY, declared its main task in 1946 to be securing youth participation in renovation and construction.[18] As noted above, volunteer labor brigades had originated during the war and continued afterwards partly in order to preserve the wartime sense of urgency and energy. Party agitprop leaders urged the formation of volunteer labor brigades in neighborhoods, the PFY, the League of Trade Unions, and the AFW, but especially among youth in the PYY in order to exploit their exceptional energies and lack of other employment.

Youth brigades began their postwar work immediately after the liberation of Belgrade but, as Milijan Neorečić complained in January 1946, were often spread so thinly that their effect was not felt. According to Mihailo Švabić, the idea of creating a few enormous federal youth brigades to supplement the local and smaller ones was his. "I thought to myself: since we're already working, let it be on something big." Although his plan faced much resistance from members of the government who felt the costs would be prohibitive, it found support from Tito.[19] Consequently, in the spring of 1946, the PYY created two large-scale federal youth brigades: one to construct a rail line between the Bosnian towns of Brčko and Banovići and other to build the "Highway of Brotherhood and Unity" between Zagreb and Belgrade.[20]

Party and youth activists throughout the spring of 1946 focused enormous attention on popularizing and mobilizing youth for participation, especially on the Brčko-Banovići Youth Railway, describing it as a demonstration by youth of its conscientious responsibility, love, and loyalty for the homeland. Ultimately some 62,000 youth working in three shifts of two months long each participated in construction of the 88 km–long railway.[21] As soon as the Brčko-Banovići Brigade had completed its work in November 1946, preparations began for the following year's major youth action, the Šamac-Sarajevo Youth Railway, which would be even bigger (242 km) and would require the participation of more than three times as many youths. Mobilization, therefore, needed to be three times as effective, and already in January 1947, Belgrade University's party committee ordered that every department and faculty adopt the slogan "All Students to the Brigade."[22]

Although the original locally based labor brigades had served mainly economic purposes, the federal brigades were created for their role in the political, ideological, professional, and cultural education of youth. The leaders of agitprop departments thus instructed local People's Councils and mass organizations to provide brigade participants with books and cultural and sports equipment before departure. One cartoon showed youth heading to the brigades carrying picks and shovels and returning from them carrying pens and books, and the slogan adopted by youth participants on the Brčko-Banovići line was "We Built the Railroad—The Railroad Built Us" (*"Mi smo izgradili prugu—pruga je izgradila nas"*).[23]

Indeed, federal brigades, at least, did devote considerable attention to cultural-educational work. They were especially diligent in their efforts to eradicate illiteracy among brigade participants, but also offered training in many useful skills, and provided other educational and cultural opportunities for youth who might not otherwise have had them. According to various reports, out of 5,896 illiterate youths on the Brčko-Banovići Brigade, 5,163 learned to read and write, while some 4,000 learned trades through technical and professional courses in such fields as welding, bulldozer driving, surveying, and masonry. In addition, brigade participants attended 1,650 lectures on political and educational topics, 950 on popular science, and 908 on various professional topics. Cultural activities included the formation of 304 choirs, 142 amateur art societies, 235 performances by visiting artists, and 133 film showings, as well as daily physical training exercises and numerous sports competitions in track and field, soccer, and basketball.[24]

Thanks to these benefits, participation on the federal brigades was to be considered an honor and, according to Švabić, only the *best* youths who had already proven themselves on local brigades were permitted to join. Living and working conditions on the federal brigades were also better than on the local ones, although even they faced numerous logistical and health-related problems. Švabić notes, for example, that the Šamac-Sarajevo brigades experienced epidemics of typhus and dysentery resulting in 10 deaths.[25]

Meanwhile, cultural-educational work on the smaller brigades was far less developed. Smaller brigades not only had less access to such cultural-educational supplies as newspapers, books, films, and sports equipment but also seemed more inclined to neglect cultural-educational work in order to concentrate entirely on the physical tasks at hand.[26] Moreover, living and working conditions on the smaller actions could be truly horrendous.

Even so, both contemporary accounts and diaries from youth on the brigades indicate a high level of morale among most participants. While many of the diaries were clearly written pro forma and lack conviction, one from a youth brigade sent to Albania during the late summer and fall of 1946 was evidently composed before official diary standards had been established and it exhibits an unmistakable air of sincerity. This diarist described frankly and without hesitation horrifying examples of poor working and living conditions in terms of health, sanitation, and nutrition, while at the same time demonstrating a deep tolerance for the situation, an indomitable will to continue, and a seemingly boundless ability to enjoy life.[27]

He noted the poor quality and insufficient quantity of food: "People are hungry. Macaroni not fried in grease or in only a little, with a few bits of meat or without it, is very poor food for eight hours of physically difficult and stressful work, so people are getting noticeably weaker and feel rather exhausted." But he then added that they all knew how poor the area was and that macaroni was the staple food source for the region. He described long miserable days of breathing in dust so thick that the youths grew gray from it and their eyes teared, but said, "all the same we work and sing." Likewise, when the girls' tent leaked in the rain, he said, they just huddled together and sang all night. The exhaustion, he explained, was eased by collective life so that even after 12 hours of work they still sang and danced. "Although we are tired, together, and with song, it is easier." While one might suspect that this diarist was only an incurable optimist or even a masochist, other reports, diaries, and the author's conversations with contemporaries of the era have upheld his version of the prevailing mood.[28]

Youth participation on the brigades was supposed to be strictly voluntary, of course, and certainly it often was. Not only was youth enthusiasm extremely high, but the brigades offered an opportunity for many young and poor peasants to escape village life and gain useful skills for the future. And while party leaders intended the brigades to have a positive moral and educational impact on youth, many young people probably saw the entire affair more as a great lark and an opportunity to get out from under the watchful eye of their parents. Unsurprisingly, then, parents were often among those most opposed to the brigades, citing concerns about moral supervision and sanitary conditions. Some went so far as to suggest that their children were being kidnapped.

Thus even as CPY poets described the brigades as a "Forge of Dreams," regional party leaders recruiting youth for them often faced resistance. Consequently, recruitment methods based on coercion were not uncommon. Some parents who refused to send their children were threatened with the loss of their jobs or ration cards, and one call for participation read, "Whoever does not respond and does not come to the brigade will be held legally responsible."[29] While CPY memos regularly denounced such incidents and methods, central party and PYY organs continued to set numerical quotas for each local organization, specifying exactly how many youths must be sent to each work action. Given the authoritarian structure of the party and considering the fact that the numerical quotas in industry were backed up by force of law, it is no surprise that local organs (correctly) considered these quotas directives to be fulfilled, not mere suggestions.

The use of coercive recruitment techniques undoubtedly helped local leaders to fulfill their brigade quotas. They also, however, had the effect of diminishing public support for volunteer labor that was voluntary in name only. Party leaders were well aware of both the use of forced recruitment techniques and their harmful effect on public support for the regime. Already by early 1947, some party leaders began publicly to speak against the use of force in recruitment campaigns. Even more significantly, youth leader Rato Dugonjić specifically informed local youth organizations that they should avoid the use of force even if it meant that they would not fulfill their brigade quotas since it threatened to destroy the entire meaning of volunteer labor. Similarly, in a later meeting, Dugonjić again insisted that it was better to send fewer brigades than to rely on coercive recruitment techniques.[30]

Over time, then, official enthusiasm for the brigades and for massive youth participation in them grew less and less pronounced—especially in the speeches of top leaders. Beyond their concerns about forced recruitment, party leaders were also responding to reports that poor working and living conditions on many brigades had damaged the health of the young volunteers. Finally, and perhaps most worrisome, was the fact that the youth organization's excessive concentration on volunteer labor distracted it from another equally if not more important task—education.

Economic Tasks and Education

Party rhetoric concerning the importance of education in 1946 and 1947 was clearly related to its immediate economic value. One of the main changes in the new educational curriculum was to shift it away from the humanities and liberal arts and toward greater emphasis on applied and natural sciences. As Serbia's minister of education, Mitra Mitrović, stated, the object of obligatory schooling was not to turn miners' children into officials or intellectuals (although it would have a positive effect on the social content of those cadres), but mainly to spread the knowledge and culture necessary for all jobs in the factory or on the farm.[31]

With the adoption of the Five Year Plan in April 1947, party emphasis on education—especially technical education—increased even further. After all, the phenomenal rates of economic growth foreseen by the plan would require the existence and cooperation of large numbers of technical and professional cadres. The plan itself called for the development of cadres to secure its fulfillment and to direct the work of academic and scientific institutions toward "the practical solution of scientific and technical problems."[32]

Party leaders intended for many members of the new technical intelligentsia to be drawn from the ranks of high-level workers by increasing their education and specialized knowledge. Thus the minister of industry and mining, Rade Žigić, recommended the formation of schools for workers in the industrial basins. "We will in that way hasten the creation of our worker-peasant intelligentsia."[33] These workers' schools offered preferential enrollment to shockworkers and other leading figures in hopes that it would result in the more rapid development of scientific innovations and inventions. Some workers thus educated were also expected to continue their self-development in the university and become qualified professionals.[34] Despite such efforts to increase working-class education, reports from 1948 and 1949 complained that schools set up by trade unions had an inadequate social content and included mainly employees, peasants, and craftsmen rather than workers.[35] In any case, party leaders accepted that the vast majority of the new "technical" intelligentsia would necessarily come from the ranks of youth educated in the standard school system. Therefore, party rhetoric also worked to impress upon youths the importance of education.

This emphasis, however, inevitably collided with the party's simultaneous demands for political activism and volunteer labor by young people. The first signs of such a conflict showed up in the extremely poor grades achieved by students in the first years after the war. While partly a consequence of material difficulties and the continuing unsettled atmosphere, low academic performance was especially evident among youth activists, shockworkers, and brigade participants.[36] In response to these indicators, numerous articles and memos stressing the importance of studying began to appear already in mid-1946 and continued throughout the following year. Even the Pioneer organization, directed at children under 15, initiated a campaign for studying and against poor grades in the fall of 1946; and in June 1947 it called for a war against "D"s with the slogan "A good pupil is a good pioneer."[37] Leaders of the PYY also conceded by the fall of 1946 that youth had thus far neglected their education and asked that in the future they study, learn, and acquire a specialty as their first priority.

Many such memos were explicitly directed at CPY and SKOJ organizations for, to the CPY's embarrassment, party and SKOJ members earned the highest percentage of poor grades. One document from Belgrade University's party committee in late May 1946 pointed out that only two out of 20 party members in the agricultural school had received good grades, and another conceded that Communist students were often failing one or more courses. Youth leaders Dugonjić and Neorečić also complained in the fall of that year that most youth leaders, whether students or not, did not study enough. According to Neorečić, some had not read a single book in months, evidently believing that they already knew enough and did not need further education.[38]

To his credit, Dugonjić, at least, quickly pointed to the inordinate numbers of meetings attended by youth activists and excessive concentration on volunteer labor as partial sources of the problem. In a January 1947 article in *Borba*, he described the letters of complaint he had received from parents concerning this problem. One father said his daughter attended 23 meetings in just over two weeks and another claimed that his daughter's grades dropped because she spent so many hours per week at meetings, often returning home late at night. When she complained, her party superior yelled at her and called her an opportunist. In the future, Dugonjić insisted, "a student no longer has to be in any leadership or in any apparatus either youth oriented or of a front organization, but only in secondary school."[39]

Such warnings were often ignored, however, and rhetoric directed at youth continued to focus on political actions and volunteer labor. For example, while in December 1946, agitprop leader Veljko Vlahović emphasized to youth the importance of education and acquiring a specialty, he also pointed to the glorious example of the martyred youth leader Ivo Lola Ribar, who had worked constantly on self-improvement but did not limit himself to book learning and managed also to participate in "real every day practical tasks." The example of the youth brigades, Vlahović continued, showed that cadres could be formed more quickly by combining physical work with study than by just attending courses. Likewise, reports from Belgrade University's party committee even up through May 1947 continued to attack the "opportunistic line" of those who believed they could not study, be politically active, participate in cultural activities, and join work brigades all at the same time.[40]

Only the adoption of the Five Year Plan brought about a real, though gradual, de-emphasis on volunteer labor since it not only called for increased attention to the education of cadres, but also delegated the necessary resources to achieve industrialization by means of paid labor. Only then could the long-term duty of youth to provide future cadres for socialist development outweigh their direct responsibility for renovation and reconstruction.[41] Even so, the task of volunteer labor continued to dominate youth agendas throughout the spring and summer of 1947 since by the time the Five Year Plan had been adopted, mobilization and propaganda for the Šamac-Sarajevo line were already in full swing and could not be halted. Thus, although newspaper articles and internal reports regularly stressed the importance of improving grades, they did not reduce their emphasis on participation in youth brigades.[42]

Finally, in the fall of 1947, the Central Council of the PYY confessed that errors in its activity had become extremely serious and were endangering its adherence to the correct party line. Three-quarters of its activity, it now admitted, was taken up by volunteer work actions leading to serious neglect of other important issues. In the future, it concluded, although some volunteer actions would continue, there would be nothing on the order of the Youth Railways.[43] Three weeks later, the central agitprop department firmly established a new balance of priorities for youth, coming down resolutely on the side of those who emphasized studying over politics and volunteer labor. Demanding that Belgrade University's party committee reduce both the number of political meetings among students and its concentration on volunteer labor, the central agitprop department formalized a shift in the party's goals for and expectations of youth. No longer would the short-term benefits of youth activism be emphasized at the expense of youth's long-term role in the transformation of society and culture.[44]

Tito fully publicized the decision to de-emphasize youth volunteer labor in his speech at the opening of the Šamac-Sarajevo line in November 1947. In it, he thanked youth for their heroic efforts but said that the party must no longer ask them to do the impossible. Perhaps alluding to the adverse effects of the brigades on health, he stressed that youth represented the country's most valued wealth, and that, therefore, the party must guard it and show concern for its physical and mental development. In the future, he said, the tasks required would be easier and aid in the construction of the state would take second place: the first duty of youths from now on was to study and gain the knowledge necessary to serve their country.[45]

The decision by party leaders to de-emphasize youth labor brigades was both a pragmatic response to feedback from below and a reflection of the party's evolving strategy for the construction of socialism. Party leaders had been aware of and concerned by abuses in the youth volunteer labor brigade system at least as early as the fall of 1946. Yet as long as those brigades had contributed to the party's most urgent priority (at that time economic reconstruction), they had been unwilling to make the necessary changes. Once the economic situation stabilized and the Five Year Plan provided the economic resources required, party leaders were free to address their earlier concerns and work to mitigate the brigades' deleterious moral impact.

The party did not now free youths to study whatever they wished, but consciously guided them toward those professions most needed by the state. Since middle-level technical and professional cadres came mainly out of professional schools, party rhetoric worked to increase enrollment in them at the expense of gymnasiums, which offered mainly a liberal arts education and prepared students for the university. As one internal report put it, "who needs thousands of gymnasium-educated students, incapable of specialized work and recruited from the ranks of the enemy."[46]

Professional and technical fields within the universities also prospered as party leaders instructed teachers and youth organizations to direct students toward those schools and faculties of particular relevance to the new order and economy. Indeed, the Five Year Plan provided quotas for university enrollment—including the placement of students in particular schools and colleges. Distribution of financial aid also facilitated planned enrollment in specific colleges and departments. Since nearly all stipends were assigned through the colleges or departments, students who changed their majors were likely also to lose their stipends. Finally, the class curriculum itself contributed to the general economic plan by permitting greater specialization in technical fields. Even theoretical work was more closely connected to practice through increased lab time and greater emphasis on the practical applications of science.[47]

Education among the nonstudent population also took on a distinctly practical character in this period. Even the ostensibly "ideological-political" education provided in trade unions now addressed mainly economic questions. Likewise, lectures in public forums were designed to help popularize science and useful knowledge, while correcting old ideas and prejudices. Lectures were to address current issues and tasks like how to prevent typhus and malaria or how to apply new agricultural techniques, avoiding abstract and irrelevant themes as well as those that were too heavily technical.[48] Agitprop departments also worked to popularize science through the formation of amateur technical clubs in such fields as radio science, meteorology, navigation, and aviation technology.

Culture and the Media

Emphasis on such explicitly pragmatic goals in 1946 and 1947, however necessary, had a deadening effect on party rhetoric, its media, culture, and eventually the entire population. As party leaders concentrated on fulfilling concrete tasks, they became ever less tolerant of the kind of deviations typical of the first postwar year. For while rhetoric inspired by radicalism and characterized by partisanstvo and improvisation was more rousing, it was also more prone to error. Likewise, those persuasive policies designed to show CPY tolerance for pluralism inevitably risked diverging from the party line. As the party's hold on power increased, it had less need to show such tolerance; and as its concern for the successful achievement of specific tasks sharpened, it became less forgiving of political errors. The party's consolidation of power, moreover, necessarily led it to formalize rules and relationships and to institutionalize policies and programs. As a result, CPY rhetoric, while following party dictates ever more reliably, became simultaneously ever less inspiring as a means of persuasion.

Problems associated with the more pluralistic and tolerant policies of the immediate postwar period had been especially evident in the area of culture. In the first years after the war, CPY leaders had deliberately tolerated a degree of cultural pluralism in order to prove their broadmindedness and willingness to work with non-Communists. Naturally, culture produced by non-Communist writers and artists, even when politically correct, did not display the required ideological bias or Marxist worldview. However, even Communist cultural personnel did not always produce up to party expectations. It seemed that they, too, had individual tastes and preferences in art that did not always coincide with party dictates. For example, we have seen that party leaders held great hopes for Miroslav Krleža as a Communist and an artist of unquestioned talent. Yet despite the Croatian Central Committee's conviction that he had "the conditions to master our line," Krleža consistently refused to bow to party dogma and retained his own unique style. As a result, the Belgrade party's City Committee felt obliged to remove his play, *U agoniji* from the repertoire of the National Theater in 1946 as a "formalistic and decadent error of bourgeois taste."[49]

CPY cultural ambitions had also suffered at the hands of many newly inducted (and in some cases newly literate) Communist cultural figures, who often lacked either sufficient knowledge of Marxism-Leninism to ensure the ideological purity of their work and/or the necessary artistic skills to secure its aesthetic quality. Thus already in 1945, one young writer, Dušan Kostić, published an extremely critical article about the amount of bad poetry being widely recited in Belgrade. These primitive poems, he said, were composed by poets who looked for words like "bomb," "Partisan," "freedom," and "hateful occupier," considering them sufficient to make stupid lines into poetry and art. He thus recommended that cultural performances include quality works from the domestic and world classics rather than poems that, even if well intentioned, could not possibly evoke enthusiasm in anyone.[50]

Finally, the enormous variety in the form, content, and quality of cultural works produced immediately after the war reflected uncertainty, even among well-educated Communists, as to exactly how socialist realist art should look. The theoretic and programmatic principles were clear, but when it came to putting those principles into practice, even the most orthodox seemed to falter. In some cases, their efforts were as crude and narrow as those of the novices they so often rebuked, while in others, they were more aesthetically pleasing, but were then subject to criticism as insufficiently ideological, militant, relevant, or optimistic. Consequently, the vast majority of literary and artistic criticism in the late 1940s consisted of various high-level party cultural figures pointing out to one another the ideological or aesthetic inadequacies of their creative efforts.[51]

This confusion greatly complicated the efforts of CPY leaders to direct culture, while it simultaneously offered greater creative opportunities to cultural personnel. Some artists and popular performers thus devised clever methods by which they appeared to toe the orthodox line while in fact doing as they pleased. Vladimir Dedijer, for example, has recalled that the modernist painter Vojo Dimitrijević, upon learning that a prominent party leader planned to attend his first postwar exhibit, quickly penned in appropriate titles for all of his clearly modernist paintings, including, for example, the title "Dream of a Wounded Partisan at the Battle of Sutjeska" under a picture of some Parisian hallucination. The party member in question was reported to have exclaimed after viewing the exhibit, "Today for the first time I understood the essence of modern painting."[52]

Various Western and "decadent" art forms also had continued to prosper, though often under false pretenses, as may be seen in the cartoons published in the party's satirical journal, *Jež*. For example, one 1946 article sarcastically explained that in the old days, cafe music had been performed in bars free of charge so that the customers would drink more, but that now all that had changed.

> In the first place, cafe singers no longer work under such names as "Star" [*Danče*], "Lady" [*Kirče*], "Blondie" [*Beli*], "Blackie" [*Crni*], and "Beauty" [*Lepi*], but advertise themselves as members of the Union Branch of Educational Workers; they don't sing in cafes, but in halls for cultural performances; they don't collect tips, but charge an entrance fee of 20–40 dinars; in short they behave like renowned artists.

The repertoire, it continued, had also changed only in name and was now called "artistic" folk music rather than "cafe" folk music. "They pour out one 'hit' after another—a man could easily get the impression that he has just made the rounds of every bar in what used to be called Aleksandar Street. Finally they reverberate songs from 'Sunny Spain' clicking their castanets and the audience can imagine just how Franco's troops are feasting today."[53]

In response to such outrages, party rhetoric in late 1946 and 1947 increasingly urged artists to contribute more directly to the party's immediate tasks by visiting factories or volunteer labor brigades and by popularizing such activities through art, literature, or music. One article in a youth journal called on musicians to draw inspiration from the work of youth brigades digging railroad tunnels. "Comrade composers," the author exhorted them, "you who write the sounds of the songs that we are singing, come here. Do not seek melodies in the city streets or in the empty beauty of nature. Come here to see nature and people united, to hear the most beautiful music."[54] Under such directives, high culture gradually lost much, though not all, of its variety and creativity in this period, becoming ever more a "cultural means of propaganda."

Yet while the party's demands that art adopt the form and content of socialist realism became increasingly rigid and peremptory, its expectations for artistic quality grew. No longer satisfied with amateur theatrical performances and crude peasant poetry, party cultural leaders demanded that art be both technically proficient and politically correct.[55] The problem was that this feat seemed impossible to achieve and in their efforts to meet party exactions, cultural personnel sacrificed not only their artistic freedom but also their spontaneity and originality. Even more serious, the party's increasing ideological demands meant that official culture lost whatever popular appeal it had had, leading many (especially among youth) to seek out alternative and underground forms of art and entertainment.[56]

In the media too, the variety and unpredictability of the immediate postwar period now came under greater fire. For example, Srdja Prica, the editor of the trade union journal *Rad,* has recalled getting into trouble for taking the initiative in selecting a title and subtitle for one of Tito's speeches. Djilas, Zogović, and Dedijer called him into the central agitprop department and asked, "Who are you to decide what is important in Tito's speech?"[57] Under such pressures, the editors and journalists of republic and local newspapers became ever more reluctant to risk high-level censure and so relied more and more on direct instructions from agitprop departments and on models provided by the central party press. As a result, the number of local newspapers and journals declined, while those remaining became increasingly homogeneous and monotonous in both form and content.[58] Newspapers and journals thus forfeited the spontaneity of the earlier period and overflowed with tedious economic statistics; "enthusiastic" but clearly pro-forma reports from factory competitions; repeated exhortations for workers to become shockworkers, innovators, and rationalizers; and insistent pleas for increased production and savings in order to fulfill the Plan.

By late 1947, party leaders could look with some satisfaction at the results of their persuasive policies: renovation and reconstruction of the economy was well under way, production had increased, youth brigades had fulfilled their function, academic performance was slowly improving, and the first six months of the Five Year Plan had been reasonably successful. At the same time, however, they knew that in many more important ways their rhetoric had failed. Popular enthusiasm for the new regime, for politics, and for community service was on the decline, and official cultural-artistic activity, while quantitatively impressive, was artistically disappointing and unpopular.[59]

Moreover, state-society relations, which had earlier been so lively, had deteriorated into a dull monologue. Party activists were still talking, but there was less and less reason to believe that anyone was listening. CPY rhetoric, it was now clear, had not resulted in the acquisition of new values, morals, goals, aesthetics, or modes of behavior. While the party had for some time successfully exploited postwar enthusiasm and energy for its own purposes, ultimately it had stifled that enthusiasm and sapped that energy. To effect any further social change, party leaders knew that they would have to recharge their rhetoric's ideological batteries and reignite the population's ardor.

Notes

1. "Izveštaj o štampi No. 4—Listovi okružnih organizacija JNOF-a Srbije," 31 March 1945, ACKSKJ, VIII II/5-b-13; "Osvrt na slovenačku štampu iz meseca jula 1945," July 1945, ACKSKJ, VIII VI/1-b-7; "Izveštaj o listu Pobjeda," 1945, ACKSKJ, VIII VI/1-b-9.
2. "Za novi stil u radu: Ograničavajmo vreme sednica!" *20. oktobar*, 9 March 1945.
3. *Glas*, 6 March 1945.
4. Milovan Djilas, Speech at the Second Plenum of the USAOJ, 5–8 Sept. 1945, AJ, SSOJ-27.
5. "Izveštaj o štampi No. 4"; "Osvrt na slovenačku štampu"; "Izveštaj o listu Pobjeda"; "Maršal Tito primio je delegaciju CO USAOJ-a," *Politika*, 16 Jan. 1946.
6. "Izveštaj o listu *Naprijed*," 1946, ACKSKJ, VIII VI/1-b-19.
7. Ivo Sarajčić, "Nešto o zadacima političkog i kulturno-prosvetnog rada na selu u vezi sa setvom," *Borba*, 22 April 1947.
8. Milovan Djilas, "O daljem radu na ideološkom i političkom podizanju komunista i ideološkom i političkom podizanju radnih masa," 21 Sept. 1946, ACKSKJ, VIII I/1-a-6.
9. Josip Cazi, "Kulturni život radničke klase njegovan kroz sindikati," *Rad*, 8 May 1946.
10. On the Stakhanovite movement in the Soviet Union see Lewis Siegelbaum, *Stakhanovism and the Politics of Productivity in the USSR, 1935–1941* (Cambridge: Cambridge University Press, 1988); for a discussion of its use in Poland see Padraic Kenney, *Rebuilding Poland: Workers and Communists, 1945–1950* (Ithaca, NY: Cornell University Press, 1996).
11. Milijan Neorečić, "Savetovanje PK SKOJ za Srbiju," Spring 1945, ACKSKJ, CKSKOJ IIa-2/1; Djuro Spoljarić, "O takmičenju," 8–9 June 1946, AJ, CV SSJ F1-plenume; "Govor Maršala Tita na prvom sletu udarnike Srbije," *Rad*, 10 Feb. 1948. See also "Udarnike i zaslužne radnike treba pravilno i na vrijeme nagradjivati," *Rad*, 7 Aug. 1946, p. 1; "Govor Maršala Tita u Jesenicama," *Rad*, 24 Aug. 1946, p. 1.
12. Spoljarić, "O takmičenju"; Živorad Djurić, "Neprekidno takmičenje—novi metod rada," 1946, AJ, CV SSJ F1-plenume. Indeed, while agitprop for competitions naturally focused on workers, it also stressed the importance of teamwork and comradely relations with the directors. Spoljarić, "O takmičenju"; Slogans about competition, 1946, AJ, CVSSJ-F1-plenume.
13. Takmičenje beogradskih berbera i frizera: Najbolji beogradski berberin uspeo je da završi brijanje za 32 sekonda," *Politika*, 2 Jan. 1946. See also Dr. Leo Gersković, "Takmičenje—metod rada narodnih vlasti," *Politika*, 24 Jan. 1946, p. 1.

14. Djuro Spoljarić, "Uredba o radnicama i platama nepravilno se primenjuje," *Rad*, 26 Dec. 1945 (italics in the original); Zaključna reč druga Djura Salaja na Kongresu JSRNJ za Hrvatsku," *Rad*, 1 June 1946; Leon Geršković, "Za pravilnu primjenu uredba o prinadležnostima," *Borba*, 21 Oct. 1947. On the complex system of wage determination for workers see Dušan Bilandžić, *Historija Socijalističke Federativne Republike Jugoslavije: Glavni procesi, 1918–1985* (Zagreb: Školska knjiga, 1985), 122–123; Susan Woodward, *Socialist Unemployment: The Political Economy of Yugoslavia 1945–1990* (Princeton: Princeton University Press, 1995), 86–89.

15. Djuro Salaj, "Zadaci jedinstvenih sindikata u svetlosti odluka drugog kongresa NFJ," 9 Nov. 1947, AJ, CV SSJ F2-plenume; Milan Janjušević, "Takmičenje—metod rada sindikalnih organizacija," *Pobjeda*, 28 May 1947.

16. Spoljarić, "O takmičenju."

17. See "Izvještaj OK KPH Brod," 6 April 1946, HDA, CKKPH; Neorečić, "Savetovanje PK SKOJ za Srbiju"; Djurić, "Neprekidno takmičenje"; "Diskusija po referatu o takmičenju," 8 June 1946, AJ, CV SSJ F1-plenume; Janjušević, "Takmičenje—metod rada sindikalnih organizacija."

18. Milijan Neorečić, Speech at the Third Plenum of the CO USAOJ, *Politika*, 11 Jan. 1946.

19. Ibid.; Mihailo Švabić, in Milomir Marić, *Deca komunizma* (Belgrade: Mladost, 1987), 203.

20. "Zapisnik sa sastanka CK SKOJ-a," 18 Jan. 1946, in Petar Kačavenda, ed., *Kongresi, konferencije i sednice centralnih organa SKOJa (1941–1948)* (Belgrade: Izdavački centar Komunist, 1984) (hereafter *KKSKOJ, 1941–1948*); "Zahvaljući ideji rukovodstva USAOJ-a koju je prihvatila celokupna omladina stvorena je mogućnost da se u program ovogodišnjih novogradnja unese podizanje 'omladinske pruge'," *Politika*, 10 April 1946; Švabić in Marić, 203. Švabić admits that he knew nothing about railroad construction and consequently often provoked both laughter and horror among the engineers in charge. One experienced engineer swore that he would kiss Švabić "where even [your] mother never kissed [you]" if the youth brigades actually succeeded in completing the Brčko-Banovići line. Švabić did not hold him to his promise. Švabić in Marić, 205.

21. *Youth Railway*, Publication of the Central Council of the People's Youth of Yugoslavia (Belgrade: 1947).

22. "Zapisnik sa sastanka Sekretarijat CV NOJ," 26 Nov. 1946, AJ, SSOJ-55; Mihailo Švabić, "Izgradnja omladinske pruge Šamac-Sarajevo," 20–24 Jan. 1947, AJ, SSOJ-28; "Zapisnik sa sastanka UK," 25 Jan. 1947, in Momčilo Mitrović and Djordje Stanković, eds., *Zapisnici i izveštaji univerzitetskog komiteta Komunističke Partije Srbije, 1945–1948* (Belgrade: 1985) (hereafter *ZIUKKPS*), 156.

23. "Izvještaj OK SKOJ za Dalmaciju," 1 April 1946, HDA, PKSKOJ-H-2; "Zapisnik sa sastanka organizacionih sekretara KK i GK SKOJ-a za Dalmaciju," 13 June 1946, HDA, PKSKOJ-H-2; *Jež*, 14 Aug. 1948.

24. *Youth Railway*; Josif K. Prikelmajer, "'Mi smo izgradili prugu—pruga je izgradila nas'," *Republika*, 12 Nov. 1946. Statistics on cultural-educational activity for the Šamac-Sarajevo line were even more impressive. See Slavko Komar, "Značaj omladinske pruge za Narodnu omladinu Jugoslavije," *Politika*, 8 Nov. 1946; Švabić, "Izgradnja omladinske pruge Šamac-Sarajevo"; Kosta Grubačić,

"Vaspitni značaj rada na čmladinskoj pruzi," *Savremena škola*, 2, No. 2–3 (Feb.-March 1947); Slavko Komar, "Veliki radovi naše omladine," *Jugoslavija-SSSR*, 20 (June 1947); Brana Perović, "Rad omladinskih radnih brigada u 1948 godini," 1–3 Dec. 1947, AJ, SSOJ-28.

25. Švabić in Marić, 203–204.

26. "Zapisnik sa sastanka CK SKOJ-a," 19 June 1946, in *KKSKOJ, 1941–1948*, 207–211; "Zapisnik sa prvog sastanka Pretsedništva CV NOH—o idejno političkom radu na čmladinskoj pruzi," 12–13 Sept. 1946, AJ, SSOJ-37; "Zapisnik sa savetovanje rukovodilaca kulturno-prosvetnog rada," 12 May 1947, AJ, SSOJ-76; "Izveštaj o pregledu radilišta omladinskih brigada," July 1947, AJ, SSOJ-209; Dnevnik radne brigade NOJ—na gradnji omladinskog pruga Kuks-Peškopija u Albaniji," August-November 1946, AJ, SSOJ-125.

27. "Dnevnik radne brigade NOJ u Albaniji."

28. "Dnevnik Prve Banjalučke udarne brigade 'Danke Mitrović'," April to June 1947, AJ, SSOJ-127; "Dnevnik rada Druge Cazinske omladinske radne brigade," June to August 1947, AJ, SSOJ-127.

29. Mihailo Švabić, "O omladinskoj pruzi," 15–16 April 1947, AJ, SSOJ-37; "Izvještaj OK SKOJ Osijek," 4 June 1947, HDA, PKSKOJ-H-4; "Izvještaj OK SKOJ Bjelovar," 24 June 1947, HDA, PKSKOJ-H-4.

30. Rato Dugonjić, "Diskusija o referatu Švabića," 15–16 April 1947, AJ, SSOJ F37; "Zapisnik sa pretsednicima glavnih odbora," 24 June 1947, AJ, SSOJ F57.

31. Mitra Mitrović, "Kome i kakvo vaspitanje i obrazovanje," *Savremena škola*, 1, No. 1 (July 1946).

32. "Zakon o petogodišjem planu razvitka narodne privrede FNRJ u godinama 1947–1951," No. 280, *Službeni list*, 3, no. 36 (30 April 1947).

33. "Govor ministra industrije i rudarstva Rade Žigić," *Vjesnik*, 9 July 1947.

34. "Govor ministra industrije i rudarstva Rade Žigić;" Kosta Grubačić, "Naši radnici dobijaju škola za opšte obrazovanje," *Borba*, 8 Jan. 1947.

35. M. Mijušković, "Škole za opšte obrazovanje radnika," *Borba*, 7 April 1948; "Analiza o radu tetvero-razrednih škola," 1949, ACKSKJ, VIII II/8-d-55.

36. Rato Dugonjić, "Zadaci organizacije NO u novoj školskoj godini na srednjim, učiteljskim i drugim školama," 25–27 Sept. 1946, AJ, SSOJ-27; Danilo Purić, "Savetovanje OK SKOJ-a po pitanju rada srednjih škola," 1946, ACKSKJ, CKSKOJ II-a-2/3; Rato Dugonjić, "Površan i slab rad organizacija Narodne omladine na srednjim školama," *Borba*, 18 Jan. 1947; "Zapisnik sa sastanka UKKPS," 13 Feb. 1947, *ZIUKKPS*, 162–164; "Zapisnik prve konferencije KPJ na beogradskom Univerzitetu," 26 May 1947, *ZIUKKPS*, 219–237; "Zapisnik sa sastanka UK," 11 Nov. 1947, *ZIUKKPS*, 286–288; "Zadaci organizacije NO za poboljšanje uspeha u školama," 5 March 1948, AJ, SSOJ-98.

37. Stana Tomašević, "Poboljšanje rada pionirske organizacije," 25–27 Sept. 1946, AJ, SSOJ-27; "Dan pionira—radosna manifestacija stvaralačkog života," *Borba*, 8 June 1947.

38. "Zapisnik sa sastanka UK KPS," 31 May 1946, *ZIUKKPS*, 57–59; "Mesnom komitetu KPS," 19 July 1946, *ZIUKKPS*, 90–92; Concluding Speech of Rato Dugonjić, "Stenografske beleške sa savetovanja," 28 Sept. 1946, in *KKSKOJ*,

Constructing the Framework: Mobilization and Control 135

1941–1948, 285; Milijan Neorečić, Speech at "Savetovanje predstavnika SKOJ-a iz svih krajeva Jugoslavije," 28 Sept. 1946, in *KKSKOJ, 1941–1948,* 279.

39. Rato Dugonjić, "Površan i slab rad."

40. Veljko Vlahović, "Kakva treba da bude omladina naše Republike," 2 Dec. 1946, ACKSKJ, LFVV II/4-e-1. See also *ZIUKKPS,* 6 May 1946, 53; 25 Jan. 1947, 156; 26 May 1947, 222, 226.

41. Dugonjić, "Diskusija o referatu Švabića"; "Najkrupniji je zadatak omladinskih organizacija pomoć omladini u stručnom uzdizanju," *Narodni list,* 8 June 1947.

42. "Slabih ocena," *Borba,* 29 May 1947.

43. Četvrti sastanak Pretsedništva CV NOJ," 15–17 Sept. 1947, AJ, SSOJ-37.

44. "O radu partijske organizacije na univerzitetu," 7 Oct. 1947, *ZIUKKPS,* 270.

45. "Govor Maršala Tita na svećanosti prilikom puštanja u saobraćaj omladinske pruge Šamac-Sarajevo," *Borba,* 17 Nov. 1947.

46. "Osnovne smjerice naše prosvjetne politike," 1947, HDA, CKKPHAP. See also "Konferencija prosvetnih radnika Srbije, Vojvodine, i Kosovsko-Metohijske oblasti," *Borba,* 16 Oct. 1945; "Referat Marice Kresojević na sastanku komisije na srednje škole," May 1946, AJ, SSOJ-2; "Savetovanje omladinskih rukovodilaca o radu u novoj školskoj godini," *Prosvetni radnik,* 15 Sept. 1947; Milislav Mijušković, "Srednjoškolska omladina pred izborom poziva," *Prosvetni radnik,* 15 June 1948.

47. Boris Ziherl, "Zadaci našeg školstva i naučnih ustanova," *Savremena škola,* 1, no. 3 (September 1946); Vlahović, "Kakva treba da bude omladina"; "Zapisnik prve konferencije KPJ na beogradskom Univerzitetu," 26 May 1947, *ZIUKKPS,* 219–237; "Sistem nastave na Beogradskom univerzitetu," after 1 June 1948, ACKSKJ, VIII VI/2-e-3.

48. "Idejno-politički rad u masama," 1947, ACKSKJ, VIII II/6-10; R. Uvalić, "O radu naših rejonskih univerziteta," *20. oktobar,* 7 Sept. 1945; "Zadaci narodnih univerziteta u okviru rada domova kultura," *Borba,* 14 Jan. 1947; "Organizacija, dosadašnji rad i zadaci kulturno-prosvjetnog rada na selu," 1947, HDA, CKKPHAP.

49. Marko Lopušina, *Crna knjiga: Cenzura u Jugoslaviji, 1945–91* (Belgrade: Fokus, 1991), 26.

50. Dušan Kostić, "O jednoj 'poeziji' koja nije poezija," *20. oktobar,* 17 Aug. 1945.

51. In an ironic contrast, the young painter Božidar Ilić, who received widespread official praise for his massive painting on a wartime theme in 1949, later admitted that he had no idea what socialist realism was but that he read the works of socialist art critics and watched Soviet films. Marić, 230.

52. Vladimir Dedijer, *Novi prilozi za biografiju Josipa Broza Tita,* Vol. 3 (Belgrade: Rad, 1984), 218–219. See also "U duhu vremena," *Jež,* 8 Dec. 1945.

53. "Nalik gajde na muziku," *Jež,* 27 April 1946.

54. Skupština Udruženja književnika Srbije," *Naša književnost,* 2, no. 4 (April 1947); Mira Alečković, "Novoj pruzi naš pozdrav," *Mladost,* 3, no. 4 (April 1947). See also "Filmski pregled: Film o mladim junacima s pruge," *Borba,* 10 March 1947; "Književnici Srbije na omladinskoj pruzi," *Naša književnost,* 2, no. 11–12 (November-December 1947): 464.

55. "Savetovanje rukovodilaca Sekcije pozorišnih radnika," *Prosvetni radnik,* 1 Nov. 1947.

56. For more on this topic see Chapter 9.
57. Srdja Prica in Marić, 149.
58. "Kratka analiza naše štampe, sa savetovanja iz republike," 1 Oct. 1947, ACKSKJ, VIII VI/1-b-24; Vladimir Dedijer, "Uloga štampe i njeno mesto u partiskom radu," 24 Oct. 1947, ACKSKJ, VIII IV-a-2.
59. For more information on the decline in public enthusiasm see Chapter 6.

6
The Cultural Transformation Begins

CPY persuasive policies in the first three years after the Second World War had focused on the party's immediate political and economic rather than long-term transformative goals. Concerned less to modify people's thoughts than their actions, party rhetoric had not so much endeavored to change Yugoslavia's culture as to manipulate it for the party's benefit. In other words, up until late 1947, the CPY did not truly attempt ideological indoctrination of the Yugoslav population; it expected people to do the right thing but did not insist that they do so for the right reason. In the fall of 1947, however, the CPY entered a further stage on its journey to the "new and better future." Taking advantage of the new opportunities offered by its increasingly strong position in power, the party now stepped up its program of socialist development and took on new tasks that required also modifications in the form and content of its persuasive policies.

By late 1947, party leaders had publicly admitted their goal of building socialism and could therefore increase efforts to attain that goal. In addition, the party initiated, in late 1947, its campaign for socialization of the countryside, thereby setting the stage for a likely confrontation with the peasantry. Finally, and at the same time, the party came face-to-face with the declining level of enthusiasm and energy among Yugoslavia's populace. These combined pressures forced party leaders to advance their progress toward socialism and to address now the more complex tasks of ideological reeducation and indoctrination. As a result, they reexamined their persuasive policies and began not only to demand more of them, but also to consider the kinds of cultural and educational changes necessary if those demands were to be fulfilled. Consequently, CPY rhetoric in late 1947 began to focus more directly on the party's long-term transformative goals, which it now admitted to be explicitly based on Marxist-

Leninist ideology. While such rhetoric was supposed to be inspirational, it was more often self-consciously pedagogical. After all, Yugoslavia's citizens could participate in and contribute to the cultural and social transformation only if they truly understood and accepted Marxist-Leninist principles as the basis of that transformation. Thus, although party and agitprop leaders were concerned by stagnating state-society relations, their increasingly didactic rhetoric did nothing to invigorate them.

New Goals and New Expectations

In the first years of Communist rule, fearing to alienate the population and provoke Western hostility, CPY rhetoric had camouflaged the party's socialist intentions with a kind of "people's liberation struggle" vocabulary. By mid-1947, however, CPY concern for its domestic and international political position gradually diminished, and public statements about the party's ideological goals began to appear. The party first openly admitted that it was building socialism in connection with passage of the First Five Year Plan in April 1947. Such assertions did not become widespread and commonplace, however, until the fall of that year, by which time all important rivals for power had been successfully marginalized, co-opted, or eliminated.[1] After late 1947, the party no longer disguised its intentions, but openly and proudly declared its goal of building a socialist, and eventually Communist, society.

CPY acknowledgment of its plan to build socialism necessarily influenced the form and content of its persuasive policies. On the most superficial level, it meant discontinuing some, though not all, of its linguistic maneuvers. While previously emphasized principles about community service and "brotherhood and unity" remained strong, the new rhetoric also emphasized many values and goals much more explicitly connected with socialism. For example, the country's increasingly close ties with the Soviet Union and other Eastern bloc countries were now justified in ideological (not pan-Slavic) terms. More importantly, however, the party's open avowal of Marxism-Leninism allowed, and indeed required, party rhetoric to become more honest about its ideological foundations. For if the CPY were to build socialism, its persuasive organs must explain what that meant; they must inform people about Marxist-Leninist ideology—its values, goals, attributes, and necessary preconditions. Such rhetoric inevitably took on a strongly pedagogical tone.

A second factor influencing the party's persuasive policies in late 1947 and early 1948 concerned its past economic progress and future goals. By late 1947, the party had managed to reestablish the country's infrastructure and economy through the concentrated mobilization of material and human resources. In addition, it had laid the economic foundations for socialism through legislation on nationalization, agrarian reform, wages, and peasant cooperatives. Most recently, party leaders believed, the Five Year Plan had secured the country's socialist future, specifying not only the direction and pace of further economic growth but also the resources required to achieve it.[2] Now party leaders faced only one further stumbling block in their economic construction of socialism—the continuing private ownership of agricultural land. Hence, party rhetoric now spoke openly about the abolition of private ownership of property as an integral part of Marxist-Leninist ideology.

CPY leaders unquestionably anticipated full socialization of the countryside in Yugoslavia, including the eventual elimination of small-scale private farming.[3] Some form of collectivized agriculture not only made up an integral part of what the CPY understood socialism to mean, but was also the only known means of introducing the peasants and agricultural production into a planned socialist economy. Up until late 1947, however, party leaders had repeatedly denied any such intention, fearing to alienate the peasants and provoke Western hostility.[4] Moreover, while party leaders had not hesitated to use force against peasants in their mandatory grain requisitioning policy known as the *otkup*, they also clearly wished to avoid the kind of violence and social disorder that had characterized Soviet relations with the peasantry. Socialization of the countryside in Yugoslavia, they believed, would follow a different, slower, and less violent path, through voluntary enrollment in various forms of peasant cooperatives. With the co-ops, Kardelj explained, "we would find our own special path toward collectivization in the village."[5]

The party even took a relatively cautious approach toward the cooperative movement in its first years. Most cooperatives formed just after the war offered members improved access to credit or various supplies, while only a very few—the "Peasant Working Cooperatives" (PWCs)—provided for common cultivation of land. Although party rhetoric had not particularly urged the formation of PWCs in the first years after the war, adoption of the Five Year Plan enhanced their economic importance as organizations that would secure the food and industrial crops necessary for further industrialization.[6] Party leaders also expected PWCs to serve a political and ideological purpose by including peasants in the construction of socialism and making them more active in state affairs. "The cooperative will, in fact, be a school which will teach the peasant administration of the state," Kardelj asserted. Finally, as mass organizations dedicated to the peasantry, PWCs would enlighten peasants, raise their consciousness, and nurture a spirit of collectivity and solidarity leading to ideological progress.[7]

Yet despite the PWCs' importance for the Five Year Plan and Yugoslavia's socialist development, rhetoric about them remained minimal throughout most of 1947. It began to increase only in November of that year, once party leaders had initiated the move toward socialization of the countryside by calling for the construction of 6,000 village cooperative centers. These centers, which were to be built by local volunteer youth labor brigades, were to provide the material basis for the later socialization of agriculture. At this point, however, the campaign was clearly in its embryonic stage, and although rhetoric for PWCs did gradually increase, it remained relatively low-key, directed more at the youth who would build the new centers than at the peasants who would later join them.[8]

One explanation for the party's cautious approach on this issue may have been its awareness of likely failure. Indeed, even such limited advocacy of PWCs as did exist in early 1948 met stern resistance from peasants who said they didn't want to live *"po diktatu"* (by decree).[9] That peasant resistance further influenced party leaders to modify their demands on agitprop departments and other persuasive organs. For if peasants were to enter PWCs voluntarily—as the party intended—they would have to accept fully the values of collectivism and believe in the party's plan to realize a better future. Not only, then, would party rhetoric have to focus more on peasants, it would have to become more educational, more inspiring, and above all more convincing.[10]

One final development in late 1947 and early 1948 that compelled party leaders to reassess their persuasive activities was the evident sharp decline in the population's enthusiasm and willingness to sacrifice for the future. Exhausted from four years of war and another three of feverish postwar activity, intimidated by CPY coercive policies, and frankly bored by ceaseless party rhetoric, Yugoslav citizens had apparently begun to lose interest in politics. As one speaker at a meeting of the central agitprop department complained, "there is no more that intense political life as occurred during the war and directly after liberation."[11] Yugoslav citizens now often ignored CPY calls for constant political activism and self-sacrificing labor, expressing instead their desire to return to "normal life." In order to revive that sense of enthusiasm and self-sacrifice and hence revitalize the moribund state-society relations, party leaders knew that they would have to enhance the role and hone the efficacy of their persuasive policies.

Culture and Ideology

Essentially, CPY leaders now had to admit that their persuasive policies had failed in many important respects. The rhetoric's narrow economic and political focus, they now realized, had made it dry and dull, while centralized control over its form and content had made it uniform and

The Cultural Transformation Begins 141

stereotyped. Moreover, party rhetoric, which concentrated almost entirely on specific tasks often without explaining their larger implications or relationship to the overall future of the country, lacked any educational and inspirational impact. One indicator of failure by CPY persuasion was the disappointingly low circulation figures for the party press. While problems of transportation and distribution had long plagued the party's persuasive efforts, by 1948 party leaders could no longer blame only logistical problems for continuing low subscription and readership. Another such indicator concerned the party's efforts in the fields of high and popular culture.

By late 1947 and early 1948, party leaders were increasingly aware that cultural personnel were failing to live up to CPY expectations. For example, although party cultural leaders had incessantly stressed the need for new dramatic works and had held regular competitions designed to produce them, the resulting manuscripts were admitted to be crude, narrow, trivial, unrealistic, and filled with characters who, according to the Communist theater critic Velibor Gligorić, spoke "like newspaper articles."[12] Nor were party leaders satisfied with their persuasive impact on writers, as may be seen in Tito's later confession to Louis Adamic:

> Frankly, our writers are not producing anything substantial. Drug Kardelj is worried too. He and Djilas and I talked about it the other day. I don't know what the matter is. In Old Yugoslavia scarcely anybody made a living writing.... Now poets, novelists, and journalists are well paid for everything they do; in fact, they receive huge honoraria for books they wrote before the war which are being reprinted; *but*—[13]

While the results of CPY policies directed at high culture were disappointing, their consequences in the realm of popular culture were truly alarming. Bored by the officially produced and promoted "ideological entertainment," Yugoslavia's citizens, and especially youth, had quickly returned to more traditional forms of amusement. Throughout late 1947 and 1948 numerous articles and reports recorded a desperate lack of "quality" entertainment. Although the party had stressed that the working man should "spend his free time in a cultural manner," and that "in our life today, there is no place for entertainment without a purpose," both internal reports and published articles nonetheless complained that cultural performances were often followed by parties with alcohol and dancing. The dances themselves were, moreover, often of the "warped Western variety," and although jazz music theoretically did "not at all come into consideration for use," it was evidently quite common at parties and performances for youth. In the spring of 1948, the Philosophical Faculty of Belgrade University booked a jazz orchestra to ensure that its spring dance made a profit. Worse yet, jury members for an artistic competition in February of that year complained that even a song from the voluntary youth labor brigades had been put to jazz music.[14] The very thought makes one shudder!

Ultimately, it became clear that the party's combined demands on culture—that it be ideologically correct, highly aesthetic, and popular—were impossible to achieve. Postwar cultural figures could create works of art, literature, or film that were popular, but which lacked aesthetic quality or correct ideological content or both. Or they could create works with high ideological content, but which were then utterly unappealing or unaesthetic or both. Or they could create works of high aesthetic quality, but which then lacked the correct ideological component or were unloved by the masses or both. Thus the CPY found itself facing two serious problems with regard to its cultural activities. It could not induce its cultural personnel, either by carrot or stick, to produce quality socialist realist culture, nor could it persuade the Yugoslav population to use and appreciate the poor quality but politically correct materials they did provide. Rather, the "masses" seemed stubbornly attached to "vulgar," "apolitical," or "decadent" forms of culture and entertainment.

In short, the party found that it had not been able to eliminate the gap between high and popular culture. Artists and writers of talent could not help but wish to create and enjoy art and literature that corresponded to their own elevated tastes. Thus, even on those rare occasions when the officially sanctioned culture met with public approval, it often drew fire from the more educated cultural personnel for its technical or artistic inadequacies.[15] In any case, the Yugoslav public showed a clear preference for cafes, alcohol, light music, jazz, and dancing to concertos and operettas, and for newspapers full of light news and sports to heavy-handed political journals. Women still preferred fashion journals with pictures of the latest Parisian evening gowns to those women's magazines that emphasized the role of new socialist females in the construction of socialism; and youth preferred comic strips and cowboy movies to socialist realist classics about resistance to "enemies of the people."

As young people, in particular, became less active in the political and social sphere, they focused more on satisfying personal needs and interests. And while CPY leaders counted on youth to become great producers and consumers of socialist realist culture, they most often satisfied their cultural and entertainment needs with Western popular culture, despite (or perhaps because of) party attempts to prohibit it. In other words, the party's cultural policies had not created new people with new values and aesthetic tastes. If anything, those policies counteracted party ends by forcing many producers and consumers of culture into a stance of opposition. For when Yugoslavia's artists and citizens rejected the official fare and sought out alternative or underground forms of culture, party leaders assumed that they were also rejecting the party's vision of the future or at least its path toward that future. The alternative and underground culture thus acquired both within the party and among the broader population the mystique of a counterculture and a political relevance it might otherwise have lacked.

The party's growing concern over the failure of its cultural policies coincided with its first efforts in late 1947 and early 1948 to initiate the transformation of society and culture in accordance with Communist values. The party's persuasive activities, its leaders now realized, had successfully mobilized existing energies and manipulated existing cultural agendas, but they had not imbued the population with new values, goals, aesthetics, and behavioral norms, nor would they. The party's new tasks required new forms and methods of persuasion. For if it were to usher enthusiastic peasants into the cooperatives, inspire the population to continued acts of self-sacrifice, and ultimately achieve full communism, party rhetoric would have to become far more complex and sophisticated; it would have to be less directive and more explanatory, less injunctive and more educational, less formulaic and more flexible. Rhetoric that had so far aspired only to make people do the right thing would now have to try to make them think the right way.

The leadership's initial guidance in this budding effort to transform the Yugoslav population through educational persuasion was rather vague and uncertain. Party leaders produced, for example, no fundamental programmatic statement detailing the new functions and tasks of agitprop departments. Rather, just as party leaders had signalled a change in goals after the November 1945 elections by criticizing the excessively broad rhetorical strategy and calling for more economic work, it now condemned the limited focus and "dry practicism" of persuasive activities over the preceding two years and demanded that they become more ideological, more educational, and more effective. Rhetoric for the Five Year Plan, for example, came under attack from central agitprop leaders because "it did not . . . lead a struggle for reeducating the people, for raising the political and ideological consciousness of the masses, for introducing a socialist concept into work." Likewise a report on trade unions complained that ideological work in them was "often neglected before the ongoing economic tasks." Even the pioneer press—directed at children under 15 years of age—drew fire from the leadership of the PYY for its inadequate political and ideological content.[16]

The party's first new demand of its persuasive organs was that they pay more attention to the role and significance of Communist ideology in new Yugoslavia. Party leaders called for greater emphasis on Marxism-Leninism in nearly all party, state, and mass organizations.[17] They urged the press to avoid all "dry practicism" and to strive for the ideological reeducation of the population through expanded treatment of Marxism-Leninism and increased attention to the party's broad perspectives for the future.[18] They demanded that the educational curriculum show increased ideological content beginning even in first grade readers.[19] And while demands for ideological content in high culture had been more or less standard (although unsuccessful) since mid-1946, party cultural leaders now greatly heightened their emphasis on ensuring the proper content of popular and mass culture. One trade union report complained, for example, that amateur cultural-artistic societies showed considerable petty bourgeois influence since trade union and party leaders treated them as entertainment organizations rather than as ideological-political and educational forums.[20]

In conjunction with the party's campaign for socialization of the village, CPY rhetoric now also began to demand ideological content even in peasant culture. An article in a journal dedicated to the cooperative movement, for example, recommended that the books in village libraries be carefully scrutinized for their ideological, scientific, and artistic value, since

> it is not irrelevant whether the libraries will hold various horoscopes, cheap travelogues from hot Africa, five-penny novels of criminal content, farcical theatrical pieces, and useless, non-ideological, backward, and reactionary literature, or real, useful, good, socially positive, artistically and scientifically valuable books, folk poetry, realistic stories, novels or chronicles, popular science, and political books or brochures.[21]

By mid-1948 some party rhetoric also began to urge that village culture come closer to the city and move beyond the boundaries of folklore. According to Serbian agitprop leader Bora Drenovac, folkore was a part of history and should be studied, but need not necessarily be included in all programs.[22]

In concert with the party's heightened concern for Marxism-Leninism, some party activists also called for a harder line in relation to the party's ideological opponents. Several speakers at a conference of the Committee for Schools and Science in the spring of 1948 expressed deep displeasure that the struggle against religion in the schools had eased off, and they worried that the number of students attending religious studies courses was far too high.[23] Likewise, CPY conciliation of the Croat Republican Peasant Party and its followers gradually waned as memos from the central agitprop department now warned against mixing the party line with that of the Radić brothers. "It is necessary to use some positive sides of 'Seljačka sloga', but we must not create a Marxist-Radićist ideological line."[24]

Beyond calling for increased ideological content, party leaders also urged persuasive personnel to adopt more educational methods. After all, if rhetoric were to change people's minds, it would have to move beyond slogans and posters to more substantial explanations of and arguments for Communist ideology. Once party leaders had openly acknowledged their goals, they expected all citizens of Yugoslavia to learn the basic tenets of Marxism-Leninism and to develop a whole new way of looking at the world. By learning the foundations of historical and dialectical materialism, they believed, Yugoslavia's citizens would come to understand and accept fully the rational necessity and inherent validity of the regime's new values and social norms. Subsequently, they would behave "correctly" not because they had been told to but because they now understood the purpose of such behavior and saw it as contributing to their own interests.

In the future, therefore, not only would newspaper articles and public lectures have to offer greater depth, but agitprop departments would have to provide more forums for the teaching of Marxism-Leninism. Previously restricted almost entirely to CPY and SKOJ members, Marxist-Leninist education now could and must be made available to the entire population through courses and lectures in all state and mass organizations, public schools, trade unions, and peasant cooperatives.[25] Several party activists even suggested that Communists and non-Communists now study together in order to avoid duplication of efforts.[26]

Finally, realizing that shouted slogans and blatant propaganda would not change anyone's mind, party leaders demanded that the persuasive rhetoric become more effective by raising its level of sophistication, originality, and popular appeal. Consequently, some activists now began to couch their calls for more ideology in somewhat more elevated terms, warning against the adoption of a "moralizing and didactic tone" and suggesting that the ideological message be carefully integrated within each subject so that it seemed a natural part of the topic and not something external to it.[27]

Faced with lagging public enthusiasm, some party leaders also began gradually to accept that the rhetoric would have to be made more enticing and would have to reflect the interests of the population as well as those of the party. After all, even the best party newspapers could not fulfill their educational role if no one read them. The Central Committee critique of the Macedonian paper *Nova Makedonija* thus argued that it had not become an organizer and leader of the masses because it was "insufficiently interesting and lively."[28] Another consequence of party demands that the press become more popular was its increased attention to the role of humor and satire. Already in 1945, the party had resumed publication of a prewar satirical paper, *Jež* (Hedgehog), despite Djilas's concern that the party was not yet ready for satire. "I do not see how we can publish a humorist and satirical paper," he worried, "if it is not permitted to touch the government, army, and police. And it is not!" Indeed, the resulting newspaper was in many ways appallingly crude and blunt, leading to jibes from *Demokratija* that *Jež* had apparently lost many of its previously razor-sharp quills.[29] In 1948, a series of articles by top CPY cultural leaders in the central literary journal *Književne novine* addressed the problem directly and admitted that CPY humoristic efforts had thus far been largely illogical, superficial, and one-sided, offering characters so stereotyped that they lost their emotive power and failed to inspire the necessary hatred. The authors now called for fighting and realistic satire that would discover and reproduce typical characters instantly recognizable as representatives of a particular class or group.[30] Not surprisingly, such politically correct satire produced on demand remained distinctly unappealing, uninspiring, and, most of all, unfunny.

In their quest for more inventive, elevated, and persuasive rhetoric, party leaders now began also to doubt the value of the Soviet example. Up to this point, and with some exceptions, CPY agitprop leaders had generally followed the cultural and educational models established by Soviet agitprop departments. By late 1947, however, party leaders were beginning to see that the Soviet rhetoric was not only often inappropriate for Yugoslav circumstances but was too simplistic and crude to bring about real social or cultural change. Consequently, they began warning agitprop personnel against the indiscriminate application of Soviet models to their own work.

Vladimir Dedijer, for example, argued in October 1947 that while the Soviet and Yugoslav press shared the same ideological line, not even *Borba* was directive to the same extent as Soviet newspapers. "Our press has more of an initiative character, it influences the masses to invest as much as possible into the completion of individual tasks, not in the form of directives but by explaining the need for those tasks to be completed."[31] Several months later, Djilas warned against publishing inappropriate materials from the Soviet Union:

> It is always necessary to take into account our specific path of development, our specific method of building socialism, and not automatically seize on everything that is Soviet. We agree in essence with the positions and critiques of the Central Committee of the All-Union Communist Party (Bolshevik), but the path, the form in which it is given does not correspond to our situation. Therefore it is necessary to proceed cautiously with the publication of such things!

He especially criticized the November 1947 translation and publication of a highly nationalistic article by the head of the Soviet Writers' Union, Aleksandr Fadeev. The article, Djilas insisted, should not have been published because "in our opinion it is incorrect, or at least does not agree with us."[32]

In the arts, too, party cultural leaders became increasingly disillusioned with Soviet models. A disastrous early attempt at collaboration in film-making had ended all further discussion about the establishment of a joint Soviet-Yugoslav film company, and already in March 1948 the government's cinematography committee replaced a course on socialist realism in its film school with one on aesthetics.[33] Party leaders now also discovered that Soviet "hit" music was often no better than that from the West. At an agitprop meeting in December 1947, Djilas advised radio stations to take from Russia only its very best light music, and two months later Serbian Minister of Education Mitra Mitrović stated bluntly that "in the U.S.S.R. works can be created that are more decadent than those in America . . . Serving up slogans as art is decadent."[34]

Finally, the party's concern to improve its persuasive policies led to calls for "greater initiative from below" and less direct interference by agitprop departments. In an October 1947 report, Dedijer worried about the uniformity of existing newspapers and the dangerous tendency to eliminate papers. Rather, he insisted, as life becomes more complex, there should be ever more newspapers. Already the previous May, he explained, Djilas had tried to decrease the involvement of agitprop departments in day-to-day decision making, but as a result, some departments had ended all their contact with the press while others continued to act as editorial boards and daily censors. Both occurrences, he stressed, were incorrect; editorial boards were not to halt all contact with the agitprop departments, but neither were they to bring every article to them for approval. Rather, they were to act as independent political bodies, reacting to events on the basis of their own initiative.[35] Djilas reiterated this position at the Fifth Party Congress in July 1948 when he insisted that agitprop departments should not try to exert their authority over everything. "This concept acts as a brake on the ideological struggle and leads to the fact that some agitprop departments kill the initiative that has appeared in various fields either from below or from the side."[36]

Yet official ambiguity over the role and authority of agitprop departments remained since middle- and lower-level activists still could not be trusted to grasp and apply the party line correctly. Left on their own, such activists too often made serious political or ideological "mistakes." Moreover, they seemed incapable of composing persuasive rhetoric that was simultaneously correct, sophisticated, original, and appealing. It was this gap between policies as dictated at the top and as applied in the field that finally led party leaders to address what they now saw as an underlying source of their failures in the field of persuasion—the low educational and ideological level of those assigned to carry out the party's persuasive policies.

Educating the Educators

The leaders of agitprop departments in the postwar period regularly complained about the low priority granted to their work and the low caliber of personnel assigned to persuasive tasks. Djilas later confirmed that agitprop departments did not receive the same attention as more important sectors like the army, police, and economic bodies, nor, according to him, should they have.[37] In any case, since there simply were not enough well-educated loyal Communists available to implement the party's persuasive policies, the CPY had to make do with many less-qualified individuals. It was partly for this reason that agitprop departments accepted the continued employment of many non-Communists in several important fields of persuasive activity.

Non-Communist, though cooperative, journalists, for example, long remained active in both the party and nonparty press. In the fall of 1947, a document from Croatia complained that only 10 of 26 journalists on the staff of the Croatian Communist party's organ, *Vjesnik*, and only 5 out of 27 journalists at Zagreb's main local organ were Communists. Other reports from central agitprop organizations claimed that anywhere from 33 percent to 81 percent of the journalists of various important newspapers (including *Borba*) were prewar cadres who exerted a strong "petty-bourgeois influence" on their newspapers.[38] Meanwhile, party activists in educational institutions referred to the weak authority of party and SKOJ members in schools and universities. Many elementary schoolteachers had close ties to the church, and Croatia's minister of education in the first years after the war was a member of the Croat Republican Peasant Party. CPY influence was even more uncertain among university professors since there were so few Communists among them. Even by the end of June 1948, only 7 percent of the teachers and administrators at Belgrade University were members of the CPY.[39] Persuasive activities in mass organizations also relied heavily on the participation of non-Communists. Although such activities theoretically took place in "cultural-educational departments" under direct leadership of the party, in the trade unions, for example, cultural-educational departments not only did not always exist in the first years after the war, but where they did exist they were not always under party control. According to a union report from late 1946, the cultural-educational departments of many trade unions contained no Communists at all.[40]

In the first years after the war, use of nonparty cadres had served CPY interests by demonstrating the party's tolerance and willingness to work with non-Communists. But while cooperative and capable non-Communists might satisfactorily repeat and promote party policies, they could not be trusted accurately to explain Marxist-Leninist ideology or properly to imbue their speeches, articles, and cultural productions with its content and values. Consequently, party leaders in late 1947 and 1948 increasingly complained about the continued presence of non-Communists in many crucial areas of Yugoslav cultural and public life. Non-Communist journalists, many activists now claimed, could not help Yugoslavia's newspapers fulfill their role as mobilizers and organizers of all forces in the country; nor could teachers with backward, reactionary views carry out the proper socialist education of youth. Indeed, the title of one article in the leading literary newspaper read "The Educators Themselves Must be Educated."[41]

Party leaders hoped now to rectify the situation both by reeducating the existing cadres and by creating new ones who would be well versed in the principles of Marxist-Leninist ideology. In the future, party leaders explained, journalists would need to have both a broad general education and sufficient political and ideological qualifications to see objects and events dialectically in their ceaseless connections and processes.[42] Consequently, the first meeting of the Union of Journalists' Associations, held in December 1947, declared its main task to be the ideological-political construction of journalistic cadres and recommended formation of a journalism school. By the end of 1948, the recommended school had been created and offered a curriculum replete with courses on Marxism-Leninism.[43]

CPY concern for the proper ideological education of teachers also increased in late 1947 and early 1948, since party demands for greater ideological content could not be met by the existing educators. In fact, party leaders had recommended the formation of special courses on Marxist-Leninist theory as early as 1946, yet documents through 1949 continued to report that they were not being held because there was no one qualified to teach them.[44] By late 1947 and early 1948, party rhetoric began instructing teachers that they must now master the principles of Communist education and the theories of Marxism-Leninism in order to become "conscious builders of the new society." It called on teachers to reeducate themselves through theoretical study of the classics of Marx, Engels, Lenin, Stalin, and Tito, both individually and in courses organized by the Union of Educational Workers. Communist educational leader Marijan Stilinović explained, it is "absolutely necessary that each of our teachers and directors have the works of Comrade Tito constantly at hand, and that they serve as a guidebook in their work."[45]

In accordance with their heightened attention to the role of cultural cadres, party leaders now also began to urge a modification of the educational curriculum, away from excessive specialization in technological fields and back toward an appreciation for the liberal arts. After all, as one unsigned article in *Borba* stressed, building human resources was just as honorable as building technical and material ones. Several other articles in *Borba* further complained that too many university students had enrolled in the departments of technology and law, while too few were in those for philosophy, mathematics, and education; and by the spring of 1948, the ministry of education had agreed to reactivate at least one classical gymnasium in each republic in order to create new cadres in the fields of philosophy, archeology, history, classical philology, and art history.[46] In addition, the curriculum for teachers' schools was now modified to include courses on both "aesthetics" and "moral upbringing," the latter of which offered sections on the development of patriotism, the nurturing of humanism, the encouragement of collectivism and discipline, and the development of willpower.[47]

Finally, and perhaps most importantly, party leaders now also applied themselves more seriously to the general and ideological education of party members themselves. For while non-Communists understandably often failed to live up to the party's increasing ideological demands, so, too, did many party members. Having joined the party during or after the war and lacking the educational basis necessary to take up philosophical studies, many party members were clearly unprepared to explain and defend Communist ideology.

CPY leaders had understood the need for and importance of ideological education among lower cadres from the very outset, and they had immediately organized lectures, reading groups, courses, and even schools for party members at all levels. Yet the success of those efforts remains uncertain. Given the very low level from which many began, some improvement was inevitable; yet one report on such work from the Croatian agitprop department admitted that only half of those enrolled in evening courses had finished and that of 558 students who had enrolled in the party's correspondence school in 1948, only 89 had actually taken and passed the exam.[48]

Certainly, CPY work on the ideological education of its members was fraught with difficulties. Not only did party educators often lack the necessary material resources, but both they and their students lacked the time and energy to devote to educational efforts. Party members were, after all, among the most overburdened members of postwar Yugoslav society. Many held numerous different responsibilities within party, state, and mass organizations, and they truly had little free time for self-improvement. A report on cultural and political life in the trade unions claimed that many of its functionaries did not have time even to read *Borba*, while an organizer of the lower party correspondence school in Croatia proposed dropping demands for written work because members simply did not have time to do it.[49]

Moreover, many party and especially SKOJ members apparently showed little interest in furthering their education. Party and youth leaders regularly complained about the lax attitude toward studying among their members, and the leaders of one local party committee even claimed that the main task of their theoretical department consisted in trying to get party cadres regularly to attend lectures and study circles. Nor was the situation much better at the higher levels; in a speech to the Central Committee of SKOJ, Neorečić claimed that some youth leaders had not read a single book in over six months.[50]

Only in late 1947 and early 1948 did CPY leaders seem to realize the extent of the problem and begin fully to grasp the importance of individual cadres for the ultimate success of their policies. After all, if party persuasive policies were to become more complex and sophisticated, so too must the personnel responsible for their execution. Likewise, party demands for greater "initiative from below" had to be accompanied by increased ideological training of lower cadres if they were not to result in serious deviations from the party line. Finally, as it had become increasingly clear that poorly educated and badly behaved cadres often served only to discredit the party and its program for change, CPY leaders now placed greater emphasis on the importance of party members as role models. An internal circular from 1947, for example, explained that Communists should serve in the People's Front as respectful, modest, well-behaved, tactful teachers. In fact, however, it complained, some Communists were not even formal members of the Front and did not attend its meetings or carry out its tasks. Some party members, the memo continued, refuse to give up their own grain surplus, talk about reading but don't do it, do not know the basic articles of the Constitution and other laws, and are drunks. "Can such people be leaders of the PFY?" it asked. Obviously not.[51]

Consequently, CPY leaders now stressed the need for increased ideological education in order both to make party members better able to fulfill new and more complicated tasks and to transform them into model members of society, capable of inspiring others. Memos from agitprop departments urged party members to increase their education not only through organized course work but also and especially through independent study. They did not explain, however, how party and SKOJ members were to be induced to show concern for self-development; nor did they offer a solution to the problem of time. Rather they simply insisted that more ideological education was necessary and that party members must find time for it. Finally, such memos did not explain how Communists, who often had only a minimal general education or were even illiterate, could possibly engage in independent study of Marxism-Leninism.[52]

Party leaders did, however, further increase their emphasis on the importance of education in general, arguing now even more forcefully for the precedence of education over political activity and volunteer labor. In the first place, teachers and professors were encouraged to place primary emphasis on their educational function. Already in June 1947, Djilas sent a memo from the central agitprop department to republic agitprop departments explaining that although the party badly needed people in the universities who were both highly qualified and loyal, the few Communist professors it could claim were terribly overburdened with functions in trade unions, mass organizations, cultural-educational clubs, and so on. As a result, they often came to class unprepared and developed a reputation as bad lecturers who considered educational tasks secondary to political ones. Meanwhile, professors hostile to the regime increased their authority by attending class well prepared, providing excellent lectures, working in scientific institutions, and meeting regularly with students. Djilas concluded that Communist professors must be relieved of other duties, because "one professional and politically-qualified teacher educating the new generation of people's specialists contributes much more to the construction of our country than [he does] by fulfilling any kind of secondary job in the mass organizations."[53] Later that year and into 1948, other leading Communists in various educational organizations also took up the plea, urging that teachers at all levels be relieved of other duties so that they could improve themselves and their courses.[54]

Students, too, were now clearly directed to privilege educational over political or economic goals. A meeting between central agitprop members and Belgrade University's party committee in the fall of 1947, for example, concluded that the committee must reduce both the number of its political meetings among students and its concentration on volunteer labor in order to facilitate the educational process. Indeed, students at Belgrade University were released from participation in the following summer's work brigades so that they might catch up on their school work.[55]

The party's new approach to the proper goals for youth was in part another indicator of its evolving strategy for the construction of socialism. Youth political activism and volunteer labor had been crucial in helping to achieve the party's initial goals of political power and economic stability. By late 1947 and early 1948, however, those aims had been realized and the party's long-term plans for youth as new socialist people could take precedence over its short-term exploitation of youth activism. Party leaders now became convinced that in order to achieve their ultimate goal, both Communist and non-Communist youth must concentrate on raising their professional and ideological qualifications by more formal education in the school system.

These changes also, however, reflected the CPY's continuing ambivalence about and ultimately its refusal to accept the unpredictable consequences of genuine activism from below. While many youth had heeded the party's call to remake society, they did not always limit their activism to its precise prescriptions. In taking the initiative, they made "mistakes" and contradicted party policies. Unwilling to tolerate such errors, party leaders now decided that what they needed from young people was not more initiative, but more obedience and a greater willingness to learn from their socialist elders.

Apparently as a consequence of this conclusion, party leaders began to consider a merger of SKOJ and the PYY in late 1947. CPY dissatisfaction with SKOJ had been building steadily due both to its excessive radicalism and its members' disdain for hard work, discipline, and study. SKOJ reports, meanwhile, regularly complained of CPY neglect in terms of both ideological and material aid.[56] Indeed, relations between the two organizations were so tense that a report from Belgrade University's party committee stated bluntly, "In SKOJ there is no love toward the Party."[57] More important, however, was the changing attitude of the CPY toward youth vanguardism. Although party leaders had valued SKOJ's leading role in carrying out CPY tasks, by mid-1947 the political needs of the CPY as a party in power had changed. SKOJ had outlived its usefulness. The Fourth and last Congress of SKOJ was held in October 1948, followed in December by the First Joint Congress of SKOJ and the PYY. The leading role of Communists within the PYY did not change after the merger, yet complaints about youth vanguardism and separatism gradually diminished as former SKOJ members—many of whom were not yet members of the CPY—lost the institutional basis for their privileged status. The PYY remained one of the most active and ideologically oriented persuasive organs in postwar Yugoslavia, but the ability of youth activists to do harm by warping or ignoring the official party line was greatly reduced.

Conclusion

The party's initial steps toward reformulating the focus and methods of its persuasive policies were uncertain and resulted in very little real progress by mid-1948. CPY rhetoric did become more openly ideological and pedagogical, while calls for action and increased economic production declined. The rhetoric did not, however, show signs of becoming more elegant or entertaining; it did not result in massive popular enthusiasm for party goals or a more dynamic relationship between the party-state and its citizens. To be fair, party leaders had very little time for their changes to take effect before the Soviet-Yugoslav split disrupted their plans. The continued failures in the field of persuasion also, however, reflected party leaders' continued reluctance to tolerate "mistakes." Nonetheless, the changing expectations and demands with regard to persuasive policies did indicate the party's awareness of its successes and failures. They also show the continuing—and indeed increasing—concern of CPY leaders to realize the long-term benefits predicted by Communist ideology. The party's changing demands on its persuasive apparatus thus clearly reflect both its concerns about growing public apathy with regard to the Communist agenda and its evolving strategy for socialist development.

Up until mid-1948, this evolution remained unarticulated, perhaps even unnoticed, by party leaders. At the Fifth Party Congress in July 1948, however, Tito explicitly referred to its existence, explaining that only now, after the party had won the war, built up state power, and renovated the economy, could it truly begin to construct socialism on the basis of Marxist-Leninist principles. "That is our fourth and greatest task, whose realization should make the life of the people of Yugoslavia happier, more prosperous, and much more cultured than it is today."[58] By that time, however, the CPY was deeply enmeshed in its conflict with the Soviet Union and Eastern European "People's Democracies." Despite Tito's apparent confidence that the party could proceed smoothly with the next phase of socialist development, the split interrupted the party's plans, forcing it in some cases to retreat to an earlier stage of development, while propelling it in others even further along the path already mapped out.

Notes

1. The fall of 1947 saw the trial and imprisonment of the party's last serious opponent within Yugoslavia, Dragoljub Jovanović. The more confident posture of the CPY at this time may also have been connected to the increasingly aggressive stance taken by the Soviet Union in its relations with the West.

2. Those resources relied heavily on credits from and trade with the Soviet Union and other Eastern European socialist states.

3. For a thorough discussion of the CPY's postwar agrarian policies see Melissa Bokovoy, *Peasants and Communists: Politics and Ideology in the Yugoslav Countryside,*

The Cultural Transformation Begins 155

1941–1953 (Pittsburgh: University of Pittsburgh Press, 1998) and Momčilo Pavović, *Srpsko selo 1945–1952: Otkup* (Belgrade: Institut za savremenu istoriju, 1997).

4. "Razgovor Maršala Tita sa stranim novinarima," *Politika,* 13 Aug. 1945; "Odgovori Maršala Tita na pitanja američkih novinara," *Politika,* 17 Oct. 1946; P. Jerehonov, "Lična svojina u Sovjetskom Savezu," *Seljačka borba,* 12 Sept. 1945; "Napomene Milovana Djilasa za uvod programa," Spring 1948, ACKSKJ, VIII IV-c-42.

5. Edvard Kardelj, "Zemljoradničko zadrugarstvo u planskoj privredi," *Narodno zadrugarstvo,* 1, no. 6 (November 1947).

6. Edvard Kardelj, "The Struggle for the Fulfillment of the First Five Year Plan," Speech delivered in the People's Assembly, 25 April 1948, Hoover Institution Library; Kardelj, "Zemljoradničko zadrugarstvo." See also Ante Bojanić, "Značaj zadruge novog tipa za ekonomski i kulturni preobražaj našeg sela," *Narodno zadrugarstvo,* 1, no. 2 (April 1947); Mico Rakić, "Seoska omladina u novoj Jugoslaviji," *Jugoslavija-SSSR,* 20 (June 1947); Josip Broz Tito, "O Petogodišnjem planu," *Komunist,* 2, no. 3 (September 1947).

7. Kardelj, "Zemljoradničko zadrugarstvo"; Bojanić, "Značaj zadruge novog tipa."

8. "Zapisnik sa sastanka sa drugovima Kardeljom, Djilasom, Kidričem, i Krstom Popivodom," 1947, AJ, SSOJ-28; Milijan Neorečić, "II Kongres NF i zadaci NO," 1–3 Dec. 1947, AJ, SSOJ-28; Rato Dugonjić, "Osmo plenarno zasedanje Centralnog vijeća Narodne omladine," *Borba,* 2 Dec. 1947, p. 1; Pero Kulundžija, "Narodna omladina i zadrugarstvo," *Narodno zadrugarstvo,* 2, no. 2 (May 1948); Zdenka Šegvić, "Problemi naše štampe od oslobodjenja do danas i njezine slabosti," May 1948, ACKSKJ, VIII II/5-b-25; "Izvještaj o radu teoretsko-predavačkog sektora," 6 May 1948, HDA, CKKPHAP.

9. "Izvještaj KK KPH Petrinja," 5 Feb. 1948, HDA, CKKPHAP.

10. "Zapisnik sa savjetovanja kulturnog sektora u agitpropima CK i PK po pitanju kulturno-masovnog rada," 20 Jan. 1948, ACKSKJ, VIII II/4-d-4; Braca Kosovac, "Izvještaj o agitaciji na selu," March 1948, ACKSKJ, VIII II/5-b-24.

11. "Zapisnik sa sastanka agitpropa," 5 Feb. 1948, ACKSKJ, VIII II/2-b-6. See also "Sistem nastave na Beogradskom univerzitetu," no date, after 1 June 1948, ACKSKJ, VIII VI/2-e-3.

12. "Resultat konkursa MP Narodne republike Srbije za dramsko delo," *Naša književnost,* 1, no. 12 (December 1946): 591; Velibor Gligorić, "O nekim pitanjima naše dramske književnost," *Naša književnost,* 1, no. 12 (December 1946): 545–551.

13. Louis Adamic, *The Eagle and the Roots* (New York: Doubleday and Co., 1952), 115. See also "Rezultat konkursa časopisa *Mladost,*" *Mladost,* 4, no. 1–2 (Jan-Feb. 1948), 97–98; M. P., "Skupština Udruženja književnika Srbije," *Književnost,* 5–6 (May-June 1948), 394–398.

14. Sergej Petrović, "Kulturno-umetnička društva treba da posvete veću pažnju radu svojih dramskih grupa," *Prosvetni radnik,* 1 Jan. 1948; Ivan Curl, "Muzika za ples," 16 Dec. 1946, HDA, CKKPH; "Problemi muzičkog odeljenja Radio-Beograda," 22 Dec. 1947, ACKSKJ, VIII II/4-d-2; Predrag J. Marković, *Beograd izmedju istoka i zapada, 1948–1965* (Belgrade: 1996) 468–469; "Zapisnik sa savjetovanja sa članovima žiria za nagradjivanje naših umjetnika," 2 Feb. 1948,

ACKSKJ, VIII II/4-d-5. See also J. P., "Tri nekulturne pojave," *Borba*, 18 Jan. 1947; Dj. K., "Nešto o radu kazališnih družina," *Naprijed*, 12 April 1947.

15. See, for example, the debate concerning Yugoslavia's first full-length motion picture, *Slavica*. Eli Finci, "Filmski pregled—*Slavica*—naš prvi umetnički film," *Borba*, 15 May 1947; Branko Drašković, "Još jednom o *Slavici*," *Borba*, 8 July 1947; "*Slavica* naš prvi umetnički film," *Film*, 3 (August 1947): 11–19.

16. Šegvić, "Problemi naše štampe"; Trade Union report, no date, after May 1947, AJ, CVSSJ F1/J3 KPO; "Savetovanje CV NO o pionirskoj štampi," *Prosvetni radnik*, 15 June 1948. See also Vladimir Dedijer, "Uloga štampe i njeno mesto u partiskom radu," 24 Oct. 1947, ACKSKJ, VIII IV-a-2; "Organizacione primjedbe na našu agitaciju i propagandu," 1947, HDA, ZV NOH-29; "Izvještaj o radu teoretsko-predavačkog sektora"; Veljko Vlahović, "Rad plenuma Saveznog odbora NFJ," *Borba*, 21 June 1948; Djuro Salaj, "Zadaci jedinstvenih sindikat u svetlosti odluka drugog kongresa NFJ," 9 Nov. 1947, AJ, CVSSJ-F2.

17. One exception to the party's demands for increased attention to ideology in late 1947 and early 1948 may be seen in its approach to the AFW. Far from calling for more political-ideological education among women, party leaders urged AFW activists to pay greater attention to issues of immediate concern to women. They should attract women's interest by becoming involved with work that was close to them—like care of children, hygiene, and so on—and should assign women to concrete, small-scale, practical tasks. AFW activists should not be afraid of so-called petty tasks, one document explained, because "the lives of women, housewives, peasants, and the lives of mothers and children are full of such ostensibly petty questions." Apparently, party members felt that women (or perhaps their menfolk) were not yet prepared to accept female political activism. Vida Tomšić, "Za učvršćenja organizacije AFŽ," *Borba*, 6 May 1948; "Govor Vide Tomšić," at the Second Meeting of the Executive Council of the CO AFŽ, 6 April 1948, AJ, AFŽ 141-8-21; "Zakljucna reč drugarice Vide Tomšić," 19–20 Sept. 1948, AJ, AFŽ 141-6-14.

18. Šegvić, "Problemi naše štampe." See also "Pojačati propagandno-agitacioni rad na selu," *Partiska izgradnja*, 1, no. 2 (April 1949).

19. Edo Vajneht, "Bukvari, čitanke i gramatike u osnovnim školama," *Savremena škola*, 3, no. 2–3 (1948); Milan Mirković, "Nastave poznavanja prirode i zemljopisa," *Savremena škola*, 3, no. 2–3 (1948); Radovan Teodesić, "Nastava istorije u osnovnoj školi," *Savremena škola*, 3, no. 2–3 (1948); Marijan Stilinović, Concluding speech at the federal conference of the KŠN on the question of gymnasiums, 18–21 May 1948, AJ, SSOJ-98; Ivo Frol, "O idejnosti i naučnosti u nastavi," *Savremena škola*, 3, no. 5–6 (1948); "Savezna konferencija o pitanjima opšte obrazovanih srednjih škola znači krupan doprinos u razvoju našeg novog školstva," *Prosvetni radnik*, 1 June 1948"; "Referati i diskusije sa V. Kongresa KPJ 21–29 Jula 1948 godine koji se odnose na univerzitet," in Momčilo Mitrović and Djordje Stanković, eds., *Zapisnici i izveštaji univerzitetskog komiteta Komunističke Partije Srbije, 1945–1948* (Belgrade: 1985) (hereafter *ZIUKKPS*), 430–439.

20. "Izveštaj o radu sindikalnih kulturno-umetničkih društava," 1947, ACKSKJ, VIII II/8-a-2. See also Trade Union report; "Osnovan je Savez kulturno-prosvetnih društava NR Srbije," *Borba*, 15 March 1948.

21. Toman Brajović, "Izgradnja zadružnih domova i dužnost učitelja na kulturno-prosvetnom podizanju sela," *Narodno zadrugarstvo*, 2, no. 4–5 (July-August 1948). See also "Izvještaj o kulturno-prosvjetnom radu," no date, fall 1947, HDA CKKPHAP; "Izdavačka delatnost za selo," no date, late 1947, ACKSKJ, VIII VI/2-g-7.

22. Bora Drenovac, "Povodom Festival Narodne omladine Jugoslavije," November 1948, ACKSKJ, VIII II/8-1-4. See also Najdan Pašić, "1948—Godina kulturnog preporoda u našem selu," *Mladost*, 4, no. 5–6 (May-June 1948): 405–407; "Zapisnik sa savetovanja kulturnog sektora."

23. Stenographic notes of the federal conference of the KŠN on the question of the gymnasium, 18–21 May 1948, AJ, SSOJ-98. See also "Zapisnik," 10 June 1948, HDA, CKKPHAP.

24. "Zapisnik sa savjetovanja kulturnog sektora"; Discussion of the work of agitprop in various cultural fields," 15 Dec. 1948, ACKSKJ, VIII II/5-c-76.

25. "Referat o ideološkom odgoju komunista," 8 Dec. 1946, HDA, CKKPH; "Teoretsko-predavački sektor," 10 Feb. 1947, HDA, CKKPHAP.

26. "Instrukcije u vezi sprovodjenja orijentacijonog plana i programa za ideološki odgoj članstva na selu i u grad," 1947, ACKSKJ, VIII VI/2-a-12; "O radu partijske organizacije na univerzitetu," 7 Oct. 1947, *ZIUKKPS*, 269–272.

27. Mirković, "Nastave poznavanja prirode i zemljopisa"; "Savezna konferencija o osnovnoj nastavi uspešno je završila svoj rad," *Prosvetni radnik*, 1 Feb. 1948; Frol, "O idejnosti i naučnosti u nastavi"; "Tematika i uputstva za izradu novih čitanka osnovnih škola," 1948, AJ, KŠN-77.

28. "Direktivno pismo CK KPJ upućeno CK KP Makedonije u vezi stanja i rada u sektora agitacije i štampe u Makedoniji," 1947, ACKSKJ, VIII I/1-a-19.

29. Milomir Marić, "Prkosne strofe Radovana Zogovića," Part 2, *Duga*, 312 (8 Feb. 1986): 63; "Ježu-koji je oćelavio," *Demokratija*, 1 Nov. 1945. Lopušina points out that since *Jež* was never censored, it must have adhered faithfully to Djilas's warning. Marko Lopušina, *Crna knjiga: Cenzura u Jugoslaviji, 1945–91* (Belgrade: Fokus, 1991), 263.

30. Velibor Gligorić, "O karikaturi—povodom izložbe jugoslovenskih karikaturista," Radovan Zogović, "Uloga karikatura i njen razvitak," and Branko Drašković, "Karikatura i njeno mjesto u novinarstvu," all in *Književne novine*, 8 June 1948.

31. Dedijer, "Uloga štampe."

32. Milovan Djilas, "O liniji naše štampe," 23 Feb. 1948, ACKSKJ, VIII II/2-b-15. See also Šegvić, "Problemi naše štampe."

33. Milovan Djilas, *Rise and Fall* (New York: Harcourt Brace Jovanovich, 1983), 77–81; Ivo Škrabalo, *Izmedju publike i države: Povijest hrvatske kinematografije 1896–1980* (Zagreb: 1984), 93–151; "Zapisnik sa savjetovanja iz Komiteta za kinematografiju," 2 March 1948, ACKSKJ, VIII II/4-d-9.

34. "Zapisnik sa savjetovanja sa drugovima iz Radiokomiteta i Radiostanice," 22 Dec. 1947, ACKSKJ, VIII II/4-d-2; "Zapisnik sa savjetovanja po pitanju muzičkih škola," 27 Feb. 1948, ACKSKJ, VIII II/4-d-7.

35. Dedijer, "Uloga štampe." See also "Kratka analiza naše štampe," 1 Oct. 1947, ACKSKJ, VIII VI/1-b-24.

36. Milovan Djilas, "Izvještaj o agitaciono-propagandnom radu," in *V. Kongres Komunističke partije Jugoslavije, Izvještaji i referati* (Belgrade: 1948), 203.

37. Milovan Djilas, Interview with the author, Belgrade, 17 November 1988.

38. "Organizacione primjedbe na našu agitaciju i propagandu"; "Kratka analiza naše štampe"; Dedijer, "Uloga štampe"; "Pregled *Rad-a*," 12 Nov. 1948, ACKSKJ, VIII II/4-d-14; Šegvić, "Problemi naše štampe."

39. Dragiša M. Ivanović, "Zapisnik sa pretkongresne konferencije partijske ćelije nastavnika i administratora Beogradskog univerziteta," 19 June 1948, *ZIUKKPS*, 386; "Mesnom komitetu KPS," 5 Nov. 1946, *ZIUKKPS*, 118–120; "Zapisnik sa sastanka UK KPS," 3 April 1947, *ZIUKKPS*, 178; "Zagrebačko sveučilište," Dinko Tomašić Collection, Hoover Institution.

40. "Referat o ideološkom odgoju komunista," 8 Dec. 1946, HDA, CKKPH.

41. See, for example, "Izvještaj agitpropa MK KPH Rijeka," 19 Sept. 1947, HDA, CKKPHAP; "I sami vaspitači moraju biti vaspitani," *Književne novine*, 2 March 1948.

42. Marijan Stilinović, "Dvadeset pet godina *Borbe*," *Borba*, 19 Feb. 1947; Šegvić, "Problemi naše štampe."

43. "U Sarajevu je održana prva godišnja skupština Saveza udruženja novinara Jugoslavije," *Borba*, 23 Dec. 1947; "Zapisnik sa savjetovanja sa KŠN po pitanju novinarske i diplomatske škole," 5 May 1948, ACKSKJ, VIII II/4-d-13.

44. "Idejno-politički rad u masama," 1947–48, ACKSKJ, VIII II/6–10; "Zapisnik sa savjetovanja sa drugovima iz Komiteta za škole i nauku," 2 March 1948, ACKSKJ, VIII II/4-a-10; "Sistem nastave na Beogradskom univerzitetu"; "Obrazovanje našeg čoveka," 1949, ACKSKJ, VIII II/8-d-35.

45. Stilinović, Concluding speech on the question of gymnasiums; Martin Mencej, "U novu školsku godinu," *Prosvetni radnik*, 15 Sept. 1947; Frol, "O idejnosti i naučnosti u nastavi"; Notes from a meeting of Communist and SKOJ teachers in Slavonski Brod, 10 June 1948, HDA, CKKPHAP; Ivanović, "Zapisnik sa pretkongresne konferencije," 388. See also "Ideološko i stručno usavršavanje treba planski i sistematski sprovoditi," *Prosvetnik radnik*, 15 Oct. 1947; "Osnovne smjerice naše prosvjetne politike," 1947, HDA, CKKPHAP; "O nekim problemima učiteljskih škola," *Prosvetni radnik*, 1 April 1948; Bogdan Svilokos, "Kako organizovati i proraditi rad u kružocima (sindikalnim grupama) za idejno-političko uzdizanje prosvetnih radnika," *Prosvetni radnik*, 1 April 1948; Diskusija u Saveznoj konferenciji KŠN po pitanju gimnazije," 18–21 May 1948, AJ, SSOJ-98; "Gimnazija, klasična gimnazija i učiteljska skola," no date, AJ, SSOJ-102.

46. "Za bolje rezultate upisa na Filozofski fakultet i Višu pedagošku školu," *Borba*, 12 Oct. 1947. See also "Savetovanje rukovodilaca Narodne srednjoškolske omladine iz cjele zemlje pre početak nove školske godine," *Borba*, 20 Aug. 1947; "Nerazmjer u raspodjeli studenata na pojedini fakulteti Beogradskog univerziteta," *Borba*, 17 Sept. 1947. Even in the technical faculties, the educational curriculum began slowly moving away from its previous emphasis on early specialization, although real progress in this direction would not come for another

year. See Vlajko Begović," O specializaciji u nastavnim planovima za tehničke i ekonomske škole," *Borba,* 30 Sept. 1947; "Stanje univerziteta i visokih škola i njihova reorganizacija," 1948, ACKSKJ, VIII VI/2-b-2.

47. "Nastavni plan i program za učiteljsku školu," May 1948, AJ, KŠN-77.
48. "Teoretsko-predavački sektor."
49. "O kulturno-političkom životu privrednih preduzeća," 27 May 1948, ACKSKJ, VIII II/8-a-3; "Teoretsko-predavački sektor."
50. "Izvještaj OK KPH Daruvar," 24 Jan. 1947, HDA, CKKPHAP; Milijan Neorečić, Speech at the Meeting of CK SKOJ, 28 Sept. 1946, ACKSKJ, CKSKOJ II a I/1. See also Report from the Divisional Commander of KPH of the 7th Shock Division of the JNA," 2 Aug. 1945, HDA, CKKPH; "Program dvomjesečnog teoretskog plana za partijske ćelije, kotarske i mjesne komitete," 15 Aug. 1945, HDA, CKKPH; Milovan Djilas, "O daljem radu na ideološkom i političkom podizanju komunista i ideološkom i političkom podizanju radnih masa," 21 Sept. 1946, ACKSKJ, VIII I/1-a-6.
51. "Narodna fronta kao platform Partijskog masovnog rada," 1947, HDA, RKSSRNH-1.
52. A document from late 1947 claimed that many Communists were still illiterate, while one from December 1948 admitted that 49 percent of youth leaders possessed only an elementary education. "Organizacija, dosadašnji rad, i zadaci kulturno-prosvjetnog rada na selu," Fall 1947, HDA CKSKHAP; "Stenografske beleške: Komisija za agitaciju i propagandu," 17–18 Dec. 1948, ACKSKJ, CKSKOJ Ib-2/2.
53. Milovan Djilas, Memo from the CKKPJAP, 17 June 1947, HDA, CKKPHAP.
54. Martin Mencej, "Savetovanje rukovodilaca Saveza prosvetnih radnika," *Prosvetni radnik,* 1 Oct. 1947. See also Pavle Radoman, "Prosvetno-politički zadaci Saveza," 15 July 1946, AJ, KŠN-17; "Za svakodnevnu brigu o našem članstvu," *Prosvetni radnik,* 15 Sept. 1947; Kosta Grubačić, "O nekim nedostacima rada na polju narodne prosvjete," *Borba,* 4 Oct. 1947; "Savetovanje školskih instruktora Srbije, Kosovo-Metohijske oblasti i Vojvodine," *Prosvetni radnik,* 15 Oct. 1947; Ante Miletić, "O nekim nepravilnostima prema prosvetnim radnicima i našim organizacijama," *Prosvetni radnik,* 15 Jan. 1948; "Govor Bakarića na II zemaljskoj konferenciji za Hrvatsku SFR Jugoslavije," *Prosvetni radnik,* 15 March 1948; Vladimir Bakarić, "U Zagrebu je održana zemaljska konferencija Saveza prosvetnih radnika Hrvatske," *Borba,* 2 March 1948.
55. "O radu partijske organizacije na univerzitetu," 7 Oct. 1947, *ZIUKKPS,* 270; "Mesnom komitetu," December 1947, *ZIUKKPS,* 300; Vjera Kovačević, "Mesnom komitetu KPS," 28 June 1948, *ZIUKKPS,* 406.
56. "Izvještaj GK SKOJ Split," 1 June 1945, HDA, PKSKOJ-H-1; "Izvještaj OK SKOJ Varaždin," 5 Oct. 1945, HDA, PKSKOJ-H-1; "Izvještaj OK SKOJ Brod," 12 Oct. 1945, HDA, PKSKOJ-H-1; "Zapisnik sa sastanka članova PK SKOJ-a za Makedoniju s članovima CK," 14 Jan. 1946, in Petar Kačavenda, ed., *Kongresi, konferencije i sednice centralnih organa SKOJa (1941–1948)* (Belgrade: Izdavački centar Komunist, 1984), 111–115.

57. "Zapisnik sa sastanka UK," 21 June 1946, ZIUKKPS, 78. Youth leader Rato Dugonjić has also since admitted to many conflicts between SKOJ and the CPY. See Milomir Marić, *Deca komunizma* (Belgrade: 1987), 156–157.

58. Josip Broz Tito, "Politički izvještaj CK KPJ," in *Peti kongres KPJ, 21–28 jul 1948, Stenografske beleške* (Belgrade: 1949), 104.

7

The Cultural Transformation Delayed

The previous three chapters have described the evolution of CPY persuasive policies from the end of the Second World War up until the Soviet-Yugoslav split of June 1948. Those policies reflected both the party's graduated strategy for the construction of socialism and its often ad hoc responses to the changing domestic and international context. They reveal a rather different view of the CPY in the immediate postwar period than that typically described by the literature. Although unquestionably devoted to Marxist-Leninist ideology and the Soviet Union, the CPY's leaders were above all pragmatic politicians willing to adapt their short-term goals and policies in accordance with the extant culture and in response to feedback from below. Well before the split with the Soviet Union, they showed an awareness that not all aspects of the Soviet model were worthy of emulation or suited to Yugoslavia's circumstances. At the same time, however, CPY leaders persistently pursued their long-term goal of transforming Yugoslavia's society and culture.

The party's progress toward that goal was interrupted and delayed by the Soviet-Yugoslav split of June 1948. The following chapters describe the immediate and secondary consequences of that split for CPY rhetoric and the party's overall approach to the construction of socialism. Eventually, as we will see, the Soviet-Yugoslav split made possible a whole series of reforms that would forever alter the outlines of the party itself and its program for change. While the split facilitated those reforms, their precise form and content were clearly dictated by the party's previous experiences and persuasive failures. The party's immediate reaction to the split, however, was far from coherent and reflected the confusion and fear that many party leaders clearly felt as they contemplated their future without the aid and support of the Soviet Union.

The Soviet-Yugoslav Split

The Cominform split that broke out into the open on June 28, 1948, was unquestionably a defining moment in the evolution of postwar Yugoslav history. More than any other single event, it changed the direction of the Yugoslav Communist party's domestic and foreign policies, ensuring that Yugoslavia would ever after attain recognition as the exception to all rules about postwar Eastern Europe and as the tiny and seemingly helpless David who stood up against the monstrous Goliath of the Soviet Union. Even so, the role of the split in postwar Yugoslav politics has been overstated; often it has been portrayed as an iron curtain, indelibly dividing two apparently unconnected regimes. In fact, however, lines of continuity between pre- and post-split Yugoslavia may be found by examining party policies in the context of its graduated strategy for the development of socialism. During the first two years following the split that strategy was interrupted, resulting in an era of considerable confusion and even chaos. Under such circumstances, state-society relations revived somewhat, although the party clearly retained its dominant status.

Given the CPY's evident devotion to Stalin and the Soviet Union, the split came as an enormous shock to the entire international community and, indeed, to CPY leaders themselves. Admittedly, certain tensions between the two Communist organizations had developed already during the Second World War, but no Yugoslav leader took them seriously until the first months of 1948 when Soviet leaders began quite deliberately to provoke a conflict. In a series of letters sent during the spring of 1948, Stalin and Molotov accused CPY leaders of such serious errors in their behavior and policies as an anti-Soviet attitude, a lack of internal party democracy, a tendency to hide behind the People's Front, and an incorrect agricultural policy that encouraged the development of "capitalist elements" in the countryside. Ultimately, Stalin invited CPY leaders to respond to these accusations at a meeting of the Communist Information Bureau—an organization of select European Communist parties that had replaced the Communist International dissolved during the war. Although steadfastly denying all of the accusations, CPY leaders declined to attend the Cominform meeting held in Bucharest that June, insisting that they would not receive a fair hearing and fearing that they might not return from it alive.[1] On June 28, 1948, the Cominform meeting published a resolution that repeated the accusations previously leveled at CPY leaders by Stalin and Molotov and further called on all good Communists within Yugoslavia to overthrow their leaders, replacing them with others more loyal to the Soviet Union and socialism.

The origins, causes, and detailed progress of the split have been documented and analyzed in numerous published sources and need not be reviewed here other than to note a general agreement that the real source of Yugoslavia's expulsion from the bloc lay in its leaders' potential for independent thought and activity.[2] More relevant to our endeavor is that literature that addresses the consequences of the split. Most early works on this topic focused on the split's long-term significance in leading Yugoslavia to adopt a milder form of socialism (labeled "workers' self management") while simultaneously maintaining a posture of stubborn independence from both the Soviet and Western blocs.[3] Inasmuch as these works mentioned the immediate post-split years, they described mainly the CPY's valiant acts of resistance and the Yugoslav public's overwhelming support for its leaders. Recently, other scholars have studied more closely the split's immediate consequences for Yugoslavia's domestic policies, describing the period from mid-1948 to 1950 as a continuation and intensification of the earlier "Stalinist" era. As evidence, they point to the party's attempts to collectivize agriculture and its brutal treatment of ideological enemies (especially the so-called Cominformists) on the prison island of Goli Otok.[4]

Though correct in noting the lag time between the split and the party's later innovative reforms and in emphasizing the repressive nature of many party activities in the first 18 months after the split, these works have not offered a coherent explanation for either the increased use of coercion or the party's new agricultural policies. Many have ascribed them to the Yugoslav Communists' psychological need to prove their loyalty to the Soviet Union and demonstrate their continued adherence to orthodox Stalinist methods.[5] Such psychological motivations may, indeed, have inspired the activities of individual leaders or cadres and probably did help sharpen the tone of CPY rhetoric. Yet it seems unlikely that party leaders, whose sense of independence has been widely recognized and who had thus far determined their policies on a combined basis of idealism and pragmatism, would now throw all past experiences out the window and begin blindly to copy the very Soviet policies they had previously described as flawed or inappropriate for use in Yugoslavia. More convincing are those who explain the party's post-split agricultural policies as a response to the threat of external invasion and the material hardships caused by the Soviet and Eastern European economic blockade. In particular, the recent works of Susan Woodward and Melissa Bokovoy do much to elucidate the changes in the party's agricultural policies.[6] A similar effort to explain the party's increased use of coercion based on Soviet pressure following the split, however, bears a clearly apologetic tone that diminishes its credibility.[7]

The period just after the split is indeed difficult to assess given its array of confused and often contradictory directives, statements, and policies. It *was* a time of admirable courage in response to unjustified attacks, but also one of brutal repression against real or presumed opponents. It was an era of optimism, when many hoped the country would move further away from the Soviet model; yet, it was also marked by what seemed to be the most blatant imitation of Soviet methods, especially in the party's campaign for socialization of the countryside. These contradictions were real; the confusion was genuine as CPY leaders sought desperately to hold on to both power and their dreams for a better future. Yet the choices they made and the policies they devised were not arbitrary, nor were they divorced from the party's previous experiences and intentions.

To make sense of CPY policies in the first 18 months after the split, one must consider them in the context of the party's graduated strategy for the transition to socialism. The Cominform split threw the party's previous achievements into doubt, reviving once again concerns about its political and economic security. Thus, regardless of its later significance for reform, the split's first impact was to return the CPY to its initial stages in the transition to socialism. Now facing serious security concerns and enormous material hardships engendered by the military posturing and economic blockade of the Soviet Union and Eastern bloc countries, CPY leaders suspended their progress toward the transformation of society and focused once again on the primary requirements of maintaining power and a stable economy. In this context, the party's increased use of coercion against ideological and political opponents, as well as its renewed emphasis on economic self-sacrifice, is both logical and unsurprising. Indeed, many policies in this period closely resembled those of the 1944–1947 era. As in the first year after the liberation of Belgrade and up to the November 1945 elections, party leaders again worked to eliminate all sources of political opposition by means of blatant coercion. Simultaneously, as in the years from late 1945 to late 1947, CPY rhetoric appealed to Yugoslav citizens' sense of pride and independence (this time in resistance to Soviet threats) and again sought to channel it toward self-sacrificing labor in the interests of accelerated economic production.

Yet, if the CPY took two steps backward following the split, it also took three steps forward, for party rhetoric in the period from mid-1948 to late 1949 did not simply duplicate that produced in 1944–1947. After all, conditions had changed and party leaders had learned from their past experiences. The first feature that distinguished the party's persuasive policies in 1948–49 from those in 1944–1947 was the more open role ascribed to the Communist party itself, including its continued emphasis on ideology and especially ideological education; the second concerned the party's intensified rhetoric aimed at socialization of the village; and the third was the increasingly critical attitude in party rhetoric toward the Soviet Union and its policies. Each of these trends represented a continuation and strengthening of those initiated by CPY leaders in late 1947 and early 1948. An elucidation of these connections, however, should not lead one to presume that either the policies or the rhetoric designed to promote them were always coherently devised or consistently implemented. They were not. It does, however, allow for a more informed analysis of those policies and for a clearer perception of their intentions and further development.

The impact of CPY rhetoric on the Yugoslav population during this period is difficult to assess. For as in the immediate postwar era, contemporaries of the time have described the atmosphere from mid-1948 to 1950 as either exciting and hopeful or repressive and frightening, depending on their individual experiences and political affiliation. In either case, it seems that the confusion of the era generated a degree of public activism previously lacking. Whether manifested as support for or opposition to the regime, such activism served to revitalize state-society relations.

Two Steps Backward

Attacks on the Opposition

One of the most immediate and tangible consequences of the June 1948 Cominform split was the party's increased reliance on force in dealing with political and ideological opponents. The party apparatus not only persecuted those members of the party and society who openly or secretly supported the Cominform resolution (known as Cominformists), but also applied blatantly coercive measures to all potential opponents of the party leadership both in and outside the CPY. The purpose was not only to squelch pro-Soviet elements within the country but to reemphasize the party leadership's dominant position. Consequently, party leaders now renewed their attacks on many old opponents—including prewar party factionalists, the clergy, "kulaks," and other "class enemies." As in 1945, numerous purges of "enemy" youth were conducted in the universities. The ground for increased repression against potential opponents outside the CPY had been prepared in the immediate pre-split period when party leaders openly admitted their socialist intentions and increased official emphasis on their guiding Communist ideology. The dramatically heightened rhetoric, arrests, and trials, however, came only after the split and focused first on real or suspected Cominformist agents within the party.[8]

Immediately after the split broke out into the open, the leadership asked rank-and-file members to express their opinions and take sides in the conflict with the Soviet Union and other "People's Democracies."[9] While the leadership allowed certain highly placed party members the time and liberty to rethink an unfortunate first choice, many others were expelled from the party, fired from their jobs, and in some cases, arrested and imprisoned or shot almost immediately.[10] Of those arrested, some were indeed true supporters of Soviet Stalinism and the Cominform resolution. Even they, however, often accepted only certain aspects of the resolution—usually those sections relating to the CPY's lack of internal democracy and tendency to hide behind the PFY. According to later reports, such Cominformists mainly feared for the fate of Communist Yugoslavia should it be isolated from the socialist community, and they felt that CPY leaders should have attended the Cominform meeting in order to demonstrate more clearly their desire to resolve the dispute.[11] Others arrested as Cominformist agents had committed such minor infractions as reading Cominformist leaflets, listening to shortwave radios, or neglecting to report suspect conversations.[12]

Regardless of the seriousness of their infractions, party leaders condemned these real and suspected Cominformists with extraordinary ferocity. In his monograph on the split, Banac presents a rich selection of the terms commonly applied to Cominformist agents:

> Stalin's "internationalists" became the official KPJ's [CPY's] "handful of renegades, ambitious and demoralized elements" (Djuro Pucar); "vacillators and careerists" (May Day slogan, 1949); "speculators, cold and soulless intellectuals who never had any understanding of the struggle of our working masses, ... old opportunists, liquidators, and cowards ... anti-party elements ... Trotskyites ... spineless characters who aspire to a comfortable life" (*Borba*); "spies enlisted by who-knows-whom" (Petar Stambolić); and even "non-humans" (*neljudi*, Djilas).[13]

What is striking about these labels is their lack of emphasis on the target's actual relationship to the Soviet-Yugoslav split. Rather, they seem intended to identify Cominformists with a variety of other "enemies of the people." It is, of course, typical of orthodox Communist rhetoric to tar all enemies with a single brush. For the most dogmatic Communist ideologues, all enemies **were** alike. All of them, regardless of their individual sins, were "objectively" class enemies and could be described in similar if not identical terms. In this case, however, CPY leaders also were seeking to minimize the appearance of internal backing for the Cominform resolution.

Banac's monograph notes the difficulty in estimating accurately the number of Yugoslav citizens caught up in the Cominformist purges. He suggests, however, that the proportion of party members involved may have reached almost 20 percent.[14] A reader of Yugoslav newspapers and journals in 1948 and 1949, however, would undoubtedly have made a much lower estimate. One consistent feature of party rhetoric was the leadership's claim to have the solid support of the overwhelming majority of the Yugoslav population. Consequently, the media rarely publicized incidents of real Cominformist support and, when it did, always associated them with other "deviations." Public documents describing Cominformist agents always referred to them as "scattered individuals," "isolated bands," and "tiny, insignificant groups" who invariably had a long history of enemy activity. Internal party documents also consciously sought to associate accused Cominformists with other "enemies of the people." The 1948 annual report from the Regional SKOJ committee for Serbia recorded the elimination of several members from youth work as Cominformists, but added that most had been poor leaders, under consideration for expulsion anyway. Likewise, a report on Belgrade University's party committee noted that in connection with the Cominformist threat, it had purged 164 members and expelled 206 students whom it described as Nedićists, Ljotićists, Četniks, and so on.[15]

The veracity of such statements is highly disputable. Certainly any open Četniks had been long since eliminated. Moreover, biographical lists of Cominform agents in Montenegro indicating their past association with wartime enemy units and any previous party punishments do not in most cases reveal a history of enemy activity. Indeed, a report from Montenegro's regional party committee admitted that a "considerable number" of those arrested, if judged by their social origins and past activities, should not have ended up in any conflict with the party.[16]

Yet party leaders also clearly expected the Cominform split to inspire other "enemy elements" to renewed activity. Another report from the regional party committee of Montenegro thus noted that supporters of the Cominform resolution had begun to gather around themselves all kinds of malcontents, including "speculators, thieves, and class enemies."[17] Tito addressed the issue directly at a Politburo meeting in late May 1949 when he stated that the struggle against Cominformists was really a fight against counterrevolution and was one that all Četniks and Ustaše would soon join. He therefore urged that the purges be taken further and sharpened, without, however, going to extremes or "characterizing everything as Cominformism."[18]

Ultimately, therefore, many of those arrested as Cominformist agents were not publicly denounced for their support of the Soviet position because that was not their crime. Many suffered for sins unrelated or only indirectly related to the Soviet-Yugoslav split, including their unacceptable views on the national question, their position in prewar factional debates, their evident dissatisfaction with the regime's economic policies, or simply their opposition to the party or its leadership.[19] Moreover, the hostile rhetoric and increased used of coercion typical of the immediate post-split era, while focusing on CPY members, also targeted a wide variety of potential opponents outside the party. In particular, party activists became increasingly hostile toward the clergy, "kulaks," and other "class enemies," by which they meant anyone opposed to the party's guiding ideology as well as its political, economic, or cultural policies. The party's increased use of coercion against Yugoslavia's peasants will be addressed below in our discussion of agrarian policy. The years after mid-1948 also, however, saw a dramatic increase in public attacks on bearers of "bourgeois ideology." According to the memoirs of non-Communist intellectual Dejan Medaković, the Soviet-Yugoslav split was followed by terrible purges in the departments of law and medicine at Belgrade University. Those faculty expelled were not Cominform agents, but merely members of the bourgeoisie.[20] Likewise, a number of trials in 1949 and 1950 indicted high school and college students for the creation of liberal organizations. One of them described his arrest and imprisonment for helping organize the Union of Democratic Youth of Yugoslavia, which called on young people to nurture a spirit of resistance and prepare for the struggle against communism with the help of Western democracies.[21]

In some cases, it seemed that party leaders employed the anti-Cominformist purges as an excuse to rid themselves of other old or potential opponents. The expulsion, arrest, imprisonment, and possible murder of top Croat leader Andrija Hebrang was one case when top CPY leaders almost certainly used the split to rid themselves of a troublesome rival.[22] Overall, however, it is misleading to suggest that party leaders saw the split simply as an opportunity to eliminate other enemies; rather, the split induced in them strong feelings of political insecurity to which they responded, in good Communist style, with enhanced repression. Party leaders who equated the success of communism in Yugoslavia with their own survival naturally saw all forms of resistance as equally dangerous. Tito was no doubt sincere when he said that the struggle against Cominformists was really a fight against counterrevolution.[23]

One clear indicator of growing anxiety about ideological opponents both inside and outside the CPY came in a contentious meeting between the Politburo of the CPY and the Politburo of the Slovenian Communist party in early January 1949. According to Slovenia's minister of the interior, Boris Kraiger, "things were not critical" but were "getting out of hand." Kraiger began his description of rising "reactionary tendencies" by noting increased activity by the church, which had "tried to activate some associations, choirs, and so on," and now included "even workers' choirs." He then pointed to increasing problems with youth: "Students threatened to strike . . . once after drinking, 100 students shouted slogans against the fascist militia and fascist regime." He further related a growing incidence of "petty bourgeois deviations" developing "under the slogan of 'independence'" and worried about the growth of nationalism, arguing that "the [cultural-artistic] group *Javorinka* is dangerous because it says in its program that Slovenes have nothing in common with the other South Slavs . . . and it thinks that the time has come to work for the break up of Yugoslavia."[24]

The Slovene report would seem to indicate that one consequence of the Soviet-Yugoslav split was the revitalization of state-society relations in Yugoslavia—even if manifested only as open conflict. Many long-standing opponents of the regime may have seen the Cominform dispute as increasing the vulnerability of the CPY and providing them with an opportunity for renewed resistance. Certainly, few observers imagined that Tito's party could survive in isolation from the Soviet bloc. According to Dedijer, the split generated "profound excitement" among Yugoslav exiles in the West who, believing that Tito's downfall was imminent, increased their activities inside the country.[25] On the other hand, it is not clear that enemy activity increased at the same level as did the party's use of coercion. It may be that CPY leaders simply felt so vulnerable following the split that they were no longer willing to tolerate any areas of autonomous activity. Here again, the party's coercive activities countered any moves toward revitalized state-society relations. Certainly, one goal of the arrests and trials was to frighten all other potential opponents into passivity once more. While the party's increased tendency toward repression represented one response to its vulnerability, another may be seen in party leaders' efforts to renew a sense of Yugoslav patriotism that could then inspire the self-sacrificing labor needed to secure a stable economy.

Pride and Productivity

The primary task of party rhetoric in the immediate aftermath of the split was to persuade Yugoslavia's citizens to stand by their leaders and support their resistance to Soviet pressure. It did so, first of all, by appealing to the same sense of pride and independence that had inspired the partisan movement during the Second World War. In this effort, CPY rhetoric was rather more effective than usual. In contrast to Soviet expectations that CPY leaders would seek to hide the conflict from Yugoslavia's citizens and the world, party leaders immediately brought it out into the open, publishing the entire earlier correspondence between themselves and Soviet leaders, as well as the Cominform resolution and their response to it.[26] According to Dedijer, they also chose quite deliberately not to jam the hostile radio broadcasts coming from the Soviet Union. By allowing Yugoslavia's citizens to read the documents themselves and hear both sides of the conflict, CPY leaders projected a sense of confidence in themselves and their constituents. That approach, in itself, may have attracted the support of some citizens. As Dedijer put it, "That had an immense effect among the Yugoslavs, for it was obvious that Yugoslavia's only strength lay in the free decision of her citizens as to who was right and who wrong."[27]

Moreover, the hostile and bullying tone of the letters and accusations increased popular support for the CPY. Stalin's belief that he could "shake [his] little finger and there will be no more Tito" was obvious in his correspondence with CPY leaders. Indeed, the entire Cominformist approach was designed to show the weakness and insignificance of the CPY. This attitude backfired, however, as it called up long-standing resentments in Yugoslavia of the typical relations between great and small powers. Thus Dedijer cited his mother, who said that CPY resistance to the resolution reminded her "of little Serbia rejecting the ultimatum of the Austro-Hungarian Empire in 1914." Djilas, too, claimed that non-Communists suffered no dilemma whatsoever in the split as it represented the traditional use of force by the great against the small. For those who believed that the split had nothing to do with communism and everything to do with typical relations between large and small countries, Tito's words, "However much each of us loves the land of socialism, the USSR, he can in no case love his own country less," rang true.[28]

If the tone of the Soviet letters facilitated the work of persuasive personnel in Yugoslavia, so did at least one Cominform accusation. While CPY leaders tended to ignore the specific content of the Cominform resolution, they were quick to publicize Soviet claims about the role of the Red Army in the liberation of Yugoslavia. According to the resolution, CPY leaders showed unwarranted arrogance in their claim to have liberated Yugoslavia by their own efforts when in fact the involvement of the Red Army had been crucial. This was undoubtedly the least effective (and least intelligent) of all of the Cominform accusations as it directly attacked the pride of all those who had sacrificed for the liberation of Yugoslavia. According to Dedijer, "the disparaging attitude toward the struggle and sacrifices the Yugoslavs had made during the war" was "what most embittered the ordinary people of Yugoslavia."[29] Former partisans were especially hurt and, according to one observer, it directly influenced the reactions of the top leadership. "It hit [Tito] hardest when the Russians tried to minimize our People's Liberation Struggle. If they hadn't made that stupid mistake, I don't know how things would have turned out."[30]

Having successfully inspired a sense of Yugoslav patriotism in many citizens, CPY rhetoric in 1948–1949, as in 1946–1947, sought to channel it toward the fulfillment of concrete economic tasks. The Soviet and Eastern European economic blockade and the party's own modernization and reconstruction policies required that the party refocus its attention on the needs of the Yugoslav economy. The CPY's Five Year Plan adopted in April 1947 had assumed access to substantial Soviet and Eastern European credits and trade arrangements that had now been withdrawn or renounced. This meant that Yugoslavia would have to fulfill the plan by means of its own resources, exporting whatever it could in order to purchase the necessary machinery and industrial raw materials from an unforgiving West. Moreover, the removal of Soviet protection and, by mid-1949, the rising threat of Soviet invasion meant that a much larger percentage of the country's resources had to be devoted to its defense industry.[31] The party's persuasive organs reflected this new economic reality almost immediately, calling once again for greater concentration on economic priorities and for economic self-sacrifice by all members of the population.

At the First Congress of the League of Trade Unions held in October 1948, Boris Kidrič launched the first volley of rhetoric aimed at urgent economic reconstruction. As chairman of the Economic Council, minister of industry, and the Five Year Plan's greatest advocate, Kidrič related Yugoslavia's economic performance and fulfillment of the Five Year Plan to its defense against Cominform attacks. At this early stage of the split, he did not focus directly on the material difficulties it had engendered. Not all agreements had been formally breached by this time and many (including Tito himself) still hoped the conflict could be smoothed over. Rather, he urged economic progress as a means of proving Yugoslavia's continued commitment to socialism despite accusations to the contrary. High economic performance in 1948 was important, Kidrič explained, not only to cover the year's necessarily large imports of machinery and wheat, but because it would provide the "manly and socialist response of our working class to the unprincipled and unsocialist campaign against us." The best way to refute slanders in the Cominform resolution and to prove Yugoslavia's loyalty to orthodox socialism, he argued, was to continue along the path of socialist construction through the development of an industrial economic base. Accordingly, he claimed that the main purpose of the congress was to inspire even greater mobilization for the struggle to fulfill planned tasks and to realize increased productivity, discipline, competition, and mechanization.[32]

Kidrič and other speakers at the congress were not entirely blind to the changes that had occurred in Yugoslav society over the past several years. Understanding that the immediate postwar sense of enthusiasm and energy had waned and that working-class demands for improved material conditions were steadily rising, they also tried to show how increased productivity would contribute to higher living standards.[33] Union leader Ivan Božičević, for example, drew special attention to the role of work norms in this process. Although often misunderstood due to their abuse as a means of capitalist exploitation in old Yugoslavia, he explained, they were now a means of increasing productivity and thereby raising living standards for the working class. Ultimately, however, the primary message was a plea for continued economic self-sacrifice. In his speech, Božičević also warned that the development of conscious working discipline could not always be achieved by education alone. Rebuking those who were "opportunistically" inclined to avoid using punishment against violators, he insisted that such measures were not only justified but necessary.[34]

Even the statute of the League of Trade Unions focused its attention less on the material or ideological needs of the working class than on the demands of the Yugoslav economy. The first task of the League according to its statute was "to educate the working class in a spirit of marxism-leninism *with the goal of mobilizing them for the socialist construction of our country*"; its second was to be "the direct organizer of the struggle of the working class for increased production and productivity."[35] Only later did the statute address the League's responsibility to show concern for the needs of workers; organize the study of Marxism-Leninism and raise the ideological-political, cultural, and professional level of workers and employees; educate the working class in a spirit of international proletarian solidarity; confirm the union of workers and peasants; and further develop the equality, brotherhood, and unity of the peoples of Yugoslavia.[36]

This emphasis on the role of trade unions in stimulating economic productivity was, of course, not new; that had been the focus of most union activity from 1945 through 1947 as well. During the spring of 1948, however, there had been signs of a shift in union priorities away from methods designed only to increase productivity and toward those that sought greater worker participation in and satisfaction with the union. For example, the League of Trade Unions' Sixth Plenum in March 1948 had introduced secret ballot voting for elections of union functionaries. The union had done so, one article explained, in order to strengthen its internal democracy, increase worker participation in the unions, and build an atmosphere of trust between workers and union officials. The plenum also underscored the importance of persuasion in dealings between union functionaries and workers, criticizing the activities of many past functionaries as bureaucratic and commandeering.[37] These concerns now seemed to fall by the wayside as emphasis recentered on economic production achieved by any means necessary. Thus, the themes established for educational work in factories in 1949 ignored issues of democratization or even ideology, focusing instead on: 1) the Five Year Plan, 2) the use of domestic resources, 3) the need for more rationalizers and innovators, 4) the struggle for increased production, and 5) the struggle for heightened discipline.[38]

The League of Trade Unions' congress established both the model and plan for party persuasion, directing its focus squarely on fulfillment of the Five Year Plan, the achievement of current production tasks, and the development of socialist competition, shockwork, and discipline.[39] Over the next 14 months, party and mass organizations, public speakers, and the media converged more and more narrowly on economic issues, frequently restating Kidrič's argument about the role of economic construction in disproving Cominform accusations and endlessly repeating his calls for the fullest possible mobilization of all domestic human and material resources and increased productivity through competition, shockwork, and heightened discipline.[40] The Second Plenum of the Central Committee of the CPY narrowed these general calls, specifying which sectors of the economy required particular attention: heavy industry, mining, transportation, military objects, electrification, and the state and cooperative sectors in agriculture.[41]

By the late spring and summer of 1949, party publicists were cranking out innumerable articles devoted to these sectors and the achievements of individual workers became front-page news, exceeding even the coverage of such issues in 1946–1947. Campaigns for shockwork, innovators, and rationalizers occupied pages previously dedicated to political and cultural affairs, while the results of economic competitions stood alongside those of sports events. Numerous articles referred especially to competitions and shockwork inspired by Alija Sirotanović, a miner from Breza who came to be known as the Yugoslav Stakhanov. Sirotanović broke Stakhanov's third record of 102 tons of coal dug when, on July 24, 1949, his brigade removed 152 tons of coal. In the following months, miners all over Yugoslavia successfully competed to surpass his record.[42]

Meanwhile, party leaders revived the volunteer labor brigades, reversing the earlier diminution of their role. The party's previous decision to reduce its reliance on volunteer and especially youth labor brigades had reflected its sense of economic self-confidence, as well as its growing awareness of the brigades' harmful physical and moral impact. Having initiated the third phase in the construction of socialism—the cultural transformation of society—many party leaders had come to believe that the brigades did more harm than good since the use of forced recruitment techniques had a counterproductive political impact while their economic value was dubious. Now, as that sense of economic security eroded, party leaders reverted to old priorities and applied old methods. Thus, rhetoric for labor brigades once again increased, with fewer and fewer reports focusing on the need to uphold the principle of voluntariness in recruitment practices. In the fall of 1948 and throughout 1949, newspapers and journals hailed the heroic efforts of the volunteer labor brigades, calling for even greater participation in them. Meanwhile, internal reports complained that brigade quotas for federal youth actions (and especially Tito's pet projects—construction of a highway between Belgrade and Zagreb and a modern addition to Belgrade on the north side of the Sava River) were not being fulfilled.[43] In February 1949, the Central Committee of the People's Youth strongly emphasized the need for more active mobilization for youth brigades the following year:

> In order that the full potential of the youth brigades be realized, organizations *must* scrupulously adhere to the mobilization plan. Further, leaderships must understand that construction of the [Belgrade-Zagreb] highway and of [New] Belgrade is critical and must be accomplished this year. Each unit is assigned youth quotas and arrival dates in accordance with operational plans. If sufficient manpower is not allocated in a timely fashion as required in the mobilization plan, then it will be impossible to fulfill the planned tasks at the construction sites.[44]

Although full mobilization was supposed to be accomplished without coercion, lower-level youth leaders correctly concluded that fulfilling brigade quotas should once again become their top priority. Consequently, by late 1949, there were again complaints of forced mobilization techniques—now referred to by some as "sharper agitation."[45]

One also finds fewer reports in late 1948 and 1949 that showed concern for living and working conditions on the brigades. It seems unlikely that conditions on the brigades had improved so radically as to render such reports unnecessary. But whereas party and youth leaders in late 1947 had frequently warned brigade leaders and workers not to overdo it and work themselves into a state of exhaustion, now many articles hailed the seemingly impossible achievements of brigade heroes. One article, for example, lauded the superhuman efforts of a young sailor, Suljo Maljević, who, when demobilized from the navy, convinced his best friends to join him on the Belgrade-Zagreb Highway brigade. There they worked three shifts a day for 20 days on only the most difficult tasks, ostensibly overfulfilling their norm in one case by 750 percent.[46]

Real economic problems had prompted the renewed emphasis on economic self-sacrifice, yet the results achieved were also hailed for their political role in "smashing the slanders" of Cominformists.[47] In describing the accomplishments of the youth labor brigades, Neorečić said that while the Cominform countries could verbally attack Yugoslavia, no slanders or lies could wipe out the bridges, roads, factories, buildings, and railways they had built. Likewise, the contributions of shockworkers, innovators, and rationalizers were said to have a clear political and ideological function. Tito himself insisted that shockwork no longer represented only the efforts of an individual who wished to stand out from the crowd; rather, he explained, "to be a shockworker . . . means having a socialist consciousness, it means understanding one's attitude toward work as a duty to the socialist homeland."[48]

These trends toward increased use of coercion and economic self-sacrifice following the Cominform split clearly harken back to party policies in the earlier stages of its transition toward socialism. As earlier, the primary purpose of such policies was to secure the party's position in power and the country's economic viability. Yet, other policies applied in those months were more closely linked to the period beginning in late 1947 and continuing in early 1948. These policies sought to expand the party's ideological influence and further the transformation of culture and society in accordance with Communist values.

Three Steps Forward

Strengthening the Role of the Party

A first indicator of the party's continued determination to advance its progress toward socialism may be seen in the increasingly open posture adopted by the CPY in Yugoslav society. Up until mid-1947, party leaders had not publicly admitted that they were building socialism, and the party itself had retained much of its prewar and wartime conspiratorial secretiveness. After mid-1947 and especially in early 1948, the party's visibility had begun to increase. Even so, Soviet accusations in the spring of 1948 that the CPY had hidden behind the PFY were essentially correct, although, of course, no one had been fooled. This was a flaw that party leaders, while denying, could easily rectify since to do so corresponded to their own interests and program.

Before the conflict erupted, CPY activists and publicists had already begun to discuss the party's role and intentions, as well as its guiding

Communist ideology, far more openly than they had immediately after the war. As soon as party leaders recognized the approaching conflict with the Soviet Union, they furthered that progress, most importantly by announcing on May 25, 1948, the first party congress to be held in 20 years.[49] At the Fifth Party Congress, convened in late July 1948, the CPY publicly stated its role as the leading force in society, emphasizing its predominant position with regard to the PFY. The party also now decided to allow public, nonparty attendance at its meetings.[50] Such open meetings, while not overly emphasized in the first years, were intended to demonstrate the party's increasingly public position and project a sense of self-confidence.

Meanwhile, internal party documents urged greater CPY involvement at all levels of society in order to enhance its political control and improve economic efficiency. The insecurity caused by the split, combined with party leaders' awareness of previous failings, had apparently convinced them that in order to maintain power and achieve socialism the party would simply have to become more active and more efficient in the realization of its goals. Consequently, numerous documents throughout late 1948 and 1949 called for greater party presence in and more structured party supervision over all aspects of society, from legislation to industry to culture.

This emphasis was clearly evident, for example, in the previously cited meeting between the Politburos of the CPY and the Communist Party of Slovenia. The response of top CPY leaders to Kraiger's report revealed both their security concerns and their plan to eliminate domestic threats by strengthening the party's internal unity and increasing its level of social activism. Central leaders took their Slovene comrades to task first for allowing such deviations to persist and then for failing to accept responsibility for their errors. Kardelj set the tone:

> The results are shown as the causes. These occurrences are not the result of our line, but of our inactivity in fighting for that line. The Central Committee of the CPY has always said: the line can succeed only if the CPY is active and united, if there is a struggle for each individual, and that is possible only if every communist is active. The Central Committee of the Communist Party of Slovenia has erred: there has been opportunism toward enemies and sectarianism toward waverers.... In the Politburo itself there has been support for nationalist deviations.... Who brought the clericalists to power in the writer's association? Our people.... Teachers have not been taken in hand. The teaching ranks need to be purged. The excuse that we lack teachers is insufficient.... The situation isn't critical, but not carrying out the line and inactivity by the Party is.[51]

Tito continued Kardelj's critique, but carefully moved the discussion to a larger context, offering a self-critical examination of the leadership's difficulty in balancing its pragmatic and revolutionary aims.

> We are a leninist Party and only with its help and with the help of democratic centralism can everything be held together.... Everything is in the Party, and the main fault is in the leadership. It has lost itself in practicism. It has lost its revolutionary vigilance.... These occurrences in Slovenia are typical but are most evident in Slovenia. We still have a long struggle before us (for example, the problem of the village). As soon as we broke with the Russians, we knew there would be much danger. The influence of the West must not be underestimated. The more relations we have with the West the more mobilized our Party must be and the more it must explain things.... Even among us at the top there have been errors in that we were not sufficiently energetic in carrying out some things. Now we need to make a change and cooperate more and have more faith in the Central Committee of the CPY. We have faith in you too, but we have the right to criticize you. You must further solidify your Party and do more political work.... Cleanse the Party of compromisers and rotten elements. Return to the Party its revolutionary spirit.... Precisely now, when we are deciding to follow a democratic path, the Party must be mobilized and unified as a centralized organism.[52]

Ranković followed up on this theme in his speech on organizational problems in the party at the Second Plenum of the Central Committee in January 1949. Complaining that Politburo and Central Committee members were not sufficiently involved in party work and that republic leaders did not send them enough information or reports, he urged party leaders to be more vigilant in following "what our party organizations are doing and how they are working."[53] Finally, Tito adopted the same approach in his critique of the Croatian Communist party in late May 1949. Reminding Croatia's leaders that most of their cadres were young and inexperienced, he instructed them to send their strongest members out to the districts and local regions. Speeches, articles, and circulars, he insisted, were not sufficient; practical daily work was needed.[54]

One element of this attempt to enhance the efficacy of party policies was greater emphasis on planning as a mode of operation. Planning was certainly not a new approach among orthodox Communist parties, and calls for its increased use had surfaced previously in CPY documents. Now, however, these calls became more frequent, insistent, and specific. For example, countless reports in the fall of 1948 that bemoaned the disorganized unplanned work and chaotic conditions in agitprop departments paved the way for a variety of party directives instructing those departments to develop detailed three-month work plans at all levels and submit them to higher organizations for approval by the end of that year.[55]

The party's increasingly visible role and party leaders' heightened demands for more supervision both served to perpetuate and enhance the already noted trends in rhetoric for more emphasis on ideology, especially ideological education, and for greater attention to the qualifications and development of party cadres. In other words, despite party leaders' concerns about their position in power and the stability of the economy, they persisted also in their determination to expand ideology's sphere of activity, increase the masses' familiarity with Marxism-Leninism, and improve the ideological qualifications of educators, propagandists, and party members. Indeed, they now had concluded that their survival in power depended on such improved cadres and increased ideological activity. Signs of this continuing commitment may be seen in numerous discussions and activities, including the October 1948 addition of an ideological-educational sector to the People's Front; a resolution from the First Congress of the League of Trade Unions to overcome occurrences of apoliticalness and lack of ideology in cultural-artistic work; a call for systematic work in teachers' *activities* to discuss the elimination of ideological deviations and the connection of theory to practice; a request from the central agitprop department for reports on ideological-educational work in all organizations of the party, PFY, PYY, AFW, and League of Trade Unions; and a directive sent to all agitprop departments to assess the ideological work of local social-political and professional journals.[56] Yet in evaluating these efforts to improve ideological-political education, most party leaders acknowledged that activists were still overburdened with "practical work," while the party's persuasive activities remained overwhelmingly "practicist," providing "too little theoretical explanation of individual questions."[57] Even ideological-educational work among party leaders tended, according to one report, to focus on party policies rather than on Marxism-Leninism.[58] The correct balance between daily politics and the transformation of society remained elusive.

An uninterested observer might suggest that party leaders were unrealistic in demanding that persuasive personnel give *top* priority to so many different tasks—that they secure the party's political position, the country's economic stability, and the public's ideological orthodoxy all at the same time. Unable or unwilling to reduce their demands, however, party leaders instead argued that the failings of party persuasion lay in the inadequate ideological qualifications of those assigned to initiate and guide the cultural transformation, including writers, musicians, artists, filmmakers, journalists, teachers, and the leaders of agitprop departments themselves. Thus, the union leader responsible for cultural issues, Mišo Pavičević, worried about the dangerous cultural infection spread by old bourgeois intellectuals who "are alien or even enemy-oriented in relation to the worker's movement, not only in their artistic conceptions but their political positions."[59]

Here again, party leaders relied on youth to resolve their dilemma. While admitting that some prewar intellectuals might be reeducated, most leaders now recommended replacing them with new and younger cadres with a more correct social background and more loyal to the Communist cause. The strongest appeal for such a focus issued from the pen of Veljko Vlahović in the spring of 1949. In a pair of lectures presented to the higher party school in Belgrade, Vlahović emphasized the need to replace old, professional, but ideologically dubious cadres with younger, perhaps less refined, but more reliable ones. Though conceding that some older intellectuals sincerely tried to grasp Marxism-Leninism and might succeed, many, he insisted, were hindered by their heritage and previous education. Moreover, he continued, the so-called apolitical intellectuals spread "unhealthy germs," the source of "various alien ideological influences in our midst." He thus urged that large numbers of the children of workers and poor peasants, "who are just as gifted as the sons of the petty bourgeoisie . . . be sent to art schools so that they may later become the pillars of culture in our country." He further called on party leaders to seek out and assist those young writers in whose hands, he said, Yugoslavia's literary development must lie.[60]

Other leaders, meanwhile, worried about the ideological background of journalists and filmmakers. Djilas, for example, now insisted that "journalistic cadres must be Party members, because if a journalist is not a Party member, that is, does not have the possibility of becoming one, he can not grasp the problems or write about them either." Similarly, another speaker declared that camera men "must be politically healthy and, if possible, Communists."[61]

The most intensive efforts to improve the quality of party ideological education, however, were aimed at teachers and at agitprop departments themselves. Several reports in late 1948 and throughout 1949 addressed the problem of teaching cadres, starting from the assumption that current educators lacked the necessary ideological qualifications to fulfill their tasks. The concluding speaker at a federal conference on the question of teachers' schools held in mid-October 1948 stated:

> Let's not fool ourselves, comrades, we inherited our teaching cadres from the past. . . . We know how they were educated, under what conditions, under what political regime, and in what social circumstances. All those factors left traces on them. . . . The process of ideologically reeducating old cadres

and the old intelligentsia isn't so easy.... it is most difficult to eliminate the traces of the past precisely in education. It was easy to force reaction from power, it is even easier to build the economy than it is to build people.[62]

Solutions offered at the conference most often aimed at improving education through the use of more politically and ideologically correct materials in lectures, courses, and texts. From now on, not only was Marxism-Leninism to be studied as a special subject, but dialectical materialism was to be introduced into all class plans and textbooks as the only correct worldview. A similar approach could be seen in the November 1948 creation of a new "sector for schools" within agitprop departments whose purpose was to supervise the development of more unified and ideologically correct class plans, textbooks, and pedagogical journals.[63]

Both the conference and agitprop departments also recommended improving ideological and general education through the elevation of new teaching cadres—preferably from the loyal working classes. This priority finally inspired party leaders to address the serious material hardships endured by teachers, especially in rural areas. A cacophony of voices now denounced the unfavorable working conditions, which, they said, not only impeded the efforts of even loyal and dedicated educators but hampered attempts by the regime to recruit new people into the profession. In order to achieve both good teaching and recruitment, party leaders concluded, educators must no longer be assigned such extraneous tasks as assisting with the *otkup* or passing out ration cards. Nor should they have to take on second jobs for strictly financial reasons. In response, several republics began gradually to reduce their demands on teachers and provide perks for rural educators, including, for example, the introduction of special stores, subsidized apartments and heating, and hardship pay for service in especially poor regions.[64]

Agitprop departments themselves were also a target for party criticism. Many failings in ideological education, the leadership now argued, were directly related to the weakness of agitprop departments, which were often incomplete and organizationally unstable, while their cadres were poorly qualified and overburdened with other assignments. Such complaints about agitprop departments had been a constant feature of local and regional party reports since the end of the war. Now, however, central party organizations had taken up the call, were expressing the same concerns both publicly and privately, and were demanding action. Central reports on party organizations in Montenegro and Slovenia, for example, noted with outrage that their agitprop departments had changed seven times in one year.[65] Even more serious, a report on ideological education revealed that only two leaders in the theoretical sectors of all district agitprop departments had completed even the lower party school.[66] The quantity and vigor of these reports reflect the increased priority that party leaders now attached to its persuasive activities. That same report thus concluded that "the organizational consolidation of agitprop and the elevation of its new members is one of the most important tasks for the further development of ideological education, not only in the Party but in general."[67]

Beyond urging regional party organizations to stop undervaluing their agitprop departments, party leaders also now suggested new criteria for the selection of agitprop personnel, based less on communication skills and more on political and ideological reliability. As Vlahović explained,

> Until now the dominant opinion has been that people could participate in agitation and propaganda work who had a certain level of education, who know a little bit about marxism-leninism . . . who are literate and have had some schooling. . . . As a result, we have had a whole series of errors in our agitation and propaganda work. . . . we need to introduce in that work, people, above all party members, above all good communists, who have a certain amount of party experience, and not just people who are literate and know how to speak well. . . . We need to struggle so that people from the ranks of the workers participate in agitational work, regardless of whether they are intellectuals or not.[68]

In such documents, party leaders declared openly what they had begun to say privately even before the split—that it was no longer sufficient for those who would guide the cultural transformation to be cooperative and literate. Now they needed also to possess certain ideological qualifications and considerable ideological zeal.[69] And since it seemed likely that not all propagandists could be reeducated, some might have to be replaced by others who would be more reliable, even if also less articulate. What was at issue here was not *political* reliability—the teachers, journalists, and agitprop activists under criticism had already proven their loyalty and obedience to the Communist regime. Under examination was not how they voted or how eloquently they could present the party line, but how they *thought*, how they viewed the world.

As in previous years, however, the party's failures in persuasion, though stemming in part from the inadequate qualifications of its personnel, also reflected uncertainty and disunity in policy determination at the top. For CPY policies now, as earlier, even when roughly corresponding to an overall plan, also represented ad hoc and hastily constructed responses to specific events—responses that were not always consistent over time or among individual leaders. Confusion among top CPY leaders was most clearly reflected in party rhetoric concerning two important issues: socialization of the countryside and the treatment of the Soviet Union and other People's Democracies.

Socialization of the Countryside

In marked contrast to the immediate postwar era when party leaders sought to woo and conciliate their rural constituents, much of the hostile rhetoric so prevalent among party publicists in the first year and a half after the Cominform resolution was aimed precisely at the party's ideological opponents in the countryside. Among those most often attacked were wealthy peasants (termed "kulaks" by party leaders), clericalists, "speculators," and "saboteurs." Often, however, such rhetoric seemed uncertain, spontaneous, and not in accordance with the party's overall strategy. Indeed, the confusion that surrounded CPY policies toward the peasantry in 1948 and 1949 provides one of the best examples of the often impulsive and uncontrolled nature of CPY activity.

Party leaders had decided already in late 1947 and early 1948 to initiate socialization of the countryside through expansion of the cooperative movement. At that point, party leaders anticipated a relatively slow process, beginning with the construction of cooperative centers as a necessary element of the socialist infrastructure.[70] Following the Cominform split, however, party leaders reluctantly decided that they would have to accelerate that process. Accordingly, the Second Plenum of the Central Committee held in January 1949 publicly called for socialization of the countryside to proceed "with greater boldness and at a faster tempo."[71] The reasons for this decision are still a matter of some controversy. One common perception of the party's behavior is that it represented a knee-jerk reaction to Stalin's accusation that the CPY was soft on the peasantry and was designed mainly to prove Yugoslavia's loyalty to Stalinist methods.[72] More recent scholarship, however, denies that CPY leaders ever intended to copy Soviet agrarian methods and attributes the changed policies to the party's need for economic self-sufficiency and an abiding (if misplaced) faith in the peasants' revolutionary nature.[73]

Whatever the cause, the change in party rhetoric directed at the countryside was unmistakable. In the first part of 1948, agitprop departments in rural areas had been instructed to focus mainly on the creation of cooperative centers through voluntary labor actions, and up until the fall of that year they did so. Following the Cominform resolution, however, both internal and public documents began to call more frequently for a "sharpening of class struggle in the village." A memo sent to the central agitprop department about persuasive activities in Kosovo and Metohia in October 1948, for example, suggested that party leaders must occasionally adopt a "harsher" approach in their relations with the peasantry. Too often, it remarked, they seemed excessively tolerant, willing to delay socialization of the village "'until conditions are ripe' without having any idea how long that might take."[74] This kind of "persuasion" may well have reflected a knee-jerk response by certain agitprop departments reacting to Soviet accusations of CPY lenience toward kulaks. That approach, however, was not dictated or endorsed by the top leadership. On the contrary, throughout 1948, CPY leaders responsible for agrarian policies stubbornly defended their previous policies toward the village and reiterated their determination to pursue socialization of the countryside through gradualist and strictly voluntary methods.[75] Accordingly, a Central Committee directive criticized recent campaigns by some agitprop departments for the common tilling of land since, it said, the party leadership had not yet given a definite decision on that matter. The same directive rebuked agitprop departments more generally as too inclined to follow their "own agitprop line, approaching party problems in a one-sided manner."[76]

By the end of January 1949, however, the party leadership did declare its intention to pursue socialization of the countryside "with greater boldness and at a faster tempo." Most students of this period have interpreted that statement made at the Second Plenum of the Central Committee as a call for mass collectivization à la Stalin of January 1930.[77] In fact, however, those damning words had been carefully surrounded by warnings and caveats intended to avert the errors and violence of Soviet-style collectivization. Kardelj's speech at the Second Plenum indeed called for more rapid growth of the socialist sector in agriculture, but continued to insist on the voluntary nature of the campaign and on the continued need for transitional institutions on the path to socialism.[78]

Despite these precautions, the party's middle and lower cadres clearly heard the decisions of the Second Plenum as a call to action and understood that their task was to get as many peasants as possible into the highest form of cooperatives—Peasant Working Cooperatives or PWCs—by whatever means necessary. Their perception was shaped in part by the atmosphere of tension in post-split Yugoslavia, the unquestionable desire of many Yugoslav party members to prove Stalin wrong, and the repressed radicalism of many young Communists. It also, however, reflected quite accurately the content and form of directives aimed at the countryside from the central agitprop department. For not only were lower and middle cadres confused by the mixed message of Kardelj's speech, so too were colleagues at the top. Djilas, the *head* of the central agitprop department, later claimed, "I was confused about collectivization. I never really understood that question. There is almost no important event that I didn't write about after 1948. I didn't write about collectivization.... I said to myself: Kardelj and the others know it better." Nonetheless, he continued, "I called my colleagues from the press to agitprop and insisted that they popularize it."[79]

Djilas's words, though self-serving, ring true. Djilas, indeed, wrote nothing on collectivization, and party rhetoric directed at the village remained exceptionally unfocused and ambiguous. When Djilas and Vlahović met with the Croatian agitprop department in early February to pass on the conclusions of the Second Plenum, they again sent a clearly mixed message. On the one hand, both stressed that the decisions of the Second Plenum did not represent a break in party policy and they emphasized the importance of all forms of cooperatives, both higher and lower. Djilas, in particular, warned against overestimating the extent of peasant movement into the working cooperatives and urged agitators to make the general cooperatives seem attractive, since it would then be easier for peasants to move to higher forms of cooperatives. He further insisted that agitators stick firmly to the principle of voluntariness, as all else would only hinder the party's work. Yet he and Vlahović also called for much more intensive party activity in the village, for a sharper struggle against kulak influence on middle peasants, and for "ceaseless" agitation toward the formation of working cooperatives. In one sentence Djilas displayed the essential ambiguity of both the party line and the rhetoric designed to promote it: "Our tactic toward the kulak," he said, "must not be a general offensive; in each concrete case we must determine the means of limiting, or rather eliminating him."[80]

Responding to these unfocused but insistent demands, agitprop departments, mass organizations, and the media rapidly expanded both the volume and intensity of their rhetoric against "kulaks" and for cooperative forms of agriculture. Yet here, too, the focus was unclear. Many activists, still relying on directives from the past, were loathe to state too openly the class nature of the regime and its struggle. In his concluding speech to the Twelfth Plenum of the PYY, Neorečić even referred directly to certain errors in the Soviet collectivization drive that the CPY did not wish to reproduce.

> Do we have to take the same forms adopted in the Soviet Union, so that we de-kulakize someone in the morning, create a kolhoz in the afternoon, and do only harm? We don't have to adopt the same forms, we don't have to make the same mistakes.... We must carry it out so that not one meter of land is damaged, the yield remains the same, we don't reduce our livestock reserves, and not one sheep is slaughtered. This means that we will have to adopt more flexible forms in the struggle.[81]

He then called on youth agitators to struggle against capitalist elements in the village not as kulaks, since that would allow them to create a united kulak front, but as "people's enemies."

> We will carry out the same kind of struggle as we did during the war. After the war we liquidated the capitalist bourgeoisie, not fighting against them as such, but as enemies. We must unmask and punish the rich peasants as enemies of the people. If one doesn't fulfill his obligation to the state we need to punish him as an enemy.... We will liquidate them as a class if we liquidate them as people's enemies.[82]

Only one month later, however, in an meeting held in the central agitprop department to discuss newspaper and journal articles concerning the village, Politburo member Mijalko Todorović criticized those articles in which, he said, "one does not see class struggle, and that might allow the peasants to remain asleep." Similarly, Djilas insisted that editors understand that the socialization of agriculture is the essential question of the economy because "it brings in class struggle which does not exist in industry or in the other branches."[83] A report addressing "propaganda-agitational work of the PYY in the village" urged that it stop idealizing the situation and show the difficulties and the course of the class struggle. "One often gets the impression," its unnamed author worried, "that the development of the village is proceeding peacefully and smoothly, without class conflicts. Such a style of writing only blunts the cutting edge of our struggle."[84] These many and often contradictory approaches to socialist construction indicate that persuasive leaders at all levels remained unclear as to the purpose or main direction of their party's agrarian policies. They did not know whether class conflict should be provoked or avoided and they did not understand what, exactly, a kulak was or what they should do with one if they found him.

Treatment of the Soviet Union

The confusion typical of CPY rhetoric toward the village was matched by its equally ambiguous attitude toward the Soviet Union. For although CPY leaders began defending themselves against Soviet and Eastern bloc accusations instantly, they did not go on the offensive in their relations with the Soviet Union until late March 1949. Up to that point, lower-level party leaders were left rudderless, uncertain as to precisely what their attitude toward the fraternal socialist countries should be. Consequently, some continued to praise the Soviet Union and Eastern bloc countries as prolifically as ever, while others simply fell silent on the issue. By mid-

1949, however, top CPY leaders had finally settled on a more active and aggressive response to the split and the Soviet Union. At that point, they began to evaluate and openly denounce not only Stalin's foreign but also his domestic policies. In so doing, the CPY leadership freed itself from the constraints of the Soviet model, opening the door to reforms and innovations in its own approach to the construction of socialism.

Although CPY rhetoric concerning the Soviet Union would eventually take a 90-degree turn away from what it had been before the split, this change developed only slowly and after much initial confusion. Given the extremely rancorous exchange of letters between the CPY and CPSU party leaderships, and following the Cominform's virtual excommunication of top CPY leaders from the ranks of orthodox communism, one might have expected CPY rhetoric to reflect these altered relations almost immediately. In fact, that was not the case. Rather, it initially combined self-righteous indignation at both the content and form of the accusations and a stubborn determination to resist such "unjust" attacks with evident confusion at the sudden turn of events and continued loyalty to and respect for Stalin and the Soviet Union. One intent of such rhetoric was to show that the CPY itself had not changed: it had always been and would remain a loyal member of the socialist bloc. Thus, party persuasion presented the Cominform accusations as the obvious result of misinformation, implying that the entire conflict could be easily resolved if only the accusers would listen. Meanwhile, articles and speeches continued to describe Soviet literature, films, economic achievements, and policies toward capitalist countries in panegyric fashion. Tito himself ended his speech to the Fifth Congress of the CPY held in late July 1948 with "Long live the Soviet Union, long live Stalin!"

According to Dedijer, Tito and top CPY leaders adopted this tone deliberately, understanding that the population of Yugoslavia would have to acclimate to new conditions gradually and come to see on their own the failings and sins of the Soviet Union.[85] In fact, however, far from being either calculated or deceptive, this rhetorical approach seems to have reflected accurately the feelings and expectations of the party's top leaders. As Rusinow (a far more reliable observer than Dedijer) put it, "if ordinary Yugoslav Communists needed time to unlearn love of the Soviet Union and faith in Stalin's benevolent omniscience . . . so did their leaders."[86] One convicted Cominformist later recalled that Blaže Jovanović, the leader of Montenegro's regional committee, had absolutely assured them that Tito and Stalin would work it out and that the conflict would soon be over.[87] Indeed, several sources have noted that Tito, in particular, long held hope that his party's relations with Stalin and the Soviet government could be repaired.[88]

Moreover, even internal party discussions of the conflict revealed uncertainty about the appropriate treatment of the Soviet Union. As we have seen, many top CPY leaders had begun to criticize Soviet models in private well before the split. Now, however, even those criticisms seemed to subside, as if the leaders feared to validate Cominform accusations by displaying any sentiments that might be construed as anti-Soviet. For example, leaders at a meeting of the central agitprop department in December 1947 had worried about the overuse of Soviet material on radio broadcasts and in February 1948, Djilas had condemned excessive reliance on the Soviet line in the press. In December 1948, however, the central agitprop department complained that too few Soviet and Eastern bloc pieces had been represented in the 1948–1949 drama repertoire.[89]

While the party's reluctance to face reality may be understandable, the resulting uncertainty left CPY persuasive personnel floundering as they received no real instructions concerning the correct approach to Stalin, the Soviet Union, and the other People's Democracies. Left on their own, party publicists followed the path of least resistance and, as a result, relatively few articles in the first year and a half after the split addressed the conflict head on and none offered any explanation for its occurrence. The split, when mentioned, was described as the consequence of slanders and defamations so inexplicable that they literally could not and need not be explained.

There were two exceptions to this general neglect of the Cominformist accusations. We have already discussed party rhetoric concerning the relative roles of the Red Army and the Partisan movement in the liberation in Yugoslavia. The other exception concerned those accusations of CPY disloyalty to the Soviet Union. Here party leaders could easily document the extraordinary lengths to which they had gone to show their dedication to Stalin and the Soviet Union. Only two weeks after publishing the resolution, Dedijer provided statistics in *Borba* clearly demonstrating the prominence of all things Soviet in the Yugoslav press, publications, and film industry. He noted for example that *Borba* had devoted 7.4 percent of its space to the Soviet Union, while in comparison the Communist newspapers of France and Bulgaria set aside only .88 percent and 6.5 percent of their space for articles on the Soviet Union. Further, he noted that in the first four months of 1948, 78.39 percent of the foreign books published in Yugoslavia had been translated from the Russian, with only 9.8 percent being of English, French, or American origin. Corresponding figures for Czechoslovakia were 20.58 percent and 60 percent respectively. Likewise, during the first four months of 1948, 71.2 percent of the films shown in Yugoslavia were of Soviet origin, while only 2.6 percent were American. In contrast, during the week from the 9th to the 15th of July, 31 American, 18 Soviet, 17 English, and 10 French films were showing in

Prague.[90] However accurate, this kind of rhetoric directly contradicted the party's simultaneous attempts to highlight its independence.

In any case, top CPY leaders eventually had to consider the causes and significance of the split more seriously. Louis Adamic records Tito as having stated already in January 1949 that something had gone wrong in the Soviet Union, that it had "blundered into the rankest type of nationalism" and was meandering into revisionism that was counterrevolutionary in effect, if not in intent.[91] Djilas also spoke of Soviet revisionism in his report to the central agitprop department after the Second Plenum of the Central Committee in January 1949.[92]

A real change in the party's rhetorical approach to the Soviet Union and Cominform split, however, came only after a pivotal meeting of Djilas and Kardelj with the central agitprop department on March 28, 1949. In his opening speech, Djilas complained that thus far agitation and propaganda directed against the Cominform resolution and its supporters had come only from *Borba*, while other newspapers simply reprinted its articles or, more often, stayed silent as if the question did not concern them. In the future, he instructed them, the conflict must be the main political question since people were confused. They demanded an explanation that would not limit itself to addressing only the slanders printed in the resolution, but would "explain the essence of things." Thus, party rhetoric directed against the resolution must cease to be purely defensive, concerned only with denying lies. It was time, he said, to go on the offense and actively unmask the split's causes and roots.

> Our weakness is that we suppressed facts about the USSR. . . . The essence of the conflict is between us and the USSR and we must make no exceptions to that perspective. . . .
>
> The weakness of our propaganda is seen also in our domestic radio broadcasts which still play mainly light music, Soviet songs, and the like which again convince people of our loyalty to the Soviet Union. We need to broadcast instead our own songs from the war and construction which will stimulate our masses to socialist construction.

Djilas now restated his earlier insistence that it was wrong to accept uncritically everything that came from the USSR and People's Democracies and, finally, he urged party organs to work out the theoretical questions systematically and to read once again the works of Marx, Engels, Lenin, and even Stalin.[93]

Kardelj confirmed the new approach, emphasizing also that the conflict was not accidental and not due to mistakes by the CPY but was the consequence of new occurrences that must follow the construction of socialism. "The question," he asked, "is whether the construction of socialism now and in the future has to repeat everything that happened in the

USSR . . . or if it can bring in something new. . . . I don't mean to say that we in our party have found a genius who is realizing a new stage in marxism," but, he continued, "we want to fight for [its] creative application."[94] From this point onward, CPY persuasive organs began to address the issue of the split in more depth and became progressively less hesitant in their criticism of the Soviet Union.

Over the course of 1949, various articles, especially in *Borba* and *Komunist*, sought to show the origins of the split in the nonsocialist behavior of the Soviet Union, especially in its foreign relations. By September 1949, Djilas had published a direct attack on Soviet revisionism that concluded that each state must find its own road to socialism and that fall, Moša Pijade argued for the first time that the roots of the Soviet deviation lay in its internal policies.[95] The Yugoslav Communists' more direct approach was undoubtedly aided by the onset of the "Titoist" purges in Eastern Europe and by the increasingly aggressive verbal attacks launched against Yugoslavia by the Cominformist countries during the summer and fall of 1949. The incredible barrage of anti-Yugoslav invective published in the second Cominform resolution on November 29, 1949, must have finally dashed any hopes that the split could be smoothed over and driven the last nail into the coffin of Soviet-Yugoslav friendship. In any case, the CPY's open counterattacks on the Soviet Union and its policies did much to free party leaders from their psychological dependence on the Soviet model as the only path to socialism. Having publicly stated that the Soviet Union had deviated from Marxism-Leninism, it now remained for CPY leaders to explain how their own policies would differ and in what ways they would reflect more accurately the intentions of their ideology's founders.

Conclusion

It is difficult to assess the precise effects of CPY rhetoric concerning the split; overall, however, the campaign must be judged a success. After all, despite all expectations to the contrary, the CPY and its leadership did survive. Certainly, official and anecdotal sources indicate that most Yugoslav citizens supported their own leaders in the conflict. Even those who were otherwise unenthusiastic about the regime seemed to feel that they'd rather suffer under their own Communists than under Stalin's. Djilas described his conversation with an at best apolitical female member of the Belgrade bourgeoisie who said, "So long as the Russians don't run the show. At least you are *our* people."[96] Yet these indications of CPY popularity must be weighed against the simultaneous growth of coercion described above. If all Yugoslav citizens supported their leaders, why the heavy reliance on force? Why so many arrests?

One problem in evaluating this era is that nearly all sources for it are either blatantly pro- or anti-Tito. Communist and pro-partisan sources, of course, all attest to a mood of enormous enthusiasm and energy very similar to that which prevailed after the war. Perhaps the most glowing of these comes from the socialist Slovene-American, Louis Adamic. Adamic's book, *The Eagle and the Roots,* based on his 1949 visit, abounds in descriptions of the love and devotion shown for Tito by Yugoslav citizens. He notes, for example, that the word *TITO* had been painted everywhere from store walls, to airplane wings, to a chimney visible only to a few top-floor apartment dwellers. With regard to the latter, when he asked the residents about it, they claimed not to have noticed it since there were so many such signs. They also insisted, however, that the signs were not propagandistic but undoubtedly expressed the true feelings of those who had painted them. Similarly, Adamic's brother admitted that while some slogans had been inscribed by the agitprop department, many were written spontaneously by average Yugoslav citizens. Adamic himself claimed at first to have been suspicious of and somewhat repelled by these expressions of loyalty and devotion. Eventually, however, he seems to have accepted them as more or less genuine.[97]

In contrast, anti-Tito sources—usually anti-Communist emigrants or Cominform supporters—insist that all such displays of enthusiasm were manufactured by agitprop departments and enforced by the constant presence of the secret police. For example, open Cominformist Petar Komnenić also described the enormous growth of the cult of personality around Tito in the months following the split but gave it a rather different spin. At the Fifth Party Congress, he insisted, all political leaders were chosen solely on the basis of their personal loyalty to Tito, while any delegates of uncertain affiliation were prevented from speaking. Moreover, he claimed that the congress was packed with agents of the secret police, who followed delegates around, recording their movements, meetings, and conversations. Secret police agents also attended all congress proceedings "and if they found someone who didn't clap for every declaration and at the appearance of every speaker, especially if that speaker were Tito, later that person would be accused of a serious crime for which he might get a year or two of 'socially corrective labor'."[98]

Both types of sources are likely expressing reality as they saw it. As in the first years after the war, extreme emotions on both sides of the political fence coexisted (though, again, on an unequal basis). How "most people" felt is much harder to discern. What does seem clear is that the split had a destabilizing effect on society. Consequently, it is no surprise that state-society relations in this period overcame the inertia that had settled in by 1947. In some cases, that inertia was replaced by a renewed sense of cooperation and partnership in a shared future; in others, it gave way to blatantly hostile relations and the open use of force. To the extent that many Yugoslav citizens were reinspired with a sense of pride, the split and the rhetoric designed to explain it did revitalize relations between the party-state and society. The mere fact that CPY leaders asked Yugoslav citizens to read the documents and decide the issue for themselves indicated the reestablishment of dialogue. The pride and enthusiasm generated by shared and successful resistance to the local bully also produced a more active and dynamic atmosphere. That more active atmosphere was also, however, reflected in the apparent growth of open resistance to the Communist regime. In either case, more dynamic relations did not mean more equal relations. As in the past, party leaders maintained a monopoly over organs of both persuasion and coercion and while they welcomed signs of renewed public enthusiasm, they aggressively persecuted any who dared oppose their program for change.

The 18 months from mid-1948 to the end of 1949 were a crucial transition period in the CPY's path toward reform. The party's harsh treatment of opposition elements and its renewed emphasis on Yugoslav pride and independence channeled especially toward the achievement of economic stability unquestionably represented backward steps in its strategy for socialist construction. Meanwhile, however, the enhanced role of the party and attempts at socialization of the countryside reflected CPY leaders' determination to move forward along the path to socialism, but also their still limited ability to act beyond the constraints of the Soviet model. The inconsistencies in CPY rhetoric during this period illustrate most accurately the confusion that party members at all levels felt as they sought to resist Soviet domination while remaining loyal to their guiding ideology. Only in mid-1949 when party leaders began openly to attack Soviet domestic as well as foreign policies could they confront the source of and gradually diminish that confusion. By announcing that Stalin's Soviet Union had deviated from the intentions of Marx, Engels, and Lenin, party leaders were now free to move beyond the constraints of the Stalinist model not only in thought but in deed. That freedom allowed and required them to devise their own blueprint for the construction of socialism in Yugoslavia.

Notes

1. Stephen Clissold, *Yugoslavia and the Soviet Union 1939–1973: A Documentary Survey* (London: Oxford University Press, 1975); Vladimir Dedijer, *Tito* (New York: Simon and Schuster, 1953), 357.

2. Clissold, *Yugoslavia and the Soviet Union*; Milovan Djilas, *Conversations with Stalin* (New York: Harcourt Brace Jovanovich, 1962); Milovan Djilas, *Rise and Fall* (New York: Harcourt Brace Jovanovich, 1983); Ivo Banac, *With Stalin Against Tito,*

Cominformist Splits in Yugoslav Communism (Ithaca, NY: Cornell University Press, 1988); Dennison Rusinow, *The Yugoslav Experiment, 1948–1974* (Berkeley, CA: University of California Press, 1977); Vladimir Dedijer, *Dokumenti 1948* (Belgrade: 1980); Dedijer, *Tito;* Vladimir Dedijer, *The Battle Stalin Lost, Memoirs of Yugoslavia, 1948–1953* (New York: Viking Press, 1970); Vladimir Dedijer, *Novi prilozi za biografiju Josipa Broza Tita,* Vol. 3 (Belgrade: Rad, 1984); A. Ross Johnson, *The Transformation of Communist Ideology, The Yugoslav Case, 1945–1953* (Cambridge, MA: The MIT Press, 1972).

3. Dedijer, *Tito;* Dedijer, *The Battle Stalin Lost;* Djilas, *Conversations with Stalin;* George W. Hoffman and Fred Warner Neal, *Yugoslavia and the New Communism* (New York: Twentieth Century Fund, 1962); Phyllis Auty, *Yugoslavia* (New York: Walker and Company, 1965).

4. Banac, *With Stalin Against Tito;* Venko Markovski, *Goli Otok, the Island of Death: A Diary in Letters* (Boulder, CO: Westview Press, 1984). Since 1989 there has been a virtual explosion of new books, mainly memoir accounts and novels, dealing with Goli Otok. Among them are Rosa Dragović-Gašpar, *Let iznad Golog otoka* (Belgrade: Akvarijus, 1990); Milinko B. Stojanović, *Antologija golootočke misli i riječi* (Belgrade: Stručna knjiga, 1996); and Mihovil Horvat, *Goli Otok: Stratište duha* (Zagreb: Orion Stella, 1996).

5. Banac, *With Stalin Against Tito;* Rusinow; Dedijer, *The Battle Stalin Lost;* Dušan Bilandžić, *Borba za samoupravni socijalizam u Jugoslaviji, 1945–1969* (Zagreb: 1969); Pero Morača and Stanislav Stojanović, eds., *Povijest Saveza komunista Jugoslavije* (Belgrade: Izdavački centar Komunist, 1985).

6. Susan Woodward, *Socialist Unemployment: The Political Economy of Yugoslavia 1945–1990* (Princeton: Princeton University Press, 1995), 100, 108–121; Melissa Bokovoy, *Peasants and Communists: Politics and Ideology in the Yugoslav Countryside, 1941–1953* (Pittsburgh, PA: University of Pittsburgh Press, 1998).

7. Radovan Radonjić, *Sukob KPJ sa Kominformom i društveni razvoj Jugoslavije (1948–1950)* 2d ed. (Zagreb: 1976).

8. One notable exception to this rule were the Dachau trials in Slovenia, which began in May 1947 and continued through July 1950. In at least 10 separate court proceedings, over 30 seasoned Communists, all of whom had been prisoners of war in Dachau, Buchenwald, and Mauthausen and many of whom were also Spanish Civil War veterans, were tried and convicted as spies and agents of the Gestapo and other foreign services. While none were openly accused of Cominformist activity, the later trials, at least, seem also to have been connected to the Soviet-Yugoslav split, though exactly how remains uncertain. One author has suggested that the arrests were designed to placate Stalin's suspicions of anyone imprisoned by the Nazis, while another argues that they may have occurred because Tito suspected the top defendant of being a Soviet informant. Others yet suspect that someone in the top leadership simply considered them to represent a potentially dangerous faction due to their previous experiences and close mutual relations. See Ljubo Sirc, *Between Hitler and Tito, Nazi Occupation and Communist Oppression* (London: Andre Deutsch Limited, 1989), 128; Banac, *With Stalin Against Tito,* 187; Rajko Danilović, *Upotreba neprijatelja: Politička sudjenja 1945–1991 u Jugoslaviji* (Valjevo: Valjevac, 1993), 112–119; Boro Krivokapić, *Dahauski procesi* (Belgrade: 1986).

9. Woodward, 127.

10. Djilas has described the not always successful efforts that top party leaders made to retain the loyalty and services of certain valued colleagues, including Stefan Mitrović, Radovan Zogović, Veljko Vlahović, Boris Ziherl, and Rodoljub Čolaković. Djilas, *Rise and Fall*, 194–197. In contrast, Sreten Žujović, Andrija Hebrang and many others were given no leeway and suffered immediate consequences. Banac, *With Stalin Against Tito*, 118–119, 129, 155–156.

11. Žarko Bulajić and Radivoje Vukićević in Stojanović, 371–372, 426–454.

12. Djilas, *Rise and Fall*, 240.

13. Banac, *With Stalin Against Tito*, 145–146.

14. Ibid., 146–151.

15. "Rad PK SKOJ-a za Srbiju u 1948 godini," December 1948, ACKSKJ, CK SKOJ IIIb–1/18; "Stanje i rad partijske organizacije na univerzitetima," 18 Jan. 1949, ACKSKJ, V-KII/13.

16. Stojanović, 608–651 passim; "Referat na plenum CK Crne Gore od nepoznatog autora i datuma," in Stojanović, 654.

17. Memo from the Regional Committee of the Communist party of Montenegro to the Control Commission of the Central Committee of the CPY, 17 Sept. 1949, in Stojanović, 604–605.

18. Meeting of PB CK KPJ, 30 May 1949, ACKSKJ, III/41. See also Veljko Vlahović, "Zapisnik plenum Komisije za agitaciju i štampu Saveznog odbora NFJ," 6 June 1949, AJ, SSRNJ 142-27-82.

19. Banac, *With Stalin Against Tito*, 145–220.

20. Dejan Medaković, *Efemeris III: Hronika jedne porodice*, 3rd ed. (Belgrade: 1993), 230.

21. Borislav Pekić, *Godine koje su skakavci pojeli* (Belgrade: 1987); Danilović, 122–126.

22. For information on that case see Banac, *With Stalin Against Tito*, 119–123; Jill Irvine, *The Croat Question: Partisan Politics in the Formation of the Yugoslav Socialist State* (Boulder, CO: Westview Press, 1993), 199–203. According to Milomir Marić, the arrests of Rade Žigić, Duško Brkić, and Stanko Opačić, all Serbs from Croatia, also had little or nothing to do with the Soviet Union, but most likely represented a "settling of old accounts" initiated by Vladimir Bakarić. Milomir Marić, *Deca komunizma* (Belgrade: 1987), 293–296.

23. Meeting of PB CK KPJ, 30 May 1949, ACKSKJ, III/41.

24. Meeting of PB CK KPJ with PB CK Slovenia, 15 Jan. 1949, ACKSKJ, III/39.

25. Dedijer, *Tito*, 367.

26. Ibid., 362.

27. Ibid., 385.

28. Ibid., 363, Djilas, *Rise and Fall*, 206; cited in Rusinow, 28.

29. Dedijer, *Tito*, 360.

30. Ivo Matija Maček, "Iz Moskve je stigao 'Borsalino'," in Marić, 102.

31. Susan Woodward points out that the shift to economic self-sufficiency had actually begun already in March 1948 when the Soviet Union reneged on its promise to deliver military hardware and withdrew its military advisors. Woodward, 108.

32. "Govor Borisa Kidriča," at I. Kongres, 24–29 Oct. 1948, AJ, CVSSJ F3/J.

33. Ivan Božičević, "Uloga i zadaci JSRNJ," at I. Kongres, 24–29 Oct. 1948, AJ, CVSSJ F3. For more information on party-worker negotiations concerning wage scales see Woodward, 84–95.
34. Božičević, "Uloga i zadaci JSRNJ."
35. "Statut Savez Sindikata Jugoslavije," 24–29 Oct. 1948, AJ, CVSSJ F3 (emphasis added).
36. Ibid.
37. "Za dalje jačanje i učvršćenje sindikalnih organizacija," *Borba*, 31 March 1948, p. 1; Mišo Pavičević, "Značaj šestog plenuma za dalji razvoj Jedinstvenih Sindikata," *Rad*, 8 April 1948, p. 2.
38. "Predlog plana," late 1948–early 1949, ACKSKJ, VIII II/2-c-20.
39. "Rezolucija o neposrednim zadacima organizacija Saveza sindikata," 24–29 Oct. 1948, AJ, CVSSJ F3.
40. For example, the third expanded plenum of the Central Committee of the Communist Party of Croatia that met in Sept. 1949 limited its work to the following economic topics: "Some problems concerning the *otkup*," "Main problems of the labor force," and "Problems of the local economy." "Zasedanje III redovnog (proširenog) plenuma CK KPH," *Socijalistički front*, 2, no. 5 (Oct. 1949): 3–44.
41. "Rezolucija o tekućim zadacima u oblasti privrede," in Branko Petranović, Ranko Končar and Radovan Radonjić, eds., *Sednice Centralnog komiteta KPJ (1948–1952)* (Belgrade: Izdavački centar Komunist, 1985), 280; Stevo Tomić, "O kulturno-masovnom radu danas," *Socijalistički front*, 2, no. 2 (April 1949): 25.
42. "Širimo pokret Alije Sirotanovića," *Omladina*, 7 Aug. 1949, p. 2; "Rudar Džemal Ramović iz Kaknja postavio novi rekord u kopanju uglja," *Politika*, 20 Aug. 1949, p. 1; "Rista Mijatović—ponos ugljenokopa Kakanj," *Borba*, 5 Sept. 1949, p. 3; M. J., "Omladina u borbi za visoku produktivnost rada," *Politika*, 19 Dec. 1949, p. 3. For more on Sirotanović see Marić, 13–16.
43. "Zapisnik sa sastanka PK SKOJ-H," 3 Sept. 1948, HDA, PKSKOJ-H-3; "Rad PK SKOJ-a za Srbiju u 1948 godini," December 1948, ACKSKJ, CKSKOJ IIIb-1/18; Stojan Bjelajac, "O mobilizaciju omladine za izgradnju Autoputa i Beograda," *Partijska izgradnja*, 1, no. 3 (May 1949): 45–49.
44. Stojan Bjelajac, "Naši privredni zadaci u trećoj planskoj godini," at XII Plenum, 20–21 Feb. 1949, AJ, SSOJ F28.
45. "Izveštaj o agitaciji i propagandi," 1949, ACKSKJ, VIII II/5-a-6; "Zaključci XIV Plenum Centralnog komiteta Narodne omladine Jugoslavije," 7 Jan. 1950, AJ, SSOJ F29.
46. M. Ž. "Razbijači kleveta," *Omladina*, 28 June 1949, p. 3.
47. Ibid.
48. Milijan Neorečić, "Narodna omladina Jugoslavije pretstavjla sastavni deo velike Titove armije svesnih boraca za pobedu socijalizma," *Omladina*, 16 Oct. 1949, p. 1; "Maršal Tito primio istaknute udarnike, novatore i racionalizatore i pretstavnike fabrike i preduzeća iz Skoplja," *Omladina*, 7 Aug. 1949, p. 2.
49. Plans for the congress had begun already on May 9, but the announcement was delayed to coincide with Tito's birthday. Woodward, 126.
50. "Direktiva CK KPJ o proradi i sprovodjenju u život Statut KPJ," 6 Sept. 1948, ACKSKJ, II-KI/43 and VIII I/1-a-8.

51. Meeting of PB CK KPJ with PB CK Slovenia.
52. Ibid. Given this clear restatement of the party's loyalty to "democratic centralism" and a Leninist approach, it is uncertain what exactly party leaders meant by the "democratic path," obviously not greater tolerance for non-Communists or a relaxation of the party's ideological commitment.
53. Aleksandar Ranković, "O organizacionim pitanjima naše partije," in Petranović, Končar, and Radonjić, 194.
54. Meeting of PB CK KPJ, 30 May 1949.
55. "Izveštaj sa obilaska aparat RK KPJ za Bosnu i Hercegovinu," 30 Oct. 1948, ACKSKJ, V-KIII/1; "Zapisnik sa sastanka održanog u agitpropu po pitanju organizacije rada agitpropa," 26 Nov. 1948, ACKSKJ, VIII II/2-b-11; "Uprava za agitaciju i propagandu," no date, late 1948?, ACKSKJ, VIII II/1-a-43. See also Woodward, 132.
56. "Izveštaj o radu NF," 14 Oct. 1948, AJ, SSRNJ 142-19-60; "Rezolucija o neposrednim zadacima organizacija Saveza sindikata," 24–29 Oct. 1948, AJ, CVSSJ F3; "Gimnazija, klasična gimnazija i učiteljska škola," no date, AJ, SSOJ-102; Veljko Vlahović, Memo from UPA CK KPJ, 29 Oct. 1949, ACKSKJ, VII II/1-b-56; Veljko Vlahović, 16 Nov. 1949, ACKSKJ, VIII II/1-b-57.
57. "Izvještaj o stanju aparata CK KPH i CK KP Slovenije," 30 Oct. 1948, ACKSKJ, V-KII/9; "Izveštaj o ideološkom vaspitanju članova Partije," 1948, ACKSKJ, VIII II/6-13; "Savjetovanje u Upravi za agitaciju i propagandu CK KPJ po nekim aktuelnim pitanjimâ agitacije i propagande," 28 March 1949, ACKSKJ, VIII II/4-d-18.
58. "Izveštaj o agitaciji i propagandi," 1949, ACKSKJ, VIII II/5-a-6.
59. Mišo Pavičević, "Ideološko-politički i kulturno-prosvetni rad Jedinstvenih sindikata," at I. Kongres, 24–29 Oct. 1948, AJ, CVSSJ F3.
60. Veljko Vlahović, "Rad Partije na ideološkom vaspitanju partiskog članstva," 21 April 1949, ACKSKJ, LFVV II/4-a-3/ and VIII IV/a-9. See also Veljko Vlahović, Memo to All UAP CKs, 14 April 1949, ACKSKJ, VIII II/1-a-17.
61. "Pregled Rad-a od I.VIII.-I.X. 1948" and "Zaključci sa savjetovanja po pitanu lista Rad," 12 Nov. 1948, ACKSKJ, VIII II/4-d-14; "Pitanje radio propagande," 15 Dec. 1948, ACKSKJ, VIII II/5-c-76.
62. Puniša Perović, Concluding speech at Federal Conference on the Question of Teacher's Schools, 14–15 Oct. 1948, AJ, SSOJ F98.
63. "Zapisnik sa sastanka održanog u agitpropu."
64. "Društveni položaj učitelja i profesora," no date, AJ, SSOJ-102; "Stanje nastavnog kadra u školama," 1949, ACKSKJ, VIII II/8-d-36; "Izveštaj o stanju učiteljskog kadra," no date, AJ, SSOJ-102; "Izveštaj o stanju nastavnog kadra u gimnazijama," no date, AJ, SSOJ-102; "Materijalni položaj prosvetnih radnika," no date, AJ, SSOJ-102.
65. "Izvještaj o obilasku partijske organizacije Crne Gore," 12 Oct. 1948, ACKSKJ, V-KV/21; "Izvještaj o radu nekih sreskih i reonskih komiteta u Hrvatskoj i Sloveniji," 26 Oct. 1948, ACKSKJ, V-KII/8. See also Veljko Zeković, "Marksističko-Lenjinističko vaspitanje kadrova," Borba, 7 July 1948, p. 2; "Izveštaj o organizaciji i problemima aparata KP Srbije," 20–23 Oct. 1948, ACKSKJ, V-KIV/18; "Izvještaj o stanju aparata CK KP Hrvatske i CK KP Slovenije," 30 Oct. 1948, ACKSKJ, V-KII/9; "Zapisnik sa sastanka održanog u agitpropu."
66. "Izveštaj o ideološkom vaspitanju članova Partije."

67. Ibid.
68. Veljko Vlahović, "Pitanje agitacije i propagande," 20 April 1949, ACKSKJ, VIII IV/a-8.
69. Susan Woodward notes a similar development in the factory where party leaders began to sneer at "prewar experts" while lauding the efforts of devoted and ambitious production workers "who, like 'the field soldier,' go into the trenches and 'fight'." Woodward, 142.
70. For a detailed accounting of party debates and conclusions concerning the peasantry see Bokovoy, 55–100.
71. "Rezolucija o osnovnim zadacima partije u oblasti socijalističkog preobražaja sela i unapredjenja poljprivredne prizvodnje," at the Second Plenum of the Central Committee of the CPY, 30 Jan. 1949, in Petranović, Končar and Radonjić, 275.
72. See, for example, Rusinow, 36; Banac, *With Stalin Against Tito*, 134–135.
73. Susan Woodward elaborates the economic argument most completely. Woodward, 100, 108–121, 137–138. Melissa Bokovoy, while citing economic issues, also draws attention to party leaders' belief that the Yugoslav peasantry represented a revolutionary force, would rally around the party, and join the cooperatives voluntarily. Bokovoy, 102–103.
74. "Agitaciono-politički rad—Izveštaj iz Kosova i Metohije," 26 Oct. 1948, ACKSKJ, VIII II/2-c-67. See also "Plan ideološko-vaspitnog rada sa komunistima na selu," 18 Nov. 1948, ACKSKJ, VIII II/6-12; Blagoje Nešković, "Organizacioni problemi Narodnog fronta," 26 Nov. 1948, AJ, SSRNJ 142-16-44.
75. Bokovoy, 86–100.
76. Directive to agitprop, 1948, ACKSKJ, VIII II/1-a-13. See also Meeting of CK KPJ, 10 Jan. 1949, ACKSKJ, II/38.
77. Woodward and Bokovoy are exceptions.
78. Edvard Kardelj, "O politici KPJ na selu," in Petranović, Končar and Radonjić, 6–47; For more evidence see Bokovoy, 101–108, and Woodward, 137–138.
79. Momčilo Djorgović, *Djilas, Vernik i Jeretik* (Belgrade: Akvarijus, 1989), 155.
80. "Zapisnik sa savetovanja održanog pri UPA CK KPH po pitanju sela," 9 Feb. 1949, ACKSKJ, VIII II/4-d-17.
81. Milijan Neorečić, Concluding speech at XII Plenum NO, 20–21 Feb. 1949, AJ, SSOJ F28.
82. Ibid.
83. "Zapisnik sa sjednice održane u Agitpropu po pitanju primjedbi na pisanje štampe o selu," 29 March 1949, ACKSKJ, VIII II/2-b-19.
84. "Propagandno-agitacioni rad Narodne omladine na selu," 1949, AJ, SSOJ F95.
85. Dedijer, *Tito*, 378–380.
86. Rusinow, 33.
87. Vukićević, in Stojanović, 432–433.
88. Dedijer, *Novi prilozi*, 295–296, Louis Adamic, *The Eagle and the Roots* (New York: Doubleday and Co., 1952), 125.
89. Meeting with Comrades from the Radio Committees, 22 Dec. 1947, ACKSKJ, VIII II/4-d-2; Milovan Djilas, "O liniji naše štampe," 23 Feb. 1948, ACKSKJ, VIII II/2-b-15; "Zapisnik sa sastanka Agitprop po pitanju repertoara pozorišta i izdavačke delatnosti," 20 Dec. 1948, ACKSKJ, VIII II/2-b-12.

90. Vladimir Dedijer, "Još jedna ilustracija nepravilnosti optužbe informbiroa," *Borba*, 13 July 1948, p. 2.
91. Adamic, 102–103, 120.
92. Cited in Rusinow, 52–53, fn. 59.
93. "Savjetovanje u Upravi za agitaciju i propagandu CK KPJ po nekim aktuelnim pitanjimâ agitacije i propagande," 28 March 1949, ACKSKJ, VIII II/4-d-18.
94. Ibid.
95. Rusinow, 54–55; Djilas, *Rise and Fall*, 254–255. Apparently, Pijade nonetheless went too far in one critique. According to Lopušina, one of the four cases of judicial censorship concerned an article by Pijade in *Književne novine* in September 1949 that was too critical of the role played by the Soviet Union in international affairs. Marko Lopušina, *Crna knjiga: Cenzura u Jugoslaviji, 1945–91* (Belgrade: Fokus, 1991), 28.
96. Djilas, *Rise and Fall*, 206.
97. Adamic, 23–43.
98. "Osvrt Petra Komnenića na Peti Kongres KPJ," in Stojanović, 37–39.

8

The Cultural Transformation Transformed

1950: A Turning Point

Nineteen-fifty was a watershed year in Yugoslavia. The beginning of that year—or more accurately, the end of the preceding one—saw the first steps toward real change in the CPY's ideological principles and strategy for the construction of socialism as well as in its persuasive and cultural policies. Essentially, that year marked a paradigmatic shift in the perspective of CPY leaders, beginning with Edvard Kardelj and Milovan Djilas. The policy changes they would initiate in the course of that 12 month period, though not welcomed by all, launched the country onto a radically new program of development that was now characterized by its opposition not only to capitalism but also to Soviet-style socialism.

The reforms of the 1950s have been traditionally described as a direct consequence of the Soviet-Yugoslav split. They were necessary, it has been argued, first to justify party leaders' resistance to Stalin, and second to ensure continued domestic stability in the face of increasing external threats.[1] Undoubtedly, the split was a crucial factor. Indeed, the need to defend their resistance to Soviet pressure and figure out what had gone wrong inspired top CPY leaders like Djilas, Kardelj, and Kidrič to begin rereading the classics of Marxism-Leninism. As a result, by mid-1949, they began to adopt an increasingly critical stance toward the Soviet Union that, though initially concentrating on the Soviet Union's "imperialist" foreign policies, gradually expanded into other areas as well. The next step beyond mere denunciation of Soviet practice was to articulate the CPY's own program for the construction of socialism. And while CPY leaders invariably claimed that their policies had always drawn on Yugoslavia's revolutionary traditions, it was clear that now, freed from the constraints of Soviet practice, they were in a much stronger position to use those traditions and devise their own interpretation of Marxism-Leninism.

Yet the foundations for this new approach had been laid earlier in CPY leaders' ability to think (if not always act) independently from the Soviet Union. Moreover, in some cases at least, the form and direction that those reforms took reflected the party's previous experiences and especially an awareness among some party leaders of flaws in their policies of persuasion. After all, as early as late 1947, party leaders had realized that the rhetorical strategies adopted thus far could not realize the party's long-term goal of transforming society and creating new people. That goal had not changed, nor had the party's graduated strategy for the construction of socialism.

On the contrary, by the end of 1949, party leaders prepared once again to resume the transformation of society delayed by the Soviet-Yugoslav split. Now, however, they had a rather different understanding of what that transformation might entail. Perhaps reassured of socialism's inevitable victory after rereading the Marxist classics, CPY leaders sought to replace the Soviet-inspired voluntaristic methods of achieving cultural change with a more deterministic, hands-off approach. The reforms of the 1950s certainly were not intended to lessen the role of Communist ideology in Yugoslav society. Rather, they reflected party leaders' extraordinary faith in it. In the ongoing struggle to balance daily political needs with their long-term goal of transforming society, CPY leaders now placed their hopes in the power of Marxism-Leninism.

This approach presumed a reduced role for coercion, while persuasion would become ever more important, but would have to change its tone. Party rhetoric would remain educational but would be less directive. To put it in pedagogical terms, group discussion and hands-on experience would replace lectures and exams. Party activists must seek to convince Yugoslavia's citizens of the rightness of Marxism-Leninism, not simply by telling them that it was so, but by allowing them to see it for themselves. Thus, they must worry not so much about preventing mistakes as using them to inspire thought, dialogue, and correct ideological conclusions. Under such conditions, state-society relations would necessarily become more active. Indeed, by trusting Yugoslavia's citizens to "see the light," CPY leaders created the possibility for a more equal and reciprocal relationship with their constituents. They also, however, opened the door for challenges to their authority.

The Third Plenum

The first steps in this new approach to the transformation of society were taken by Djilas in his speech on educational policy at the Third Plenum of the Central Committee of the CPY in late December 1949.² According to Djilas, the inspiration for his speech came in the fall of that year while he was on a boat to attend a meeting of the United Nations in New York. As Djilas explained it, he spent most of his time on that boat sorting through two enormous canvas sacks filled with reports and analyses of Yugoslavia's educational system.

> I read from morning til late at night, despite the repetitiveness and triviality of the material. But I continued reading in New York. I never quite finished the final neatly organized, all encompassing survey... Tired and dubious, I skipped to the proposals and conclusions. They were, indeed, methodical and consistent. At first glance I liked them... Then suddenly I had a flash of insight—I think it dawned on me overnight—that such a mountain of work was unnecessary to determine a Central Committee position. From that critical, "heretical" realization my thoughts spiraled onward.... It finally struck me that our whole direction, our whole educational methodology needed to be turned around—and that sack of proposals and conclusions along with it. Instead of schools of indoctrination on the Soviet model, we needed gradually to reconstitute schools along traditional, freer lines.³

Having first received Kardelj's approval, Djilas prepared for the Third Plenum a speech filled with terms and phrases like "self-management," "socialist democracy," "the free exchange of opinions," and "ideological struggle," which, although not entirely new, would now become constant signposts along the party's new path toward socialism. The basic goal of the educational system, Djilas explained, was not to create bureaucrats but truly new people, "free socialist people, people who think and work boldly and courageously, who are broad and diverse in their comprehension, and not people whose minds have all been cut according to the same pattern."⁴ The problem, he said, was how? Human consciousness could not be changed according to any schedule or by administrative means. Nor could the administrative apparatus take for itself a monopoly on ideology "without simultaneously violating the principle of socialist democracy, curbing the initiative of the masses, and inhibiting the growth of a healthy ideological struggle between the old . . . and the new."⁵ Rather, he explained, schools should work from the theoretical bases and principles of the Yugoslav revolution in order not only to liquidate capitalist elements but also to reduce the role of bureaucracy, further broaden the initiative of the masses, and strengthen self-management of the people.⁶

Djilas also now began to argue against the excessive use of censorship. While agreeing that it might be necessary to prevent the propaganda of "those who would establish the exploitation of man by man or damage the equality of our people," he insisted that it was no less necessary, and perhaps even more so,

> to provide to those who wish honestly and loyally to fight for the blossoming of our socialist country [and] the progress of science and culture ... all the means and conditions to express their efforts, so that in the free exchange of opinions and the verification of ideas in practice, they may find the most diverse and fruitful forms for further development. Because there is nothing more senseless and dangerous for socialism than the stifling of initiative and the adoption of ready-made bureaucratic forms and administrative measures in the field of human thought.... There can be no development and no progress without ideological struggle, that is, if the further development of productive forces and changes in social relations are not also accompanied by a struggle in the field of human thought.[7]

Beyond these broad injunctions, Djilas offered a number of specific recommendations in his speech. First, he called for a greater reliance on Yugoslavia's pedagogical traditions, rejecting the notion that their entire inherited school system had been worthless.[8] Second, Djilas urged a broader degree of decentralization in the school system to permit both greater independence for and initiative from Yugoslavia's republics. Although the broad educational program would be the same for the entire country, the texts need not be, even for subjects like physics, math, and chemistry. He also urged that textbooks based on translations from Russian be replaced with domestic productions as soon as possible.[9] Perhaps most important, Djilas recommended decentralizing Marxist-Leninist education at the university level so that it would be taught as an integral part of every subject and not as a separate course, because "every separation of Marxism-Leninism into a special teaching subject ... would lead to the separation of dialectical and historical materialism from their applications and that is the path to inevitable dogmatism."[10] Finally, Djilas urged yet again that the working and living conditions of teachers be improved, along with their academic qualifications. Teachers and university faculty, he insisted, must acquire their positions on the basis of their knowledge and accomplishments, not party membership, and were then to be freed of all other administrative, economic, and political duties. Teachers in rural areas, he suggested, should be provided with apartments and heating fuel free of charge.[11]

Indeed, in the following months a series of legal decrees and measures did improve the material position of educational workers, although not always as quickly or comprehensively as party leaders had hoped.[12] At first, however, those less tangible aspects of Djilas's speech, which mandated an entire new approach to education, were given only lip service or were ignored altogether. A long report on education from a speaker at the Fourth Plenary Meeting of the Central Committee of the Communist Party of Croatia, for example, addressed a whole slew of practical problems, but said nothing about democratization, decentralization, or the struggle of opinions. The resolutions from that meeting repeated all of the concrete directives of the CPY's Third Plenum, but barely mentioned its ideological, attitudinal aspect.[13] Gradually, however, more articles and reports began to adopt the party's less injunctive and more dialogic approach to education. For example, the resolutions from a conference of the law faculty about the ideological and professional elevation of teachers urged that all law classes be freed from dogmatism and that questions that are debatable not be presented as absolute truths. Likewise, a report from the PYY called for greater decentralization and more tolerance for free discussions among students, "because it is hard to imagine a university without a sharpening of the struggle of opinions."[14]

Although Djilas's speech at the Third Plenum initiated the party's new approach to the construction of socialism, it took CPY leaders another six months to work out and set in place the next, far more definitive, steps in that direction.[15] One can, however, trace their progressively imaginative rhetorical approach to ideological and cultural questions in a series of lectures, reports, and articles presented over the course of that late winter and spring.

Already in late 1949 and continuing throughout the spring of 1950, many leaders had become increasingly aware of the need for changes in the party's persuasive style and approach. Vlahović, for example, while still calling for more planning and preparation, worried already in late 1949 that persuasion had too often been replaced by administrative methods and that weak political work was stifling the initiative of the masses. One problem, he explained, was that district party committees tended to neglect persuasive work, leaving it entirely up to the agitprop departments.[16] Activists in trade union agitprop departments similarly complained that their work was too isolated from the remaining activities of the trade unions and argued that it would be more effective if led by one of the more general political figures. Too often, one activist complained, union leaders in the field saw cultural-educational work as an extraneous burden to be carried out only if other tasks permitted. These leaders also urged that agitators in the field be allowed more independence and more opportunity to develop their self-initiative.[17]

After the Third Plenum these kinds of discussions became even more common and more self-confident in tone. In March 1950, for example, an unsigned article in *Borba* sharply criticized the tendency of the Union of Cultural-Artistic Societies to act as an organ of cultural control. Replacing education with administrative measures and censorship, it insisted, was incorrect and unacceptable. Rather, the Union must seek to develop more self-initiative in its members.[18] Vlahović also criticized the tendency to replace persuasive work with censorship and to separate party activities into discrete sectors. In an internal party report, he now argued that the work of agitprop departments was so closely connected with other sectors of party activity, it would be senseless to ask which was more important. He thus urged that persuasion become a constituent part of daily party work, requiring the activity of a much larger number of members. Finally, Vlahović complained that the state tasks often assigned to activists from agitprop departments (such as carrying out the *otkup* or tax collection) served to discredit them and hampered their more important job of explaining such measures and mobilizing the masses.[19] Vlahović raised similar complaints at a meeting of the Commission for Agitation and the Press in the PFY. The centralized administration of persuasive work, he claimed, had warped its character, reducing the circle of activists and leading to political passivism in lower organizations.[20]

Another example of the party's more adventurous and imaginative approach to the construction of socialism came in a lecture on party cultural and educational policies at the Party School. Here Vlahović addressed for the first time since the Second World War the question, "What is culture?" All previous reports, articles, and lectures on cultural policies assumed that this question had been resolved in the Soviet Union long ago and needed no further explication. Although Vlahović's exposition on culture propounded a clearly Marxist perspective, it certainly represented the most sophisticated discussion of that topic in all of postwar Yugoslavia's Communist rhetoric.[21]

Meanwhile, Djilas prepared the ground for the more substantive reforms to come, relating them to the need for increased education. The main source of Soviet revisionism, he argued, was in its attitude toward the state in socialism. Strengthening the state under socialism, he insisted, should not mean increasing its bureaucratic apparatus as had occurred in the Soviet Union, but enhancing the role of direct producers in the economy, thus allowing certain functions of the bureaucratic apparatus to wither away. While agreeing that the party must continue to lead the state, he emphasized that it must also work to organize and elevate the consciousness of the masses so that they could more quickly take over the functions of the state.[22]

Restructuring Party and Mass Organizations

These developing trends in the party's ideological and persuasive agenda found their culmination in June 1950 with the Law on Worker's Self-Management and the restructuring of party and mass organizations.

Since they affected the party's economic policies and very mode of operation, these reforms represented a far more concrete modification of the party's program than had the Third Plenum. Although presented as a first step toward the gradual withering away of the state, the law insulated the state and economy from the inexperience or unreliability of the workers through carefully constructed organizational forms. It remains uncertain, as Rusinow has explained, whether Tito intended the Law on Self-Management as a mere ploy to create the illusion of popular participation in government or "a very cautious first step" that would eventually lead to *real* workers' control.[23] Djilas, I am certain, believed it to be the latter, as it coincided with and helped justify his own rapidly advancing notions about how to realize the transformation of society.

The Law on Self-Management was accompanied by a Central Committee declaration urging a sharper separation between the party and the state. According to the June 1950 declaration, since the new economic measures would allow for much greater involvement by working masses in leadership of the economy, the party could no longer afford to "lead party and state activities by bureaucratic means but must direct its entire work toward mobilization of the masses ... the elevation of the masses' socialist consciousness, the development of criticism, and so on."[24] Party activists who had too often focused only on the fulfillment of concrete tasks associated with government were now to regain their ability to evaluate government decisions and work on political mobilization of the masses.

The move to clarify and more firmly establish the boundaries between party and state activity required also an alteration in the position and activities of mass organizations. Just as the party reform of June 1950 separated the party and the state, later reforms that year sought to divorce the functions of the People's Front from those of the state. The PFY had thus far given enormous support to the government, helping out with pre-election campaigns, tax collection, and *otkup* actions. Indeed by 1949 and 1950, Front leaders and organizations had become so closely associated with the state that its meetings were sometimes confused with official government ones. However helpful in the short run, this kind of activity had compromised the Front's role as an organ of persuasion. In accordance with the party's enhanced faith in ideology, the reforms of 1950 sought to de-emphasize the Front's economic and governmental tasks and revitalize and decentralize its activities in the sphere of ideological and political persuasion.[25]

One manifestation of this shift was a reduction in voluntary work actions at the federal level. In 1949 and to a lesser degree in 1950, the organization of volunteer labor brigades had made up much of the content of PFY work. This emphasis on volunteer labor had coincided with the sense of economic urgency engendered by the Soviet and Eastern European economic blockade. By November 1950, however, a Central Committee letter indicated the need for stronger political work and directed the PFY to restrict its volunteer labor brigades to local work actions such as the repair and construction of nearby schools, playgrounds, housing, streets, waterworks, bridges, sports fields, cooperative centers, and reading rooms.[26]

Similarly, PFY organizations began to focus their political activities on concrete issues affecting their local region. According to a report from 1953, in the years from 1948 to 1950, both the form and content of the Front's ideological work had been planned and decreed from above. After 1950, however, Front organizations began to adapt their work to local events and conditions. By way of example, the report described the organization in Istria of protest meetings in response to an Italian irridentist campaign for Trieste. The increased attention to local conditions also led the PFY to more closely adapt its forms of political activity to local audiences. It turned out, for example, that political lectures by experts worked best in cities, while in smaller towns and villages, broader, less specialized, and less formal Front meetings were more effective.[27]

But if the PFY and state were to be separated, the Front's ties to the Communist party now had to be made stronger than ever. Blagoje Nešković, president of the Front's Executive Council, thus complained at an October 1950 meeting that the PFY's persuasive rhetoric had not generally been coordinated with that of the party. The party, he admitted, was at fault since it had simply relied on its control over the state to ensure popular compliance with its wishes. "As long as [the party] sat in power," he explained, "it pushed and was the government and everything, it didn't sense the needs of the Front, it resolved matters administratively." Now, however, as the party was relinquishing its position of state authority, it would have to reestablish firm connections with the Front so that the PFY "will truly be an organ of the Party and will be led by it." Only thus could it serve the party as its "weapon in the political struggle."[28]

The reorganization of party and mass organizations prepared the ground for a solution to the isolation of agitprop departments so often bemoaned in the previous six months. In a further elaboration of the party reorganization in October 1950, Aleksandar Ranković directly addressed the future form and tasks of agitprop departments. At the highest level, the Departments for Agitation and Propaganda in the Central Committees were now officially renamed Administrations for Propaganda and Agitation (Uprave za propagandu i agitaciju or UPAs), presumably to emphasize a stronger role for long-term ideological propaganda in relation to short-term political and economic agitation.[29]

Republic UPAs would consist of four or five paid professionals who would then supervise the activities of various unpaid members in institutes, enterprises, and mass organizations. At the lower levels, the changes in structure were more substantive and directly addressed long-standing complaints that agitprop departments had been neglected and were excessively isolated from other sectors of party work. Persuasive work in district committees was now to be led directly by the party secretary, assisted by a commission of three or four nonprofessionals, while in basic party organizations, separate agitprop sectors were eliminated altogether. Rather, persuasion was now established as an essential part of general party activity. From now on, persuasive tasks were to be assigned to every member of a party organization and the progress of those tasks was to be discussed at every party meeting.[30]

Persuasive work in the PFY was also reorganized, first to combine and reduce the apparati of the Central Commissions for Agitation and the Press and for Ideological Work. Then in 1950 and 1951, agitprop committees, first in district, city, and regional PFY organizations, and then at the republic and federal levels were simply abolished. As in the basic party organizations, responsibility for persuasion now lay with the general leadership—in this case, the Executive Council of each front organization. The purpose, once again, was to make mobilizational work the daily activity of the body and to engage the entire membership of the PFY in its fulfillment.[31]

By decentralizing persuasive work and thus "ending the practice of the administrative transmission of directives from above and the empty practicistic fulfillment of those directives from below," party leaders hoped to raise the level of ideological-political leadership and encourage independence and initiative among lower party leaders. A later report optimistically explained,

> Our party is today so ideologically elevated and has been so enriched by the experiences of our practice that we can ... expect party leaderships and most basic party organizations to find inventive ways of realizing the basic party line and to be independent and expeditious in dealing with occurrences and problems in the field.... Besides, the purpose of party leadership is not only to ensure the achievement of this or that task but, through the fulfillment of various concrete tasks, to realize the education and elevation of party organizations.[32]

In effect, party leaders were relinquishing a degree of their centralized control. They had decided to trust in the abilities of their lower party and front cadres, believing that if required to carry out tasks independently, those cadres would live up to the responsibility and learn from their mistakes. Apparently, the consequences of those mistakes were now considered to be less important than the value gained from direct hands-on experience.

Reforms of the Press

CPY leaders' increased willingness to trust not only party cadres but Yugoslavia's citizens may be seen in a further and crucial reform of the press and other periodical publications in 1950. Public and internal reports had demanded for some time that the press become more varied, interesting, and attractive. In June 1950, however, a meeting of the central agitprop department devoted to problems of the press took those demands a step farther. Calling for an end to empty party phraseology and plans and norms in newspapers, it now urged the education of professional and self-directed journalists who "can go anywhere, establish broad ties, and seek explanations without waiting for directives." At another meeting that fall, activists complained that the editors of *Borba* promoted too few young journalists and did not base hiring and promotion decisions on the quality of their work.[33]

Meanwhile, Djilas and others worried about distribution of the press, noting that some papers were being artificially forced on readers by party organizations who required subscriptions along with party dues and by the leaders of mass organizations who went door-to-door promoting their own particular organs. One problem with this approach, they explained, was that it wasted paper, which was in short supply. According to an article in *Borba* by Olga Biljanović, it was not unusual to find a huge quantity of unclaimed papers often several months old in the regional councils of mass organizations. Another problem was that it led to local favoritism and rivalries among newspapers. Biljanović noted, for example, that distributors in Novi Sad refused to put *Borba* and *Politika* on the stand until *Slobodna vojvodina* had sold out. The press, Djilas insisted, should be spread only by professional salesmen and on the principle of demand; party and PFY leaders should agitate for the press but must not, themselves, become salesmen.[34]

Without doubt, the low purchase rate of party newspapers and magazines worried CPY leaders. One might easily imagine a number of possible explanations for the failure of Yugoslav citizens to buy newspapers in the expected quantity, including the still high illiteracy rates, tight budgets in a time of great economic difficulty, or even passive resistance. Party leaders were certainly correct, however, in pointing to another potential cause for low readership—the papers and magazines were unbearably dull. Not only were the topics covered unvarying and predictable (the heroic efforts of shockworkers and youth in fulfilling the

Five Year Plan, the aggressive imperialist policies of the Soviet Union, the support of the Yugoslav populace for the party leadership and its program for the future) but the language used to describe them was equally formulaic and programmatic. The editors and journalists of these newspapers and articles were clearly more concerned about following CPY directives to the letter and thus avoiding errors than they were about reader response. As a result, the press lost its reading public and hence its value as a means of persuasion. Again, party leaders now hoped that they could resolve this problem by trusting in the abilities of lower cadres. Although CPY leaders had no intention of freeing the press from its political obligations, they had come to believe that responsible and ideologically correct newspaper personnel, if allowed greater initiative, would be able to follow the party line in a way that was both innovative and interesting.

Therefore, a meeting of the central agitprop department in early December 1950 concluded that all newspapers and journals must become profitable and support themselves from their own fully voluntary sales.[35] Though introduced without much fanfare or further discussion, this decision would have deep and lasting consequences for the form, content, and very future of the party's persuasive agenda. For in effect, it meant accepting the predominance of consumer demands over ideological dictates and, as such, it signified a fundamental change in party leaders' perspectives. The cultural transformation, they now seemed to believe, could not be achieved by fiat, but must take place more gradually through the manipulation of existing values and tastes.

Finally, in that same month, the Federal Assembly passed laws eliminating official censorship for children's and youth literature and press. According to the law's explanation, though censorship had originally been necessary to ensure the proper education of children and youth, today such supervision could be fulfilled by youth and school organizations as well as by simple public criticism.[36] Again, this law reflected an approach to the construction of socialism, which now relied less on the power of negative actions like censorship and more on positive persuasion. It also showed the party's desire to involve Yugoslav citizens in their country's social transformation and its willingness to trust them to do the right thing.

Further Reforms

As may be seen by the number and significance of the above-described reforms, 1950 marked a true turning point in the CPY's approach to the construction of socialism. Party reforms were not, however, confined to that year alone but were further elaborated and articulated in the course of the following two years. In June 1951, for example, the state gave up its monopoly on the purchase of artistic works, opening up their sale to museums, galleries, republic and city cultural institutions, and economic enterprises.[37] Censorship of films also gradually declined. In June 1951, the central agitprop department first recommended replacing the censorship commission for films with a selection committee. That advice was finally realized in the spring of 1952 with the formation of a less directive "Committee for Cinematography" that was to give suggestions and opinions about imports, exports, and the distribution of raw materials. Perhaps the most significant change here was that from now on the opinions of the minority in the committee were also to be noted and passed on to the relevant state institutions. Finally, in December 1952, the Committee for Cinematography was simply abolished. Notes from the accompanying agitprop department meeting explained that in the future, film imports were to be selected on the basis of specific requests from the republics, allowing for greater choice and fuller utilization of the information and experiences of Yugoslav citizens abroad.[38]

Meanwhile, party leaders further strengthened their efforts to stimulate ideological debate. As explained by Djilas, the "Resolution on Theoretical Work in the CPY," passed at the Fourth Plenum of the Central Committee of the CPY in June 1951, was to end the party's monopoly on ideological questions and make possible true inner party democracy.[39] Djilas also presented a number of speeches throughout the country in 1952 that further elaborated and expanded upon the party's new role and theoretical perspective. In a June 1952 speech in Priština, Djilas outlined his view of the stages through which the CPY was passing in seeking to realize the transition to socialism. In the first stage, he explained, the party had prepared for and carried out the revolution, while in the second it had focused on "the construction of state power and the liquidation of capitalist property in the cities." Only recently, he continued, had the party embarked on the third stage, which he described as social democracy or workers' management of the economy. According to Djilas, during the first two phases the party's primary role had been organizational—that is, it had organized and led the class struggle—while its educational function had been necessarily reduced. Now, in the third phase of the transition, the party no longer needed to organize against capitalist owners and could focus entirely upon educating and raising the socialist consciousness of the masses.[40]

In that speech and in several others, Djilas also discussed the future "withering away" of both the state and the party. While agreeing with Tito and Kardelj that this would not happen quickly and would mean only a withering away of the state's functions,[41] Djilas also made it clear that neither the state nor the party was an end unto itself. The working class, he asserted, was the main force in society, while the party and state were only tools in its hands. It would be wrong, he said, to think that "since we are the avant-garde of the proletariat . . . we know better than the proletariat what it should do and can therefore decide what its tasks should be." Rather, he continued, the party must "determine its new line from the practical struggle and interests of the proletariat."[42] This was a far cry from the party's 1945 assertion that as the leading unit of the working class, only *it* could "determine the direction of class struggle."[43] Consistent with his other efforts to revitalize state-society relations, Djilas was now calling on Yugoslavia's working class to play a much more active role and was trusting it to help bring about the social transformation.[44]

The Sixth Party Congress and the Fourth Congress of the People's Front

The high point of the party's reform policies came at the Sixth Congress of the CPY, now renamed the LCY, held November 2–7, 1952, and at the Fourth Congress of the People's Front in late February 1953. According to Djilas, he had proposed changing the party's name from the Communist Party of Yugoslavia to the League of Communists of Yugoslavia because the word *Party* would inspire narrow, Leninist forms, while *League* better suited their eventual expectation that it would wither away. Only later did Kardelj remind him that the League of Communists had been the name of the original Marxist organization. With the approval of Kardelj and Tito and the acquiescence of Ranković, the congress passed the name change, declaring that it was no mere formality but corresponded to the party's new role at a new level in the development of the Communist movement.[45]

The Sixth Congress also confirmed and strengthened earlier efforts to separate party and state functions. The LCY would now take on a more clearly ideological and political-educational role. Its primary task would be raising the socialist consciousness of the working masses by means of persuasion and personal example. The LCY, one article explained, must now be the "political leader, teacher, and educator of the workers" and must wage a merciless struggle against all that reduced the power of the masses, including especially bureaucratic and commandeering methods.[46]

The Fourth Congress of the PFY, now renamed the Socialist Alliance of the Working People of Yugoslavia (SAWPY), further expanded the line laid down at the Sixth Congress. In agreement with previous reforms and declarations, speakers at the Fourth Congress now referred to SAWPY as a political tribune or, in Kardelj's words, an "all people's parliament" that would permit the broadest possible participation by the masses and the free struggle of opinions. The most remarkable advance, however, was seen in the new description of the role of the party within SAWPY. All now agreed that SAWPY was the main political organization through which the party would work and that the party would represent only its "most ideologically consistent section." The role of party members within the organization would be to serve as "ideological educators and bearers of the true spirit of socialism." They would lead not by dictating or commanding methods but by example and persuasion. Indeed, Djilas now claimed that party members would be evaluated primarily by their work in the front, that is, by how well they were able to convince the masses.[47]

Kardelj took the reforms a step further yet, seeming almost to deny the leading role of Communists altogether. In the future, he argued, the party should confine itself mainly to dealing with ideological questions, while concrete political and social issues would be resolved directly by organs of SAWPY. The party, in his view, would not even be responsible for determining the general line of political activity.

> The League of Communists of Yugoslavia does not consider that confirming the line of struggle for the construction of socialist relations in our country is its monopoly alone. That struggle and its direction affect all those who honestly contribute to the united efforts, that is, the enormous majority of our working people. Therefore, the political line of our struggle for socialism will be the result of the conscious and active cooperation of the working masses organized in the Socialist Alliance. . . . In short: the League of Communists has no pretensions of ruling in the place of the working masses, but wishes to inspire and educate the masses so that they will know how to lead their own government, their own factories, and their own social organs and organizations.[48]

Accordingly, he continued, the party must now end its old practice of making decisions that the front would only confirm. He even went so far as to say that the party could no longer assume that it was always right and that it must be willing to learn from the masses. "The conscious activity of the most progressive social forces and the spontaneous social movements of the masses act upon each other in a mutual fashion. They are for each other teachers."[49] Here Kardelj seemed to be making a direct appeal for more equal and reciprocal relations, referring to Yugoslavia's citizens as the party's partners (or at least advanced graduate students) rather than its pupils.

It remains unclear exactly what motivated Kardelj's extraordinary renunciation of the party's leading role in politics. A. Ross Johnson has suggested that the speech, which he considers a contradiction to the Sixth Party Congress, either resulted from Kardelj's tendency toward abstraction or represented a deliberate overstatement of the role of SAWPY aimed at foreign observers. Alternatively, Kardelj may have considered his elaboration of the party's role completely consistent with the line presented at the Sixth Party Congress. Certainly Djilas would have seen it in that light, and he has suggested that Kardelj stood with him in such matters.[50] Whatever the explanation, there is no doubt that Kardelj's speech at the Fourth Congress marked the apex of the reform process and that the expectations it engendered were unrealistically high.[51] For taken to its logical extreme, such a statement would seem to threaten the party's position in power. After all, the legitimacy of the Communist party's monopoly on power was based on its unique grasp of the laws of history and its unerring prescription for progress toward the new and better future. Such a suggestion of the party's fallibility would challenge its right to maintain a monopoly on power. Not surprisingly then, Tito began almost immediately thereafter to lead the party down a new path, away from such radical reform measures and toward the reestablishment of firm political control by the party.

In fact, it seems clear that Tito had begun to worry about the new reforms already by the Sixth Party Congress. His speech to the congress thus called attention to certain weaknesses that had developed along with the decentralization of ideological-educational work. He especially worried about party members' inattention to the growth of bourgeois and clerical activity and called for greater vigilance. As ties with the West increased, Tito pointed out, more and more ideas that were "outdated" and "alien to socialism" would appear. Under these conditions and since the CPY "no longer interferes in everything as a supreme arbiter and judge," he explained, it must pay more and more attention to ideological education as a means of ensuring the correct development of socialist society. "The broader our democratization, the greater must be the vigilance of party members toward such occurrences, whether they are found in the press, in oral propaganda, in the form of some action and so on."[52] He also expressed concern about the warped values and growing demoralization among some cadres who seemed to think that their personal life was completely independent from the party, and he pointed to the spread of various "alien ideological, political, and cultural concepts" among those who "misunderstand our democracy."[53]

Tito restated these concerns at a meeting of the Central Committee held on his island retreat of Brioni in June 1953. The purpose of the meeting was to reconsider and evaluate the conclusions of the Sixth Party Congress. At its end, a directive letter was sent to all party organizations, pointing to two serious errors that had developed since the Sixth Congress. One was the continued tendency of some middle and higher party cadres to work in the old way, treating the conclusions of the Sixth Congress as a mere rhetorical tactic. The other, which received far more attention, was the almost complete inactivity among lower party cadres who had apparently absolved themselves of all responsibility for the construction of socialism. These cadres, the letter explained, seemed to believe that they no longer needed to fight anti-socialist tendencies and that their role as Communists had been reduced to holding lectures. The letter did still worry about excessive bureaucratization and the use of administrative methods, but only because it meant that Communists had lost their revolutionary fervor and will to direct political action.[54]

Conspicuously absent from the letter were calls for ideological debate and the "struggle of opinions." Indeed, an article in *Komunist* further elaborating on the letter noted instead the growth of harmful criticism. Some Communists, it explained, attacked the weaknesses of the old system without recognizing that many of its aspects had been necessary and that "without the use of many administrative measures we would not have been able to resolve many issues." As a result, some party members now showed a reluctance to attack the enemy with sufficient energy or "to carry out those revolutionary measures which are sometimes necessary and unavoidable." Finally, the article addressed head-on the crucial danger of the new reforms, which, by exposing the fallibility of the party, challenged its exclusive right to power. "With such criticism we only do harm to ourselves, because the working people will reasonably ask, 'Who can guarantee that everything you are doing and saying now is so smart, when up until now you have worked so poorly and made so many foolish mistakes?'"[55]

Although this first step away from democratization was almost certainly related in part to the death of Stalin in early March 1953, which reduced the threat to Yugoslavia's security, such comments suggest that the reversal stemmed more directly from internal problems associated with the reforms. As Johnson has explained it, the reforms so demoralized the party's rank and file that the party seemed to face the possibility of its own "internal disintegration." The new methods of work were simply too difficult for most cadres to master, and in any case, there was little evidence that the party was "capable of achieving its leading role in society in a new way, by 'persuasion,' and that the population was ready and willing to follow it."[56] In fact, however, these developments were not entirely new, and could not be attributed solely to the conclusions of the Sixth Party Congress. The party's entire reform period had been punctuated by debates over these very issues.

Playing by New Rules

The new reforms initiated in 1950 and continued throughout the course of the following three years had an extraordinary impact on the development of social and cultural life in Yugoslavia. They resulted in an immediate blossoming of cultural production and distribution and in the proliferation of lively and heated debates at all levels. The party's broadened ideological perspective was evident mainly among top leaders of the CPY, whose discussions of Marxism-Leninism became increasingly adventurous. For example, in one meeting of the central agitprop department in late 1950, Djilas discussed numerous routes to socialism, including the possibility that it might be achieved by peaceful means and without blood. "For the victory of socialism," he explained, "what is essential is not Marx's or Lenin's ideology, what is essential is what form it will take (and it could take some completely liberal form, even Quakers)."[57] Simultaneously, the leading figures of various party, state, professional, and cultural forums debated such topics as the changing tasks of the People's Front and its relationship to the state, the new role of trade unions and their appropriate relationship to the workers' councils, the best way to teach Marxism-Leninism and other philosophies, the role of the press and agitprop departments, the future development of cultural-artistic societies, and party policies toward youth and with regard to high and mass culture. At the center of many of these debates were the key, but not often articulated, questions of how to engage in and win the "struggle of opinions" on a more level playing field and exactly what kind of victory was attainable.

Debates About Censorship

Many of the debates that addressed these questions revolved around the opposition between political censorship and consumer choice in the media, arts, and entertainment. After Djilas's speech at the Third Plenum, most party directives called for a reduction in attempts to control published materials by means of direct censorship. Instead, party leaders were to allow editors, journalists, writers, dramatists, filmmakers, and others more independence so that they might learn to think for themselves, react swiftly to current events, and develop a sense of social responsibility. The declared purpose was not to mimic Western-style democracies and their views on freedom of the press; openly anti-socialist and enemy elements still would not be given free rein. The new liberties would, however, be available to all "loyal and patriotic" individuals honestly working for the future of a socialist state. While recognizing that errors in judgement and improper analyses were inevitable, party leaders now believed that their publication was not fatal and might even be beneficial as it would provoke corrections and more accurate analyses from elevated members of society. In the ensuing contest, the validity of the Marxist-Leninist perspective would become clear to all; those who had erred in their analysis would be reeducated and those who had never believed might now come to do so.

An additional goal of the new approach was to achieve more lively and less stereotyped publications that would not only be more convincing but would increase readership. The latter became especially important after the December 1950 decree that all publications must become financially self-supporting. As noted previously, the purpose of the decree was both to reduce waste under conditions of an acute paper shortage and to increase the quality of publications by subjecting them to consumer scrutiny. Again, however, this was a risky enterprise as it relied upon the willingness and ability of Yugoslavia's consumers to make the "right" choices and demand the "right" kind of articles, reports, and other printed materials.

Already by the fall of 1951, numerous internal and public party reports began to complain that newspapers and journals were abusing their new freedoms, were pandering to the public's lowest instincts, and had begun to resemble the decadent bourgeois press both in form and content. Thus, for example, the leader of Serbia's agitprop department, Bora Drenovac, while agreeing that the appearance of *NIN (Nedeljne informativne novine)* as one of the first new publications to emerge under the new conditions had "been felt like a breath of fresh air," expressed disappointment at its low cultural level. The journal, he claimed, while proving that articles could be interesting, had quickly moved beyond interesting to sensational, "showing in the process less and less culture and ever fewer ideological-political criteria, until finally it has begun to publish things which are absolutely unbelievable in a socialist country."[58] Similarly, Nerečić, speaking at a meeting of the PYY executive bureau concerning the youth newspaper *Omladina,* asserted that although the paper had become more independent and interesting, it had recently "slid toward a position of petty bourgeois anarchism." By mid-1952, one internal report from the central agitprop department worried about the growing evidence of regionalism in the nationally specific press, and another openly admitted that "the press is slipping out of our hands and it is not clear who or what it serves."[59]

At the same time as the party's direct political control over the press declined, its expectations for it grew. Party documents now increasingly called on editors and journalists to be more independent and active in their criticism of middle- and lower-level party and government officials. In mid-1951, for example, Djilas urged that journalists be sent out to the source of events and discuss them on the spot. They don't need someone to give them the line, he argued; "they need to be there where the line is being created." Later that year, he insisted that the most important task of the press at that moment was to provide criticism and to "give more space for discussion."[60]

Djilas also made it clear, however, that such criticism had to come from an unmistakably socialist perspective. The press, he explained, must be an independent factor in social life but must not operate outside of or beyond the party. Consequently, the need for journalists who were both loyal and well educated became even more evident. The editors and journalists sent out to the field, Djilas explained, must always be good Communists, selected on the basis of their "party-mindedness." They were to be literate and intelligent people who would push the new party line, but who would also be unafraid to point out and criticize errors in the field, even if threatened by members of the district committee. Djilas therefore recommended that correspondents in the districts hold the same party stature as members of the district party committee.[61]

Yet, as in the past, such loyal and able cadres were hard to come by. Many reports thus blamed errors in the press on the continued presence of "enemies" among journalistic cadres and called for a purge of their ranks.[62] A central agitprop department report from May 1952, for example, claimed that over half of *Borba*'s correspondents were weak and should be replaced. The problem, it admitted, was finding people who were politically elevated and held sufficient authority to resist pressure by individual organs of government or the directors of enterprises. Likewise, another agitprop report noted that most of the editors at *Politika* were still prewar journalists, while the new journalists were young and had been accepted into the party only after 1948. All of them, it claimed, were petty bourgeois in their outlook.[63]

An additional explanation for the failings of the new and more liberal press concerned the activity, or lack thereof, of Communists in that field. Djilas, for example, sharply denounced the apparent reluctance of many Communists to become involved in the intense cultural debates that had emerged in the absence of direct censorship. Noting that "Slovene clericalists" had taken over the Writer's Association, he reminded the leaders of agitprop departments that they still had many enemies and that "the revolution falls when those who bear it fall."[64]

The uncertain response of party members to the new policies was indeed disturbing. Yet it was also understandable given certain basic ambiguities in the party's policy. One such ambiguity lay in the party's simultaneous desire both to encourage and to win the struggle of opinions. While on the one hand, party leaders sought to stimulate debate, opening up the field to a variety of unauthorized and potentially "incorrect" views, on the other hand they wished to unmask those views in the strongest possible terms, pointing out their errors and reactionary bases. Under more neutral conditions, such a strategy might have been feasible, if not necessarily successful. But conditions were not neutral. The party's position in power, as well as its history of censorship and repression, was not so easily forgotten. In fact, the party's new attacks on "unhealthy" trends differed little in tone and content from the official denunciations of the past, leading those who dared engage in the struggle of opinions first to retreat into a frightened silence (thus ending the debate) and later to accuse party leaders of returning to Soviet-style administrative and bureaucratic methods. In neither case did the party achieve its goal of proving the validity of Marx's theory "fair and square" by means of persuasion.

One of the first cases to reveal this contradiction, as well as the uncertainty, even among top party leaders, about the limits of the new cultural freedom, concerned Branko Ćopić's "Heretical Stories," published in the August 1950 issue of *Književne novine*. Ćopić's satire, which poked fun at high muckety-mucks and their privileged lifestyles, caused an uproar among party cultural and political leaders. In the following weeks, Ćopić was summoned to the central agitprop department for a personal meeting with Djilas and was threatened by security guards, while his story was denounced in *Borba* and by Tito himself. Ultimately, the satire was banned for a period of 30 years.[65]

The question on everyone's mind was, "What next?" Would Ćopić be arrested or blacklisted? What did a party denunciation mean under these new conditions? Would the regime return to methods of censorship or would it indeed rely only on persuasion?[66] Even top party leaders seemed uncertain and divided on this issue. After all, the reformers had agreed that open enemies would not be tolerated. But where was the line between an open enemy and a recalcitrant intellectual or misguided youth? What kinds of experimentation needed only to be criticized and what kinds had to be forbidden?

In this case, it seemed that the crime, while serious, was forgivable. Although the novella was banned, Tito made it clear in his speech that Ćopić would not be arrested, and indeed he suffered no official persecution and continued to publish.[67] Others, however, were not so fortunate. According to Vladimir Dedijer, the Slovenian poet Edvard Kocbek was blacklisted for years after the publication of his "decadent" and "individualistic" war stories in 1951.[68] Apparently, Ćopić's party credentials and close relationship with many top party leaders protected him, whereas Kocbek's Christian Socialist past made him particularly suspect.[69] Even in Ćopić's case, however, verbal attacks by such high officials were sufficient to stifle further attempts at satire for some time. As Djilas would later remark, "We saw with Ćopić that when we struck, all fell silent."[70]

Over time, however, as Ćopić suffered no official persecution and as top CPY leaders reiterated their promises of tolerance, the representatives of alternative cultural trends became increasingly bold. Only one year after the attack on Ćopić, Drenovac published a scathing attack on the new political and cultural journal *NIN*. The fact that Drenovac had placed his remarks in the first person plural strengthened the attack, suggesting that his views were those of the entire Serbian agitprop department. Yet the editors of *NIN* not only did not prepare a self-criticism but published a vigorous article in self-defense, denying the accuracy or validity of Drenovac's complaints. This unprecedented response resulted not only in a second, much more serious and hostile article from Drenovac, but also in a summons to the editorial board from the Serbian agitprop department and a comment from Djilas that *NIN* was the seat of an enemy group, all sons of the bourgeoisie.[71] One of the editors, later recalling that meeting, reported the agitprop department's warning that *NIN* was not only harmful but was acting as an "enemy" in the field, adding, "Imagine what such a judgement meant in those times!"[72] Obviously, Djilas and other party leaders had difficulty accepting the consequences of their reforms.[73] Again, however, the journal was not closed down, nor was the editorial board removed.

Similar attacks by high-level party members on other journals, including *Mladost, Svedočanstvo, Krugovi,* and *Duga*, also drew counterattacks and self-justifications rather than apologies and self-criticism.[74] It now seemed that winning the struggle of opinions would be more difficult than anticipated. By mid-1952, some journals even targeted their satire on the party. The Zagreb literary journal *Krugove,* for example, had written in one issue, "in the time of socialist democracy freedom, ha-ha-ha. . . " Nonetheless, Drenovac insisted that they couldn't close the press down on that basis but must simply work to discredit such publications.[75] In other words, despite their difficulties, party leaders did not abandon the new approach. On the contrary, new reforms continued to appear.

After the party's renunciation of its monopoly on ideological questions following the Fourth Plenum in June 1951, party leaders continually reminded themselves and others that their criticisms of a given cultural work did not represent any official denunciation but only their own personal contributions to the struggle of opinions. These efforts at self-limitation were particularly evident in discussions about the role of the central literary newspaper, *Književne novine*. Djilas first described the party's attempts to broaden the paper's circle of participants in an October 1951 meeting of the central agitprop department. "That," he explained, "is why we pushed Belić and Andrić. Now we need to push Krleža and Ristić. Then it remains to broaden our collaborators in Zagreb and Ljubljana."[76] A few months later, the editorial board of the paper itself, headed by Milan Bogdanović and Skender Kulenović, published a lengthy dissertation on its role and perspective, denying rumors that the paper wished "to establish a monopoly on literature and culture" or that it was "some kind of 'official organ'." Rather, the editors noted, Yugoslavia's cultural life had entered a new and important stage of development "in which various creative aspirations, concepts, and directions are increasingly being taken to the public and are appearing in all their obvious dissent." The editors claimed to approve this development as a positive expression of the strengthening of socialist democracy, although they also devoted much space to attacking recent occurrences of "reactionary, antisocialist, anational, morbid, and decadent aspirations and concepts" and to defining their own policy as one that would resist all decadence whether of Soviet or Western origin. At the end of their treatise, however, the editors again emphasized that there were no longer any official or sacred authorities in the realm of culture whose opinions and judgements could not be publicly criticized and that, therefore, despite their own high positions in the establishment, they must be allowed to contribute to the debate just like anyone else.[77]

That the ambiguity remained, however, was made clear in a scandal that developed during the summer of 1952. The controversy in this case revolved around the withdrawal from the Belgrade National Theater's repertoire of Jean Anouilh's French vaudeville, *The Ball of Thieves,* at the request of Mitra Mitrović, then acting as both minister of education and head of the agitprop department in Serbia. Mitrović later claimed that she had acted after receiving outraged phone calls from several politicians, including Moša Pijade, who shouted, "What is your theater doing? Are we really all thieves?"[78] Fearing, she said, for the fate of the entire theater, she asked its manager and the play's director to pull the piece. "Conscious of my high party and state position, they took my 'suggestion' as a decree and withdrew the presentation from the repertoire."[79]

But if the theater's directors were willing to submit quietly to such official interference, other cultural figures were not. Within weeks, literary critic Eli Finci denounced the withdrawal in the new Belgrade journal *Svedočanstvo* as a "ban on laughter." Drenovac then responded with a strong defense of Mitrović's action in *Književne novine*. Indeed, as Ratko

Peković argues, the controversy around *The Ball of Thieves* was really only an excuse for a confrontation between the two journals and their conflicting cultural concepts.[80]

Mitrović finally ended the debate, though not the mutual hostility, by publishing her own explanation and self-defense.[81] Although Mitrović later admitted that she had actually agreed with Finci, at the time she concurred with Drenovac in criticizing Finci's attitude that once the party had opened up the ideological struggle, Communists should no longer be able to express their views. Had Finci stuck to arguments about dogmatism in art, bad repertoire policies, or even undeveloped taste, she insisted, it would have been fine. It became clear to her, however, that even had she only offered her opinion, Finci would have rejected it simply because it came from a state functionary. Thus, she concluded, Finci's struggle against bureaucratization really came down to "preventing communists from defending their concepts simply because they hold this or that state or party function."[82] The assessment may have been correct, but it is also true that by asking the theater to withdraw the piece in her official capacity as minister of education, Mitrović had revealed to all the continued ambiguity of the party's position and its apparent inability to achieve its ends solely by means of persuasion.[83]

Perhaps seeking to minimize the damage to his reforms without giving up the ideological struggle, Djilas now entered the fray with an article in *Književne novine*. Although his piece represented an unambiguous attack on an article by Aleksander Vučo in *Svedočanstvo* and indeed on the journal itself, Djilas prefaced his remarks with a lengthy caveat. He had been planning to publish his article in *Književne novine* for some time, he explained, but had been told that given the ongoing polemics between the two journals, it might look as though he were officially endorsing *Književne novine*'s views. He had then briefly considered publishing his critique in *Svedočanstvo*, but had decided against it since he really did not support its positions. After further delays he had finally decided to go ahead with the article in *Književne novine* but wanted to make it clear at the start that it did not represent an official attack on *Svedočanstvo*.[84]

The conflict finally ended when both journals ceased publication in the fall of 1952.[85] Editors from both journals (although more from *Književne novine*) then sought to overcome their hostility through joint participation in *Nova misao*, an all-Yugoslav journal dedicated to questions of science, philosophy, and art that published its first issue in January 1953. According to Djilas, *Nova misao*, though Marxist in its perspective, would be anti-dogmatic and would "analyze their inherited stock of ideas." Indeed, in the course of the following year, *Nova misao* became increasingly adventurous in its concepts and stimulated much ideological and intellectual ferment among party members. But as articles for *Nova misao* increasingly occupied the time and attention of Djilas and other persuasive activists, the agitprop department itself "faded away as a bureaucratic party organization."[86]

The Response by Agitprop Departments

Without question, the new reforms had seriously confused any understanding of the role and function of agitprop departments. How could they work to "channel correctly the aspirations of the populace for culture," once the party had given up its cultural monopoly and if its leaders now spoke out only as equal participants in the struggle of opinions? This dilemma, clearly evident though never openly discussed in debates at the top, also explains the behavior of the members of agitprop departments at middle and lower levels of the party.

In the first year after the reorganization of the party and its agitprop departments, internal and public documents reported numerous instances of both under- and overreaction to the new policies. Many bemoaned the continued absence of a struggle of opinions and complained that everything was still accepted from above without thought.[87] Others, however, worried about trends toward passivity and demoralization in response to the new policies. As early as January 1951, for example, an article by Drenovac in *Partijska izgradnja* complained of stagnation in agitprop departments, noting that while many organizations had ceased working "in the old way," they had not yet begun to work "in the new way." Likewise, an internal report from Niš remarked that some members seemed to think that the new policies simply meant less work. "Committees have grasped that they can no longer lead in the old ways, but it is not sufficiently clear to them how to establish the leadership system on new bases and simultaneously carry out all the economic tasks before them (the otkup and so on)."[88]

By late 1952, the trend toward passivism had apparently triumphed over blind subordination to directives. Several reports now complained that while a few local and district committees still worked in the old ways, addressing in detail questions that ought to be left to other organs, most had lost interest even in those issues that ought to concern them, apparently believing that everything they had done in the past was no good. Fears of violating socialist democracy, one report complained, now led many members to react with complete indifference when confronted with enemy actions. Worst of all, the new policies had even affected internal party discipline. Some party committees, the reports claimed, now believed that they could, but did not have to, carry out the decisions of the upper leadership, while their members showed similar laxity and often neglected to attend meetings, pay dues, or carry out specific assignments.[89]

The end result, then, of the party reforms in the field of persuasion and culture was precisely the opposite of what had been intended. As with social ownership of property, what the party proclaimed to be everyone's responsibility soon became no one's. Rather than involving all loyal Yugoslavs in the transformation of society, the new reforms had only led to a sense of demoralization among party members who simply could not figure out how they were simultaneously to "play fair" and "win at all costs." Yet, the decline in party persuasion came not only because the rules of the game had changed; it also reflected an evolving sense of what kind of victory might be possible.

A further, and in many ways more profound, effect of the party's reforms was to diminish its expectations for culture as a means of propaganda and to delay (if not derail altogether) its hopes of creating new people with new values, beliefs, and behavioral norms. The party's evolution toward this less ambitious but more pragmatic approach may be seen in a series of debates about youth and culture that developed in the period from 1950 to 1953.

Notes

1. See, for example, Dennison Rusinow, *The Yugoslav Experiment, 1948–1974* (Berkeley, CA: University of California Press, 1977), 32.
2. In the same month Kardelj, speaking to the Slovene Academy of Sciences, criticized Soviet science and argued for freedom in the field of scientific creation. Predrag J. Marković, *Beograd izmedju istoka i zapada, 1948–1965* (Belgrade: 1996), 325.
3. Milovan Djilas, *Rise and Fall* (New York: Harcourt Brace Jovanovich, 1983), 260–261.
4. Milovan Djilas, "Problem školstva u borbi za socijalizam u našoj zemlji," at the Third Plenum of the Central Committee of the CPY held 29–30 Dec. 1949, in Branko Petranović, Ranko Končar, and Radovan Radonjić, eds., *Sednice Centralnog komiteta KPJ (1948–1952)* (Belgrade: Izdavački centar Komunist, 1985), 295.
5. Ibid, 289.
6. Ibid., 292.
7. Ibid., 295–296.
8. Ibid., 293.
9. Ibid., 300, 307–308.
10. Ibid., 302.
11. Ibid., 312–314. Kardelj's speech to the Third Plenum focused mainly on foreign policy, but he did urge the press to be less sectarian in its treatment of Yugoslavia's relations with the West. Ibid., 474–475.

12. Dr. Ivo Babić, Report on the work of the Ministry of Education of Croatia in 1949, 1950, AJ, MNK F61; Dj. Bogojević, "Mostarska oblast—primer pravilnog sprovodjenja odluka trećeg plenuma CK KPJ," *Borba*, 5 April 1950, p. 2; "Zapisnik sa sastanka održanog u UPA CK KPJ za drugovima iz SK Mostar," 10 April 1950, ACKSKJ, VIII II/2-b-30; "Izveštaj o obilasku partiske organizacije u AP Vojvodini," 6–30 April 1950, ACKSKJ, V-KIV/62.

13. Nikola Sekulić, "Prosvetni problemi i školstvo," at Četvrto plenarno zasedanje CKKPH, held 17 April 1950, *Socialistički front*, 3, no. 3 (June 1950): 10–45; "Rezolucija o školstvu," from Četvrto plenarno zasedanje CKKPH, held 17 April 1950, *Socialistički front*, 3, no. 3 (June 1950): 3–8.

14. "Rezolucija Treće interfakultetske konferencije pravnih fakulteta o ideološkom i stručnom uzdizanju nastava," *Politika*, 20 Jan. 1950, p. 2; "Informacija o problemima u vezi sprovodjenja odluka III plenum CK KPJ u organizacijama Narodne omladine na univerzitetima," June 1950, AJ, SSOJ F330. See also Veljko Vlahović, "Kulturno-prosvjetna politika partije," no date, 1950?, ACKSKJ, LFVV II/4-d-1; "O nekim ideološko-političkim i unutarpartiskim pitanjima, na osnovu zaključaka CK KP Crne Gore," no date, ACKSKJ, V-KV/27.

15. In fact, party leaders created workers' councils as a first step toward the later self-management reforms already in December 1949. At that point, however, they were limited in scope and apparently intended mainly as an experimental measure. Letter to all Central Committees from Organizational-Instructors Bureau, 21 Dec. 1949, ACKSKJ, V-KI/66.

16. Veljko Vlahović, "O radu odeljenja za agitaciju i propagandu," *Partijska izgradnja*, 9–10 (1949): 13–19.

17. Mišo Pavičević, "Neposredni zadaci ideološko-političkog rada u sindikatima," at X Plenum CV SSJ, 11–12 Dec. 1949, AJ, CVSSJ F17; Mirko Milojković, "Organizacioni problemi kulturno-prosvetnog rada," no date, 1949–1950?, AJ, CVSSJ F83 KPO.

18. "Povodom jedne beleške," *Borba*, 5 March 1950, 5.

19. Veljko Vlahović, "Predmet: Partiska izgradnja," 16 May 1950, ACKSKJ, VIII IV/a-16.

20. Veljko Vlahović, "Zapisnik sa sastanka Plenuma Komisije za agitaciju i štampu Saveznog odbora NFJ," 29 May 1950, AJ, SSRNJ 142-27-82.

21. Vlahović, "Kulturno-prosvjetna politika partije."

22. Milovan Djilas, "Savetovanje propagandista," 6 May 1950, ACKSKJ, VIII II/2-d-20; Milovan Djilas, "Naša dosadašnja iskustva u borbi za socijalizam," *Savremene teme* (Belgrade: Borba, 1950), 41–50.

23. Rusinow, 57–59.

24. "Pismo o radu i ulozi sreskih komiteta," 22 June 1950, ACKSKJ, II-KI/59; Odluke i direktive CK KPJ, Svim Centralnim komitetima KP Republika," 22 June 1950, *Partijska izgradnja*, 6 (1950): 55–60.

25. "Informacije o radu Narodnog fronta Jugoslavije od V. Kongresa pa do danas," 1953, ACKSKJ, XII 10/3 and AJ, SSRNJ 142-3-10; Edvard Kardelj, "Uloga i zadaci Socijalističkog saveza radnog naroda Jugoslavije u borbi za socijalizam," Speech at IV Kongres NFJ, 23 Feb. 1953, *Komunist*, 5, no. 2–3 (1953): 104.

26. "Informacije o radu Narodnog fronta Jugoslavije"; Kardelj, "Uloga i zadaci Socijalističkog saveza radnog naroda Jugoslavije"; Krsto Popivoda, "Izveštaj o radu NFJ," 23 Feb. 1953, AJ, SSRNJ 142-3-10.

27. "Informacije o radu Narodnog fronta Jugoslavije"; Kardelj, "Uloga i zadaci Socijalističkog saveza radnog naroda Jugoslavije." Also, like the party, the PFY now took steps to reduce its administrative apparatus. A meeting of the Executive Council of the People's Front in late June 1950 thus reduced the number of its commissions from 13 to 7 and the size of its professional apparatus from 26 to 17. "Zapisnik sednice Sekretarijata Izvršnog odbora NFJ," 29 June 1950, AJ, SSRNJ 142-20-65.

28. Blagoje Nešković, "Stenografske beleške: Sednica Sekretarijata Izvršnog odbora NFJ," 23 Oct. 1950, AJ, SSRNJ 142-20-65. Nešković's criticism of the role of the party within the Front is perhaps unsurprising given his ambivalent response to Stalin's attack on the CPY, which had specifically accused the party of hiding behind the Front and failing to carry out its leading role. According to Djilas, Nešković had initially suggested that the CPY should attend the Cominform meeting, had rejected the idea of ever fighting the Red Army, and maintained his devotion to Stalin long after the split. Despite all this, party leaders did not move against him immediately; by late 1952, however, after Nešković expressed his opposition to improving relations with the West, he was expelled from the party and returned to his prewar occupation as a laboratory physician. Djilas, *Rise and Fall*, 199–201, 219–221; Svetozar Vukmanović-Tempo, *Revolucija koja teče: Memoari*, Book 2, (Belgrade: 1971), 94. Even so, there is no evidence that Nešković's line on party/front relations was, at that time, out of step with the rest of the party leadership.

29. Memo to all CKs from A. Ranković, 14 Oct. 1950, ACKSKJ, VIII I/1-a-12. Already since March 1949 the departments had been called Uprave za agitaciju i propagandu, and in fact, agitprop documents even after 1950 often referred to them by that title rather than as the Uprave za propagandu i agitaciju. For the sake of simplicity I will continue to refer to it as the central agitprop department.

30. Ibid.

31. "Zapisnik sednice Sekretarijata Izvršnog odbora NFJ," 29 June 1950, AJ, SSRNJ 142-20-65; "Zapisnik sednice Sekretarijata Izvršnog odbora NFJ, 23 Oct. 1950, AJ, SSRNJ 142-20-65; Djuka Julius, "Problemi političko-prosvjetnog rada u Narodnom frontu," no date, AJ, SSRNJ 142-27-83.

32. Bora Drenovac, "O reorganizaciji agitpropa," *Partijska izgradnja*, 1 (1951): 46–54.

33. "Zaključci sa sastanka o problemima u novinarstvu održanog u Agitpropu," 2 June 1950, ACKSKJ, VIII II/2-b-31; "Zapisnik sa sastanka Uprava za agitaciju i propagandu CK KPJ, 16 Oct. 1950, ACKSKJ, VIII II/2-b-39.

34. Olga Biljanović, "Kvalitet štampe—osnovno merilo u njeno rasturanju," 5 Nov. 1950, ACKSKJ, VIII II/5-b-51; Memo about distribution of the press, 10 Oct. 1950, ACKSKJ, VIII II/5-b-50; Memo to all CKs from Milovan Djilas, 10 Oct. 1950, ACKSKJ, VIII I/1-a-11.

35. "Zapisnik sa sastanka o štampi," 2 Dec. 1950, ACKSKJ, VIII II/2-b-41.

36. "Peta sednica Saveznog veća," 29 Dec. 1950, *Drugo redovno zasedanje Saveznog veća i Veća naroda, drugi saziv, 27–29 Dec. 1950, Stenografske beleške* (Belgrade: 1951).

37. "Zapisnik sa sastanka Uprava za agitaciju i propagandu," 9 June 1951, ACKSKJ, VIII II/2-b-51; "Zaključci na sastanku kod druga Djilasa," 22 Dec. 1951, ACKSKJ, VIII II/2-b-63.

38. "Zapisnik sa sastanka Uprava za agitaciju i propagandu"; "Rešenja o osnivanju odbora za kinematografiju," No. 115, *Službeni* list, 8, no. 11 (7 March 1952); "Rešenje o ukidanju odbora za kinematografiju," No. 675, *Službeni* list, 8, no. 58 (3 Dec. 1952); "Zapisnik sa sastanka u Agitpropu po pitanju filma," 10 Dec. 1952, ACKSKJ, VIII II/2-b-76.

39. "Rezolucija Četvrtog plenuma CK KPJ o teorijskom radu u KPJ," and Milovan Djilas, "O teorijskom radu naše partije," 3-4 June 1951, in Petranović, Končar and Radonjić, 639, 589-597.

40. Milovan Djilas, "O Partiji," 6 June 1952, ACKSKJ, VIII IV-a-22.

41. Cited in A. Ross Johnson, *The Transformation of Communist Ideology, The Yugoslav Case, 1945-1953* (Cambridge, MA: The MIT Press, 1972), 201.

42. Djilas, "O Partiji"; Milovan Djilas, Speech in Titograd, part 2, 19 April 1952, ACKSKJ, VIII IV-a-19; Milovan Djilas, "Partija u prelaznom periodu," 23 May 1952, ACKSKJ, VIII IV-a-22.

43. "Šta je i kakva treba da bude naša komunistička partija," 15 Aug. 1945—but clearly written much earlier, between June 1941 and May 1943, HDA, CKKPH.

44. In so doing, Djilas may have been moving beyond what other party leaders believed acceptable. His support for the notion of the "withering away of the state" apparently contributed to his expulsion from the party in 1954. (See Rusinow, 75.) In 1952, however, no one openly disputed Djilas's arguments.

45. Djilas, *Rise and Fall*, 292; Momčilo Djorgović, *Djilas, Vernik i Jeretik* (Belgrade: Akvarijus, 1989) 151-152; "Značaj Šestog Kongresa Saveza Komunista Jugoslavije," *Komunist*, 5, no. 1 (1953): 5-8.

46. "Značaj Šestog kongresa," 6. See also "Rezolucija Šestog kongresa KPJ o zadacima i ulozi Savez komunista Jugoslavije," 6 Nov. 1952, ACKSKJ, I/VI-K2/90, and in *Komunist*, 6, no. 5-6 (Sept-Dec. 1952): 1-8.

47. "Govor Maršala Tita," at IV Kongres SSRNJ, 22 Feb. 1953, AJ, SSRNJ 142-3-10; Milovan Djilas, "O zaključcima Šestog kongresa Saveza komunista Jugoslavije i odnosu izmedju Saveza komunista Jugoslavije i Socijalističkog saveza radnog naroda Jugoslavije," 1 Dec. 1952, ACKSKJ, VIII IV-a-26; "Rezolucija Šestog kongresa."

48. Kardelj, "Uloga i zadaci Socijalistickog saveza radnog naroda Jugoslavije," 109-114.

49. Ibid.

50. Johnson, 203-209; Djilas, *Rise and Fall*, 320.

51. That the significance of the Fourth Congress was clear to all may be surmised from the fact that Belgrade's most independent newsmagazine, *NIN*, paid more attention to it than it had to the Sixth Party Congress. Marković, 50.

52. Josip Broz Tito, "Borba komunista Jugoslavije za socijalističku demokratiju," Speech at the Sixth Party Congress of the CPY, 3 Nov. 1953, in Josip Broz Tito, *Govori i članci*, Vol. VII (Zagreb: 1959), 256-258.

53. Ibid.

54. "Svim organizacijama Saveza komunista Jugoslavije," *Komunist*, 5, no. 7 (July 1953): 451–456.

55. "Drugi plenarni sastanka Centralnog komiteta Saveza komunista Jugoslavije, *Komunist*, 5, no. 7 (July 1953): 457–464.

56. Johnson, 213–215.

57. "Beleške sa sastanka Uprave," 25 Dec. 1950, ACKSKJ, VIII II/2-b-44.

58. Bora Drenovac, "Beogradski 'NIN' i jedna rdjava pojava u novinarstvu" *Književne novine*, 4, no. 41 (12 Oct. 1951): 2. For information on the origins of *NIN* see "Neposlušno čedo agitprop," in *Dva veka srpskog novinarstva*, Mihailo Bjelica ed., (Belgrade: Institut za novinarstvo, 1992), 274–276.

59. "Zapisnik sa sastanka Biroa CK NOJ," 3 Oct. 1951, AJ, SSOJ F56; "Problemi kulturno-prosvetnog rada," 1952, ACKSKJ, VIII II/8-d-61; "Zapisnik sa sastanka Komisije za štampu o problemima štampe," 29 Aug. 1952, ACKSKJ, VIII II/2-a-8.

60. "Zapisnik sa sastanka održanog kod druga Djilasa"; Stenografske beleške sa sastanka, diskusija Djilasa o odnosu izmedju štampe i državnih organa," 1951, ACKSKJ, VIII II/4-c-4.

61. "Zapisnik sa sastanka održanog kod druga Djilasa"; "Zapisnik sa sastanka u upravi agitacije i propagande CK KPH po pitanju unutrašnje-političke rubrike," 20 Aug. 1951, ACKSKJ, VIII II/2-b-54. See also "Stenografske beleške sa sastanka, diskusija Djilasa o odnosu izmedju štampe i državnih organa," 1951, ACKSKJ, VIII II/4-c-4.

62. "Zapisnik sa sastanka Agitpropa," 25–26 Dec. 1951, ACKSKJ, VIII II/2-b-64.

63. "Zapisnik sa sastanka Potkomisje za štampu CK KPJ," 7 May 1952, ACKSKJ, VII II/2-a-15; "Zapisnik sa sastanka Komisije za štampu o problemima štampe."

64. "Zapisnik sa sastanka Biroa CK NOJ," 3 Oct. 1951, AJ, SSOJ F56; "Zapisnik sa sastanka Agitprop-komisije," 19 Dec. 1951, ACKSKJ, VIII II/2-b-62.

65. Djilas, *Rise and Fall*, 270–271; Marko Lopušina, *Crna knjiga: Cenzura u Jugoslaviji, 1945–91* (Belgrade: Fokus, 1991), 29–30.

66. Lopušina, 120.

67. Ratko Peković, *Ni rat ni mir: Panorama književnih polemika* (Belgrade: Filip Višnjić, 1986), 83–86; Djorgović, 24. According to Lopušina, they had to let him publish because without him they couldn't put together a single elementary school reader. Nonetheless, Ćopić did not emerge unscathed. Lopušina cites Erih Koš as saying that Ćopić began to drink heavily after this experience. Then, in 1954, Ćopić once again found himself in trouble with the authorities, this time over a lecture he'd given at the university and over three short stories, one of which was clearly satirical. Finally, by the late 1950s, as his refusal to conform became clear, Ćopić was expelled from the party. In March 1984, Ćopić committed suicide by jumping off the Sava bridge onto the concrete below. Despite the lengthy intervening time period, Koš directly blamed the censorship for his death. Lopušina, 120; Marković, 179–181.

68. Vladimir Dedijer, *Novi prilozi za biografiju Josipa Broza Tita*, Vol. 3 (Belgrade: Rad, 1984), 522.

69. For more on the Kocbek case see Edvard Kocbek, *Dnevnik 1951–1952*, ed. Dimitrij Rupel (Zagreb: Globus, 1986).

70. "Zapisnik sa sastanka Agitprop-komisije."

71. Drenovac, "Beogradski 'NIN' i jedna rdjava pojava u novinarstvu"; Bora Drenovac, "Još jednom o 'NIN'-u," *Književne novine*, 4, no. 42 (27 Oct. 1951): 7; "Zapisnik sa sastanka Agitprop-komisije."

72. "Neposlušno čedo agitpropa," in Bjelica, 276.

73. In his diary, Kocbek noted that in one *Borba* article Djilas called simultaneously for "sharp discipline" and more democratization and legality. Lopušina also noted Djilas's hypocrisy in calling for "the free struggle of opinions" while he censored Živorad Stojković's brochure *O jednom ćutanju u književnosti*, which sought to show that literature was lagging behind the reforms in politics. Kocbek, 165; Lopušina, 120. However, given that Djilas, both before and after this period, was inclined to be consistent to a fault, I would attribute his contradictory policies to genuine uncertainty and confusion rather than deliberate deception.

74. Bora Drenovac, "'Mladost' mračnija od starosti," *Književne novine*, 5, no. 53 (29 March 1952): 1, 4; "Zapisnik sa sastanka Komisije za štampu o problemima štampe"; Milovan Djilas, "Vučovi 'Dokazi' slobode," *Književne novine*, 5, no. 65 (14 Sept. 1952): 2–3; "Problemi kulturno-prosvetnog rada," 1952, ACKSKJ, VIII II/8-d-61.

75. "Stenografske beleške Savetovanja članova Centralnih komiteta NO republika po pitanju rada u srednjim školama u narednoj godini," 16 Aug. 1952, AJ, SSOJ F58.

76. "Zaključci sa sastanka UPA," 15 Oct. 1951, ACKSKJ, VIII II/2-b-56.

77. "Osnovno danas," *Književne novine*, 5, no. 47 (6 Jan. 1952): 1.

78. According to Lopušina, the play was banned not because it suggested that party leaders were thieves but because it portrayed thieves as heroes. The latter explanation makes more sense given the content of the play, which has nothing to do with governing elites but is a light romantic comedy about three thieves who set out to con an upper-class family but fall in love with the daughters instead. Mitrović's version, however, would better explain the party's paranoid reaction. Perhaps Pijade had not actually seen the play but only guessed at its content from the title. Lopušina, 31–32.

79. Djorgović, 219–221.

80. Bora Drenovac, "Da ne ostane bez odgovora," *Književne novine*, 5, no. 59 (24 June 1952): 4.

81. Peković, 128–130; Mitra Mitrović, "Povodom diskusije o skidanju 'Bala Lopova' sa reportoara, upućeno 'Svedočanstvima' i 'Književnim novinama'," *Književne novine*, 5, no. 65 (14 Sept. 1952): 1; Djorgović, 220–221.

82. Mitrović, "Povodom diskusije o skidanju 'Bala Lopova'."

83. Further proof that party leaders still often influenced cultural politics in a direct manner may be seen from a 1952 agitprop meeting on publishing at which Djilas absolutely forbade publication of the works of Jean-Paul Sartre. "Zapisnik sa sastanka po pitanju izdavačke delatnosti," 5 March 1952, ACKSKJ, VIII II/2-b-69.

84. Djilas, "Vučovi 'Dokazi' slobode," 2–3.

85. Lopušina lists several other journals banned at approximately the same time, including *Pogledi, Medjutim, Krugovi, Zapisi, Književni jadran, Literatura,* and *Galerija* due to their disagreement with party policies or because they were not sufficiently "ideološki pure." Lopušina, 31–32.

86. Djilas, *Rise and Fall*, 287, 329–330, 350.

87. See, for example, "Izveštaj ekipe CK KPJ o obilasku partiske organizacije u Makedoniji od 13 do 29 Juna 1951 godine," June 1951, ACKSKJ, V-KIII/22; "Informacija o sprovodjenju rezolucije o školstvu III plenuma CK KPJ, 1951, ACKSKJ, VIII II/8-d-60.

88. Bora Drenovac, "O reorganizaciji agitpropa," *Partijska izgradnja*, 1 (1951): 46–54; "Kratka informacija o obilasku Niške oblasti," 1951, ACKSKJ, V-KIV/48.

89. "O nekim problemima rada partije," mid-1952, ACKSKJ, V-KII/26; "Teza za diskusiju na Upravi 1952 g.," 1952, ACKSKJ, VIII II/2-c-63; Aleksandar Ranković, "O predlogu novog statuta KPJ i nekim organizacionim pitanjima partije," 6 Nov. 1952, ACKSKJ, I/VI-K2/68. Similar discussions took place in documents relating to the People's Front and the trade unions where, again, reorganization and deprofessionalization caused much confusion about what exactly they were expected to do and who should do it.

9

The Cultural Transformation Abandoned

As we have seen, CPY leaders counted heavily on both cultural personnel and youth to help realize the transformation of society. Yet, as we have also seen, party leaders were often disappointed by their achievements in the field of culture as well as by the attitudes and behavior of youth. New cultural creations fell far below party expectations, and Yugoslavia's youth seemed equally far from becoming the new more socialist people. The party's concerns about youth were especially serious since its expectations for them had been so high. Indeed, the party's failure to mold youth's character and values called into question its entire vision for the future. The party's problems with youth were, however, closely associated with its cultural policies since youth often revealed their nonsocialist views in their production and selection of high and mass culture. The recalcitrance of young people in their approach to culture thus displays more clearly than anything else the party's inability to transform either youth or culture, whether by means of direct orders and coercion or more subtle persuasion.

CPY leaders had begun to confront the failure of Soviet-style rhetoric to create new people with new values already in late 1947. The reforms of the early 1950s represented a renunciation of negative techniques like censorship and a decision to let the positive power of Marxist ideology effect change on its own. The failure of this approach to transform either youth or culture gradually led party leaders to give up on culture as a direct means of indoctrination and to temper their expectations for the creation of new people with new socialist values.

Youth and Culture After the Soviet-Yugoslav Split

CPY policies toward youth and culture did not change dramatically in the first 18 months following the Soviet-Yugoslav split. By late 1949, however, one can see the first signs of reform in that area as well. As was the case more generally, however, these initial signs of change were rather tentative and reflected the party's still ambiguous reaction to the split. For example, in late 1949 the central agitprop committee began to compile reports about and hold meetings with young writers, critics, and the editors of youth journals. These meetings and reports reflected party leaders' considerable disappointment and frustration with the literary efforts of young writers whose work, they said, continued to show narrowness, a lack of education, and the influence of decadent and formalist literature.[1] Party cultural leaders called attention to two sets of errors typical of youth's cultural creations. One concerned the politically correct but aesthetically unappealing works of young writers that were frequently characterized by "phrase-mongering optimism" and which led to sentimentalism and an idealization of social relations. Such works, they complained, were conventional and colorless in style with bloodless and schematically formed characters. The other set of errors were typical of those young writers who had fallen under the influence of prewar bourgeois formalist and surrealist poets. The works of these young artists, while often showing considerable talent, were politically and ideologically unacceptable as they consisted of "individualistic," "pessimistic," and "reactionary" love poetry or "animalistic" portrayals of life couched in "crude naturalistic" terms.[2] Once again, party leaders faced their apparent inability to make artists out of party hacks or party hacks out of artists.

The solutions offered to this dilemma reflected the ideological confusion within the CPY following the Soviet-Yugoslav split. The formal conclusions adopted by the conference called, in typical Stalinist style, for a greater connection between youth and the new socialist reality they were expected to describe. As a necessary condition for their success, it explained, young writers "must study more deeply and broadly the lives of our working people.... In that way they will become real interpreters of the struggle which our peoples ... are leading against the Informbureau's counterrevolution." Thus, the report urged that young writers spend time in industrial enterprises, mines, and peasant working cooperatives so that they might experience firsthand the daily heroism of the working classes.[3] This approach differed not at all from earlier demands in 1945 and 1946 that writers seek their inspiration in factories, mines, and volunteer labor brigades.

At the same time, however, many speakers seemed to be moving toward a new approach to literary creation, condemning a dogmatic view of aesthetics and rejecting preconceived recipes for literature. Moreover, reflecting the party's more recent emphasis on education as the means to socialism, conference leaders also called for increased study of both

Marxism-Leninism and the works of Yugoslav and world classical literature in order to improve youth's ideological and professional qualifications. In a notable contrast to many past documents, this report did not specify which elements of Yugoslavia's literary heritage were appropriate for study and which must be rejected out of hand.[4]

Ultimately, as we shall see, this trend toward a relaxation of cultural policies prevailed. It was evident already at the Second Congress of the Union of Yugoslav Writers held in December 1949, where speakers not only openly condemned Soviet cultural policies, but now suggested that art could not and must not be subordinated to politics. The union also began to accept that artistic themes and subjects might be apolitical. Petar Šegedin, for example, pleaded for more of the spiritual human essence in party-minded literature and insisted that political practice could not serve as a direct criterion for artistic value. As one poet later put it, the congress "officially established that poets can write even about pretzels."[5]

Over the following two years, the reforms that occurred in all spheres of Yugoslav society led also to greatly increased tolerance for the creation of nonsocialist and alternative culture. Indeed, once adopted, these reforms engendered an immediate blossoming of new cultural production at all levels. Critics became increasingly bold in their indifference and resistance to Soviet and socialist-realist models, while writers and artists, especially among youth, now freed from the constraints of socialist realism, experimented with a variety of styles previously censured. Some even ventured into the sphere of satire, now directing their jibes not only at the old bourgeoisie but at the new administration and its functionaries. By the end of 1950, several new literary journals openly supported a variety of modernist and non-socialist-realist artistic trends and by mid-1951, writers and poets were applauding their new freedom to write not only about politics, shockworkers, and youth brigades but also about feelings, love, and flowers.[6]

Just as important was an increasingly indulgent attitude toward Western and "petty bourgeois" popular culture that seemed to reflect the party's evolving attitudes toward both culture as a form of propaganda and youth as the bearers of the new culture. To begin with, party leaders had apparently concluded that the gap between high and popular culture could not be eliminated by artificial and coercive methods and that since the two forms of culture must coexist, they might as well live up to their names—that is, high culture should be of high aesthetic quality and popular culture should be popular. Perhaps they had concluded that it was better to permit artistic freedom than to destroy culture's aesthetic value or drive it underground and into a stance of political opposition. At the same time, the new policies seemed to reflect a reconsideration by party and youth leaders of the role of entertainment and popular culture in the development of youth psyches.

Although party leaders had long recognized the natural need of children to play and have fun, they had generally expected youth over 15 to devote far more energy to constructive activities. Admittedly, youth organizations offered their members ample opportunity to participate in and attend such leisure-time activities as sports, concerts, cultural performances, movies, and dances; yet those activities were often self-consciously educational and had excluded the concept of entertainment for its own sake. Now, however, in accordance with the party's new approach toward socialist construction, many party leaders seemed to accept that "fun for fun's sake" was a legitimate form of culture, at least for youth.[7]

Thus, beginning in early 1950, the party gradually relaxed its restrictions on imports of new Western films and jazz music and on domestic production of light and popular culture. One report from the PYY even argued that the music schools should focus especially on creating good jazz orchestras as a means of recruiting youth.[8] As party restrictions relaxed, the public, and especially youth, eagerly lapped up the new Western delicacies now available in the entertainment world. Whereas in January 1950, four out of 10 films showing in Belgrade were Soviet made, after March of that year only one or two Soviet films were playing at any given time, while the number and percentage of American and Western European films steadily increased.[9] One of the first new Hollywood films shown in Yugoslavia after the war—Esther Williams's *Bathing Beauties*, translated as *Bal na vodi*—was outrageously popular when it debuted in December 1950; Yugoslav citizens lined up for blocks to see it over and over again and according to one estimate, some 86–87 percent of all Belgrade citizens saw it at least once.[10] Likewise, jazz music flourished and urban youths began sporting the modern fashions they had seen in Western films and fashion magazines and on foreign visitors. Perhaps the most obvious indicator of the party's new approach came in late 1950 when CPY leaders bowed to public pressure and demanded that all newspapers and journals become financially independent and support themselves from their own truly voluntary sales.[11] Concluding that the officially sanctioned newspapers and journals had become so dull and formulaic that people were refusing to buy or read them, party leaders now sought to revitalize the country's cultural life and publications by offering the public more of what it wanted. CPY leaders hoped that in so doing, these publications would lead to open ideological debate between the party and society, allowing the party convincingly to prove the values of socialism and thus effect the cultural transformation.

In other words, while the reforms clearly opened up enormous new possibilities for the creation and distribution of much apolitical and, implicitly if not explicitly, nonsocialist art and culture, they were not meant to lessen the role of Communist ideology in Yugoslav society. On the contrary, based on the premise that in a free struggle of opinions the Communist ideology would inevitably prevail, they reflected the party's continued attachment to and extraordinary faith in Marxist-Leninist ideology. Party leaders had not given up on culture as a means of indoctrination or on youth as their hope for the future. Now, however, they argued for a less intrusive approach to cultural and social manipulation. Cultural artistic trends, party leaders now admitted, could not be dictated, nor could the gap between high and low culture be eliminated by fiat. Rather, they now believed that more educational rhetoric combined with open ideological debate would persuade youth of the cultural and political bankruptcy of "petty bourgeois," "reactionary," and "vulgar" cultural forms. In the process, youth would once again become participants in the transformation of society, though now at a higher level.

Thus, several documents insisted that party persuasion, while no less important than in the past, must concentrate more on education and should not become a form of censorship. According to one unsigned report from the PYY, banning "bad" films, although tempting, would only provoke a stubborn desire among children somehow to see the film. Therefore, it concluded, parents, teachers, and others would do better to simply discuss the film and in general to show more concern for the proper education of youth. Likewise, at the Fourteenth Plenum of the People's Youth in January 1950, Milorad Pešić emphasized that physical attacks on "bourgeois decadent youth"—cutting their hair or even their clothing—were not the correct ideological-educational approach toward such individuals. Rather than blowing things out of proportion and expelling youths from the organization, party leaders should seek to uncover the causes of the problems and morally educate each individual youth.[12]

CPY cultural activists responded to this new approach in a variety of ways. Some clearly welcomed the new opportunities for cultural freedom and became fervent promoters of the "struggle of opinions." Others, however, were plainly uncomfortable with the modified policies. For many, the new approach seemed confusing since it offered no concrete information about how to create socialist culture and socialist people in daily practice. Party cadres had now been informed that they could not forbid alternative approaches to culture but that they must nonetheless prevent their harmful effects. How this was to be accomplished, no one knew. They further worried that reduced censorship would only encourage the spread of openly anti-socialist and "reactionary" culture. Thus, internal and public documents from the early 1950s speak alternately in voices of toleration and outrage, reflecting the party's uncertainty and concern about its new policies.

The publication of many new and unquestionably non-socialist-realist works throughout 1951 and 1952 provoked a series of heated debates in literary journals as Communist cultural personnel tried to work out the limits to and deal with the consequences of their new policies. After all, the old proponents of socialist realism had not all converted to modernist styles nor were they all impressed by the new atmosphere of tolerance. Many continued to demand that art and literature support political and economic efforts to build socialism on a daily basis. For example, Dušan Kostić, one of the more active poets from previous years, declined to condemn the old practice of providing "standing orders" (*porudžbina*) in literature and poetry and described the mission of art in terms identical to those so often repeated in the years from 1944 through 1949. We are living, he asserted, under a shower of slanders but we have pride, honor, and manhood. "We need a fighting spirit, energy, and shockwork. Because these are fighting times, because there are still dark forces in the world. . . . It is the duty of a poet and writer to speak to the people honestly and openly . . . to inspire and elevate them with the power of true poetic words, and not to leave them, fleeing from the battle into formalistic games and solipsism."[13] Such remarks reflected the fears of many that cultural freedom had gone too far and might endanger the party's progress toward socialism. An unsigned internal report from the central agitprop department in 1952 neatly summarized these concerns. Arguing that while in 1950 and 1951 the party had struggled mainly against the ideological influence of the Soviet Union, the document urged that the party now increase its efforts against the penetration of "bourgeois" ideology and decadence, which, it said,

> is being carried out with careful bowing to political slogans of socialist democracy and is characterized as the victory of that democracy. Ideologically, however, it attacks first of all the philosophical bases of marxism. Dušan Matić writes, for example, that "there is no marxist aesthetics just as there is no marxist physics or agronomy . . ." Dušan Nedeljković teaches "The Philosophical Synthesis of Materialism and Idealism" in the Kolarčev People's University and *Svedočanstvo* praises him for it, criticizing only the fact that he is nonetheless too exclusivist toward domestic idealists. Belgrade's *Mladost* and *Svedočanstvo* defend the ideology of anti-heroism in literature and are reviving surrealism. Zagreb's *Krugovi* declared abstract art to be "the

only contemporary art." And Kocbek in Slovenia is publishing a book of novellas which are really reactionary social criticism in literary form and which have a clearly marked personalistic existentialist position.[14]

Again, such concerns were particularly evident among those who worked with youth. After all, while young people seemed most vulnerable to the influence of Western culture and ideology, they were also expected to provide the basis for the new society. Already in January 1951, a meeting on the work of the PYY with young writers bemoaned the growing tendency of youth to support and imitate prewar decadent poetry in direct opposition to "progressive" literary art. In the ensuing discussion, Dušan Kostić noted that while the split with the Soviet Union had broadened people's perspectives, it had also contributed to the idea that "various lines" of culture were acceptable and that only decadent poetry was real poetry. Even recognizing that young people always aspire to something new, Kostić nonetheless worried that so many were running from reality into subjectivism, while so few continued the tradition of "fighting poetry."[15]

The growing divide between youth and their elders also appeared in open debates on the pages of various cultural journals. Seasoned Communists most often simply denounced the developing cultural trends among youth. Bora Drenovac exemplified this approach in his critique of the youth cultural journal *Mladost*. From its initial flirtation "with abstract and senseless poetry," he explained, the journal had declined even further, recently publishing a manifesto "imbued with its superior, unsurpassed scorn for realism in literature and art, for anachronistic social morality and ethics, for narrowness of any type." While agreeing that it was characteristic of anything new to be intolerant of the past, he insisted that *Mladost* had not, in fact, contributed anything new. Drawing its inspiration from old surrealist and modernist trends, it represented nothing but "the first step toward ... human alienation, from the very spirit of those revolutionary events which have lasted among us for more than a decade."[16]

In contrast, a few voices from the older generation called for tolerance. Oto Bihalj-Merin, a Communist writer from the prewar era, wistfully recalled the days when his elders had complained about young people. "Today in a conversation," he remarked, "I heard the same tone and it surprised me. I had to look in the mirror and see the wrinkles on my face. Have we gotten old already?" He then wondered if youth today were as critical, disrespectful, overconfident, and full of the desire for knowledge and experience as his generation had been. The older generation, he said, has always looked at youth with skepticism and reserve, but it would be more helpful if they also adopted a tone of recognition and friendship. "There is no lack of talent," he insisted, "there is a lack of understanding and readiness to accept what is new."[17]

Meanwhile, many youth leaders and writers complained that their elders simply did not and could not understand their problems and approaches. Zoran Mišić, a young literary critic who in the past had attacked youth for their lack of "revolutionary optimism," now argued that it was pointless for young writers to ask the older generation for advice on how to become poets since every generation had to find its own solution. While apparently agreeing with older critics that young writers often lacked a sense of mission and purpose, he blamed their lack of focus on the fact that "we got mixed up in [the older generation's] business, in their old discussions of ten to twenty years ago, although they are useless to us now. . . . We are thirty years old and they still call us young and we still ask them, 'how do you write poetry?'"[18]

Mišić's remarks point to another dilemma. For while Mišić and others like him fought with the older generation of Communist cultural figures over the appropriate form and content of high culture, they lost touch with the rising generation of youth, who were increasingly attracted to popular forms of culture. Far more numerous, in fact, than the debates about high culture were documents from the PYY concerned about the proliferation of "wild" jazz music, "amoral black dances," and "bad" American films, which, one said, distract youth from "our" problems and difficulties and create a myth of the West as a place where people "work very little and live very well." Others complained about the Western-inspired inclinations toward extravagant fashions and tastes, slang, and cheap entertainment. One noted the formation of various "decadent," "reactionary," and "immoral" youth clubs that called themselves *"teksas-klapen"* bands or *"sheri-brandi"* brigades and whose members engaged in such outrageous activities as adopting nicknames like Bimbo, Jumbo, Dedi, Fredi, and Judi, excitedly discussing idiotic American films and exchanging old comic books about gangsters, detectives, love, or adventure.[19]

The main characteristic of such Western deviations was, of course, that they were popular and designed to entertain the masses. They stood as proof that the gap between high and popular culture was as wide as ever and that the latter was not losing its appeal. Faced with repression in the late 1940s, popular culture had simply gone underground; now in the new and more tolerant atmosphere of the early 1950s it was back out in the open, sauntering down the street in a tight red dress, wearing spike heels and gaudy lipstick. It showed up at parties and dances where, to the horror of CPY leaders, young people would "drink brandy, roast meats, swear etc."[20] It also appeared in the youthful fascination with movie stars and pop musicians (especially Western ones) and with fashion fads. Djilas recalled, for example, that in 1949–1950 the Western fashion of wearing multicolored socks with tight pants hit Yugoslavia, causing great consternation among PYY leaders who resented its implication that ideology wasn't important.[21]

Worst of all, however, it showed up on the pages of the new, financially independent press. CPY demands that the media become financially self-sufficient had placed an enormous new burden on editors, forcing them to seek out and walk the fine line between popularity and political reliability. This new financial requirement, combined with a serious paper shortage in 1951, now plainly revealed contradictions within the party's cultural policies, forcing people to choose sides in a battle among ideology, aesthetics, and accessibility. The conflict between aesthetic and commercial criteria in culture became the subject of a heated debate among contributors to *Književne novine* in the summer of 1951.

The debate was initiated by an author from Sarajevo who blamed the financial insolvency of literary journals on their poor quality, arguing that "the question of material credits and deficits is in some way related to the question of creative credits and deficits." He then suggested that journals follow the example of a stockings factory in Sarajevo that had been operating in the red until someone pointed out that their stockings were of poor quality, unattractive, and uncomfortable. Once the factory had accepted that criticism and begun to create new higher-quality goods, it quickly made a profit.[22]

The article provoked a storm of outraged responses. The editor of Sarajevo's literary journal, for example, claimed that its financial woes resulted mainly from a shortage of literary consumers in the country (and not, he implied, from his poor editorial policies). Literary journals could not appeal to the wide masses like soccer clubs nor, he snidely remarked, could they raise their quality to the level of the sock market.[23] An article in the next issue discussed the relationship between literary production and the public in a more principled and less defensive way, but it too denied the relevance of the stockings factory example. Noting that consumers need no special skills or knowledge to judge the value of socks, it questioned whether the reading public's failure to understand literature should be a measure for its objective value; for if the taste of the average American moviegoer were the determinant for film value, then Esther Williams's *Bathing Beauties* would be worth more than *Hamlet*.[24] Clearly, while most writers were pleased with the prospect of greater liberty in their selection of form and content, they were less enthusiastic about the financial responsibility that accompanied it.

An even more virulent and widespread debate, however, revolved around the opposition between popularity and politics. Forced now to show financial solvency and having read reports that showed entertainment and sports newspapers reaping substantial profits while political and ideological journals operated in the red, the editors of many newspapers and journals sought to boost the popularity of their political and literary organs by lightening their tone and including more varied types of material.[25] These materials were not, however, always consistent with the party's ideological agenda. A document from the central committee of the PYY, for example, complained that the editors of the central youth journal *Omladina* had clearly gone too far in their efforts to enrich the content of the paper, especially with regard to increased coverage of entertainment where, it said, the journal did not differ at all from petty bourgeois newspapers.[26]

Likewise, many publishers began creating original comic strips that were either sold separately or inserted in other newspapers and journals. This innovation made a certain amount of sense, both financially and ideologically. Despite the party's revulsion toward them as media of bourgeois decadence and vulgar pop culture, Western comic strips had remained immensely popular in postwar Yugoslavia and were a regular feature of youth underground culture and black market activity. The new cultural policies of the 1950s resulted in greater tolerance toward comic strips. *Donald Duck*, for example, first appeared in *NIN* in February 1951. Still, by creating new Yugoslav comic strips, publishers could argue that they were simultaneously meeting the natural demands of youth for entertainment, providing strips that were more ideologically and politically correct than those published in the West, and increasing the circulation and profitability of their newspapers and journals. The latter claim was certainly true; the new Yugoslav strips sold out quickly and clearly contributed to publishers' financial independence. Yet CPY and especially youth leaders were far from satisfied with the strips. They worried incessantly about their criminal content; poor artistic and linguistic quality; adventurist, mystical, and sensationalist tendencies; and "vulgar" themes about the struggle for love, honor, revenge, and wealth. According to an unsigned report from the PYY about youth publications, the editors of these strips clearly did not understand issues of ideology and did not connect the strips to the problem of instilling socialist and Communist qualities in youth. The report cited the example of a new strip entitled *Our Beginnings* about athletic competitions in the Stone Age that, it said, included half-animal people and "impossible" animals, unknown to zoologists, but who wore modern sports outfits and used modern sports equipment. "How can such nonsense pretend to have ideology in its content?" it asked.[27]

That report accepted the possibility that domestic strips might be improved if based on events from Yugoslavia's history, which, it insisted, "are much more interesting and dramatic than the impossible ideas copied from the West." But it warned that editors must guard against vulgarizing or warping those events. By way of example, it referred to a strip called *The Marriage of Maksim Crnojević*, based on an event from Serbian history. The problem here, it said, was that Maksim looked more like a Hollywood film star or Tarzan than a hero from Serbia's medieval struggle against the Turks.[28]

While the report did not further elaborate on this issue, its arguments seemed to cast doubt on the party's ability to use popular culture for its own ends. Yugoslav youth might indeed read *The Marriage of Maksim Crnojević* because its form was appealing and its hero reminiscent of Hollywood superstars. Yet whatever they then learned about Serbian history and its glorious revolutionary traditions, it seemed to imply, would be overshadowed by the more potent message promoting pop culture and Western values. The medium, in other words, was the message. The CPY not only could not create new culture that was popular, it could not use the existing popular culture for its own purposes.

Despite such concerns, the CPY did not rehabilitate the more restrictive cultural policies of the 1940s. And however rancorous the debates and public attacks, the leaders of agitprop departments were now generally forced to rely on persuasion, only rarely resorting to old methods of censorship, intimidation, or arrest. After all, those policies had also failed. Moreover, top CPY leaders remained convinced of communism's ultimate victory and the accompanying cultural transformation. Thus, although Tito expressed disappointment and anger at the proliferation of jazz music in a speech to the Union of Musicians in the spring of 1953, he also made it clear that the party could not fight it "by administrative means" but only through "correct and systematic work in the musical education of our youth."[29]

Others, meanwhile, simply downplayed the deleterious effects of Western culture on youth. One author, for example, reassured his public that while youth of a certain age would always seek out adventure films and try to imitate them, they would later find them stupid and clichéd. "The Magic Sword," he admitted, had inspired many boys to play at being knights with wooden swords but, he continued, "on that basis should we really prevent the film from being shown and forbid children under 16 from seeing it?"[30]

Djilas, consistent with his past views, reiterated arguments about the importance of ideological debate and cultural freedom for the proper socialist education of youth. It was both natural and necessary, he said, for young people to have an entertainment, sports, and cultural life, for how else could they become broad and educated people? "They must pass through it," he insisted, "or they will become dried up people, who at the age of forty resemble some shaved official who understands only what has been ordered from above or a blinkered horse who cannot see to the right or left."[31] Even Drenovac gradually relaxed his position and by the summer of 1952 argued in favor of greater struggles among youth. There is nothing so terrible, he suggested, about the possibility of four answers to one question. "For me, it isn't important if a question creates chaos in the youth organization, it is good, and we should let it be discussed. . . . If some youth is excited by a theory which seems terribly important to him or if he thinks that there is no more horrible beast than a cat, let him be excited and speak out, that isn't dangerous for our youth. What is dangerous is when the struggle about such things ceases . . . what is dangerous is stagnation."[32]

Proof that the new less restrictive policies toward culture would not be reversed but continued came at the November 1952 Third Congress of the Yugoslav Writer's Union in Ljubljana. In a speech previewed and approved by top CPY leaders, Miroslav Krleža openly denounced the dogma of socialist realism and spoke out in favor of art for art's sake. He rejected the entire utilitarian approach to culture, including Stalin's description of writers as "engineers of the human soul." In a conflict between a work's political or ideological content and its aesthetic form, Krleža now spoke out firmly for the latter.[33] Unable to force Krleža to "master" the party line, CPY leaders had now decided to accept and adopt his line.

Conclusion

Yugoslavia's reformist policies in the political and ideological sphere reached their high point by the spring of 1953 and began slowly to be reversed in the following years until expanding again in the next decade. Yet the party's liberal policies toward culture and the arts remained. Indeed over time, CPY efforts to influence the form and content of culture gradually declined. Certain nonnegotiable restrictions and taboos unquestionably remained, especially with regard to the national question and Tito's personal reputation. Otherwise, however, although party and youth leaders still ranted and raved about the negative impact of vulgar pop culture, they did so no more forcefully or effectively than do those in the United States who worry about the deleterious effects of Hollywood values or pop music. By the end of the 1950s, CPY leaders had not only abandoned their direct efforts to manipulate culture, but had apparently given up altogether on its value as a means of indoctrination. Creative activities and consumer responses, it seemed, could neither be controlled nor accurately predicted. Cultural personnel—if artists—could not or would not create in accordance with party dictates, and—if party hacks—could not imbue their politically correct creations with artistic value. Likewise, cultural consumers, whether highbrow or lowbrow, stubbornly refused to modify their tastes and interests to suit party expectations.

The party's modified approach to culture developed in part as a result of its conflicts with youth, which forced party leaders to accept an extant style and tradition that they could neither eliminate nor manipulate for their own purposes. Party leaders certainly did not give up on youth as their hope for the future. They could not do so without renouncing their entire ideology and claim to legitimacy. Thus, they continued efforts to indoctrinate youth with socialist principles in schools and other educational and political forums. They also, however, apparently recognized the ineradicable existence of a style and set of behavioral traditions peculiar to youth. Young people, they now believed, simply needed entertainment, excitement, and adventure and were always inclined to rebel against their elders. As a revolutionary party, the CPY had relied on that quality in youth. As members of the establishment party, they first sought to repress it but by 1952 concluded that they could tolerate youthful rebelliousness as long as it remained within what they now saw as the relatively harmless sphere of culture and entertainment. Youth thus remained the party's main reservoir of new talent, though also its most serious challenge. Over the following decades, youth and especially student demonstrations presented the greatest threat to the Communist regime, with the exception of (and sometimes in combination with) nationalist movements.[34]

The party's new policies toward culture also gave mixed results. The CPY's response to social pressures from below meant that culture would play a very different role in Yugoslavia than in the other Communist-dominated states of Central and Eastern Europe. For CPY leaders could have rehabilitated their Soviet-style voluntaristic and restrictive cultural policies. To do so, however, would have meant accepting that the official culture would have a limited and often counterproductive impact, while alternative and underground culture would become increasingly politicized and serve as a form of protest. In contrast, by seeking to depoliticize culture, CPY leaders generally prevented it from becoming a tool of the opposition. Only when the party sought to demonize a particular cultural manifestation—as, for example, with Punk in the 1980s—did it take on importance in the political sphere.[35] Yet even when left to its own devices, popular culture and youth's adherence to it still served to undermine the regime, as it promoted a set of values very different from those espoused by Communist ideology. These values, based on individualism and self-interest, offered Yugoslavia's citizens an alternative view of the world—one that many found attractive.[36] Thus, in the sphere of culture, as with ideology, party leaders found that they could not always win the struggle of opinions.

Notes

1. "Izveštaj o umetničkom, idejnom, i političkom stanju u poeziji i prozi mladih kniževnika," no date, 1949? ACKSKJ, VIII II/8-c-23; "Savetovanje mladih književnika i kritičara u prostorijama časopisa 'Mladost'," 15 Nov. 1949, AJ, SSOJ F76; "Zaključci savetovanja uredništva omladinskih časopisa i njihovih saradnika," 14–15 Nov. 1949, AJ, SSOJ F76.

2. "Izveštaj o umetničkom, idejnom i političkom stanju u poezije i prozi mladih književnika." See also Ratko Peković, *Ni rat ni mir: Panorama književnih polemika* (Belgrade: Filip Višnjić, 1986), 68–71.

3. Peković, 68–71; "Zaklučci savetovanja uredništva omladinskih časopisa i njihovih saradnika."

4. "Zaklučci savetovanja uredništva omladinskih časopisa i njihovih saradnika."

5. Peković, 75–78; Zoran Mišić, "Prvo je: svako neka zna šta hoće," *Književne novine*, 4, no. 16 (17 April 1951).

6. Marin Franičević, "A književnost nije ni jedno ni drugo," *Književne novine*, 4, no. 21 (22 May 1951): 3; Mišić, "Prvo je: svako neka zna šta hoće."

7. "Informacija o problemima u vezi sprovodjenja odluka III plenum CK KPJ u organizacijama Narodne omladine na univerzitetima," June 1950, AJ, SSOJ F330; Report on the tasks of the PYY in schools, no date, mid-1950?, AJ, SSOJ F101.

8. "Izveštaj o pitanjima kulturnog rada i života u organizaciji NO Beograda," no date, 1949–50?, AJ, SSOJ-78.

9. See, for example, "Beogradske vesti," *Borba*, 5 Jan. 1950; 5 April 1950; 5 Aug. 1950.

10. Predrag J. Marković, *Beograd izmedju istoka i zapada, 1948–1965* (Belgrade: 1996), 450.

11. Memo about distribution of the press, 10 Oct. 1950, ACKSKJ, VIII II/5-b-50; Memo to all CKs from Milovan Djilas, 10 Oct. 1950, ACKSKJ, VIII I/1-a-11; Olga Biljanović, "Kvalitet štampe—osnovno merilo u njeno rasturanju," 5 Nov. 1950, ACKSKJ, VIII II/5-b-51; "Zapisnik sa sastanka o štampi," 2 Dec. 1950, ACKSKJ, VIII II/2-b-41. The relaxed censorship on films may also have been related to cost accounting measures. Marković refers to discussions in the central agitprop department in 1950 and 1951 that noted the evident profitability of imported films, while domestic productions rarely covered their costs. Marković, 444, 453.

12. "Moralno vaspitanje omladine," 1951, AJ, SSOJ F76; Milorad Pešić, "O nekim pitanjima ideološko-vaspitnog rada u organizacijama Narodne omladine," at XIV Plenum of NO, 5–7 Jan. 1950, AJ, SSOJ F29. See also Veljko Vlahović, "Predmet: Partiska izgradnja," 16 May 1950, ACKSKJ, VIII IV/a-16. The comment about cutting clothing may have referred to a case where youth activists cut

off the ties of a group of musicians to make them look more ideologically acceptable. Marko Lopušina, *Crna knjiga: Cenzura u Jugoslaviji, 1945–91* (Belgrade: Fokus, 1991), 247.

13. Dušan Kostić, "Dug književnika," *Književne novine*, 4, no. 35 (28 Aug. 1951): 1.

14. "Problemi kulturno-prosvetnog rada," 1952, ACKSKJ, VIII II/8-d-61.

15. "Zapisnik sa savetovanja o radu organizacije Narodne omladine sa književnim početnicima," 15 Jan. 1951, AJ, SSOJ F76.

16. Bora Drenovac, "*Mladost* mračnija od starosti," *Književne novine*, 5, no. 53 (29 March 1952): 1. See also Čedo Kis[no Haček]ić, "Mladost umorna od letova, tapka," *Književne novine*, 5, no. 56 (11 May 1952): 4.

17. Oto Bihalj-Merin, "Klima duha," *Književne novine*, 4, no. 16 (17 April 1951): 1.

18. Mišić, "Prvo je: svako neka zna šta hoće." In fact, when the article was published Mišić was still eight months shy of his 30th birthday.

19. "Informacija o Narodnoj omladini," 19 Jan. 1952, AJ, SSOJ F330; Pešić, "O nekim pitanjima ideološko-vaspitnog rada." See also "Izveštaj o omladini," 1951, ACKSKJ, V-KII/27; "Izveštaj o pitanjima kulturnog rada i života"; "Školska omladina iz godišnjeg izveštaja 1951 godine," in the section on Serbia in "Neka pitanja rada organizacije NO u srednjim školama u periodu 1949–1952," no date, mid-1952, AJ, SSOJ F101; "Informacija o delovanju propagande sa zapada i njenom uticaju," 1952, ACKSKJ, VIII II/9-36.

20. Pešić, "O nekim pitanjima ideološko-vaspitnog rada"; "Izveštaj o omladini." See also "Zapisnik sa sastanka Biroa CK NOJ," 2 Feb. 1950, AJ, SSOJ F56; "Izveštaj o pitanjima kulturnog rada i života."

21. Milovan Djilas, Interview with the author, 6 August 1991, Belgrade.

22. Miroslav Djordjević, "Varijacije na jednu novu temu," *Književne novine*, 4, no. 26 (26 June 1951): 1.

23. Isak Samokovlija, "Ko je protiv borbe mišljenja," *Književne novine*, 4, no. 29 (17 July 1951): 1.

24. Zoran Gluščević, "Nove varijacije na stare teme," *Književne novine*, 4, no. 30 (24 July 1951): 3.

25. "Pregled mjesečnog financijskog poslovanja listova *Narodne štampe*," 23 Sept. 1947, HDA, CKKPHAP.

26. "Zapisnik sa sastanka Biroa CK NOJ," 3 Oct. 1951, AJ, SSOJ F56.

27. Report about youth illustrated newspapers and comic strips, 1951, AJ, SSOJ F79.

28. Ibid.

29. Josip Broz Tito, *Govori i članci*, Vol. IX (Belgrade: 1966), 63–64, cited in Marković, 471.

30. "Moralno vaspitanje omladine."

31. Milovan Djilas, "O Partiji," 6 June 1952, ACKSKJ, VIII IV-a-20.

32. Bora Drenovac, "Stenografske beleške Savetovanja članova Centralnih komiteta NO republika po pitanju rada u srednjim školama u narednoj godini," 16 Aug. 1952, AJ, SSOJ F58. According to Djilas, although Drenovac had often appeared "rigid" and "dogmatic," by 1952 he acquired solid "democratic convic-

tions." After the party backed away from its reforms in late 1953, Drenovac, apparently suffering from "an intellectual and emotional crisis of his own... withdrew into linguistic research." Djilas, *Rise and Fall,* 353.

33. Peković, 147–150.

34. See, for example, Marković, 188–190. Youth newspapers and journals were also always among those most frequently censored. See Lopušina, 158–160.

35. Jozef Figa, "Socializing the State: Civil Society and Democratization from Below in Slovenia," in *State-Society Relations in Yugoslavia, 1945–1992,* ed. Melissa Bokovoy, Jill Irvine, and Carol Lilly (New York: St. Martin's Press, 1997), 163–182.

36. See Marković, 214.

Conclusion

CPY persuasive policies in the first nine years after the Second World War describe the party's progress within its graduated strategy for the construction of socialism. Indeed, persuasion was an integral and crucial element in the party's plan to build a new and better society. Party leaders expected their persuasive policies to contribute to both the party's short-term political and its long-term transformative goals. They thus paid close attention to the successes and failures of those policies, frequently adjusting them to match the party's evolving strategy and in response to external events and feedback from below. The most important of these adjustments concerned the relative emphasis on the party's daily political needs versus its long-term goal of transforming culture and society. While these adjustments did not noticeably increase the efficacy of CPY persuasion, they did affect the nature of relations between the party-state and Yugoslav society.

In the first stage of Yugoslavia's postwar development, from the liberation of Belgrade in October 1944 up to the November 1945 elections, the CPY concentrated primarily on achieving power. In this period, the party's policies of persuasion addressed both its long-term transformative and its immediate political goals. In order to secure popular support for the regime, CPY rhetoric focused much attention on the party's long-term vision for a new and better future. That vision, however, was described in extremely broad and general terms that often had little or nothing to do with Communist ideology. Adopting a "people's democratic" vocabulary, this approach assured Yugoslav citizens that the party was willing to compromise and would work with "all progressive forces" in the country. At the same time, however, CPY rhetoric in this early phase both reflected and exploited the revolutionary atmosphere and spontaneous enthusiasm generated by the war. It sought to direct that revolutionary fervor toward the fulfillment of such immediate political and economic goals as purging state, social, and cultural institutions of open opponents to the new regime; carrying out land reform; and securing CPY victory in the elections. Popular responses to this approach were mixed, reflecting both genuine enthusiasm for and staunch opposition to the party's program of change. As a result, state-society relations in the first year of Communist rule were both dynamic and unpredictable. Passions ran high in the immediate postwar era and Yugoslavia's citizens often expressed their hopes and fears, loves and hatreds quite openly.

Having achieved legal power through the November 1945 elections, party leaders, up until late 1947, focused on introducing the foundations for socialism through legislative means and reviving an economy decimated by war. In this stage, the party's transformative agenda, while not forgotten, was placed on a back burner. As a result, party persuasive policies became increasingly dry and repetitive as they centered on narrow political and economic issues. Moreover, disturbed by the unreliable behavior of Yugoslavia's citizens, party leaders now sought further controls over public activity. Consequently, CPY rhetoric in this period consisted mainly of appeals to Yugoslav citizens to work more and harder, and to express their loyalty to the party by repeating slogans and attending carefully staged political rallies.

As these appeals were accompanied by the open threat of coercion, all debate ceased, and state-society relations became increasingly one-sided. Constrained by escalating instructions, decrees, and even threats from above, party activists gradually lost much of their initial enthusiasm and became mere functionaries, concerned mainly to satisfy the demands of their superiors. Meanwhile, Yugoslavia's citizens responded to the growing rigidity of CPY rhetoric as well as the party's open use of coercion by avoiding interactions with the party-state. Over time, they learned to cooperate with party dictates only as much as was required and then retreat into their private lives.

By late 1947, party leaders could look with some satisfaction at the results of their persuasive efforts: CPY control was firmly established and the renovation and reconstruction of the economy were well under way. Persistent persuasion, especially when backed up by economic incentives and the threat of force, had enabled party leaders to channel and direct the energy and activities of many Yugoslav citizens. Party rhetoric had sometimes induced people to join volunteer labor brigades, vote for the "right" candidate in elections, or work on Saturdays and religious holidays. At the same time, however, party leaders knew that in many more important ways their persuasive strategies were inadequate for the more complex tasks ahead. The rhetorical methods applied in these first postwar years were simply too crude and too didactic to change people's minds or transform society. In fact, however, in these first two periods of Yugoslavia's postwar history, the party had not really tried to change society; its persuasive policies had been geared toward the achievement of political and economic, not transformative, goals. Up until late 1947, the CPY expected people to do the right thing but did not insist that they do so for the right reason. As long as the party was not so much trying to change the way people thought as the way they acted, it could get by with less sophisticated rhetoric. Nonetheless, these initial persuasive policies had serious consequences: state-society relations had become one-sided and stagnant. The party's concern to stifle its own revolutionary impulses, eliminate pluralism, and direct all political, economic, and cultural activity had deadened the popular nerve system, inhibiting spontaneous activity and destroying the very enthusiasm on which it had relied.

By late 1947, CPY leaders began efforts to rectify this problem. Having initiated the third stage in the party's construction of a "new and better future," they now began to address the more complex tasks of ideological reeducation and indoctrination. In the period from late 1947 to mid-1948, party leaders sought a new balance that would give more weight to long-term goals and reinspire Yugoslavia's population with their vision for the future. Despite evident uncertainty about exactly how to realize the cultural transformation, CPY persuasive policies reflected the changing emphasis and by early 1948 had begun to pay more attention to issues of ideology. Party leaders now urged that persuasive activists reduce their emphasis on economic activities and political slogans. Rather, they should focus on the importance of education—especially ideological education—in order to change not only people's behavior but their values, attitudes, and beliefs. Finally, and perhaps most importantly, party leaders now also insisted on increasing the general and ideological education of party members themselves. Only party members who displayed both a high level of general education and a deep familiarity with and commitment to Marxism-Leninism, they argued, could provide the necessary role models. In fact, state-society relations in this period remained one-sided, but were now more pedagogical than injunctive.

These first steps in the party's effort to transform society and culture were interrupted and delayed by the Soviet-Yugoslav split of June 1948. Faced by Soviet and Eastern European hostility as well as an almost complete economic blockade, party leaders were now forced to refocus on issues of security and economic stability. As in the immediate postwar era, state-society relations became more active and unsettled, reflecting both renewed support for and opposition to the regime. In this context, both the increased repression from mid-1948 to late 1949 and the accompanying rhetorical demands that Yugoslav citizens again express their support for the party through political activity and economic self-sacrifice are unsurprising. Yet, while many policies in this period seemed reminiscent of those in the first two phases, the period from mid-1948 to late 1949 was not simply a replay of 1944–1947. Yugoslavia's Communists had been forced to suspend their immediate plans for the transformation of society, yet they had not forgotten the lessons learned in previous years. CPY leaders now clearly understood that whatever the value of concrete political rhetoric for the fulfillment of specific tasks, it would not and could not lead them to their ultimate goal of full communism. Thus, party persuasive activists continued to emphasize also the importance of general and ideological education—both for the masses and, especially, for the party's own cadres. The uncertainty among top CPY leaders about the party's direction was evident, however, in the inadequate and often contradictory instructions that these persuasive activists received about the campaign for socialization of the countryside and Yugoslavia's relationship with the USSR.

Meanwhile, seeking theoretical justification for conflict within the socialist bloc, CPY leaders were also embarking on a reevaluation of the party's ideological principles by rereading and reinterpreting the classics of Marxism-Leninism. In the process, they developed not only a new approach to the political and economic construction of socialism but also a more sophisticated and thoughtful understanding of cultural and social change. Consequently, while the immediate post-split era did show increased levels of repression and higher demands for the mobilization of labor, it also served as an incubator for new ideas about how to achieve the transformation of society and culture through open debate and greater initiative from below.

The first signs of life to come out of the incubator were seen at the Third Party Plenum of December 1949, which sought to reconstitute the educational system in a way that would make possible the creation of truly new people "whose minds have not been cut all according to the same pattern."[1] After this plenum, party rhetoric increasingly stressed the importance of "the struggle of opinions" while reducing reliance on censorship as a means of achieving change. In the following three years a broad series of reforms would substantially alter the functions and organizational structures of the party, state, and mass organizations, as well as the relationships between them. Crucial to the party's attempts to transform society and culture were the decentralization of agitprop departments and reforms of the media that reduced censorship and accepted the primacy of consumer demand.

These reforms clearly were not meant to lessen the role of Communist ideology in Yugoslav society. On the contrary, they reflected a heightened level of faith among party leaders in the power of that ideology and of persuasion. Perhaps reassured of socialism's inevitable victory after rereading the Marxist classics, CPY leaders now sought to replace the Soviet-inspired voluntaristic methods of achieving cultural change with a more deterministic, hands-off approach. They were still determined to win the struggle of opinions, but now believed that they could do so by more democratic means. In the course of open debate, they now argued, the validity of Marxist-Leninist principles would become evident to all and would win over any remaining doubters. In practice, of course, the reforms opened the doors to much apolitical and nonsocialist thought and cultural activity. Consequently, they were unwelcome to many party members who worried about the growth of openly anti-socialist and "reactionary" elements and wondered how the transformation of society was to be realized in daily practice.

Despite these concerns, CPY leaders stayed the course, confident of their ideology's irresistible persuasive effect. CPY adherence to the new approach was confirmed at the Sixth Party Congress of November 1952 and the Fourth Congress of the Socialist Alliance of the Working People of Yugoslavia in March 1953. Yet only two months later, the Second Plenum of the Central Committee on the island of Brioni put an end to the most extreme reforms—especially those that had seemed to question the party's infallibility and hence its monopoly on power. Far from assuring the victory of Marxism-Leninism, the reforms threatened the security of party leaders, who were now reminded that initiative from below could be dangerous. The Second Plenum thus marked the end of the first phase of CPY reformism and the beginning of a limited return toward party control over society by more traditional legislative and coercive methods.

CPY leaders did not, however, return to pre-1950 approaches toward cultural and social change. While unwilling to let reliance on persuasion threaten the political supremacy of the party, CPY leaders still believed that the cultural transformation of society must come about gradually through socialist education and ideological persuasion. And yet, already by 1953 there were indications that the new methods of persuasion would be no more effective than the old. Decentralization of the persuasive apparatus had not, in fact, made it work better. Rather, by broadening the base of persuasive work, party leaders had diluted its power, focus, and intensity. Moreover, despite party leaders' expectations, it was not at all clear that Marxist-Leninist ideology would win the struggle of opinions, at least not in the near future and not with these party cadres. Most middle- and lower-level party cadres simply could not hold their own in any elevated discussion, nor were they capable of engaging in subtle persuasion.

Thus the leadership's new approach to socialist transformation and its new persuasive policies only caused confusion within the ranks. Baffled and demoralized by the leadership's seemingly impossible demands, some members simply continued to employ the old rhetoric, which was, however, now much less frightening and effective, while others gave up the struggle entirely. Thus, the innovative reforms of the early 1950s, though intended to help realize the cultural transformation, only discouraged further activity toward that end as they called into question both the value of persuasion as a means of change and the inevitability of Marxism-Leninism's ideological victory.

Moreover, when party leaders shifted the emphasis onto their long-term transformative goals in the early 1950s, they found that they had endangered their own position in power. The new model for the transformation of society had given primary consideration to Marxist-Leninist ideology, believing that political legitimacy would inevitably follow. It did not. As state-society relations became more dynamic, they also became less predictable. Initiative from below refused to remain within the prescribed boundaries, and the struggle of opinions did not effect mass conversions to Marxism. On the contrary, it seemed mainly to result in an increasingly critical attitude toward the CPY, its leaders, and their policies. Thus, the dilemma that CPY leaders faced as they sought to balance long-term and short-term goals was real. Would they maintain their grip on power at the expense of their connection to the masses and vision for the future? Or, if they wished to remain true to the principles inherent in that vision, would they have to sacrifice power? Ultimately, party leaders chose power, with Djilas, the sole exception to the rule, being purged in January 1954. Eventually, they even seemed to give up on their goal of transforming society and culture by means of persuasion, and increasingly sought to build their legitimacy on other, more political, and more attainable bases. The balance between the transformation of society and the achievement of daily political goals thus tipped irrevocably in favor of the latter.

Seen from this perspective, it becomes clear that many fundamental changes in the development of Communist Yugoslavia, though made possible by the Soviet-Yugoslav split, were inspired not by external but by internal developments. The graduated strategy for the construction of socialism that led party persuasive activists already by late 1947 to emphasize ideological education over concrete political tasks provided both the motivation and the direction for the reforms of the early 1950s. In the absence of the split, of course, these reforms might never have occurred. Yet, failing the CPY's persistent attempts to combine political pragmatism with ideological integrity, the split itself might never have occurred.

For the party's policies and even ultimately its ideology were not simply copied from the Soviet blueprint; they were also the result of a process of improvisation and negotiation (however unequal) both among elites and between elites and the broader population. Decision making was centralized and top party leaders certainly knew what they wished to accomplish but did not always agree on how; nor did they have the means to ensure that their dictates were properly applied at lower levels. Meanwhile, social pressures from below, often manifested in unorganized ways through individual acts of resistance (as with youth's stubborn attachment to popular culture), were sometimes successful in changing party rhetoric and even its broader policies. After all, since party leaders genuinely wanted their persuasive efforts to work, they solicited and listened to feedback from below.

Of course, there were limits beyond which they would not go. They would not make any changes that obviously threatened their position in power or their plans for the construction of socialism in Yugoslavia. Those boundaries expanded somewhat following the Soviet-Yugoslav split. By 1950, the party's concepts of what threatened its power and what it meant to construct socialism were substantially different from what they had been in 1946. The step backward from reform beginning at the Brioni plenum in June 1953, however, stood as proof that those essential limitations remained. Reforms that seemed to threaten the party's monopoly on power would not be tolerated. Coercion, while applied less often and less blatantly than in the past, thus remained an important element in maintaining the party's hold on power.

Party leaders also refused to renounce their socialist intentions. Yet the CPY, now the LCY, could not simply return to Stalinist methods; it had rejected them too virulently and, what's more important, too publicly. Moreover, many party leaders themselves had become fully convinced of the bankruptcy of the Stalinist system. Thus, they were forced to seek a middle ground, retaining a monopoly on power but allowing greater flexibility in such areas as culture. In the ongoing struggle to balance the party's long-term and short-term goals, the transformation of society remained on the scale, but would never again be permitted to threaten the party's hold on power.

Here, then, we may have a partial solution to one of the enduring riddles of Communist regimes: how parties originally filled with fresh and intense idealists became dull organizations made up of dry and colorless bureaucrats who apparently believed in nothing but their own position in power. In the Yugoslav case, at least, that transition away from idealism originated as a move toward it. For only when the Yugoslav Communists truly attempted to realize the promises of their ideology did they begin to lose faith in their ability to transform society, culture, and human beings by persuasive means. Party rhetoric, the leaders then discovered, was successful mainly when it relied on preexisting values and beliefs, but was much less so when it tried to instill in the population new ideas and new behavioral norms. Persuasion, in other words, could occasionally help realize the party's short-term political agenda but not its long-term transformative one.

Once it became clear that they could not win the struggle of opinions in a fair fight, party leaders seem to have relegated the transformation of society and culture to the distant future, when it would be achieved not by their own heroic efforts or powers of persuasion but by the inevitable and faceless forces of history. As Communists, then, their main task was to stay in power and ensure social ownership of the means of production long enough for those forces to develop. The Communist vision for the future, while still a necessary component of party legitimacy, thus lost its urgency, while the role of politics increased until the party's need to maintain power became its only real source of political decision making. The solution was perhaps not all bad. It allowed and required the party to develop other sources of legitimacy, including the gradual decentralization of power, a higher standard of living, and greater freedoms (including the freedom to travel abroad) than were available to the citizens of any other Communist regime. Yet that pragmatic approach to power also enabled certain segments of the LCY in the late 1980s and early 1990s to attach themselves to a new source of legitimacy—nationalism—with tragic results.

Notes

1. Milovan Djilas, "Problem školstva u borbi za socijalizam u našoj zemlji," at the Third Plenum of the Central Committee of the CPY, held 29–30 Dec. 1949, in Branko Petranović, Ranko Končar, and Radovan Radonjić, eds., *Sednice Centralnog komiteta KPJ (1948–1952)* (Belgrade: Izdavački centar Komunist, 1985), 295.

Bibliography

Books and Articles

Adam, Peter. *Art in the Third Reich*. New York: Harry N. Abrams Inc., 1992.
Adamic, Louis. *The Eagle and the Roots*. New York: Doubleday and Co., 1952.
Alexander, Stella. *Church and State in Yugoslavia Since 1945*. Cambridge: Cambridge University Press, 1979.
Andreis, Josip. *Music in Croatia*. Zagreb: 1974.
Auty, Phyllis. *Tito, A Biography*. New York: McGraw Hill, 1970.
_____. *Yugoslavia*, New York: Walker and Co., 1965.
Avakumović, Ivan. *History of the Communist Party of Yugoslavia*. Aberdeen: Aberdeen University Press, 1964.
Bailes, Kendall E. *Technology and Society Under Lenin and Stalin, Origins of the Soviet Technical Intelligentsia, 1917–1941*. Princeton: Princeton University Press, 1978.
Bakarić, Marija Šoljan, ed. *Kata Pejnović: monografija*. Zagreb: 1977.
Banac, Ivo. *The National Question in Yugoslavia: Origins, History, Politics*. Ithaca, NY, and London: Cornell University Press, 1984.
_____. *With Stalin Against Tito, Cominformist Splits in Yugoslav Communism*. Ithaca, NY: Cornell University Press, 1988.
Baum, Ann Todd. *Komsomol Participation in the Soviet First Five-Year Plan*. London: MacMillan, 1987.
Beljo, Ante. *YU Genocide*. Toronto and Zagreb: 1995.
Benigar, O. Aleksa. *Alojzije Stepinac: Hrvatski kardinal*. Rome: Ziral, 1974.
Bilandžić, Dušan. *Borba za samoupravni socijalizam u Jugoslaviji, 1945–1969*. Zagreb: 1969.
_____. *Historija Socijalističke Federativne Republike Jugoslavije: Glavni procesi, 1918–1985*. Zagreb: Školska knjiga, 1985.
Bisztray, George. *Marxist Models of Literary Realism*. New York: Columbia University Press, 1978.
Bjelica, Mihailo, ed. *Dva veka srpskog novinarstva*. Belgrade: Institute za novinarstvo, 1992.
Bokovoy, Melissa K. *Peasants and Communists: Politics and Ideology in the Yugoslav Countryside, 1941–1953*. Pittsburgh, PA: Pittsburgh University Press, 1998.
Bokovoy, Melissa, Jill Irvine, and Carol Lilly, eds. *State-Society Relations in Yugoslavia, 1945–1992*. New York and London: St. Martin's Press, 1997.

Bokun-Djinić, Sonja. *Na sudilištu agitpropa: Etatizam i književno nasledje, 1944–1952.* Belgrade: Filip Višnjić, 1997.
Borland, Harriet. *Soviet Literary Theory and Practice During the First Five-Year Plan, 1928–1932.* New York: King's Crown Press, 1950.
Brake, Michael. *Comparative Youth Culture: The Sociology of Youth Cultures and Youth Subcultures in America, Britain, and Canada.* London, Boston, Melbourne, and Henly: Routledge and Kegan Paul, 1985.
Brenk, France. "Nacrt povijesti jugoslavenskog filma." In *Povijest filmske umjetnosti,* edited by George Sadoul. Zagreb: 1962.
Brković, Jevrem. *Anatomija morala jednog Staljiniste.* Zagreb: 1988.
Brody, Richard J. "Ideology and Political Mobilization: The Soviet Home Front During World War II," Carl Beck Papers in Russian and East European Studies, No. 1104, Pittsburgh, PA: 1994.
Brown, Edward J. *The Proletarian Episode in Russian Literature, 1928–1932.* New York: Columbia University Press, 1953.
Cazi, Josip. *Komunistička partija Jugoslavije i sindikati.* Belgrade: 1959.
_____. *Nezavisni sindikati, 1921–1929.* 2 vols. Zagreb: 1962–1964.
Čengić, Enes. *S Krležom iz dana u dan.* Zagreb: 1985–1990.
_____. *The Central Committee Resolution and Zhdanov's Speech on the Journals* Zvezda *and* Leningrad. Bilingual Edition. Royal Oak: 1978.
Clark, Katerina. *The Soviet Novel.* Chicago: University of Chicago Press, 1981.
Claudin-Urondo, Carmen. *Lenin and the Cultural Revolution.* New Jersey: Harvester Press, 1977.
Clissold, Stephen. *Djilas, The Progress of a Revolutionary.* Great Britain: Maurice Temple Smith, 1983.
_____. *Yugoslavia and the Soviet Union 1939–1973: A Documentary Survey.* London: Oxford University Press, 1975.
Čolaković, Rodoljub. *Izabrani govori i članci.* Sarajevo: 1960.
_____. *Kazivanje o jednom pokoljenju.* Sarajevo: 1968.
Constitution of the Federal People's Republic of Yugoslavia. Hoover Institution Library.
Cvetković, Slavoljub. *SKOJ, 1919–1929.* Belgrade: 1979.
Danilović, Rajko. *Upotreba neprijatelja: Politička sudjenja 1945–1991 u Jugoslaviji,* Valjevo: Valjevac, 1993.
Dedijer, Vladimir. *The Battle Stalin Lost, Memoirs of Yugoslavia, 1948–1953.* New York: Viking Press, 1970.
_____. *Dokumenti 1948.* Belgrade: 1980.
_____. *Novi prilozi za biografiju Josipa Broza Tita.* Vol. 3. Belgrade: Rad, 1984.
_____. *Tito.* New York: Simon and Schuster, 1953.
_____. *Veliki buntovnik, Milovan Djilas, Prilozi za biografiju.* Belgrade: 1991.
Dimić, Ljubodrag. *Agitprop kultura, Agitpropovska faza kulturne politike u Srbiji, 1945- 1952.* Belgrade: Rad, 1988.
Djilas, Aleksa. *The Contested Country: Yugoslav Unity and Communist Revolution.* Cambridge, MA: Harvard University Press, 1991.
Djilas, Milovan. *Anatomy of a Moral: The Political Essays of Milovan Djilas.* London: Thames and Hudson, 1959.
_____. *Članci, 1941–1946.* Belgrade: Kultura, 1947.

———. *Conversations with Stalin*. New York: Harcourt Brace Jovanovich, 1962.
———. *Land Without Justice*. New York: Harcourt Brace Jovanovich, 1958.
———. *Memoirs of a Revolutionary*. New York: Harcourt Brace Jovanovich, 1973.
———. *The New Class: An Analysis of the Communist System*. New York: Praeger, 1957.
———. *Rise and Fall*. New York: Harcourt Brace Jovanovich, 1983.
———. *Savremene teme*. Belgrade: Borba, 1950.
———. *Tito: The Story from Inside*. New York: Harcourt Brace Jovanovich, 1980.
———. *Wartime*. New York: Harcourt Brace Jovanovich, 1977.
Djordjević, Dragoslav. "Socijalistički realizam 1945–1950." In *Nadrealizam, socijalna umetnost*. Belgrade: 1969.
Djordjević, Jovan. *Ustavno pravo FNRJ*. Belgrade: 1953.
Djorgović, Momčilo. *Djilas, Vernik i Jeretik*. Belgrade: Akvarijus, 1989.
Dragović-Gašpar, Rosa. *Let iznad Golog otoka*. Belgrade: Akvarijus, 1990.
Drugo vanredno zasedanje Narodne skupštine FNRJ, 20. marta–1. aprila 1946, Stenografske beleške. Belgrade: 1947.
Dunham, Vera. *In Stalin's Time: Middle Class Values in Soviet Fiction*. Cambridge: Cambridge University Press, 1976.
Ellul, Jacques. *Propaganda, the Formation of Men's Attitudes*. New York: Alfred A. Knopf, 1965.
Erlich, Vera St. *Family in Transition, A Study of 300 Yugoslav Villages*. Princeton: Princeton University Press, 1966.
Evans, Janet. "The Communist Party of the Soviet Union and the Women's Question: The Case of the 1936 Decree 'In Defence of Mother and Child'." *Journal of Contemporary History* 16 (1981): 757–775.
Farrell, Robert Barry. *Yugoslavia and the Soviet Union 1948–56*. Hamden, CT: Shoestring Press, 1956.
Feuer, Lewis S. *Marx and the Intellectuals*. New York: Anchor Books, 1969.
Figa, Jozef. "Socializing the State: Civil Society and Democratization from Below in Slovenia." In *State-Society Relations in Yugoslavia, 1945–1992*, edited by Melissa Bokovoy, Jill Irvine, and Carol Lilly. New York: St. Martin's Press, 1997.
Fitzpatrick, Sheila. *The Commissariat of Enlightenment, Soviet Organization of Education and the Arts Under Lunacharsky, October 1917–1921*. Cambridge: Cambridge University Press, 1970.
———. *Education and Social Mobility in the Soviet Union 1921–1934*. Cambridge: Cambridge University Press, 1979.
———, ed. *Cultural Revolution in Russia, 1928–1931*. Bloomington, IN: Indiana University Press, 1984.
Flaker, Aleksandar. *Sovjetska književnost u Jugoslaviji, 1918–1941*. No publisher, no date, Narodna biblioteka Srbije.
Geertz, Clifford. *The Interpretation of Cultures*. New York: Basic Books, 1973.
Gleitman, Henry. *Youth in Revolt: The Failure of Communist Indoctrination in Hungary*. New York: Free Europe Press, 1957.
Gligorijević, Milo. *Odgovor Mica Popović*. Belgrade: 1984.
Goldman, Wendy. "Freedom and Its Consequences: The Debate on the Soviet Family Code of 1926." *Russian History* 11, No. 4 (Winter 1984): 362–388.
———. *Women, the State, and Revolution: Soviet Family Policy and Social Life, 1917–1937*. New York: Cambridge University Press, 1993.

Gramsci, Antonio. *The Modern Prince and Other Writings*. New York: International Publishers, 1957.
Hall, Stuart. "Notes on Deconstructing 'The Popular'." In *People's History and Socialist Theory*, edited by Raphael Samuel. London: Routledge and Kegan Paul, 1981.
Havel, Vaclav, et al. *The Power of the Powerless*. Boston, MA: Faber and Faber Inc., 1987.
Hasanagić, E. *Nezavisni Sindikati*. Belgrade: 1951.
History of the Communist Party of the Soviet Union (Bolsheviks), Short Course. Edited by a Commission of the Central Committee of the CPSU (B). New York: International Publishers, 1939.
Hoffman, George W., and Fred Warner Neal. *Yugoslavia and the New Communism*. New York: Twentieth Century Fund, 1962.
Höpken, Wolfgang. "History Education and Yugoslav (Dis)-Integration." In *State-Society Relations in Yugoslavia, 1945–1992*, edited by Melissa Bokovoy, Jill Irvine, and Carol Lilly. New York: St. Martin's Press, 1997.
Hoptner, J. B. *Yugoslavia in Crisis, 1934–1941*. New York: Columbia University Press, 1962.
Horvat, Mihovil. *Goli Otok: Straitšte duha*. Zagreb: Orion Stella, 1996.
Informativni priručnik o Jugoslaviji, Opšti podaci o političkom, privrednom, socijalnom, kulturnom i prosvetnom životu u Federativnoj narodnoj republici Jugoslaviji. Belgrade: 1948–1951.
Irvine, Jill. *The Croat Question: Partisan Politics in the Formation of the Yugoslav Socialist State*. Boulder, CO: Westview Press, 1993.
Jelavich, Charles. *South Slav Nationalisms: Textbooks and Yugoslav Union Before 1914*. Columbus, OH: Ohio State University Press, 1990.
Johnson, A. Ross. *The Transformation of Communist Ideology, The Yugoslav Case, 1945–1953*. Cambridge, MA: The MIT Press, 1972.
Joravsky, David. *The Lysenko Affair*. Cambridge, MA: Harvard University Press, 1970.
Jovanović, Dragoljub. *Ljudi, Ljudi...* 2 vols. Belgrade: 1973, 1975.
Jovanović, Nadežda. *Sindikalni pokret u Srbiji, 1935–1941*. Belgrade: 1984.
Jowett, Garth S., and Victoria O'Donnell. *Propaganda and Persuasion*. Newbury Park, CA: Sage Publications, 1986.
Jugoslavija 1945–1964, Statistički pregled. Belgrade: 1965.
Kačavenda, Petar. *Omladina u revoluciji*. Belgrade: Institut za savremenu istoriju, 1985.
_____. *SKOJ 1941–1948*. Belgrade: 1979.
_____, ed. *Kongresi, konferencije i sednice centralnih organa SKOJa (1941–1948)*. Belgrade: Izdavački centar Komunist, 1984.
Kalezić, Vasilije. *Djilas, kontroverze pisca i ideologa*. Belgrade: 1986.
Karapandžić, Borivoje. *Jugoslovensko krvavo proleće 1945: Titovi Katini i Gulazi*. Belgrade: 1990.
Kardelj, Edvard. *Put nove Jugoslavije, 1941–1945*. Belgrade: 1949.
_____. *Reminiscences*. London: 1982.
Kenez, Peter. *The Birth of the Propaganda State, Soviet Methods of Mass Mobilization, 1917–1929*. Cambridge: Cambridge University Press, 1985.

Keniston, Kenneth. "Youth Culture as Enforced Alienation." In *The Cult of Youth in Middle Class America*, edited by Richard L. Rapson. Lexington, MA, Toronto, and London: D. C. Heath and Co., 1971.
Kenney, Padraic. *Rebuilding Poland: Workers and Communists, 1945–1950*. Ithaca, NY: Cornell University Press, 1996.
Kershaw, Ian. "How Effective Was Nazi Propaganda?" In *Nazi Propaganda, the Power and the Limitations*, edited by David Welch. Great Britain: Croom Helm Ltd., 1983.
Knežević, Zlata. *Kulturno stvaralaštvo u revoluciji*. Zagreb: 1981.
Kocbek, Edvard. *Dnevnik 1951–1952*, edited by Dimitrij Rupel. Zagreb: Globus, 1986.
Koštunica, Vojislav, and Kosta Čavoški. *Party Pluralism or Monism, Social Movements and the Political System in Yugoslavia, 1944–1949*. Boulder, CO: Westview Press, 1985.
Kovačević, K. *Muzičko stvaralaštvo u Hrvatskoj, 1945–1965*. Zagreb: 1966.
Kovačić, Olga. *Women of Yugoslavia*. Belgrade: 1947.
Krivokapić, Boro. *Dahauski procesi*. Belgrade: 1986.
_____. *Umorna levica*. Belgrade: 1985.
Kuzmanović, Rajko. *Privremena narodna skupština DFJ*. Belgrade: 1981.
Lane, Christel. *The Rites of Rulers*. Cambridge: Cambridge University Press, 1981.
Lasić, Stanko. *Sukob na književnoj ljevici*. Zagreb: Liber, 1970.
Lenin on Literature and Art. Moscow: 1967.
Lenin, V. I. *Materialism and Empirio-criticism*. Moscow: 1947.
_____. *On Culture and Cultural Revolution*. Moscow: 1970.
_____. *On Youth*. Moscow: 1980.
_____. *Polnoe sobranie sochinenii*. 5th ed. Moscow: 1959–1965.
Levine, Lawrence. *Highbrow/Lowbrow: The Emergence of Cultural Hierarchy in America*. Cambridge, MA: Harvard University Press, 1988.
Lilly, Carol S. "Problems of Persuasion: Communist Agitation and Propaganda in Yugoslavia, 1944–1948." *Slavic Review*, 53, no. 2 (Summer 1994): 395–413.
Lopušina, Marko. *Crna knjiga: Cenzura u Jugoslaviji, 1945–91*. Belgrade: Fokus, 1991.
Lukacs, Georg. *Essays on Realism*, edited by Rodney Livingston. Cambridge, MA: The MIT Press, 1981.
_____. *The Meaning of Contemporary Realism*. London, 1963.
Lukavac, Mirko. "Prvi dani kinematografije u SR Hrvatskoj (1945–1946)." *Filmska kultura* 100 (July 1975): 163–167.
Lukes, Stephen. *Essays in Social Theory*. London: MacMillan Inc., 1977.
Lukić, Sveta. *Contemporary Yugoslav Literature: A Sociopolitical Approach*, edited by Gertrude Joch Robinson. Chicago: University of Illinois Press, 1968.
Maguire, Robert A. *Red Virgin Soil*. Princeton: Princeton University Press, 1968.
Mally, Lynn. *Culture of the Future: The Proletkult Movement in Revolutionary Russia*. Berkeley, CA: University of California Press, 1990.
Marić, Milomir. *Deca komunizma*. Belgrade: Mladost, 1987.
Marković, Predrag J. *Beograd izmedju istoka i zapada, 1948–1965*. Belgrade: 1996.
Markovski, Venko. *Goli Otok, the Island of Death: A Diary in Letters*. Boulder, CO: Westview Press, 1984.

Maslarić, Božidar. *Moskva—Madrid—Moskva.* Zagreb: Prosvjeta, 1952.
Mataga, Vojislav. "Književna kritika i teorija socijalističkog realizma." *Gordogan,* 17–18 (Jan.-April 1985): 332–379.
Matvejević, Predrag. *Književnost i njezina društvena funkcija.* Novi Sad: 1977.
McCarthy, Katherine M. "Peasant Revolutionaries and Partisan Power: Rural Resistance to Communist Agrarian Policies in Croatia, 1941–1953," Ph.D. Dissertation, University of Pittsburgh, 1996.
Medaković, Dejan. *Efemeris III: Hronika jedne porodice.* 3rd ed. Belgrade: 1993.
Mitrović, Momčilo, and Djordje Stanković, eds. *Zapisnici i izveštaji univerzitetskog komiteta Komunističke Partije Srbije, 1945–1948.* Belgrade: 1985.
Morača, Pero, et al., eds. *Narodni front i komunisti Jugoslavije, Čehoslovačka, Poljska, 1938–1945.* Belgrade, Prague, and Warsaw: 1968.
Morača, Pero, and Stanislav Stojanović, eds. *Povijest Saveza komunista Jugoslavije.* Belgrade: Izdavački centar Komunist, 1985.
Nešović, Slobodan, ed. *Rad zakonodavnih odbora Pretsedništva AVNOJ i Privremene narodne skupštine DFJ (3. aprila–25. oktobra 1945).* Belgrade: 1952.
_____. *Sednice Prezidijuma Narodne skupštine FNRJ (prvog i drugog saziva, 4 februar 1946–9 januar 1953).* Belgrade: 1956.
Neuberg, Paul. *The Hero's Children: The Post-War Generation in Eastern Europe.* New York: William Morrow and Co. Inc., 1973.
Nikolić, Vinko. *Tragedija se dogodila u Svibnju.* 2 vols. Zagreb: 1995.
Pattee, Richard. *The Case of Cardinal Aloysius Stepinac.* Milwaukee, WI: The Bruce Publishing Co., 1953.
Pavlov, Todor. *Na literaturni i filosofski temi.* Sofia: 1946.
_____. *Teorija odraza.* Belgrade: 1947.
Pavlowitch, Stevan K. *Tito—Yugoslavia's Great Dictator.* Columbus, OH: Ohio State University Press, 1992.
Pavlović, Momčilo. "Dragoljub Jovanović i Komunisti." *Dragoljub Jovanović, naučnik, političar, stradalnik: Zbornik radova.* Niš: 1994.
_____. *Srpsko selo 1945–1952: Otkup.* Belgrade: Institut za savremenu istoriju, 1997.
Pekić, Borislav. *Godine koje su skakavci pojeli.* Belgrade: 1987.
Peković, Ratko. *Ni rat ni mir, Panorama književnih polemika, 1945–1965.* Belgrade: Filip Višnjić, 1986.
Peti kongres Komunističke partije Jugoslavije, Izvještaji i referati. Belgrade: Izdavački centar Komunist, 1948.
Peti kongres Komunističke partije Jugoslavije, 21.–28. jula 1948, Stenografske bilješke. Belgrade: Izdavački centar Komunist, 1949.
Petranović, Branko. *Istorija Jugoslavije 1918–1978.* Belgrade: 1980.
_____. *Političke i pravne prilike za vreme privremene vlade DFJ.* Belgrade: 1964.
_____. *Revolucija i kontrarevolucija u Jugoslaviji (1941–1945).* 2 vols. Belgrade: 1983.
_____, ed. *Zapisnici sa sednica Politbiroa Centralnog komiteta KPJ (11. Jun 1945–7. jul 1948).* Belgrade: 1995.
Petranović, Branko, Ranko Končar, and Radovan Radonjić, eds., *Sednice Centralnog komiteta KPJ (1948–1952).* Belgrade: Izdavački centar Komunist, 1985.
Petranović, Branko, and Momčilo Zečević. *Jugoslovenski federalizam: Ideje I stvarnosti.* Vol. 2. Belgrade: 1987.
Pijade, Moša. *Izabrani govori i članci, 1941–1947.* Belgrade: 1948.

_____. *Izabrani govori i članci, 1948–1949*. Belgrade: 1950.
Plekhanov, G. V. *Art and Social Life*. Moscow: 1957.
Plut-Pregelj, Leopoldina, Aleš Gabrić, and Božo Repe. *The Repluralization of Slovenia in the 1980s: New Revelations from Archival Records*. The Donald W. Treadgold Papers, no. 24. Seattle: University of Washington, 2000.
Predragović, Milenko. *Kata Pejnović*. Kragujevac: 1978.
Problems of Soviet Literature, Reports and Speeches at the First Soviet Writers' Congress. Westport, CT: 1934.
Prvi kongres kulturnih radnika Hrvatske, Topusko, 25–27 June 1944, Gradja. Zagreb: 1976.
Prvo vanredno zasedanje Narodne skupštine FNRJ, 31. januara–4. februara 1946, Stenografske beleške. Belgrade: 1946.
Radelić, Zdenko. "Organizacija i osnivačke skupštine odbora Hrvatske republikanske seljačke stranke, 1945–1947." *Časopis za suvremenu povijest*, 28, no. 1–2 (1996): 73–87.
_____. *Hrvatska seljačka stranka, 1941–1950*. Zagreb: 1996.
Radić, Radmila. *Verom protiv vere: Država i verske zajednice u Srbiji, 1945–1953*. Belgrade: INIS, 1995.
Radonjić, Radovan. *Sukob KPJ sa Kominformom i društveni razvoj Jugoslavije (1948–1950)*. 2d ed. Zagreb: 1976.
Ramet, Pedro. "Catholicism and Politics in Socialist Yugoslavia." *Religion in Communist Lands* 10, No. 3 (Winter 1982): 256–274.
_____, ed. *Religion and Nationalism in Soviet and East European Politics*. Durham, NC: Duke University Press, 1984.
Ranković, Aleksandar. *Izabrani govori i članci, 1941–1951*. Belgrade: 1951.
Reinhartz, Dennis. *Milovan Djilas: A Revolutionary as Writer*. New York: East European Monographs, distributed by Columbia University Press, 1981.
Revolucionarni omladinski pokret Jugoslavije, 1919–1979. Zagreb: 1979.
Riordan, Jim, ed. *Soviet Youth Culture*. London: MacMillan Press, 1989.
Rodzianko, Fr. Vladimir. "The Golgotha of the Orthodox Church in Yugoslavia, 1941–1951." *The Eastern Churches Quarterly*, 10, No. 2 (Summer 1953): 68–75.
Rosenberg, Bernard, and David Manning White, eds. *Mass Culture Revisited*. New York: Van Nostrand Reinhold Co., 1971.
Rusinow, Dennison. *The Yugoslav Experiment, 1948–1974*. Berkeley, CA: University of California Press, 1978.
Schapiro, Leonard. *The Communist Party of the Soviet Union*. 2d ed. New York: Random House, 1971.
Schudson, Michael. *Advertising: The Uneasy Persuasion*. New York: Basic Books Inc., 1984.
Scott, James C. *Weapons of the Weak: Everyday Forms of Peasant Resistance*. New Haven, CT: Yale University Press, 1985.
Selenić, Slobodan. *Očevi i oci*. Belgrade: 1988.
Shoup, Paul. *Communism and the Yugoslav National Question*. New York: Columbia University Press, 1968.
_____. "The Yugoslav Revolution: The First of a New Type." In *The Anatomy of Communist Takeovers*, edited by Thomas T. Hammond. New Haven, CT: Yale University Press, 1975.
Šibl, Ivan. *Sjećanja: Poslijeratni dnevnik*. Vol. 3. Zagreb: 1986.

Siegelbaum, Lewis. *Stakhanovism and the Politics of Productivity in the U.S.S.R., 1935–1941.* Cambridge: Cambridge University Press, 1988.
Sirc, Ljubo. *Between Hitler and Tito, Nazi Occupation and Communist Oppression.* London: Andre Deutsch Limited, 1989.
Sklevicky, Lydia. "Emancipated Integration or Integrated Emancipation: The Case of Post-Revolutionary Yugoslavia." Unpublished manuscript.
———. "Kulturnom mijenom do žene 'novog tipa' Antifašisticka fronta žena." *Gordogan* 6, no. 15–16 (January-April 1984): 73–111.
———. "Organizirana djelatnost žena Hrvatske za vrijeme narodnooslobodilačke borbe 1941–1945." *Povijesni prilozi* 3, no. 1 (1984): 83–127.
———. "The 'New' New Year, or How a Tradition Was Tempered." *East European Politics and Societies* 4, No. 1 (Winter 1990): 4–29.
Škrabalo, Ivo. *Izmedju publike i države: Povijest hrvatske kinematografije 1896–1980.* Zagreb: 1984.
Slijepčević, Djoko. *Istorija srpske pravoslavne crkve.* Vol. 3. Cologne: 1986.
Spehnjak, Katarina. "Hrvatsko seljačko prosvjetno društvo 'Seljačka sloga'." *Časopis za suvremenu povijest,* 29, no. 1 (1997): 129–146.
Stites, Richard. *Revolutionary Dreams, Utopian Vision and Experimental Life in the Russian Revolution.* Oxford: Oxford University Press, 1989.
———. *The Women's Liberation Movement in Russia, Feminism, Nihilism, and Bolshevism, 1860–1930.* Princeton: Princeton University Press, 1978.
Stojanović, Milenko B., ed. *Antologija golootočke misli i riječi.* Belgrade: Stručna knjiga, 1996.
Supek, Ivan. *Krivovjernik na ljevici.* Bristol: British-Croatian Review Publications, no date.
Swayze, Harold. *Political Control of Literature in the USSR, 1946–1959.* Cambridge, MA: Harvard University Press, 1962.
Thomson, Oliver. *Mass Persuasion in History, An Historical Analysis of the Development of Propaganda Techniques.* Edinburgh: Paul Harris Publishing, 1977.
Tirado, Isabel A. *Young Guard! The Communist Youth League, Petrograd 1917–1920.* New York: Greenwood Press, 1988.
Tismaneanu, Vladimir. *Reinventing Politics: Eastern Europe from Stalin to Havel.* New York: Free Press, 1992.
Tito, Josip Broz. *Govori i članci.* 12 vols. Zagreb: Naprijed, 1959.
———. *Izgradnja nove Jugoslavije.* 2 vols. Belgrade: 1948.
Tomasevic, Jozo. "Collectivization of Agriculture in Yugoslavia." In *Collectivization of Agriculture in Eastern Europe,* edited by Irwin T. Sanders. Lexington, KY: University of Kentucky Press, 1958.
Tomić, Stojan T. "Izbori u vrijeme revolucionarnog etatizma 1945–1953." In *Skupštinski izbori u Jugoslaviji, 1942–1982.* Belgrade: 1983.
Ulam, Adam B. *Titoism and the Cominform.* Cambridge, MA: Harvard University Press, 1952.
Valentić, Mirko, ed. *Spomenica Bleiburg, 1945–1995.* Zagreb: 1995.
Vasić, Miroljub. *SKOJ 1929–1941.* Belgrade: 1979.
———, ed. *Četvrti kongres SKOJ-a i Zajednički kongres SKOJ-a i NOJ, 1948.* Belgrade: Izdavački centar Komunist, 1985.
———, ed. *Kongresi, konferencije i sednice Centralnih organa SKOJ-a 1919-1924, and 1925–1941.* Belgrade: Izdavački centar Komunist, 1984.

Volk, Petar. *Svedočenje–hronika jugoslovenskog filma, 1945–1970*. Part 2. Belgrade: 1975.
Vukmanović-Tempo, Svetozar. *Revolucija koja teče—Memoari*. Vols. 1 and 2. Belgrade: 1971.
Wachtel, Andrew. *Making a Nation, Breaking a Nation: Literature and Cultural Politics in Yugoslavia*. Stanford, CA: Stanford University Press, 1998.
Williams, Raymond. "Culture." In *Marx: The First Hundred Years*, edited by David McLellan. London: Frances Pinter Publications, 1983.
Woodward, Susan. *Socialist Unemployment: The Political Economy of Yugoslavia 1945–1990*. Princeton: Princeton University Press, 1995.
Youngblood, Denise J. *Movies for the Masses, Popular Cinema and Soviet Society in the 1920s*. Cambridge: Cambridge University Press, 1992.
Youth Railway. Belgrade: Publication of the Central Council of the People's Youth of Yugoslavia, 1947.
Ziherl, Boris. *Članci i rasprave*. Belgrade: 1948.
Zogović, Radovan. *Na poprištu: književni i politički članci, književne kritike, polemike, marginalije*. Belgrade: 1947.

Archival Sources

Arhiv Centralnog komiteta Saveza komunista Jugoslavije (ACKSKJ, Archives of the Central Committee of the League of Communists of Yugoslavia), Belgrade

Agitprop/Ideološka Komisija (Department of Agitation and Propaganda/Ideological Commission): Fond VIII.
Centralni komitet Savez komunističke omladine Jugoslavije (Central Committee of the League of Communist Youth of Yugoslavia): Fond CKSKOJ.
Komisija za masovne i društvene organizacije (Commission for Mass and Social Organizations): Fond XII.
Komisija za rad medju ženama (Commission for Work among Women): Fond XVII.
Lični fond Borisa Kidriča (Personal fund of Boris Kidrič): Fond LFBK.
Lični fond Borisa Kidriča, Privredni problemi (Personal fund of Boris Kidrič, Economic Problems): Fond LFBK Privredni problemi.
Lični fond Veljka Vlahovića (Personal fund of Veljko Vlahovic): Fond LFVV, Odluke, direktive, pisma (Decisions, Directives, Letters): Fond II.
Organizaciono-instruktorska Uprava (Organizational and Instructors Administration): Fond V.
Politburo: Fond III.
Šesti kongres (Sixth Congress): Fond I/VI.
Sveslavenski komitet (All-Slavic Committee): Fond SK.

Hrvatski Državni Arhiv (HDA, Croatian State Archives, previously the Archives of the Institute for the History of the Workers' Movement of Croatia), Zagreb

Anti-fašistički front žena (AFŽ, Anti-Fascist Front of Women).
Centralni komitet Komunističke partije Hrvatske (CKKPH, Central Committee of the Communist Party of Croatia).

Centralni komitet Komunističke partije Hrvatske, Agitprop (CKKPHAP, Central Committee of the Communist Party of Croatia, Department of Agitation and Propaganda).
Komitet za društvenu aktivnost žena Hrvatske (KDAŽH, Committee for the Social Activity of the Women of Croatia).
Pokrajinski komitet Savez komunističke omladine Jugoslavije za Hrvatsku (PKSKOJ-H, Regional Committee of the League of Communist Youth of Yugoslavia for Croatia).
Raionski komitet Socijalističkog saveza radnog naroda Hrvatske (RKSSRNH, Regional Committee of the Socialist League of the Working People of Croatia).
Ujedinjeni savez anti-fašistčke omladine Hrvatske (USAOH, United League of Anti-Fascist Youth of Croatia).
Vijeće Savez sindikata Hrvatske (VSSH, Council of the League of Trade Unions of Croatia).
Zemaljsko vijeće Narodne omladine Hrvatske (ZVNOH, Land Council of the People's Youth of Croatia).

Arhiv Jugoslavije (AJ, Archives of Yugoslavia), Belgrade

Anti-fašistički front žena (AFŽ, Anti-Fascist Front of Women).
Centralno veće Savez sindikata Jugoslavije (CV SSJ, Central Council of the League of Trade Unions of Yugoslavia).
Komitet za kulturu i umetnost (KKU, Committee for Culture and Art).
Komitet za škole i nauku (KŠN, Committee for Schools and Science).
Lični fond Dragoljuba Jovanovića (Personal fund of Dragoljub Jovanović).
Ministarstvo za kulturu i nauku (MKN, Ministry of Culture and Science).
Ministarstvo prosvete (MP, Ministry of Education).
Savezna komisija za pregled filmova (Federal Commission for the Review of Films).
Socijalistički savez omladine Jugoslavije (SSOJ, Socialist League of Youth of Yugoslavia).
Socijalistički savez radnog naroda Jugoslavije (SSRNJ, Socialist League of the Working People of Yugoslavia).

Newspapers

20. oktobar (Belgrade), organ of the People's Front of Belgrade.
Borba (Belgrade), organ of the Communist Party of Yugoslavia.
Demokratija (Belgrade), organ of the Democratic Party.
Glas (Belgrade), organ of the People's Front of Serbia.
Gore srca (Zagreb), organ of the Literary Society of Cyril and Methodius.
Jež (Belgrade), humorous newspaper published by the League of Journalists' Associations of Yugoslavia.
Književne novine (Belgrade), organ of the Union of Writers of Yugoslavia.
Naprijed (Zagreb), organ of the Communist Party of Croatia.
Narodni list (Zagreb), organ of the People's Front of Zagreb.

Naš sport (Belgrade), organ of the Main Council of the Physical Culture League of Yugoslavia.
Omladina (Belgrade), organ of the People's Youth of Yugoslavia.
Oslobodjenje (Sarajevo), organ of the Land Council of the Anti-Fascist Council of People's Liberation of Bosnia and Hercegovina.
Pobjeda (Cetinje), organ of the People's Front of Montenegro.
Politika (Belgrade), ostensibly independent newspaper but clearly controlled by the CPY.
Prosvetni radnik (Belgrade), organ of the Union of Educational Workers of Yugoslavia.
Rad (Belgrade), organ of the United Trade Unions of Workers and Employees of Yugoslavia.
Republika (Belgrade), organ of the Republican Party.
Seljačka borba (Belgrade), organ of Peasants in Cooperatives and on State Farms.
Selo (Belgrade), organ of the Executive Council of the Agrarian Party.
Slobodna Dalmacija (Split), organ of the United People's Liberation Front of Dalmatia.
Slobodna Vojvodina (Novi Sad), organ of the United People's Liberation Front of Vojvodina.
Slobodni dom (Zagreb), organ of the Croat Republican Peasant Party.
Srpska Riječ (Zagreb), organ of the Main Council of Serbs in Croatia.
Vjesnik (Zagreb), organ of the People's Front of Croatia.
Zadruga (Belgrade), organ of the Main Union of Serbian Agricultural Cooperatives and the Union of Worker/Employee Producer/Consumer Cooperatives for Serbia.

Other Periodicals

Film (Belgrade), organ of the Cinematography Committee.
Glasnik (Belgrade), organ of the Serbian Orthodox Church.
Jugoslavija (Belgrade), publication of the League of Journalists' Associations of Yugoslavia.
Jugoslavija-SSSR (Belgrade), organ of the Society for the Cultural Cooperation of Yugoslavia with the U.S.S.R.
Komunist (Belgrade), organ of the Central Committee of the Communist Party of Yugoslavia.
Mladost (Belgrade), youth journal for literature and culture published by the Central Council of the People's Youth of Yugoslavia.
Narodno zadrugarstvo (Belgrade), organ of the Main Cooperative Union of Yugoslavia.
(Naša) književnost (Belgrade), literary journal.
Naša moda (Zagreb), Croatian fashion magazine.
New Times (Moscow), Soviet political journal for foreign consumption.
NIN (Nedeljne informativne novine) (Belgrade), weekly political magazine
Nova Misao (Belgrade), monthly journal on literature, science, and art.
Partiska izgradnja (Belgrade), organ of the Central Committee of the Communist Party of Yugoslavia for organizational questions.

Priroda (Zagreb), organ of the Society for Natural Sciences.
Republika (Zagreb), literary journal for Croatia.
Savremena škola (Belgrade), organ of the Union of Educational Workers and Employees of Yugoslavia.
Seljačka sloga (Zagreb), educational journal of the Croat Republican Peasant Party.
Slaviane (Moscow), organ of the All-Slavic Committee.
Slovensko bratstvo (Belgrade), organ of the Slavic Committee of Yugoslavia.
Službeni list FNRJ (Belgrade), official bulletin of the Federal People's Republic of Yugoslavia.
Socijalistički front (Zagreb), organ of the Central Committee of the Communist Party of Croatia.
Trideset dana (Belgrade), Journal on foreign policy.
Ukus (Belgrade), fashion journal published by the Central Council of the Anti-Fascist Front of Women.
Vesnik (Belgrade), organ of the Association of Orthodox Priests of Yugoslavia.
Žena danas (Belgrade), organ of the Anti-Fascist Front of Women.

Index

Abstract nature, of party goals, 115–117
Activism, 5–6, 88–92
Aesthetics, in culture, 98–99
AFW. *See* Anti-fascist Front of Women
Agitation. *See* Agitprop
Agitprop, 9, 12(n12), 73(n24), 143
 as tool for cultural change, 38–41
 economic issues, 116
 lack of leadership in, 67–68, 70
 media reform, 216
 on collectivization, 183–184
 post-reform ideological debates, 214–222
 post-reform response, 221–222
 post-split party role, 177–181
 post-split press reforms, 208
 post-split reorganization of, 205–206
 volunteer labor brigades, 120–121
Agrarian issues. *See* Collective farms
Agrarian Party, 49–50
All-Slavic Movement, 83–84, 101, 108(n17)
American culture, 187–188, 232, 236–237, 239
Andrić, Ivo, 96–97, 219
Anti-fascist Front of Women (AFW), 48, 53, 85, 121, 156(n17), 178
Anti-fascist organizations, 42
Arts, 79, 94–95, 129–130, 135(n51), 231–232
Association for Orthodox Priests, 101
Augustinčić, Antun, 96

AVNOJ. *See* People's Liberation Council of Yugoslavia

Babović, Cana, 53
Bakarić, Marija Šoljan, 108(n24)
Ballet, 99
Bihalj-Merin, Oto, 235–236
Biljanović, Olga, 207
Bogdanović, Milan, 219
Borba newspaper, 10, 40–41, 83, 148
 criticism of censorship, 202–203
 cultural pluralism expressed in, 96
 media ideology, 146–147
 media reform, 216
 on educational policy, 62–63
 post-split press reforms, 207
 post-split Soviet treatment, 187–189
 postwar activism, 87
 pragmatic party goals, 116
Bosnia-Hercegovina, 29, 62
Brčko-Banovići Youth Railway, 121–122, 133(n20)
Brioni Plenum, 24
British forces, 19–20, 107(n2)

Ćopić, Branko, 96, 226(n67)
Cadres, 66–71
Censorship, 56(n23), 57(n24), 229
 criticism of, 200–203
 official elimination of, 208
 post-reform debates over, 214–221
 reduction of, 233–234
Central Committee Plenum, 23
Centralism, 30, 61–63

Četniks, 19–20, 29–30
Čolaković, Rodoljub, 37
Čopić, Branko, 217–218
Christmas, 102, 103(fig.)–104(fig.)
Church-state relations, 84, 101
Class struggle, 80–83
Coercion, 6–7
  cultural policies, 92–100
  recruitment for labor brigades, 123–124
  volunteer labor brigades, 174
Collective farms, 24, 183–184
Comic strips, 238–240
Cominform, 21–22, 161–165
Cominformists, 165–169
Comintern, 18, 25–26
Communist Party of Croatia, 39, 68
Communist Party of Yugoslavia (CPY)
  as tool of cultural change, 35–42
  establishment of, 18–21
  ideological goals, 25
  internal disunity, 61–66
  vision for Yugoslav society, 1–2
  See also League of Communists of Yugoslavia
Competition, 118–120, 173
Constitution, Yugoslav, 47
Constitutional Assembly, 20
CPY. *See* Communist Party of Yugoslavia
Croat Home Guard, 88
Croat Republican Peasant Party (CRPP), 45, 49–50, 96, 144–145
  widespread appeal of, 81–83
Croatia, 29, 35
  class struggles, 81–83
  educational policy, 62
  post-split party role, 177
Croats, 17, 20
CRPP. *See* Croat Republican Peasant Party
Cultural change
  through CPY, 35–42
  through education, 45–46
  through mass organizations, 48–54
  through religion, 46–48
  through the state, 42–48
Cultural manipulation, 7–9, 77
Cultural policies
  early cultural pluralism, 95–96
  persuasion versus coercion, 92–100
Culture, 11(n1)
  culture gap, 231–232, 236–237
  decline of pluralism, 128–132
  impact of reforms, 214
  moving towards socialism, 140–148
  post-split relaxation of policy towards, 231–232
  volunteer labor brigades, 121–122
  See also Arts; Literature; Theater; Writers

Dachau trials, 192(n8)
Danon, Oskar, 41
Dapčević, Peko, 102
Dedijer, Milica, 108(n24)
Dedijer, Vladimir, 37, 129–130, 146–147
  media reform, 217–218
  post-split patriotism, 170–171
  post-split Soviet treatment, 186–187
Democracy, Djilas' support of, 37
Democratic Federated Yugoslavia, 20
Demokratija newspaper, 87, 106, 146
Devčić, Natko, 41
Dimitrijević, Vojo, 95, 129–130
Dissidents, 36–37
Djilas, Milovan, 54(n6), 97, 227(n73)
  agitprop, 39
  class differentiation, 81
  CRPP importance, 82
  cultural freedom and debate, 239–240
  media reform, 216
  on collectivism, 183–184
  on PFY, 50
  party role, 36–37
  post-split ideology, 179
  post-split press reform, 207–208
  post-split reforms, 209–210

post-split Soviet treatment, 188
post-split transformations, 198–199
pragmatic party goals, 117
Slavic sentiment, 108(n17)
transformation of education, 199–203
Djurić, Ljubodrag, 102
Domestic issues, 27–29
Drenovac, Bora, 243(n32)
   culture debates, 235
   media reform, 215
   on folklore, 144
   on theater censorship, 219–220
   party role, 37
   post-reform controversy, 221–222
Dugonjić, Rato, 64, 86–87, 124–125

Economic aid, 27
Economy
   as pragmatic party issue, 115–117
   economic development, 21
   increasing production, 118–120
   Law on Worker's Self-Management, 22–23, 203–207
   movement towards socialism, 138–139
   prewar poverty, 27–29
   See also Volunteer labor brigades
Education
   as indoctrination, 7
   as party goal, 125
   as pragmatic party goal, 117, 124–128
   as tool of social change, 45–46
   Communist education of educators, 148–153
   disunity in educational policy, 61–63
   Djilas's transformation of, 1 99–203
   movement towards socialism, 145
   party disunity among educators, 68–71
   post-split ideology, 179–180
   postwar politicization and purges of, 89–91

   religion and, 47
   "struggle of opinions," 248–249
   subverting religion, 102–104
   volunteer labor brigades, 121–122
Elections
   1945 elections, 20
   postelection purges, 115
Engels, Friedrich, 1, 22
Ethnic tensions, 29
Ethnicity, 17–18
External constraints, 25–31

Families, 85–86
Fascism. *See* Anti-fascist organizations
Fashion, 237
Federal structure, 29–30
Federalism, 30, 79–80
Film industry
   censorship of, 56(n23)
   early cultural pluralism, 96
   Western films, 96, 187, 232
Finci, Eli, 96, 219
Five Year Plan, 120, 124, 126, 138–140, 143
Franičević, Marin, 99

Glasnik newspaper, 102
Gligorić, Velibor, 141
Gorky, Maxim, 40
Greece, 26–27
Grol, Milan, 106
Gubec, Matija, 83

Hebrang, Andrija, 168
"Heritage of the People's Liberation Struggle," 79
Historical context, 17–25
A History of Physics from Oldest Times to Atomic Energy (Supek), 39
Home Guards, 30, 88, 107(n2)
Identity, national, 29–30, 60(n64)
Ideology, 25
   cultural realism, 93–95
   giving way to popularity, 229–240
   See also Rhetoric versus ideology

Ilić, Božidar, 135(n51)
Independent Democratic Party, 49
Industrialization, 80
Infrastructure, 28
Intellectuals, 94–100, 113(n71)
Internal constraints, 25–31

Jež journal, 130, 146
Johnson, A. Ross, 212–213
Jovanović, Arso, 102
Jovanović, Dragoljub, 117

Kardelj, Edvard, 36
  party reforms, 211–212
  post-split party role, 176–177
  post-split Soviet treatment, 188–189
  post-split transformations, 198–200
  See also Peasant Working Cooperatives
Kardelj, Pepca, 108(n24)
Kidrič, Boris, 171–172, 198
Knez od Zete, 41
Kocbek, Edvard, 217–218, 227(n73)
Komunist journal, 10, 189
Konjović, Jovan, 41
Kosovo-Metohia, 29, 71
Kostić, Dušan, 96, 129, 234–235
Kraiger, Boris, 168–169
Krleža, Miroslav, 97, 129, 219, 240
Kulenović, Skender, 219

Labor
  as community goal, 79
  revolution as inspiration for, 86–87
  shockwork and competition, 118–120, 173
  See also Volunteer labor brigades
Law on Worker's Self-Management, 22–23, 203–207
LCY. *See* League of Communists of Yugoslavia
League of Communist Youth of Yugoslavia (SKOJ), 41–42, 52
  education as party goal, 125
  extremism of, 65–66
  increasing factory production, 118
  moving towards socialism, 151, 153
  postwar party support, 88–92
  violence against clergy, 104–105
League of Communists of Yugoslavia (LCY), 2, 210–214
League of Trade Unions (LTU), 48
  cadres, 68
  election stance, 81
  party role, 50–52
  post-split party role, 178
  post-split patriotism, 171–173
  volunteer labor brigades, 121
Legal system, 23
Lenin, Vladimir, 1
Liberation, from German occupation, 17–18, 20, 75, 77
Literature, 96–100, 234–236
Ljotićists, 30
Local particularism, 30
Local party organizations, 66–71
LTU. *See* League of Trade Unions

Macedonia, 29, 62
Maček, Vladko, 82
Maljević, Suljo, 174–175
Marx, Karl, 1, 22
Marxist-Leninist ideology, 4–5, 138–139, 144–145
Mass organizations
  as tool of cultural change, 48–54
  post-split reorganization of, 203–207
Mayakovsky, Vladimir, 96
Media, public, 7, 10–11
  as tool of cultural change, 43–45
  decline of pluralism, 128–132
  denouncing CPY policy, 106
  downplaying of communism, 78
  early non-Communist press, 96
  ideology versus popularity, 237–239
  lack of leadership in, 68
  movement towards socialism, 143–146

Index   269

moving towards socialism, 141
post-split ideology, 179
post-split press reform, 207–208
post-split relaxation of policy towards, 232
See also Censorship
Mencej, Martin, 62
Mihailović, Draža, 19–20, 117
Military violence against Home Guard, 107(n2)
Mišić, Zoran, 236
Mitrović, Mitra, 108(n24), 227(n78)
   AFW, 53
   decadence in the arts, 147
   education as pragmatic party goal, 124
   partisantsvo, 91
   party role, 37
   post-reform cultural controversy, 219–220
Mitrović, Stefan, 39
Mladost journal, 218, 235
Montenegro, 29, 62, 71
Morals, 2
Music, 232, 236–237

Naša književnost journal, 10
National issues, 29
National question, 29–30
Nationalism, 62, 169–175
Nazor, Vladimir, 82, 95
Nedeljković, Dušan, 234
Neorečić, Milijan, 28, 37, 118
   education as party goal, 125
   on media reform, 215
   on youth brigades, 121
Nešković, Blagoje, 205, 224(n28)
Newspapers. *See* Media
NIN journal, 10, 215, 218, 225(n51)
Nova Makedonija newspaper, 145
20.oktobar newspaper, 10
Omladina journal, 238

Painters. *See* Arts
Partisans, 18–19, 30, 79
   postwar violence, 87–88

religious celebration, 101
violence against Home Guard, 107(n2)
Partisanstvo, 86–92
   in culture, 92–100
   religion and, 102–105
Party leaders
   functional disunity, 63–65
   post-split role, 175–182
Party-state, 4
Patriotism, 169–175
Pavičević, Mišo, 179
Pavlov, Todor, 93
PCs. *See* People's Councils
Peasant Working Cooperatives (PWCs), 139–140, 183
Pejnović, Kata, 85
Peković, Rato, 220, 226(n67)
People's Councils (PCs), 19
People's Front of Yugoslavia (PFY), 20, 48–50
   formation of, 18–19
   ideological training, 151
   media support, 45
   post-split reorganization of, 206–207
   post-split role, 175–182
   reform policies, 23
   Slavic movement, 84
   volunteer labor brigades, 121
   See also Socialist Alliance of the Working People of Yugoslavia
People's Liberation Council of Yugoslavia (AVNOJ), 19–20
People's Peasant Party, 49–50
"People's Power," 79, 81
People's Youth of Yugoslavia (PYY), 42, 45, 48, 52–53, 89–92
   education and, 125
   moving towards socialism, 153
   post-split party role, 178
   volunteer labor brigades, 120–121
Pešić, Milorad, 233
Petar, King, 19–20
PFY. *See* People's Front of Yugoslavia
Pijade, Moša, 81, 102, 219, 227(n78)

Pioneer Organization, 52–53, 125
Pluralism, cultural, 95–96, 128–132
Politika newspaper, 10, 102, 106, 207
Popović, Nikola, 98
"Popular Front" line, 18, 65
Propaganda. *See* Agitprop
Provisional Assembly, 20–21
Publishing, 47
See also Media
Purges, 89–91, 115, 193(n10)
PWCs. *See* Peasant Working Cooperatives
PYY. *See* People's Youth of Yugoslavia

Rad newspaper, 10, 81
Radić, Ante, 82
Radić, Stjepan, 82–83
Radicalism, 86–92, 102
Ranković, Aleksandar, 23, 36, 177, 205
Realism
    cultural realism, 93–95
    socialist realism, 135(n51), 240
Red Army, 19
Reforms, 161–162
    agrarian, 21
    cultural, 208–210, 229–240
    for long-term transformation, 249–250
    organizational, 23–24
    party reforms, 210–214
    post-split media reform, 207–208
Religion, 100–106, 144–145
    as tool of cultural change, 46–48
    church-state relations, 84
Republika newspaper, 10, 44–45, 87
Republika journal, 10, 44–45, 87, 97
Revolution, as inspiration for labor, 86–87
Rhetoric versus ideology
    All-Slavic Movement, 83–84, 101, 108(n17)
    class struggle, 80–83
    culture and, 140–148
    demise of pluralism, 128–132
    downplaying communism, 77–80
    for long-term transformation, 137, 251–252
    from abstract to pragmatic goals, 115–117
    increasing factory production, 118–120
    postwar ambiguity of, 105–106
    radicalism and activism, 86–92
    religion, 100–105
    socialism as party goal, 138–140
    volunteer labor brigades, 120–124
    women and families, 85–86
    See also Soviet-Yugoslav split
Ribar, Ivo Lola, 102, 126
Ristić, Marko, 96, 219
Rittig, Svetozar, 84

SAWPY. *See* Socialist Alliance of the Working People of Yugoslavia
Šamac-Sarajevo Railway, 126–127
Šegedin, Petar, 231
Šegvić, Zdenka, 68
Švabić, Mihailo, 64, 121, 133(n20)
Second Plenum of the Central Committee, 24
Serbia, 17, 19, 29
    class struggles, 81–82
    educational policy, 62
Shockwork, 118–120, 173
Simić, Vladimir, 106
Sirotanivić, Alija, 173
Sixth Party Congress, 23
    See also League of Communists of Yugoslavia
SKOJ. *See* League of Communist Youth of Yugoslavia
Slavic movement, 83–84, 101, 108(n17)
Slovenia, 29, 35
    Dachau trials, 192(n8)
    educational policy, 62
    impact of Soviet-Yugoslav split, 168–169
Social behavior, 2
Social-Democratic Party, 49
Socialism, 4–9
    as party goal, 137–154
    initial attempt at transformation, 21–23

post-split transformation of education, 199–203
Socialist Alliance of the Working People of Yugoslavia (SAWPY), 24, 210–214
  Fourth Congress, 225(n51)
Socialist Party, 49
Socialist realism, 135(n51), 240
Socialization, of the countryside, 182–185
Soviet Union, 2–3
  conflict with, 21–22
  disillusionment with, 146–147, 198–199
  early CPY ties to, 25–27
  increasing affinity with, 138–139
  post-split attitude towards, 185–189
Soviet-Yugoslav split, 2–3, 5, 26, 75
  attitude towards Soviet Union, 185–189
  effect on transformation, 247–248
  effects of rhetoric, 189–191
  historical background, 161–165
  post-split conflicts, 165–169
  post-split patriotism, 169–175
  post-split purges, 193(n10)
  relaxation of youth and culture policies, 229–240
  role of the party, 175–182
  socialization of the countryside, 182–185
Spoljarić, Djuro, 118
Stalin, Josef, 21, 23, 162–163, 170
Stalinist era, 2–3
State, as tool of cultural change, 42–48
State-society relations, 6
  cultural manipulation, 7–9
  demise of pluralism, 131–132
  persuasion versus coercion, 92–105
  postwar ambiguity of, 105–106
Stepinac, Alojzije, 20, 47, 105–106, 117
Stilinović, Marijan, 95
Supek, Ivan, 39

Territorial issues, 117
Theater, 40–41, 129
  Partisan theater, 98
  post-reform controversy, 219, 227(n78)
  religious satire, 102
Theater of People's Liberation, 95
Third Plenum of the Central Committee, 199–203
Tito, Josip Broz, 18–19, 22, 36
  dissatisfaction with writers, 141
  downplaying of communism, 78
  moving towards socialism, 154
  on Western relations, 27
  on women's roles, 85
  party reforms, 211–213
  post-split stances, 170–171, 177, 186, 188, 190
  unitarism, 80
  volunteer labor brigades, 121, 127
Tito-Šubašić Agreement (1944), 19
Todorović, Mijalko, 185
Tomašević, Stana, 91
Tomić, Aleksander, 106
Tomšič, Vida, 53, 108(n24)
Trade unions, 68, 171–173
Transformation, of policies, 137
Trieste, Italy, 26–27

Ujević, Augustin Tin, 99
United League of Anti-Fascist Youth of Yugoslavia (USAOJ). *See* People's Youth of Yugoslavia
United People's Liberation Front. *See* People's Front of Yugoslavia
United States
  economic aid from, 27
  popular culture, 187–188, 232, 236–237, 239
Ustaša, 20, 29–30, 39, 47
Utilitarianism, of high and popular culture, 92–93

Values, 2
  group versus individual good, 78–79

instilling through culture,
    92–94
  See also Ideology
Violence
  against clergy, 104–105
  against Home Guard, 107(n2)
  Partisan youth, 90–92
Vjesnik newspaper, 148
Vlahović, Veljko, 37, 83, 126
  criticism of censorship,
    203
  post-split ideology, 179
  post-split party role, 181
Vojvodina province, 29
Volunteer labor brigades, 120–124,
    127
  partisantsvo, 86–87, 91–92
  post-split reduction of, 204–205
  post-split revival of, 173–174
  role and importance of, 64

War
  as cultural theme, 98, 129
  psychological impact of, 30–31
Western democracies, 26–27
Women
  cultural-educational opportunities,
    53
  in government, 108(n24)
  in volunteer labor brigades, 123
  legal status of, 47
  party expectations of, 108(n22)
  rhetoric versus ideology, 85–86

Working class
  cultural-educational policies for,
    50–52
  rhetoric versus ideology, 80–83
  trade unions, 68, 171–173
World War II, 17–19
Writers, 96, 112(n58), 129
  media reform, 216–221
  post-split relaxation of policy
    towards, 230–231

Youth and youth movements, 7–8,
    110(n35)
  moving towards socialism, 151–153
  pop culture versus socialist ideals,
    141–143
  post-split relaxation of policy
    towards, 232–240
  postwar reliance on, 88–92
  violence against clergy, 104–105
  Western media appeal, 238–239
  See also Education; SKOJ; Volunteer
    labor brigades
Yugoslav Republican Democratic
    Party, 106
Yugoslav Republican Party, 49
Yugoslavia, new, 17
Yugoslavia, old, 17

Žigić, Rade, 124
Zhdanov, Andrei, 93
Zogović, Radovan, 37, 39, 45, 65–66,
    72(n14), 96–97, 99

For Product Safety Concerns and Information please contact our EU representative GPSR@taylorandfrancis.com
Taylor & Francis Verlag GmbH, Kaufingerstraße 24, 80331 München, Germany

www.ingramcontent.com/pod-product-compliance
Lightning Source LLC
Chambersburg PA
CBHW071347290426
44108CB00014B/1469